# Entrepreneurial Ethics
## *Values and Decision Making in Successful New Ventures*

■ ■ ■ ■

**David Newton**
*Westmont College*

**KENDALL/HUNT PUBLISHING COMPANY**
4050 Westmark Drive    Dubuque, Iowa 52002

Copyright © 1997 by David Newton

Library of Congress Catalog Card Number: 97-61024

ISBN 0-7872-3772-8

All rights reserved. No part of this publication may be reproduced, stored in a retrieval system, or transmitted, in any form or by any means, electronic, mechanical, photocopying, recording, or otherwise, without the prior written permission of the copyright owner.

Printed in the United States of America

10  9  8  7  6  5  4  3  2  1

# Contents

*Foreword  v*
*Acknowledgments  vii*
*Introduction  xi*

**Chapter**

| | | |
|---|---|---|
| One | Entrepreneurial New Ventures | 1 |
| Two | Entrepreneurs: Drivers of New Ventures | 19 |
| Three | The Entrepreneur's Idea and Vision | 33 |
| Four | The Entrepreneur's Personal Value System | 45 |
| Five | A New Model of Entrepreneurial Ethics | 67 |
| Six | Entrepreneurial Representation | 85 |
| Seven | Entrepreneurial Market Expectations | 105 |
| Eight | Entrepreneurial Financial Requirements | 125 |
| Nine | Entrepreneurial Partnering | 143 |
| Ten | Entrepreneurial Firm Culture | 159 |
| Eleven | Change and New Venture Momentum | 177 |
| Twelve | Evidences and Interactions of Ethics | 191 |

*Appendix  207*
*Notes  213*
*Glossary  225*
*Index  243*

# Foreword

Both entrepreneurship and ethics are topics of great current interest. The business press routinely features the exploits of "up and comers," while simultaneously reporting the ethical lapses of business firms and individuals. Numerous professional conferences and academic journals likewise focus attention on both new ventures and business values. This book is timely, therefore in its exploration of the linkage between these two topics of vital concern.

Because of the dynamic role of entrepreneurship in today's society, the values of entrepreneurs are critically important. Much of our current business life is driven by the forces of entrepreneurial activity. New ventures bring innovation, improved products, better services, and new jobs. If we are to realize fully these benefits of entrepreneurship, its leaders must play by rules that protect those with a stake in such activity.

Ethical issues in entrepreneurial firms must be faced in an atmosphere of rapid change. Few, if any, business ventures are isolated from the swirling currents of change. By their very nature, however, leaders in rapidly growing entrepreneurial ventures create change as well as experience it. What is the impact of such conditions on values and ethical behavior? Are there special pressures, temptations, and uncertainties that affect social awareness and ethical behavior in such businesses? Do those at the helm of rapidly growing businesses display the same sensitivity to ethical issues as do leaders in more stable business institutions? Are they inclined to skip a rung or take shortcuts to speed up the growth process? The features of rapid growth and innovation that are inherent in entrepreneurial firms make an inquiry into the implications for ethical behavior intriguing.

In any institution, the underlying culture with its perspectives on social issues provides a foundation for ethical behavior. In rapidly growing entrepreneurial organizations, that culture must be formed while the firms plunge ahead at breakneck speed. Concentration upon attractive opportunities and efforts to build a viable business in a competitive marketplace allow little time to reflect on ethical obligations or to develop ethical codes of doing business. The entrepreneur's lack of experience and the absence of ethical traditions could easily reduce the clarity of moral precepts and encourage rationalization of less ethical, but more expedient, behavior. These possibilities make it appropriate to investigate the process of ethical decision making in entrepreneurial firms.

Current discussions about effective leadership place a strong emphasis on values, replacing to some extent, an earlier preoccupation with techniques and styles. Successful leaders are thought to be those who create trust and who base their leadership on basic moral principles. Entrepreneurs, especially those in rapidly growing businesses, are obviously pursuing ideas or visions of the future. We might also wonder if they are committed to a kind of leadership that incorporates fundamental values necessary for long-term success. An examination of their ethical decision making processes should help in answering that question.

Those who lead change in entrepreneurial firms are the entrepreneurs themselves. As individuals, they see business opportunities and assume personal risks to try and exploit those opportunities. The entrepreneur, or entrepreneurs, occupy center stage. In contrast to much larger, established corporations, these ventures are marked by less bureaucracy and less sophisticated management practices. Leadership is thus highly individualistic in nature. These individual leaders are the key players in David Newton's model of ethical decision making in rapidly growing businesses. He has built his model on individual entrepreneurs—the type of people who bring firms into existence and who make them grow. Newton surveyed some 250 entrepreneurs whose companies were included in *INC.* magazine's list of the 500 fastest growing privately held companies over the last seven years. By tying the model to the experience of real entrepreneurs in rapidly growing firms, the author has sought to make the model realistic.

Present knowledge of entrepreneurial values consists primarily of bits and pieces of information about ethical perspectives of entrepreneurs concerning a variety of very specific issues. The author's contribution in this book is his proposal of a model that links the personal characteristics of entrepreneurs with the activities of the entrepreneurial firm. The book, therefore, presents a conceptual scheme for examining entrepreneurial decision making rather than a "how-to" book for improving ethical behavior.

As part of the model, Newton incorporates common features of rapidly growing ventures—for example, risk, uncertainty, innovation, and a less formal internal environment—to establish the context for decision making. These factors may together make entrepreneurial ventures, and specifically individual entrepreneurs, more susceptible to ethical compromise. The model considers the process of ethical decision making in a number of specific business areas—for example, forecasting, financing, and external partnering arrangements.

The author's presentation is enhanced by coupling the results of the survey of individual entrepreneurs with the conceptual scheme used to explain the challenges to ethical decision making. The survey results reported and discussed by the author should increase our knowledge concerning the values of successful entrepreneurs. Perhaps more importantly, the model should add to our understanding of how those values are worked out in situations that involve pressures for compromise, but that also provide opportunities for value-based decisions.

—*Justin G. Longenecker*
*Waco, Texas*

# Acknowledgments

I received tremendous support for this project from numerous professional and academic colleagues. You offered personal words of wisdom, letters with thoughts and ideas about ethics and the entrepreneurial process, and a good deal of e-mail with encouragement for the various topics I wanted to explore. For two years, you strongly encouraged me to get the data together and write this book, whether over a lunch discussion at *ICSB*, a paper presentation at *USASBE*, a journal article review for *JSBS*, or a business plan dinner with the *MIT Forum*. You endured hours of listening to me promote my concept and vision for a book like this that would deal with ethics and personal values form the entrepreneur's unique perspective in the fast-growth new venture. You stirred up my thoughts, added specific details to my ambiguity, and helped provide focus and clarity for this model and these chapters. This book reflects a wealth of input and challenge to me as a fellow inquirer about this topic we all love so dearly.

Special thanks go to Justin Longenecker who graciously agreed to lend his professional reputation by providing the opening comments for this book. Since we first met in 1990, you have always been a welcome handshake and discussion at various conferences, and always a source of new perspectives and encouragement to me in my various research. Thanks for your support.

I would also like to acknowledge the *Faculty Professional Development Committee* at Westmont College for granting me a one year sabbatical away from my normal teaching duties so that I could devote a full time effort to the research and writing of this book. This last year away from teaching would not have been possible without the help of three colleagues who filled in admirably to teach my regular course load in my absence during the 1996-97 academic year. First, I want to thank T.J. Natale for his truly outstanding job in *Entrepreneurship & New Venture Development*. Your entrepreneurial experience coupled with your current endeavor, *Reliant Ventures*, gave that sizable class a solid foundation in the entrepreneurial process and a clear perspective of what is good and right and admirable in the contemporary business environment. I also want to thank Bob Heavner for graciously stepping in and providing a first rate course in *Corporate Financial Management* even though your personal and professional schedule was changing dramatically and you had already scheduled two weeks in Europe during the fall term. The students experienced the perfect balance between the quantitative methods and the qualitative issues, and were able to draw upon a wealth of knowledge and ethical perspectives from your many years in the field of corporate finance. It was also personally rewarding to have Josh Yager agree with me, that a former student can come back five years after graduation with an *NASD* license and *C.F.P.* designation, and do an excellent job teaching *Investment Analysis and Portfolio Management*. Perhaps your PhD in finance is not entirely a long shot.

I also want to thank my good friends and colleagues from the faculty of economics and business, Roy Millender, Edd Noell, and Paul Morgan for their many years of support and encouragement. Thanks, Paul, for firing up the quantitative models, and teaching *Managerial Economics* in my place. I believe the reputation for that annual spring tradition was well maintained.

Special recognition goes out to the five student research assistants, April Myers, Keith Currier, Johan Frisell, Onesi Gnaniah, and Eric Mooney, who toiled many hours in the Small Business Resource Center during the fall semester to help me complete the primary survey phase of this research. When we first met in August and discussed the process and objectives for contacting 350 entrepreneurs from the *INC. 500*, you looked a bit shocked. And when the first two weeks were slow going and there was no momentum in sight, I am sure your asked yourselves how you could get out from under my plans. But you persevered, the momentum began to build, and the data came rolling back to Deane Hall at a steady pace for about twelve straight weeks. Every time I open up that database and look at the all those rows and columns of cases and variables I am always reminded of your effort and commitment to complete the task. I certainly hope you will read this book with a sense of pride and accomplishment for your part in helping to secure a wealth of empirical evidence for my numerous hypotheses and ideas about entrepreneurial ethics. Was feasting at the Chart House worth the wait?

I also want to acknowledge my Westmont faculty colleagues across the various academic departments. You have collectively inspired me in numerous ways to press ahead as a teacher, fellow scholar, and mentor to our students. It is truly a privilege to be a part of this faculty community, where high quality inquiry is greatly respected and where an honorable exchange of dialogue is still valued. I also want to thank Stan Gaede for his contagious commitment to pursuing scholarly inquiry. When we first met in Oregon back in 1992, your personal mentoring grabbed my attention and sparked my interests to rigorously pursue the integration of personal values with the entrepreneurial process and private enterprise development. Over the next few years, you twice edited my ethics manuscripts prepared for students. It was then very rewarding, last summer, to have you come and assume the position of Provost here at Westmont. Many of the original ideas for this book were taken directly from notes that I made during your sessions at that conference five years ago. I hope that this work will be the first of many similar endeavors still to be conceived.

I also must acknowledge a select group of faculty mentors who inspired me during my undergraduate and graduate studies. For C. Robert Clemensen, who crafted so elegantly and concisely such a persuasive values-oriented philosophy for every aspect of commerce and the business process. For Dick Burcaw, who integrated core moral absolutes into all aspects of corporate financial transactions. For Kobad Arjani, who inspired me to view my studies in economics and business as a moral prerequisite for building personal values. For Howard Vos who constantly challenged me to "never stop asking questions". For June Hagen who advocated a life-style of continuous reading, writing, and dialogue to ensure a lifetime of growing. I think of Michael Arthur and his genuine concern for me to enter the financial markets with strong personal morals and a sense of direction and purpose. And Warren Briggs, who pressed into me an appetite to question all that business offers and to seek clear and decisive answers, but do so with a sight set on commitments that never waver. To Igor Ansoff, who told me that I could truly make a timely ethics contribution to the field. And finally to Dick Harriff, who always reminded me to maintain the proper perspective between my professional academic pursuits and family, personal time, and individual growth as a person. You have all contributed to this final product.

Finally, I want to especially acknowledge my wife, Kimberly, and our four wonderful children, Jesse, Katherine, Jennifer, and Christiane. You are truly an inspiration to me. I receive so many interesting ideas from you on so many levels. You each tolerated me working at home for an entire year, and let me dominate the use of the computer. But with that came extra dividends to greet you in the afternoon as you came home from school or from teaching French. We had lunches on the back patio. I got to meet you at the bus stop. I was also able to pick you up from pre-school, shoot some basketball, drive you to ballet, or take a bike ride to the beach in the middle of the afternoon. You even took me to Magic Mountain for a day of nonstop thrill rides to break the monotony of sitting at the computer for too long. At times it got very busy with my deadlines, but it sure was a nice year of being around the house during the day. I look forward to it again on my next sabbatical.

# Introduction

Weekly news magazines are generally not lacking for stories about top managers at huge multinational corporations being involved in questionable business practices. Who can forget the 1980's and the reports of securities fraud and manipulation by the likes of Ivan Boesky, Charles Keating, and Michael Milken, or the deceit and misrepresentation displayed by the Bank of Commerce and Credit International.[1] Recently, commodities futures trader Yasuo Hamanaka at Sumitomo Corporation[2] lost $1.8 billion by entering false trades and altering financial reports, and Nick Lesson ran unauthorized and highly speculative interest rate futures trades and drove four hundred year old Baring's Bank, Ltd. out of business in less than two months.[3] *W. R. Grace* maintained policies of spying, fraud, and deception that resulted in hundreds of indictments for illegal price fixing and preferential contract allocations.[4] Systematic racketeering at Banker's Trust created client losses in excess of $500 million.[5] And *Bausch & Lomb* was caught using gray-marketing in Hong Kong to falsify annual sales growth in excess of twenty-five percent.[6] But Barry Minkow reminded everyone that fast-growth entrepreneurial ventures may not always be as "hot" as they appear.[7]

Corporate America saw a new wave of interest in business ethics about ten years ago, and business schools have since offered extensive formal ethics training for future corporate managers.[8] And yet, the more entrenched the discipline of business ethics becomes in business school curricula, the more bewildering it appears to managers.[9] The question remains: "Has a renewed interest in ethics produced measurable improvement in managerial performance?" Big business has a renewed interest in, and commitment to, the pursuit of rigorous ethical standards and guidelines to govern the fairness of commercial transactions.[10] But what about the ethical conduct of workers at small to medium sized, privately-held, fast-growth entrepreneurial ventures? Certainly they are just as susceptible (if not more so) to incredulous daily business decision making and questionable procedural challenges. Often, when the economy hits a downturn and firms encounter decreases in sales and profitability, many small to medium enterprises look for ways to cut corners and minimize their risk exposure due to increased business and market uncertainty.[11] It can be quite challenging for entrepreneurs to identify and implement a successful ethics program.[12]

Much has been said about the relative success and failure rates of firms that include a formal ethics program as part of their normal operations.[13] The chief executive of Levi Strauss and Company has stated that ethics is about the character and courage of individuals, and doing the right things even it costs more, and should be placed above all other priorities in the firm's long term planning process.[14] Evidence suggests that the benefits and costs to the firm that engages in ethical behavior are both literal and intangible. Favorable effects range from profitability, sales, and market share, to trust, loyalty, and confidence. Negative effects include everything from bad debt, negative earnings, and bankruptcy, to deceit, theft, and low morale. Many argue that there exists a long-term cost to unethical behavior.[15] It has been documented that firms which stress business ethics actually experience increased profitability[16], and higher ethical standards increase economic activity in the short run.[17] However, there are others who believe that ethical behavior will not be rewarded by the market, because such actions are in direct conflict with the very fabric of the competitive environment.[18]

It has been estimated that more than three quarters of American firms now operate with formal, ethical codes of practice.[19] Yet, many individuals and companies are not sure of how to approach the issues of compromise and integrity[20], and remain perplexed as to how ethical standards are developed and ultimately implemented. The difficulty comes in establishing a consistent code of conduct that is applicable to all business situations. Businesses recognize a wide range of variance in the types of transactions and the dynamics of the individuals involved in numerous commercial negotiations and deal making. There appears to be no way to arrive at a universally accepted procedural standard by which participants engage in business activities. What is acceptable in certain areas of business, may in turn be somewhat questionable in others. What is deemed inappropriate in one commercial transaction, may be standard operating procedure in another.

Entrepreneurs introduce newly designed products and services, launch new companies, and create new markets through innovation and the ability to recognize opportunity, often when others do not notice such openings in the competitive market. The tremendous amount of uncertainty surrounding an entrepreneurial venture may contribute to a lack of rigidity with respect to policies and procedures. How are entrepreneurs and the firms they conceive uniquely positioned with respect to the development and implementation of ethical behavior? Some suggest that a simple mathematical formula can facilitate an objective, endogenous program for measuring values-oriented activity in the firm.[21] The recent focus of the National Conference on Business Ethics dealt with the impact that mergers, takeovers, and corporate restructuring have on ethical behavior as firms are suddenly transformed into different organizations almost overnight, complete with new rules for success and failure.[22] It is important to continuously review the status of ethical practices and to make formal recommendations as to how individuals and firms can improve their behavior in the future. However, the vast majority of the research literature on business ethics is aimed at large corporations. Without clear guidelines, many firms risk significant exposure to economic loss due to employee inexperience and lack of a professional ethic.[23] Entrepreneurial satisfaction is perhaps the most fundamental measure of new venture success.[24] But how do values interact with ethical decisions to guarantee success without compromise? Many have asked over the years whether an entrepreneur's personal values have any impact on the relative success of the new venture. Others have inquired whether the new venture's success is a direct reflection of the entrepreneur. But ethical behavior remains a difficult construct to measure, and presents a significant challenge to quantify its effects on entrepreneurial decision making.

During the last two years, while I was formulating my ideas for this project, friends and colleagues offered numerous comments and opinions about what the final product should look like. The two most popular responses I received when I said I wanted to write the first book in the market dealing with *entrepreneurial ethics* were: "Well now, 'Entrepreneurial Ethics', there's an oxymoron if ever I heard one," and "Heh, that should be a pretty short book." With all kidding aside, I searched every corner of the existing book market, and found two categories devoted to entrepreneurship, and four dealing with ethics. In the entrepreneurship area, I found introductory textbooks that covered the breadth and depth of the seminal literature and research in the field for use as the primary text in a survey course in entrepreneurship, small business management, or new venture development. The other works dealt with narrow and specific issues about the entrepreneurship process, such as start-ups and business plans, new venture finance, small firm strategy, and commentaries on entrepreneurial types. In the ethics area there were books dealing with the philosophical arguments and foundational issues of morality and values, and others dealing with ethics in the political economy or society in general. There were surveys of the broad scope of *business* ethics, but these tended to focus on the large, multi-faceted corporation. The last group were case studies of large corporations, offering practical examples of different categories for ethics in accounting, marketing, finance, strategy, management, advertising, production, or legal issues.

However, there were no books about the distinct ethical issues of fast-growth entrepreneurial new ventures. My vision is that this book will meet the growing need for college and university professors to have a specific entrepreneurial ethics resource to accompany the main course textbook for both undergraduate and MBA courses in entrepreneurship, small business management, and new venture development. The book can be used to facilitate class discussions and research inquiry into numerous areas of ethics within the context of studying new ventures and the entrepreneur. It deliberately avoids the conversion of values into some form of overly simplistic discrete formula, and it is designed specifically *not* to define one person's view of ethics, or be a book of "how to do business ethics in the small firm." The model should stimulate a good deal of debate about how values affect smaller firms, and what areas of new ventures are most likely to be exposed to the pressures and increased potential for ethical compromise.

This book presents a new model that is uniquely suited for examining ethical issues from the distinct perspective of the entrepreneurs who start and manage new ventures. Careful attention is paid to the range of regular business activities that successful entrepreneurs engage in every day, as they encounter specific policy junctures within the model. My model integrates a progressive sequence of factors that have a cumulative effect on the firm's internal values profile. The entrepreneur's individual characteristics comprise the foundational component that supports core values and personal factors of influence on the new venture. This unique configuration establishes a business-level methodology for recognizing ethical issues, and offers a performance basis for five fundamental new venture ethical domains, including: a) *firm representation,* b) *market expectations,* c) *financing requirements,* d) *external partnership agreements,* and e) *firm culture.*

The model works like this. First, there are new ventures, entrepreneurs, and new ideas or concepts to introduce to various markets. Second, entrepreneurs formulate and exhibit individual perspectives and interpretations of moral judgments, core values, and ethical behavior. Third, entrepreneurs perform seven basic business actions that apply to each of the functional areas within the enterprise. And finally, as entrepreneurs move and operate in these actions within the risky and often volatile environment of the start-up venture, they experience exposure to an increased potential for compromising those individual values within five separate ethical domains of the new venture development process. Evidence will be presented that business vision is often synonymous with the personal vision and aspirations of the individual entrepreneur, and that, in many cases, the entrepreneurial new venture is essentially a subjective extension of the personal nature exhibited by the entrepreneur. The types of business operations that introduce this increased propensity for ethical concerns will be referred to as *relational transactions*. These include all those scenarios where the firm is represented in some form of negotiation or decision making process. A *relational transaction* can either include the individual entrepreneur or employees of the firm acting on behalf of the entrepreneur. It is the various configurations of these transactions that require ethical behavior and personal value judgments that are unique to entrepreneurial new ventures.

Empirical support for this model will be presented throughout the ensuing chapters. This evidence is derived from a six-month survey of nearly two hundred and fifty individual entrepreneurs whose companies were listed on *INC. Magazine*'s list of the "500 Fastest Growing Privately Held Companies" from 1990 through 1996. The final database consists of two hundred and fourteen individual entrepreneurs' responding to forty separate situational decision scenarios and seven demographic items. Findings will be presented for each of the five ethical domains of relational transactions to categorically represent a broad scope of new venture ethical issues and problem areas. How the firm interacts in each of these domains will vary due to the primary impact of the entrepreneur in establishing firm behavior. The evidence suggests that new ventures do reflect the individual entrepreneur's characteristics and as such they often develop company-wide policies and procedures that directly represent the entrepreneur's personal value system.

The chapters are organized to blend the ethics and values model into a sequential format that examines entrepreneurial value judgments as resultant effects of the firm's company-wide vision. This vision is determined by the entrepreneur's unique combination of attitudes and characteristics displayed in guiding and managing the firm. Chapter One summarizes specific characteristics that define the propensity for ethical situations in entrepreneurial new ventures. The nature of newly launched firms is profiled with respect to the product or service concept, the competitive market, and the potential for sustainable growth. Chapter Two then examines the individual entrepreneur, the driver of this new venture, and outlines those specific personal attributes that are generally conducive to ethical considerations. Links are drawn between new venture risk and uncertainty, and the unique personal characteristics of entrepreneurs. The underlying rationale is that new ventures provide a structural mechanism for individual entrepreneurs which does not exist in large corporation environments.

Chapter Three explains the bonding process of the entrepreneur, the idea, and the recognized opportunity as uniquely expressed in the entrepreneur's vision for the venture. The process of idea generation involves a distinct personal vesting system in the entrepreneur and creates a series of sequential links of commitment that draw the business and the entrepreneur closer to each other. Chapter Four then outlines how the individual entrepreneur brings to the enterprise a distinct set of personal values. These decision making value parameters are intricately associated with the entrepreneur's business idea. It is here that a secondary underlying rationale is introduced, namely that the new venture begins to reflect the personal profile, values, and ethical behavior of the entrepreneur. But an idea and vision are not sufficient to shape the entrepreneur's values.

Chapter Five sets forth the entire scope of this unique model as the basis for the ethics of new ventures. It ties together the personal values of the risk tolerant entrepreneur and the venture's risky activities, and creates a basis for bringing together an idea and an opportunity within a business vision. However, this perceived melding of the individual entrepreneur with the vision and mission of the newly launched enterprise, may present the notion that the personal values and ethical considerations of the individual become one and the same with the firm's corporate perspective. This phenomenon then contributes to how the entrepreneur and the venture deal with ethics and value-based decision making across the five previously mentioned business situations called relational transactions. Chapter Six covers the first ethical domain of *new venture representation*, where the melding of the entrepreneur with the firm's perspective produces a direct impact on all aspects of how the content and process of the new business are represented externally in the competitive market. Chapter Seven describes how this melding can have a direct influence on the degree of future *market expectations* for measuring business performance. Chapter Eight discusses the values impact on the various applications of new venture *financial requirements*. Chapter Nine demonstrates the process by which the new venture establishes the structure and frequency of external business *partnering*. And Chapter Ten explains the nature and effectiveness of the firm's internal *firm culture*.

The relative extent of entrepreneurial reflection in each of these five domains of relational transactions plays a significant role in how the venture is strategically positioned for change in the market. Ultimately, these internal capabilities for accommodating change will determine the long-term viability of the venture and its ability to maintain momentum in a changing competitive environment. Chapter Eleven brings together the entrepreneurial ethics model within the context of change and the impact that the resultant decision making can have on the firm's competitive momentum. Chapter Twelve then provides a wide range of empirical evidences and interactions of the various ethical issues covered in the previous six chapters. The detailed statistical analysis and regression results from Chapter Twelve are then summarized in an Appendix. A glossary of terminology is also provided, as well as a topical index, and comprehensive end notes for all outside sources cited throughout the book. It is hoped that this model of entrepreneurial ethics formation and decision contexts will generate numerous discussions among entrepreneurs and employees of new ventures, as well as students and faculty of entrepreneurship and the new venture development process.

— *David B. Newton*
Santa Barbara
California

# CHAPTER ONE

# *Entrepreneurial New Ventures*

## The Ethics Posture of New Ventures

Newly launched entrepreneurial business ventures generally tend to generate a good deal of excitement among investors, employees, managers, and the marketplace, because they are associated with positive expectations toward a yet unrealized sales and profit potential, innovative ideas, and prospects for rapid growth in a newly emerging market. Most, if not all, of the inherent tenets that comprise entrepreneurial ventures tend to create an environment fraught with the capacity to produce a wide range of ethical dilemmas, moral considerations, and value judgments. There are numerous fundamental characteristics that to some extent comprise all entrepreneurial new ventures. However, for the scope of this discussion of entrepreneurial ethics, Table 1.1 presents six characteristics as those that require a magnified attention to values-based decision making in new ventures. Together, they construct the unique ethical environment associated with entrepreneurial new venture development, an atmosphere that tends to position individual entrepreneurs as uniquely susceptible to ethical dilemmas.

The entrepreneurial new venture is actually an ethical conundrum, which will hereafter be referred to as a *prospective paradox*. This paradox consists of two core perspectives. First, entrepreneurial new ventures are often virtually untested, and as such, they are perched precariously upon a complex network of assumptions and probability assessments related to specific anticipated future prospects. These open-ended prospects are at the very heart of the entrepreneurial new venture. The unique nature of the organizational structure tends to create and support a form of *systematic optimism* for related stake holders, including capital providers, suppliers, distributors, employees, and customers. But, on the other hand, because new ventures are in fact untested, a distinctive form of *venture paroxysm* also serves as perhaps the greatest hindrance to clear and objective thinking with respect to the appropriate decisions and strategies necessary to successfully realize those specific anticipated future prospects. These unrealized prospects are an abstract concept, yet they directly impact decisions concerning tangible components of the enterprise such as capital investments, employment, marketing strategies, and production operations.

■ ■ ■ ■
**Table 1.1**
**Ethics Oriented Characteristics of New Ventures**

1. *a direct relationship between business risk and the entrepreneur's expected return,*
2. *a high level of business uncertainty due the "untested" nature of the company's operations,*
3. *a business that is primarily defined by a newly introduced product or service innovation,*
4. *an external competitive market that exhibits a significant opportunity for the introduction of a new product or service,*
5. *an internal environment that is less formal and lacks the structural sophistication of proven policies and procedures,*
6. *a relatively small, concentrated core of managerial decision making responsibility.*

■ ■ ■ ■

The new venture can also tend to foster a *modified rationality* among stake holders that directly impacts ethical alternatives, moral choice, and value judgments. This describes the negative impact to decisions among stake holders of entrepreneurial new ventures caused by the abstract concept of anticipated future prospects. It can even alter individual ethical alternatives , moral choices, and value judgments about tangible business decisions because the potential for significant future gain exists for those who can persevere through various levels of risk and uncertainty. The firm and the entrepreneur will encounter several primary *relational transactions* based on these new venture characteristics. Relational transactions are the points of contact where the entrepreneur interacts with the various constituencies that have stakes in the success of the new venture. It is the various interactions due to the unique characteristics of the entrepreneurial firm that create the inherent propensity for entrepreneurs to face difficult moral choices and ethical dilemmas in their decision making.

New ventures embody these characteristics and expose entrepreneurs to inherently difficult ethical considerations. These features are unique to smaller, entrepreneurial enterprises and distinguish the small company from the large corporation across several dimensions. The specific internal and external environments associated with new ventures provide a wide range of values-based decision scenarios and numerous implications for management capabilities. The internal focus deals with employees, decision processes, policies, and procedures. The external aspects include the competition, partners, and the whole of society in general. Questions have been raised as to the individual responsibility of the new venture with respect to consumers, social welfare, and quality of life. All start-up companies encounter a good deal of risk as to whether they will ultimately meet with success or failure. However, in addition, there are many today who argue that new ventures must also recognize their inherent social responsibility within the competitive environment.[1] Perhaps one of the most exciting features of the entrepreneurial venture is the realization that an idea that has not yet been tried can be implemented at the right time and in the right place to produce a brand new organization that generates jobs and investment returns.[2] Yet, beyond sales and profitability, investment and job creation, new ventures embody an entire range of personal and professional choices in the market. Evidence suggests that start-up firms must effectively merge with the established infrastructure of society in general, and that new ventures can contribute to, or detract from, a host of non pecuniary benefits and costs within the overall social context.[3]

Each of these six characteristics, when examined individually, present a whole host of potential ethical scenarios and value judgments relating to several constituencies. Business operations and ethical responsibility must go hand in hand because the firm is establishing a reputation and a following while it is telling its story to the market.[4] Perhaps the largest single characteristic dealing with ethics and value judgments involves the entrepreneur's personal belief that the venture will ultimately be very successful.[5] Certainly the most attractive characteristic of the new venture is its potential for huge rewards to those who climb on board at the ground level, and yet the flip side of this coin is fraught with a tremendous challenge and obstacles that could literally overnight bring the entire venture to screeching halt.[6] The following, is a broad list of managerial questions facing individual entrepreneurs. "Is there a measurable and recognizable innovative distinction in the new product or service?" "What is the societal mission of the new venture?" "In what ways does this organization exhibit distinctive competency relative to the competition?" "To what extent does the structure and complexity of the competitive market dictate business policy?" "Is the potential for sustained market growth adequate to support a long-term strategy?" "What is the most effective capital structure for the new venture?" "What are the inherent consequences of the available sources of venture funding?"

## Risk and Expected Return

Risk is a relative measure of the variance of expected outcomes that are likely to occur and each is assigned a respective probability relative to the comparative positions of the other reasonable outcomes under consideration. Risk management does not include every *possible* outcome that can be surmised, but only those probable outcomes which are quantified based on a relative sequential scale. Expectations for the entrepreneurial new venture will cover a wide spectrum of probable outcomes, ranging from extraordinary success through complete failure (bankruptcy and total loss). It is inherent in new ventures that a wide variance of probable outcomes confront the founding executive management team. These widely varying expectations for future returns however, serve as one of the primary motivating forces in the entrepreneurial new venture development process. This is perhaps best described through the Schumpeterian form of entrepreneurship characterized by the creation of new ventures designed either to bring innovative products to existing markets, or existing products to innovative markets, activities which incorporate a significant degree of risk.[7]

Modern finance theory recognizes a direct relationship between the accepted level of risk and *expected* return.[8] This trade-off is fundamental to understanding investment selection and portfolio management,[9] and parallels the entrepreneurial new venture development process. Figure 1.1 depicts the fundamental relationship between accepted risk (the horizontal axis) and the *expected* return (the vertical axis) commensurate with that position. Point A represents an investment position whose coordinates are a perfectly hedged and virtually risk-free exposure with a relatively low or nominal *expected* rate of return $R_A$. Point B shows a separate position whose coordinates are an average level of market diversification with a relatively higher *expected* return $R_B$. This *expected* return incorporates an additional premium beyond the risk-free position due to the increased risk exposure of the diversified position. Line AB defines the various combinations between risk and *expected* return that a rational individual would be willing to accept between a risk-free position and an average, fully diversified market position. It is probably invalid to assume that this perfect linear relationship defines all possible positions in the risk- return trade off. The correct functional form is intuitively curvilinear because there is probably only a relatively small incremental increase in marginal expected return due to increased risk exposure at Point D versus Point B (no rational individual can expect continuous linear intervals of *expected* return beyond the point of a fully diversified position, because at some point beyond an average level of risk, additional risk exposure begins a negative effect on *expected* returns).

■ ■ ■ ■

**Figure 1.1**
**The Direct Relationship of Risk and Return**

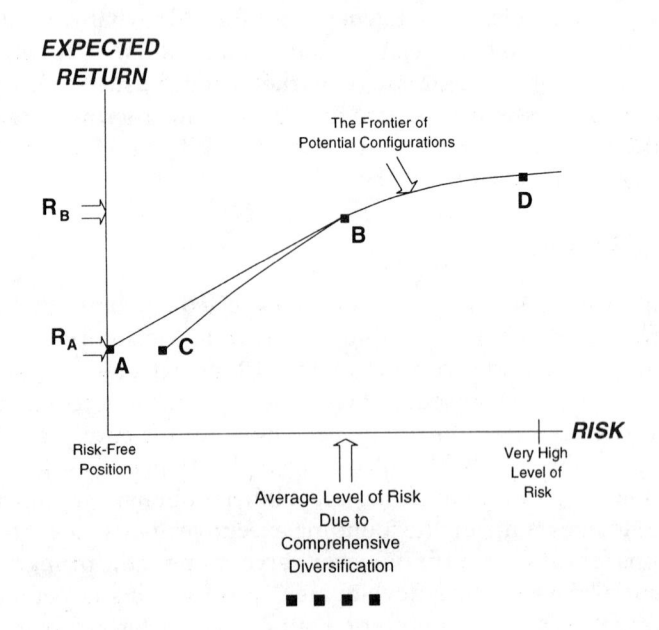

■ ■ ■ ■

The prospects of obtaining a certain anticipated level of future reward serve as the differentiating rationale when investors choose between various degrees of risky investments, such as providing funds for a new venture.[10] Risk transfer and risk premia are fundamental constructs in modern financial theory.[11] When two parties form a contract, the risk prone party (the assignee) agrees to accept the risk averse party's (assignor's) uncertain potential future outcomes in exchange for a fixed and up-front premium (normally pecuniary remuneration). The receipt of this payment signals the ultimate transfer of the risk between the two parties and constitutes an underwriting function on the part of the assignee.[12] The risk premium is constructed so as to appropriately compensate the assignee based upon the degree of uncertainty that is present across a range of probabilistic outcomes. The entrepreneur's vesting in the assignment of the actual results accrues to the risk assumption, while the assignor sacrifices assignment vesting in exchange for receipt of the risk premium. Risk assumption and assignment vesting are components of mutual coinvestment with claims to the venture results,[13] in the form of potential losses, as well as potential gains.

Two motives exist to reduce business risk. First there is a desire to reconcile the conflict of interests between owners (shareholders) and managers (agents), and second, there is an interest in reducing or eliminating certain aspects of uncertainty concerning future cash flows.[14] The former addresses the matter of agency risk transfer, while the latter represents *rate-of-return* risk. Lower business risk is directly correlated with lower rates of expected return, although no cause and effect conclusion is inferred.[15] Risk averse individuals are content to reduce the variance on *expected* future cash flows in exchange for a fixed income (e.g. a salary or a rent), with negligible potential upside variability. Entrepreneurs seek to secure assignment vesting, in that effective managing of greater risk offers the promise of greater potential return, as opposed to no risk in exchange for the lower return fixed income. Perhaps Frank Knight captured the essence of the entrepreneurial risk and return trade-off when he wrote: "Entrepreneurship characterizes how the confident and venturesome assume the risk, or insure the doubtful and timid, by guaranteeing to the latter a specified income in return for an assignment of the actual results."[16] This is the purest form of Schumpeterian entrepreneurship.

Several risk transfers occur between vertical business channels related to entrepreneurial new ventures. The eighteenth century French economist Cantillon referred to commerce organizers as "inter market operators" who undertake to mobilize imperfect markets to reduce uncertainty and risk.[17] The entrepreneurial new venture is uniquely exposed to business risk relative to expected future returns, and managing this determines bankruptcy versus profit for the venture.[18] At each successive channel there are risk transfers, where potential future cash flows are assigned to the subsequent party in exchange for an up-front fixed income. This process of assignment vesting is a fundamental component of entrepreneurial new venture development. But as such, it is also a significant source of ethical decision making issues related to personal values and relational transactions. Perhaps nowhere else is the entrepreneur exposed more directly to problems of ethical choice than in the process of clarifying and securing the ultimate risk management positions of all the interested stake holders in the new venture.

Entrepreneurs actively seek out dark, impeded, and poorly defined market environments in order to create and implement those missing links between the various disconnected business elements (each of which is marginally effective).[19] Eventually, the entrepreneur introduces a well integrated system of significant economic power that can mold and shape an emerging market and attract capital investment. Entrepreneurial risk transfer and assignment vesting are required in order to provide sufficient incentives for the individual to pursue pure Schumpeterian entrepreneurship. If no risk is transferred from the risk averse party to the entrepreneur, it is hypothesized that it is highly unlikely that the absence of the ensuing assignment of the venture's actual results will create sufficient incentive for innovative activity and risk management.

Entrepreneurs have a choice between working for a riskless wage or operating and managing a risky firm, and the futurity encountered by entrepreneurs provides incentives for entrepreneurs to create, or construct, the future as they wish it to be so that entrepreneurs push aside uncertainty, which then permits meaningful activity[20] and ask, "what are the opportunities for the greatest economic results?" Risk averse managers (as opposed to entrepreneurs) merely act as agents of the firm's owners and are supposedly motivated by the guarantee of a fixed income (salary) and job security. They seek to minimize the likelihood of bankruptcy by reducing the firm's nonsystematic business risk.[21] If these same risk averse managers are compensated based on cash flow, they will always opt for lower total compensation if the firm's future cash flows are relatively stable, as opposed to being volatile.[22] For instance, many franchisees do not appear to engage in true Schumpeterian entrepreneurship, but rather more closely resemble corporate managers, in that they are unwilling to take even moderate risks when compared with new venture entrepreneurs.[23]

## Business Uncertainty

Business uncertainty is different from business risk. Risks have already been described as a range of potential outcomes that are likely to occur and each is assigned a respective probability relative to the comparative positions of the other reasonable outcomes. Generally, entrepreneurial new ventures are launched even though specific risks have been identified. The rationale is that the entrepreneurial decision making team will be able to effectively manage these risks and navigate the new venture accordingly. But entrepreneurial enterprises also contain some elements of uncertainty. This captures the potential outcomes that cannot accurately be measured in terms of assigning probabilities of occurrence. Often, business are not launched if there exists an unacceptable level of uncertainty with respect to expectations about the firm's future sales, market penetration, production and technology capabilities, personnel competency, and potential profitability. However, some degree of uncertainty always exists with respect to the various potential future results the firm can experience after the launch. Business uncertainty remains as the truly "unknown" component of the enterprise.

Because uncertainty is an inherent characteristic of new ventures, how the firm describes it and deals with it is very important with respect to ethical considerations in decision making. Each individual entrepreneur is free to assess the nature of uncertainty within the company and define it in a personal context based on perception and the anticipated degree of impact certain factors could have on the firm. This allows uncertainty to be transformed into variable that represents an en*trepreneur-dependent assessment* (EDA). The weight or importance assigned to a matter of uncertainty determines its impact on decision making for the new venture. The personal bias and perception of the individual entrepreneur will color the degree to which this issue is taken seriously in business decision making. For instance, the founder of the venture believes there exists some level of a chance that government statutory requirements could be imposed within the next three-to-seven years that could regulate the production quality and distribution of this newly introduced product. There is no way of exacting a relative probability for this timing factor, nor the scope and content of how it might be structured. It is true *uncertainty* that does impact the expectations for the business. The entrepreneur can decide the subjective nature and composition of this uncertainty and either include it as an intangible issue that must be weighed in related decisions, or to varying degrees, dismiss this as being so unknown and intangible that no reasonable value or assessment can be determined relative to decision making. This creates a compounding effect that interacts with the greater specificity of the relative risk management of other tangible and well-identified expected outcomes.

An agency problem can exist when managers, who have no assignment vesting, try to act as agents on behalf of firm owners and pursue risky business ventures using the owners' resources. Owners and other vested parties will incur agency costs in the form of expenses to the company's creditors to write and execute protective covenants restricting the managerial pursuit of risky ventures which could profit the stockholders at the expense of the creditors. Another form involves monitoring costs, specifically the accounting function, where co-ownership exists and shareholders wish to monitor periodic owner-manager activity.[24] Risk averse managers desire a predictable stream of income (a relatively lower standard deviation of possible outcomes versus the prospects of the entrepreneurial new venture), and are therefore likely to avoid risky ventures if they were to have assignment vesting.[25] However, entrepreneurs act as agents on their own behalf and seek relatively risky or uncertain future cash flows, and put at risk their own reputation and financial resources. It is this exposure to, and acceptance of, business uncertainty that contributes to both an internal organizational environment, as well as an external environment, comprised of multiple levels of relational transactions that contain direct and indirect ethical considerations for the entrepreneur.

## Business Innovation

The vast majority of entrepreneurial new ventures are built upon some degree of either a product, service, or manufacturing innovation that forms the basis for the competitive position in the market. The effect of innovation varies tremendously across two dimensions. *Level I Innovation* deals with the substantive qualities that measure tangible performance benefits relative to similar, existing products, services, or manufacturing processes. *Level II Innovation* involves the intangible qualities that are a function of appearance, perspective, and personal interpretation. Three issues differentiate managerial fads from managerial fashions, as they pertain to managerial innovations. They include the factors that affect the rate of diffusion of the innovation, the distinctions between the early through late stages of adoption of the innovation, and the effects that adopter networks have on the process of diffusing innovation.[26]

The entrepreneur is enmeshed in the innovation diffusion process on two separate levels. At Level I, the tangible, physical properties of the newly introduced product, service, or manufacturing process produce somewhat objective and measurable performance improvements relative to those similar products, services, or process technologies already established in the existing market. Examples at this level include the superior speed of processing baggage at an airport terminal, the superior fuel efficiency of a new internal combustion engine, the 50% reduction in noise levels with a new manufacturing machine, the real time savings of sending a package with this courier, the improved communication sound quality of a new phone system, reduced costs of equipment maintenance, and the development of a longer useful life for electronic component parts. A *Level II Innovation* involves intangible, non-material properties of a newly introduced product, service or manufacturing process that produce much more subjective improvements to existing similar products, services, or processes. These are much more difficult, if not impossible, to measure because they are based solely on the individual personal interpretation and perspective of the entrepreneur and the market. Examples include improved care and attention in handling your overnight delivery, greater prestige from driving the new model year automobile, less confusion about programming a certain video cassette recorder, the enhanced and more modern looking appearance of the new control panel, and the easier technique for operating a newly modified industrial forklift.

Because business innovation carries with it components of anticipation, expectations, potential revolution in the market, and the possibility of attracting whole segments of the existing market away from prior entrants, it looms on the horizon for the entrepreneur as the single underlying factor that could propel the new venture to instant stardom and a financial windfall. It would not be inappropriate to state that the entrepreneur is "banking on" the innovation to put the company on the competitive road map as a leader in the industry. However, it must also be noted that there is never a "sure thing" when it comes to newly introduced business innovation. The entrepreneur will confront numerous opportunities to assess and represent the performance attributes of the firm's innovation to a wide range of constituencies, including potential customers, materials suppliers, marketing distribution channels, advertising and promotional underwriters, financial intermediaries, prospective capital providers, and even the competition. The untested nature of newly introduced innovations translates into various negotiation and representation situations where the entrepreneur will have to make considerable value judgments regarding costs and benefits, and ethical decisions concerning how to engage in relational transactions with the entire range of interested parties.

Consider the following scenarios. In the first case, a new venture has developed a Level I innovation consisting of a new patented component peripheral for the current best selling manufacturing machine in the commercial chemicals industry. This peripheral has performed admirably in controlled laboratory tests when utilized in conjunction with the leading apparatus in the field. There are no existing products similar to it in the market, and no known competing products in the works at other firms. The innovation has been proven to prolong the useful life of this widely used manufacturing machinery by between 35% and 50%, which translates to between three and five years. It also reduces the cost and need for regular scheduled maintenance. It could either be enthusiastically received as the most revolutionary new idea in the chemical industry in the last decade and experience a rush of new orders that immediately outstrips production capabilities, or it could be considered an unnecessary additional capital cost in the production mix, or meet with mixed reviews from actual field data at the manufacturing sites of those companies that initially adopt the product. It could do well for an initial twelve month introduction, but then encounter five similar devices that do no infringe on the patent and yet provide comparable performance results. The truth of the matter is that no one knows for sure whether the product's nascent feasibility will translate into bona fide long term viability. This places a tremendous amount of pressure on the entrepreneur to establish and effectively communicate a sense of credibility, even when the majority of new product information is still unavailable from the market. Individual optimism about future prospects can create a biased view of reality, and seep into the decision making processes of the firm.

A Level II scenario involves a similar add-on peripheral device for the same piece of manufacturing equipment in the same commercial chemicals industry. This product is an operating panel overlay circuit board that partially automates the programming sequence of buttons that must be pushed, and gauges that must be set, prior to operating the machine for a given shift. It is easily installed in less than 45 minutes and presents a very colorful, high-tech appearance to the control panel area on the front of the machine. It is thought that this device will speed up initial programming time, make the manufacturing process much easier to monitor, and improve the training of new operators because of the color-coordinated lighting scheme and the sequencing organization of the buttons and gauges. This form of Level II Innovation will encounter numerous difficulties in the marketing and promotion phases because the prescribed benefits are largely cosmetic and may lack substantive gains in operating utility.

Figure 1.2 summarizes the possible outcomes of both Level I and Level II Innovations. No formula exists to accurately predict which types of innovations have the greater likelihood of success because there are numerous subjective and values-oriented factors that impact the market's adoption process. Quadrants A and C depict *perception connections* whereby the innovator is successful in communicating the features, benefits, and costs of acquisition to the prospective buyers and the market agrees with the innovator firm's position. A "Type A" connection is often considered to be the easiest form of business innovation perception to establish, while the process of securing "Type C" agreement can be described as a manipulative selling job on the part of the innovator. The disagreement present in the "Type B" outcome is sometimes very difficult for the entrepreneur innovator to swallow because the benefits are tangible and should be easily recognized by the target market, but due to some unanticipated reasons, the market is tending to disagree with the innovator and the perception connection is never established. The "Type D" area is often referred to as the "I-Told-You-So" region of innovation introduction because the somewhat non substantive features and benefits of the innovation were difficult to sell to the prospective market, and the market proved to be unimpressed with the pitch that was offered, and no perception connection was ever established.

Personal preferences and individual perceptions will have to be won over in large num-

■ ■ ■ ■

**Figure 1.2**
**The Adoption of Innovations**

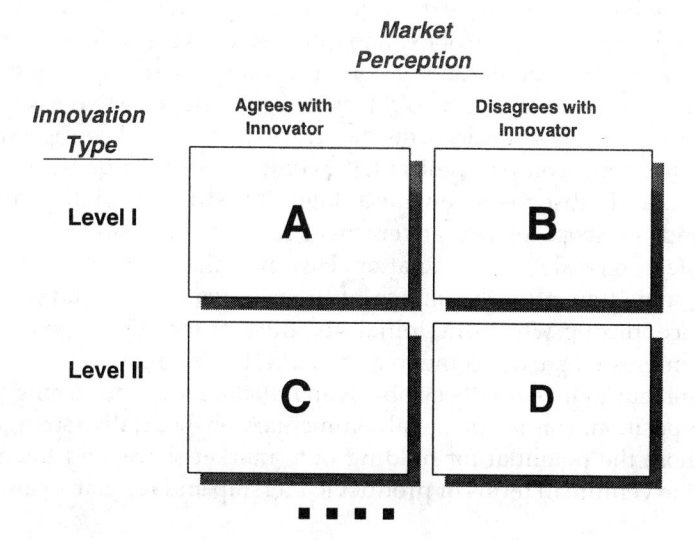

|  | Market Perception | |
|---|---|---|
| **Innovation Type** | Agrees with Innovator | Disagrees with Innovator |
| **Level I** | A | B |
| **Level II** | C | D |

■ ■ ■ ■

bers in order for this device to gain a strong foothold in the competitive market. In each of these two cases, the entrepreneur is confronted with several separate and conflicting business innovation realities. On the one hand, it could be surmised that all Level I Innovations will be readily recognized by target users and immediately adopted on a wide scale, while most Level II items meet with mixed reviews. However, on the other hand, exceptional, tangible, and measurable benefits in a Level I Innovation could go somewhat unnoticed and unrewarded by the target market due to cost or other logistical considerations, while a seemingly unnecessary cosmetic Level II Innovation add-on device could win over the vast majority of the designated users because it made an instant connection with the market's perception of the high-tech design and appearance. Business innovation is a major contributor to exposing the entrepreneur to numerous ethical considerations because of the nature of the unknown reaction to various types of innovation by the market.

## Significant Market Opportunity

Having discussed the nature of the risk return trade off, the component of business uncertainty, and various aspects of business innovation, the fourth characteristic that draws the entrepreneurial new venture into a unique position of ethical considerations involves the inherent perception that there exists significant market opportunity for the firm. This is both a function of the innovation prospects and the optimistic portion of the probable risks and returns that have been identified, as well as the positive outcome associated with any business uncertainty. The entrepreneur perceives that there exists an opening in the existing market for either a new product or service, or sufficient freedom to initiate a new market from scratch due to the nature and function of some form of innovative idea. The new venture is the vehicle through which the individual entrepreneur operates in this market and the means by which information is filtered and communicated to the stake holders and other related constituents. Why then, is this market opportunity conducive to ethical challenges?

The most common misconception about markets for new products and services is that they are inherently fast-growth in nature. True, there are many fast-growth markets that are the result of a newly introduced innovation from an entrepreneurial new venture, but not all entrepreneurial new ventures create or expand into fast-growth markets. The entrepreneur is placed in the awkward position of having both a seemingly wide open market opportunity placed before the new venture, but also a lack of complete knowledge about the *ultimate market composition* of that opportunity. This describes the eventual configuration of the relative placement of the initial company entrant, the competitive positioning of other firms (both existing companies and subsequent new candidates), the structure of the marketing distribution channels, and the scope of any government regulations dealing with the product or service, its manufacture, and its dissemination. However, this composition will not be known for certain until some time after the launch of the new venture and a period of *competitive settling* takes place, during which the initial volatility of the wide open market begins to stabilize and all interested parties come to rest in a certain manner.

The entrepreneur will generally establish an *initiator proxy* concerning the *expected* ultimate market composition. This is a personal commentary on the relative strength of the original market penetration, the potential for holding onto market share, and the anticipated final resting spot for the venture in terms of product leadership and regulatory impacts. The prospects for achieving significant gains in an emerging market opportunity present another potentially difficult ethical hurdle for the entrepreneur. The company founder is often placed in a position to assess, establish, and then represent an initiator proxy to stake holders. This occurs during the seed phase, while recruiting human resources and capital providers. And it also occurs during the launch phase while suppliers, distributors, and other stake holders try to ascertain the marketing strengths of the new venture. These interested parties may not want to admit it, but the entrepreneur is in a very powerful position to influence investor sentiment and opinion within the target market regarding the perceived strengths of the new venture. The proxy is often constructed for the first time during the writing of the business plan and the seed phase. It is often modified just prior to the launch, but that does not always mean that the entrepreneur has better objective information about the new market entry. Optimism can appear substantive and be contagious among stake holders due to the personal charisma of the entrepreneur and the choice of media used to deliver the message about the firm's forecast. But various forms of entrepreneurial hype, or touting, should only encourage greater due diligence on the part of potential capital providers.

The new venture must factor in an *erosion factor* based on the reality that, to some extent, other firms will eventually enter the market and attempt to implement either direct head-to-head competition or carve out a smaller niche built on the strength of a subsequent, but relatively minor , design or performance modification. The erosion factor is measured across two separate dimensions, speed and magnitude. It attempts to forecast the rate of decrease in the initial entrant's beginning market share as newly emerging competitors stake claims to various pockets of distinction around the position of the new venture innovator. This planning tool provides a basis for the entrepreneur to predict several ultimate market composition scenarios. The model cannot determine the actual market configuration, but it does factor in realistic prospects for the impact of competitive and regulatory components. Figure 1.3 shows how the erosion factor impacts new market opportunity relative to the speed and magnitude of deterioration. The horizontal axis represents the time duration over which the erosion takes place and the vertical axis measures the relative degree of negative impact to the new venture's initial stake in the market as the percentage decrease in market share due to factors brought about by new entrants and regulatory issues.

The erosion factor is based on a dependent relationship between the magnitude of the negative impact to the time duration as it is played out during the process of entry by competitors and the formalization of any applicable government regulations or restrictions. The Type I factor represents "massive erosion," where severe magnitude occurs over a very short duration of time, and leaves the new venture with only a small fraction of its initial stake. Type II depicts "steady erosion," where moderate to severe impact occurs over an intermediate time period, and leaves the firm with a relatively small retention of market share. The Type III example describes "intrusive erosion" where the firm experiences some intrusion into its "turf" occurring over an intermediate period similar to Type II, but market share loss is only around 50% of the initial stake, allowing the new venture to remain as a significant player in the ultimate market composition. The Type IV mode is the "erosion" where collateral damage to the initial stake is minimal and occurs over a prolonged time period, and the firm ultimately remains the leader in the industry. An example could be a Type II scenario where a firm with an initial 75% stake in a $100 million new market (first year sales of $75 million), ends up with a 28% market share within a year and a half. The 47-point drop is a 63% decrease in sales due to "steady erosion." Regardless of the degree, entrepreneurs must include an erosion factor when they examine market opportunity and make decisions to represent future expectations to interested stake holders.

■ ■ ■ ■

**Figure 1.3**
**The Erosion Factor of Market Opportunity**

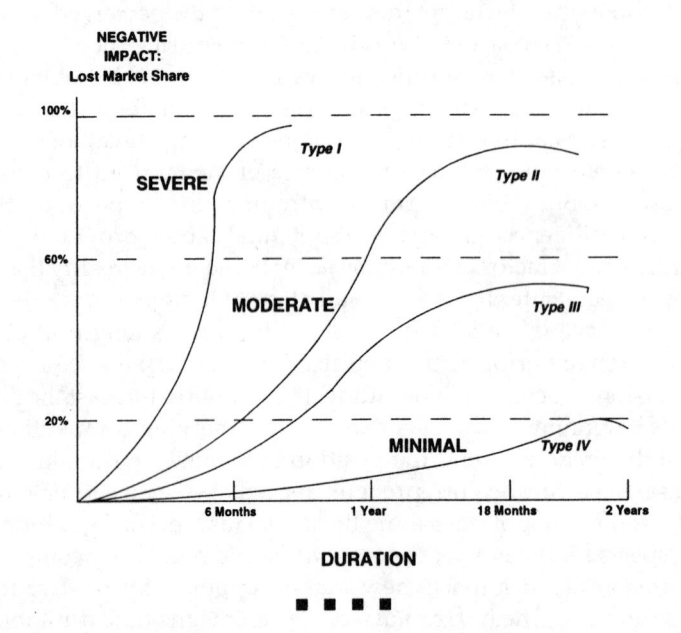

■ ■ ■ ■

## Less Formal Internal Environment

The fifth characteristic of the entrepreneurial new venture that makes the firm susceptible to difficult ethical considerations involves the less formal internal decision making and operations environment relative to more established and larger companies. The entrepreneurial organizational structure tends to be a much more flat and narrow design in relation to the taller and broader framework utilized by firms that have significantly more employees and have, over many years, developed highly formal operating policies, procedures, and information management systems. Most large and well-established companies have grown to the extent that the division of labor has progressed to an elaborate series of units, divisions, and departments each performing highly specialized tasks in support of huge sales volume and significant production and marketing logistics. Figure 1.4 shows a typical organization chart with clear channels of authority and managerial communication, and an extensive division of functional areas.

In direct contrast to the tall and wide structure of the larger, well-established firm, the typical profile of a new venture has the founder as the head of the organization generally followed by a narrow level of a few core functional areas right beneath, and reporting directly to, the entrepreneur. Figure 1.5 shows the organization chart for a flat and narrow

## Figure 1.4
### Established Firm Organization Chart

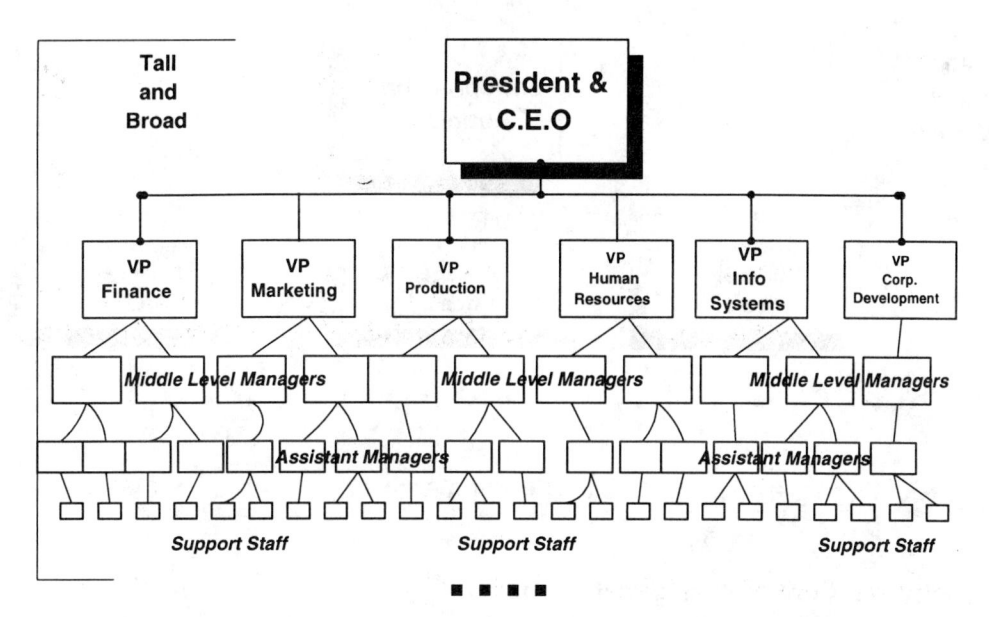

*[Organization chart showing: President & C.E.O at top (labeled "Tall and Broad"), reporting down to VP Finance, VP Marketing, VP Production, VP Human Resources, VP Info Systems, and VP Corp. Development. Below the VPs are Middle Level Managers, then Assistant Managers, then Support Staff.]*

entrepreneurial new venture. Lines of communication flow directly to the founder within a compact network of team orientation for decision making. The overall environment for this type of structure tends to be quite personal and informal with regard to how people approach each other and the channels through which decision policies are formulated. The new venture reflects this informality for several reasons. First, there are a comparatively fewer number of employees in an entrepreneurial firm. Second, the focus of the organization is promoting a new product or service, and growing sales. Initially, the entrepreneurial venture does not focus on decision procedures, information management systems, and departmental organizational charts and meeting schedules. Third, the entrepreneur wants to have instant access to news about customers and the market in order to respond quickly. Fourth, the entrepreneur tends to be flexible and able to adapt to sudden changes as the firm encounters new situations each day for which there are not yet clear policies or procedures. Many entrepreneurs state that they want their employees to imitate this flexible and spontaneous manner, even if it means acting without all the necessary and pertinent information. Fifth, an "open-door" policy often exists between the entrepreneur and the relatively few employees. This may not be able to support consistency with respect to how information is gathered and processed, how decisions are made, and who has the authority to make certain decisions in specific situations. Ethical predicaments arise because the informality may lack direction and controls.

**Figure 1.5**
**Entrepreneurial Organization Chart**

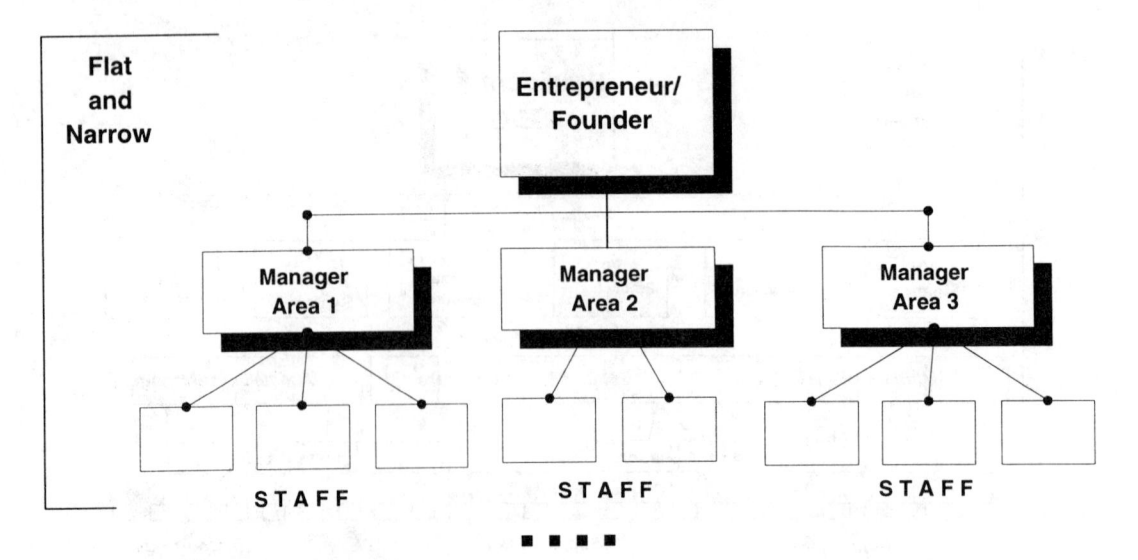

```
Flat
and                    Entrepreneur/
Narrow                 Founder
                           │
         ┌─────────────────┼─────────────────┐
      Manager           Manager           Manager
      Area 1            Area 2            Area 3
      ┌─┼─┐              ┌─┐              ┌─┼─┐
      STAFF              STAFF            STAFF
```

## Concentrated Core of Managerial Responsibility

The sixth and final characteristic that predisposes the entrepreneur to a wide range of ethical considerations is that managerial responsibility tends to exist in a highly concentrated core of individuals. Many new ventures rely almost exclusively on the entrepreneur to make virtually all decisions. There is no delegation of substantive authority to employees in the few functional areas of the firm. The entrepreneur can possess essentially 100% of the power to review and analyze a situation and implement a decision. In some cases there may be one or two other individuals that are sometimes consulted for their opinion and ideas, but the entrepreneur is "running the show" and believes that the ultimate success of the venture is dependent on his or her ability to handle all operating and strategic issues as they arise. The justification for maintaining a highly concentrated core of managerial responsibility comes from three sources. First, the entrepreneur is deeply vested in the future potential for the venture's success. Second, the entrepreneur sees the new venture as a personal extension of his or her own goals and objectives. As such, they can feel a sense of responsibility to individually shoulder the results of decisions. Third, they truly believe in the product or service, and they are already committed to persevere even in the face of substantial obstacles and business risks. This attitude can foster the belief that only they know what is best for the firm, and that employees are all essentially support personnel.

Managerial responsibility in the entrepreneurial new venture can be thought of as a series of sequential levels of decision importance. At the very core of the scheme resides the entrepreneur, with the broadest range of authority and decision making ability. Ideas, direction, strategies, and plans are all initiated by the entrepreneur at this core level. Employees are placed at incremental stages surrounding the individual entrepreneur at the core. This structure is known as *Concentric Managerial Placement*.[27] Figure 1.6 depicts the typical flow of managerial responsibility within an entrepreneurial new venture. Line AB originates with the entrepreneur at the core and is the policy directive aimed at Decision Area 1. Arc *ab* is the span of responsibility present for the support staff employee that relates to this decision at concentric Level I. Arc *cd* is the breadth of responsibility for the person at Level II, and arc *ef* and arc *gh* show the duties at Level III and Level IV respectively. In a similar manner, line AC is the management directive aimed at Decision Area 2. The four levels of concentric managerial placement handle the related issues represented by the four arcs: *a'b'*, *c'd'*, *e'f'*, and *g'h'*. The directive originates at the Core Level with the owner-entrepreneur and proceeds across the areas of responsibility for support personnel. Each staff employee understands their respective range of duties as they relate to implementing the directive and accomplishing the objective for that decision area. Most entrepreneurs operate in a manner like this because it allows them to continuously monitor the progress of activities so as to keep their finger on the pulse of important decisions as the objective procedural aspects carried out by the firm's support staff resources.

**Figure 1.6
Concentric Managerial Placement**

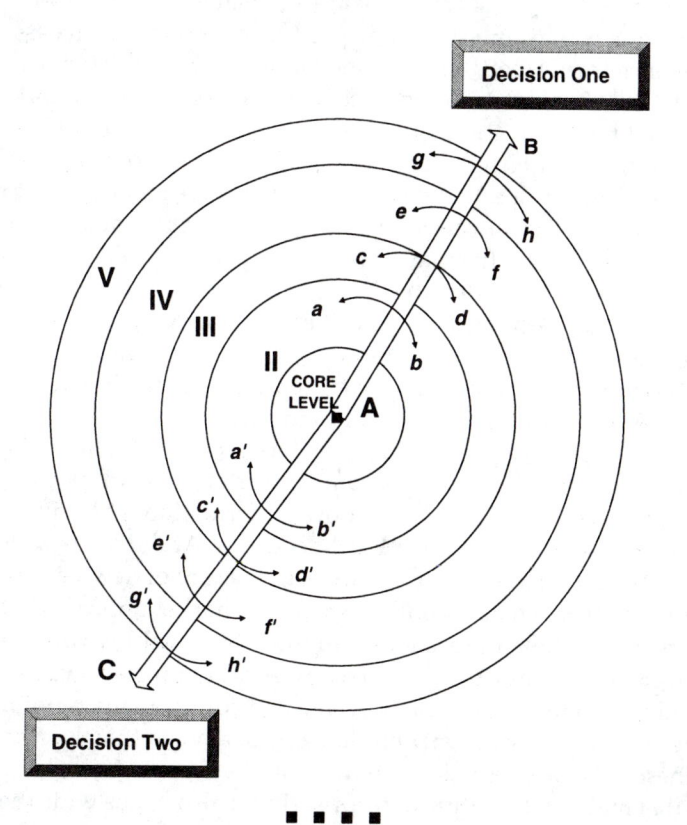

This type of concentric positioning keeps the entrepreneur at the core of all decision making directives, and allows employees to readily send questions and concerns back down along the policy line to entrepreneur. However, this is certainly not the most efficient or practical manner to operate and manage the new venture. Although similar models of this style of structure are readily found in most entrepreneurial new ventures, it tends to overburden the owner at the core with too many procedural details related to a sizable number of concurrent decisions. This accurately describes the metaphor that the entrepreneur has "too many irons in the fire" and is therefore not doing any one thing well.

## An Ethical Compounding Effect

Together, the previous six characteristics produce an ethical compounding effect that stretches the exposure of the entrepreneurial new venture into a unique position with respect to displaying values-oriented decision making. First, the direct relationship between risk and *expected* return supports the assumption that accepting increasing levels of risk will be rewarded with a higher *expected* return, and this exposes new ventures to numerous decision areas that are not clearly defined in objective black and white effects. Somewhat related to these identifiable risks are various aspects of business uncertainty that cannot be quantified. The risk and uncertainty combine to leave many decisions open to subjective criteria and personal perspectives as to what is appropriate and what is not. The firm is then engaged in marketing an innovative (and untested) new product or service or process. Because there is not yet a performance track record for the innovation, the new venture can breed an overly optimistic expectation of complete acceptance by the market, and a rapid and wide spread adoption by targeted buyers. If there exists an optimism about the role of innovation, then the determination might be inferred that a significant market opportunity is within the grasp of the newly launched enterprise. In light of these outward perceptions, the internal environment of the entrepreneurial firm can tend to be somewhat informal when compared with larger, established companies. This may appear to support an open atmosphere and a true "team" approach to decision making, but it also affords a good deal of individuality with respect to interpreting data, establishing priorities, and implementing decisions. Finally, the new venture can tend to overly concentrate on managerial decision making responsibilities exclusively within the realm of the founding entrepreneur as the initiator and catalyst at the functional core of the new venture's directives and action plans.

At this point, the first premise of this book has been established. The entrepreneurial firm is a risky venture that also includes some uncertainty as to its successful operation. These constitute two levels of relatively unknown information which increase the tendency to subject the entrepreneur to difficult ethical decisions. At the next two levels, additional unknown information exists relative to the untested nature of new venture innovation and the prospects for capturing an apparently significant market opportunity. But again, these continue to encroach on the entrepreneur's unique, personal interpretation of these matters, and as such creates a venue filled with many ethical implications. Lastly, the informality of the internal environment and the concentrated core of managerial responsibility foster more exposure to subjective interpretation and personal ethical perspectives. Taken in their entirety, these six characteristics of new ventures are compounded together to create an atmosphere that makes for exciting enterprise, but it also opens wide the door to a unique susceptibility to questionable ethical decisions, moral choices, and value judgments. Having examined the ethical characteristics of new ventures, it is now time to investigate and evaluate ethical considerations unique to the individual entrepreneur, the driver of the emerging business.

## CHAPTER TWO

# *Entrepreneurs:*
## *Drivers of New Ventures*

### Introduction

Attention will now be focused on the person behind the enterprise, the individual entrepreneur. The founder of the new firm is often *the* primary driving force responsible for the assessment and analysis at the seed stage, and the successful launch and growth of the company in the market. Historically, entrepreneurship has been linked with Protestantism, the need for achievement, and as the catalyst for economic development. There exists a wealth of empirical evidence that several characteristics appear to be common among individual entrepreneurs. Table 2.1 lists several empirically supported characteristics associated with entrepreneurial behavior. Entrepreneurs usually pursue a self-determining venture, in which they possess complete control of all decisions related to operations, and where the probability of remaining in the pursuit increases directly relative to the time that has expired since the inception of the venture.[1] The driver of the new venture displays a sense of singular responsibility, an ability to anticipate and recognize future opportunities, and a willingness to see risk acceptance not as a function of chance, but rather as a function of skill on the part of the entrepreneur, to manage it and make calculated decisions to optimize economic returns while minimizing exposure to business and financial risk.[2]

Table 2.2 outlines another group of seven entrepreneurial principles that support successful new ventures.[3] Fundamental factors of informality, personal initiative, autonomy, and optimistic aspirations are generally bound together by some degree of financial vesting in the venture. The supports the principle of *co-investment mutualism*, which supposedly insures that entrepreneurs will seriously weigh the risk factors and act in a fiduciary capacity because they represent a pool of vested stake holders and want to preserve capital asset values. However, this can also work in reverse and support more risky behavior because the entrepreneur recognizes the benefits of diversification among several stake holders. This form of general liability exposes entrepreneurs to a continuum of expected outcomes, which include immeasurable profit on the one end, and a total loss at the other.

**Table 2.1**
**Empirical Evidences of Entrepreneurs**

1. *Self-employment is independent of age or work experience.*
2. *The likelihood of departing self-employment decreases with the duration of that self-employment.*
3. *The fraction of the labor force that is self-employed increases with age until age 40.*
4. *Men with significant assets are most likely to become self-employed.*
5. *One's wage earner experience has a small return in self-employment pursuits.*
6. *Low-end (poorer) wage workers are more likely to become self-employed.*
7. *Those with an internal locus of control are more likely to become self-employed.*

**Table 2.2**
**Principles of Successful Entrepreneurs**

1. *Free-Market Philosophy*
2. *Protected Autonomy*
3. *Decentralized Organization Structure*
4. *Creative Self-Initiative*
5. *Para-Managerial Network of Contacts*
6. *Built-In Appetite for Growth, and*
7. *Co-Investment Mutualism*

Table 2.3 presents another list comprised of nine objective characteristics of individual entrepreneurs.[4] The most noticeable feature is that of *vision*, the ability to be forward looking and literally see the venture operating successfully, even though the launch is still in the future. Entrepreneurs possess the ability to see beyond apparent constraints and obstacles, and recognize new opportunities for potential successes. The visionary activities of entrepreneurs are akin to the basic constructs of modern strategic behavior, including an external adaptiveness combined with a systematic and proactive execution of action plans.[5]

Entrepreneurs migrate toward, and readily accept, uncertainty as perhaps the core component of the new venture that is most closely linked with the potential for positive future performance.[6] True entrepreneurial activity embodies a large variance of expected future returns. The risk associated with the level of uncertainty differentiates entrepreneurs from

### Table 2.3
### Characteristics of Entrepreneurs

A. *Recognize the "big" picture.*
B. *Spot opportunities.*
C. *Totally commit to their cause.*
D. *See a need for complete control.*
E. *Possess a utilitarian view of what is right in a given situation.*
F. *Welcome uncertainty.*
G. *Utilize their contacts and connections.*
H. *Embrace competence.*
I. *Possess special "know-how"*

managers in large, established corporations. The entrepreneurial role is often discussed within a managerial context, as the one component of the formal organization where an individual seeks to improve the performance of a business unit by adapting to a changing environment.[7] It is critical to distinguish that definition of managerial entrepreneurship, which are those activities involved in coordinating and carrying on the duties of a going concern (where the components of the production function are well known and operate in established and clearly defined markets), versus the Schumpeterian form of entrepreneurship, which exhibits those activities necessary to create an enterprise where the parts of the production function are only partially known and operate in newly established, volatile, and somewhat poorly defined markets. Traditional corporate managers tend to function in more well-lit, well-defined, and unimpeded environments that present fewer obstructions, whereas entrepreneurs thrive in dark, poorly-defined, impeded environments complete with obstructions.[8]

The measure of entrepreneurial motivation across these two separate and distinct functions will produce differing ethical behavioral tendencies and variable results. Evidence suggests that Schumpeterian entrepreneurship and the management function are not related. Empirical research has found that entrepreneurs disdain the management function within their enterprise, and possess relatively little managerial motivation, when compared with various strata of corporate managers.[9] Entrepreneurs have a significantly lower need for power and security.[10] Yet, on the other hand, entrepreneurship "trait" studies have generally been lacking in their attempts to systematize common entrepreneurial characteristics so as to screen individuals or businesses as being an entrepreneurial "type," or to systematically commute identifiable entrepreneurial asset stocks to individuals.[11] Entrepreneurial behavioral studies have been significant in specifying an organization's creator as one who intentionally fulfills or undertakes a dynamic role in the business venture,[12] as opposed to arbitrarily meeting the static requirements in the manner of a functional manager. There have also been attempts to define and facilitate systematic *intra*corporate entrepreneurial activity in which the players, their roles, and the process flow of new ventures are objectively quantified. However, these do not address structural differences between organization types.[13]

## 22 ■ Chapter Two

A situational approach to entrepreneurial behavioral principles recognizes that these characteristics are unstable, in that any measurable behavior is determined by the independent variables unique to the venture's situation.[14] This infers that much of the variance in successful entrepreneurship can be explained by firm-specific unique variables and the contextual circumstances peculiar to that venture case. Stanford professor Robert Burgleman however, has long advocated systematic entrepreneurship, and the concept of *corporate venturing*, defined as a "formalization of a new corporate-level activity to generate new business for the large organization, primarily through the use of internal resources."[15] The *intrapreneur*[16] was introduced to describe the individual working within a large corporate environment specifically equipped and funded to generate new ventures.[17] Eventually, *intracorporate entrepreneurship* was envisioned as a new strategic component for all large companies as a systematic process that would allow big business to recapture the original determination, creativity, innovation, and imagination of true entrepreneurs.[18] The etymologies of the terms *entrepreneur* and *intrapreneur* differ in that intrapreneurship is designed by to train key managers in entrepreneurial values and behavior in order to foster creative project development.[19] Intrapreneurs then work within the firm as individual free market agents, within prescribed limitations, utilizing specific and discretionary corporate resources (intracapital) which may place further limits on the motivation necessary for pursuing risky new ventures.[20]

It can be very difficult to transfer apparently fixed and objective principles of entrepreneurship into other environments and assume that success will occur due to the presence of these characteristics.[21] The entrepreneur operates in a unique environment and exhibits qualities that are conducive and adaptive to the volatility, uncertainty, risk, and unknown factors present in new venture development. The following six characteristics parallel the six features of new ventures discussed in chapter one.

## Managing Risk and Risk Aversion

In the previous chapter, the relationship between risk and return was presented as a direct measure of association, in that increased risk exposure will only be accepted on the assumption that it brings with it an increased level of *expected* return as a risk premium compensation. Contrary to many misconceptions, entrepreneurs are not irrational, risk *seeking* individuals who would accept just about any level of moral hazard provided there was even a small chance of realizing a substantial future gain. Instead, the typical entrepreneur is generally risk sensitive to the degree that the new venture idea must possess an inherent and measurable trade-off between a reasonable probability for upside potential versus the prospects for downside loss. But do not most corporate managers and employees exhibit similar tendencies toward risk aversion? What distinguishes the entrepreneur as unique with respect to a risk averse perspective? The crucial distinction is that the entrepreneur believes that the risk can be systematically managed so as to effectively minimize its impact to the new venture development process. The entrepreneur is convinced that risk exposure will vary over many stages of the life of the company, and that there are two separate components that comprise risk management. The first is *active risk management* and the other is *latent risk management*. Active risk management involves implementing specific strategies aimed at reducing the firm's overall net exposure to negative circumstances. The entrepreneur believes that certain levels of business and financial risk exposure can be navigated successfully, and even avoided altogether, through the use of various strategies of diversification and contingency plans. The entrepreneur recognizes that extraneous risk variables probably do exist outside the new venture, but focuses instead almost entirely on specific, identifiable risks that can be controlled or impacted by personally formulated decisions. This type of risk management assumes that success in the new venture development process is dependent on accurately assessing negative prospects and implementing appropriate strategies to reduce their impact on the firm.

Latent risk management is quite different. It asserts that levels of risk exposure will ebb and flow, like the tides, in a random fashion based on the numerous extraneous variables outside of the entrepreneur's individual control. The entrepreneur believes that certain types of business and financial risk will increase and decrease due to the interaction of outside forces that cannot be controlled or impacted by the entrepreneur's decisions or strategies. But this is often an ill-advised planning perspective because it assumes that things can "tend to work themselves out" over time and that certain risks are unavoidable and will change on their own during the course of new venture development. A common ethical problem for entrepreneurs stems from this notion that not all negative news has to be reported or acted on immediately because many aspects of bad news will, over time, tend to even out with respect to the impact they have on operations. This also supports the idea that there is sometimes nothing to be gained in responding to every negative issue that surfaces because the firm can rely on its *weathering capability* for some of the financial and operating storms that confront the new venture. This common practice involves utilizing a "wait and see" approach to various types of risk, such that the enterprise does not engage in planned responses to a potentially negative issue, but instead keeps focused on the existing operating plan that is in place and, to some degree, disregards any form of directly addressing the risk because it is deemed as exogenous to the management function, residing outside of the realm of the firm's control. This strategy carries with it many ethical concerns that will be dealt with in both Chapter Seven and Chapter Eleven.

## The Problem of Invited Uncertainty

Many entrepreneurs are somewhat enamored with the open-ended prospects of navigating unchartered waters. They tend to exhibit various symptoms of a *Kirk Syndrome*, named for the fictional intergalactic starship captain. These symptoms include a thrill and excitement experienced in taking a product or service innovation into a newly emerging market, and an overly emboldened sense of confidence that they will achieve success due to their willingness to pursue uncertainty while others are content to merely operate in well-defined markets, with known products, and clear channels of distribution. The entrepreneur is credited as one who "boldly goes where no one else has gone before." This invitation to uncertainty can be incorrectly viewed as a positive attribute of entrepreneurs, when in fact it can be the one factor that is most likely to destabilize the new venture. An entrepreneur displaying symptoms of Kirk Syndrome may be more likely to disregard objective, outside advice about the firm's potential problems, and be more apt to head straight into a new market even if certain indicators are present that define the market as highly volatile and nearly impossible to define. The entrepreneur may actually gain an adrenaline rush from pursuing uncertainty in much the same way that a patron to an amusement park is drawn to the thrill of riding the high speed attractions.

A good deal of folklore has been promulgated regarding the nature of the entrepreneur actively seeking uncertainty in the external environment. It has often been said that, as the wagon trains full of people came from the east in the early 1800's during the days of the settling of the western United States, the true pioneers where generally the ones who experienced either the greatest rewards, by making the first claims to new lands, or the greatest failures, by enduring the full brunt of various hardships that comprised the uncertainty of being the first settler to enter into a new territory. In many ways, this analogy fits the description of *entrepreneurial pioneering*, where the market landscape is wide open and few, if any, have gone on ahead into the new region. Uncertainty abounds due to extremely limited information about the environment. And any information that is available is generally not current or reliable with regard to its source. Pioneers will, at some later date, either be viewed as extremely visionary and incredibly opportunistic, or foolish and lacking in common sense, and this view will be completely dependent on hindsight some time after the uncertainty has passed away and the new market comes into focus.

Perhaps the most significant negative impact related to the entrepreneur's invitation to uncertainty is the personal challenge that it creates and maintains within the individual. The company is already, in many ways, a direct reflection of the entrepreneur. It can be argued that the process of actively seeking uncertainty and embracing it as a necessary component of the new venture development process is not a requirement of the entrepreneur, but rather a tendency of individual behavior. The invitation is often made by the individual in order to provide a sense of positive potential gain to investors, or to purport a landmark adoption of a new technology. Successful entrepreneurs do not *have* to embrace uncertainty, they merely tend to be attracted to it, and often without any fear that it could translate into the financial ruin of the new venture. The open exposure to market uncertainty brings with it a wide range of ethical considerations regarding how the unknown issues are addressed and represented to stake holders, and what actions are implemented in order to limit the negative effects to all interested parties.

## The Innovator Trap

The "open door" policy that most entrepreneurs tend to exhibit toward uncertainty may be tied directly to the position the individual takes as to the *expected* depth and breadth of market penetration for a particular innovation. The process of creating a new technology, product, or service idea is highly complex and involves numerous variables that impact the direct outcome of innovation in the competitive market. However, an *innovator trap* does exist as a potential detriment for entrepreneurial behavior, and this is characterized by the belief that *all* innovations will be readily recognized and accepted in the market. The fact that the entrepreneur pursues various degrees of innovation does not necessarily translate into immediate market acceptance, rapid growth in sales, and venture success. And on the other hand, there does not have to exist a highly sophisticated degree of innovation in order for the entrepreneur to be successful. The innovator trap describes the pull on the individual entrepreneur to overemphasize a positive evaluation of an innovation. It subjects all new ideas to a criterion that the innovation must be able to demonstrate immediate *star quality*. The entrepreneur may feel pressured to convince everyone that the innovation will have the same impact as the internal combustion engine had on the transportation markets, or that Microsoft Corporation had on the market for personal computers.

The entrepreneur is so closely enmeshed with prospects for the innovation that a subjective premium is placed on individuals who are truly ground-breaking innovators. The entrepreneur hopes to capitalize on this subjective premium with investors and other stake holders related to the innovation. However, most entrepreneurs are characterized by an ability to try something new, to make adjustments in existing products and services that add value for end-users, or to improve a process so as to make it operate more efficiently or at less cost. Ethical concerns will surface if there are questions about whether the entrepreneur is truly an innovator, or merely a good storyteller who is able to passionately embellish the relative features of the innovation into a marketable product or service. But the reality is that not all innovations have to turn the business world upside down in order to support a highly successful new venture. And conversely, not all entrepreneurs possess the ability to be radical, ground-breaking innovators.

Great attention is given to radical or revolutionary innovators by the popular press in the commercial and financial community. Tremendous accolades are bestowed upon entrepreneurs whose revolutionary designs and ideas redefine the competitive market and capture a disproportionate share of sales potential relative to other firms. Often, these entrepreneurs become "household" names within the industry as their faces grace the front covers of prestigious business, finance, entrepreneur, and small business news magazines. The innovator trap can be evaluated in reference to the reality of acceptance for the new idea in the market. There are essentially four categorical types of market innovation measured across the two dimensions of market depth and breadth. Market depth defines how far into a specific targeted niche does the innovation penetrate. Market breadth describes the scope of the range across which users are adopting the innovation. Figure 2.1 summarizes four possible configurations of innovation acceptance. The upper left quadrant is defined as *disinterested innovation*, where there are very few levels of application and use in a market with narrow limits. A few firms within a certain niche have adopted the new idea, but they represent a relatively small number from the list of potential adopters that could use the innovation in that market segment. The lower left hand quadrant represents *surface innovation* as there appears to be many different adopters across a variety of separate market sectors, but like the previous case, the number of actual users is relatively small versus potential users. Without numerous levels of adopters, the innovation begins to gain a reputation as a specialty application, rather than a universal form of invention. The upper right section shows a typical *limited innovation*, where literally every level of supplier, producer, distributor, and marketer has adopted the new idea; the only drawback is that the product or service concept has applications that are restricted to a small and unique niche in the market. The lower right quadrant then depicts the best case scenario of *saturated innovation* where adoption is happening across a wide range of different market types, and applications are being clearly recognized and used at all levels within these markets. The individual entrepreneur can get caught in the trap where a subjective personal perspective regarding the type of innovative activity undertaken can cloud the true nature of a new idea and support unmerited positive expectations among stake holders and the competitive market. Many ethical issues will have to be dealt with because the propensity for innovative activities by the entrepreneur can interpret unrealistic degrees of impact in the market.

**Figure 2.1**
**Market Innovation Acceptance**

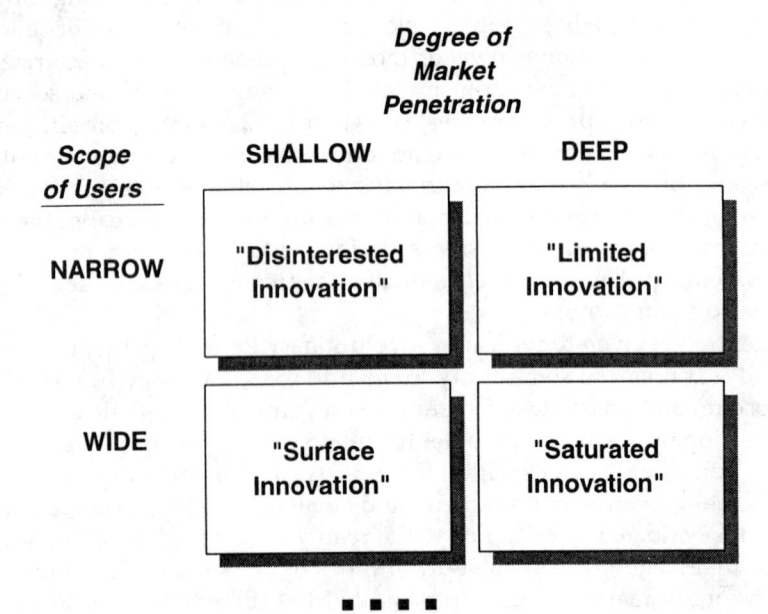

|  | Degree of Market Penetration | |
|---|---|---|
| **Scope of Users** | **SHALLOW** | **DEEP** |
| **NARROW** | "Disinterested Innovation" | "Limited Innovation" |
| **WIDE** | "Surface Innovation" | "Saturated Innovation" |

## The Flaw of Spotting Opportunity

The next characteristic of the entrepreneur that supports an increased potential for exposure to difficult ethical issues is the entrepreneur's penchant for recognizing excellent potential market opportunities. There is no way to accurately quantify an opportunity. Perhaps the most common way to try and determine a novel opening for commercial activities in a market is through assessing market potential and sales potential. A typical business plan for a new venture must be able to present convincing evidence that the entrepreneur has accurately located a wide open door in a market that is potentially vast and should support strong, consistent growth for a long time to come. But the entrepreneur's ability to spot opportunity is probably tied (to some degree) to the three prior characteristics already discussed in this chapter, and these continue to subject the new venture to a unique combination of propensities for questionable ethical behavior.

The concept of spotting opportunity is really a matter of securing a superior position in the market, or "getting the jump on" the competition. If an entrepreneur is willing to manage risks, and at the same time accept a good degree of uncertainty, a strong measure of subjectivity is introduced to the entrepreneurial process. This position is then prone to get caught in the innovator trap and the entrepreneur will once again be the primary source of insider information at the center of the new venture. Although entrepreneurs have been attributed with a knack for seeing an opportunity that no one else can see, there is no clear method to this proficiency for gaining an advantageous business position in the market. Spotting opportunity is really a question of timing, of determining *when* it is best to make the first move into the newly emerging market. Entrepreneurs are credited with either spotting the early signs of the opportunity in the making, or with creating opportunity in a market that appears to be somewhat stable. The entrepreneur is often the one who introduces the new level of volatility that deliberately disturbs the market's status quo and shakes up the present configuration of players at all levels in various vertical and horizontal channels.

Entrepreneurs are placed in an interesting ethical position with respect to spotting marketing opportunity. They can either overreact to an apparent opportunity, or under react to the potential opening in the market's fabric, and neither of these responses will be known for sure until a good deal of time has passed since the original action. An opportunity *over*reaction happens when the entrepreneur becomes too optimistic about the prospects for moving successfully into the new market and commits too many resources to the effort relative to the eventual realized return. The biggest problem with an *over*reaction is that the entrepreneur will not become aware of this miscalculation until personnel, funds, and time have already been allocated. In a somewhat similar sequence of events, an *oppor*tunity underreaction happens when the entrepreneur becomes overly pessimistic about what appears to be a very limited market potential. Figure 2.2 shows an opportunity-commitment template that compares both an entrepreneurial *over*reaction and *under*reaction to accurately spotting market opportunity. The horizontal axis measures the entrepreneur's *ex ante* assessment of a certain market opportunity (A*) and the eventual *ex post* results of the actual market performance (A). The dotted line depicts a *Type I Gap*, which is a false negative assessment, an *over*reaction to opportunity. A second example shows *ex ante* market opportunity (B*) and the actual results (B). Here the dotted line represents a *Type II Gap*, a false positive assessment, an opportunity *under* reaction. In the first case, the entrepreneur has supposedly spotted an excellent opportunity and has therefore committed significant resources to try and realize this potential. But the market was misread, and the entrepreneur is now too heavily committed due to the *over*reaction. In the second case, the entrepreneur did not recognize any opportunity, so the decision was made to restrict personnel, funding, and time allocations toward this effort because the initial sales response was deemed inadequate to support a fully funded strategy. A problem occurs when the market improves from its primary condition and requires a full scale allocation of company resources, but the time available to respond is too short relative to the time required to effectively implement the strategy. The entrepreneur faces a "catch 22" to either make a full commitment, but run the risk of pouring resources into a losing effort, or play it cautious and hold back resources, but run the risk of being unable to respond to a sudden positive shift in firm performance, and then miss the new opportunity altogether. But, the credibility of the entrepreneur's idea for the new venture is often evaluated in a highly subjective manner. Many new ideas are in fact *keepers*—business concepts linked to well-defined markets with clear potential for extended growth. Others are long on opportunity, but short on logistics and true substance. A conflict of interest exists when market expectations are based on the owner's perspective about the idea, and whether the firm can make the product or service concept a reality, and do so at a profit. Again, the entrepreneur is exposed to many ethical questions pertaining to the market interpretation, opportunity, and strategic reaction.

## Figure 2.2
## Opportunity–Commitment Template

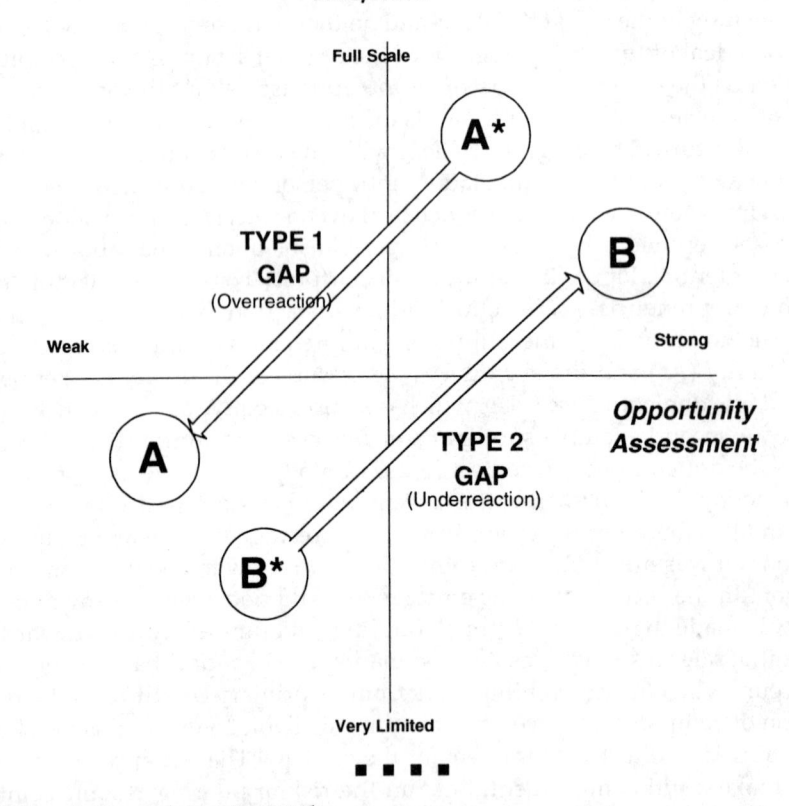

**Level of Resources Committed by the Entrepreneur**

Full Scale

A*

TYPE 1 GAP
(Overreaction)

B

Weak — Strong

**Opportunity Assessment**

A

TYPE 2 GAP
(Underreaction)

B*

Very Limited

## Concerns about Complete Control

Because entrepreneurs may display a propensity for managing risk, uncertainty, susceptibility to the innovator trap, and subjective flaws of spotting market opportunity, they need to build in distinct layers of managerial checks and balances as a precautionary measure to insure that proper perspectives are accurately determined with respect to the many unknown factors that exist in the new venture development process. The prior chapter discussed the tendency to concentrate managerial responsibility within a relatively small area in the organization. In the most extreme cases, virtually all the decision making capacity rests with the entrepreneur, a characteristic that most entrepreneurs seek. But complete control of the venture and a difficulty in delegating authority translates into yet another problem area for personal value considerations and ethical decision making by entrepreneurs. There can be a tendency for individual policy makers to be somewhat closed minded regarding outside input prior to making decisions, and various degrees of resistance to seeking out and accepting feedback after decisions are implemented. Entrepreneurs generally like to sit in the driver's seat and hold the steering wheel to direct the new venture along a certain route that is supposedly the best itinerary for achieving success. After all, the entrepreneur is the founder of the firm, and is most directly responsible for the creation of the new idea that launched the enterprise. But once operations start, and the firm defines its position in the competitive market, the quantity of time and degree of attention necessary just for the coordination of routine, daily functional operations can be very significant, and certainly strain the resources of even the most committed and diligent entrepreneur. Two ethical problems arise when the entrepreneur deliberately maintains control of all business decision making responsibilities, and these contribute directly to the ethical ramifications for the venture on a cumulative basis with the prior characteristics already discussed.

The first ethical concern is the issue of *figurative delegation*, where the entrepreneur presents the outward appearance of passing along certain aspects of decision making authority to other people in the organization, but the process is only procedural and lacks any form of true content responsibility. This plays itself out in two distinct manners with the staff managers who work directly for the entrepreneur. In one situation, the issue that was passed along to the subordinate by the entrepreneur is actually a non issue, but it has been packaged to outwardly resemble a critical matter in order to foster a sense of substantive involvement in the decision process on the part of support personnel. In another circumstance, a truly critical issue is supposedly delegated to the staff manager, but the entrepreneur never actually relinquishes control of both implementing and monitoring the directive. Although the decision was seemingly handed off to another person, the entrepreneur maintains a continuous review and close eye on every aspect of the decision so that the staff person feels that the entrepreneur is constantly "looking over the shoulder" to verify that progress is happening in a predetermined manner. This behavior by the firm owner is generally based on the premise that what matters most is that employees "feel" as if they are contributing to the decision processes in the firm, regardless of whether their assessments and input are ever actually considered by the entrepreneur. This presents a very difficult ethical issue for the new venture because it brings into question the entrepreneur's personal credibility in relationships, communication, and representation. And it is not so much that the employees have an implied perception of making contributions to decisions, but some entrepreneurs could even go so far as to explicitly state that employee input has been used in the decision, when in fact it was not even considered in the least.

A second ethical concern for entrepreneurs who seek complete control of the operation is the tendency to construct an elaborate *managerial hedge* around their decision making. The hedge can take one of two forms. In some instances, the entrepreneur shows outward signs of being receptive to input and feedback from staff personnel, but a structural buffer has been crafted within the organizational hierarchy that insulates the entrepreneur from other people's comments and concerns through the creation of special committees, the scheduling of numerous meetings, and the strategic placement of certain administrative assistants. The entrepreneur can hide behind this complex hedge and blame the procedures and other people if it turns out that staff managers feel that they are not always being heard in the decision making process. The other form of managerial hedge is not an organizational structure issue, but involves the intangible aspect of decision immediacy. This describes how the entrepreneur attributes the lack of staff input and feedback into decisions to the urgency with which certain decisions had to be made and implemented. The core issue is time. The entrepreneur hides behind the justification that there was not enough time to consult everyone about the matter and therefore the decision had to be made quickly, which made it impossible to check with the staff before hand. Each of these hedges are used to control the critical flow of information and keep responsibility overly concentrated in the realm of the entrepreneur. But the consolidation of power in one individual will expose the new venture to serious ethical matters and several moral choices dealing with authority.

## The Downside of Networking Contacts

The sixth characteristic of the entrepreneur that has a direct impact on ethical issues for the new venture is the propensity to build and utilize a complex network of outside contacts and associates that can be tapped into for advice, referrals, funding, and ideas. Most empirical research has found that entrepreneurs effectively manage several layers of individual contacts in a well-orchestrated network of related firms, suppliers, buyers, designers, financiers, and technology managers. This is generally seen as a very positive endeavor on the part of entrepreneurs, and is sometimes viewed as essential to the success of new firms. However, the positive aspects of the network are balanced by two distinct negative effects with respect to ethical decision making and personal values. The first concern is that the network can become a passive management cushion for the entrepreneur to discard responsibility for decisions that have already proven to be poor in content and results. It can become quite easy and convenient for the entrepreneur to shuttle along all the blame for miserable performance to the intangible catchall of the "outside advisers" or the "consulted specialists" related to certain decisions. The entrepreneur has found a place to deposit the negative origins of faulty decisions. There is nothing worse for the entrepreneur than seeing the new venture falter and stumble along in certain areas. Any type of negative performance is usually taken as a commentary on the personal integrity, reputation, and competence of the entrepreneur. When the firm experiences the effects of a miscalculation, an inadequate investment return, or an unsatisfactory personnel acquisition, outside stake holders such as capital providers, market channels, and end-users are apt to point the finger directly at the entrepreneur to take the blame for the poor performance. There will be a temptation for the entrepreneur to spread the blame around by relegating all, or portions of, the decision responsibility to the various individuals who serve on both a formal advisory board and as informal counsel. It is often quite interesting to listen to an entrepreneur claim limited or no knowledge about a certain decision, and try to transfer the responsibility for that incorrect move over to someone else who is advising the firm. It is generally perceived as very inconsistent behavior for an entrepreneur to be out of the loop on major decisions regarding key personnel, asset acquisitions, marketing contracts, promotional strategies, investment allocations, technology commitments, or manufacturing processes. These are all core functions of the new venture development process and very important to the owner's sense of control, direction, and vision for the enterprise. Yet, many entrepreneurs are quick to "pass the buck" to a business partner who constructed a bad deal, a financial backer who pressured the firm to go in the wrong direction, or a consultant whose forecast was poorly constructed. But ultimately, the entrepreneur must learn to view the network and referrals as resources that can provide input and feedback, rather than joint partners with equal or greater decision making clout. Final responsibility must always be the entrepreneur's. But misery loves company, and during tough times it can be tempting to search for others to share in the accountability for poor venture performance.

The second concern is even more interesting than the first. Rather than blaming some collective intangible in the network entity, the entrepreneur can actually receive really bad advice and inferior counsel from underqualified individuals that comprise the network of contacts. The difference here is that the poor performance can truly be traced back to inferior recommendations given by supposedly knowledgeable people. Entrepreneurs often surround themselves with close friends, former colleagues, family members, and recent acquaintances who appear well meaning, but who lack the necessary expertise to offer truly insightful recommendations to the firm owner. The network may not contain high quality knowledge or proficiency in the specific functional details of the enterprise. The network and referrals could also be a group of opportunistic individuals who have their sights set on a share of any future financial gains the new venture may produce. They display the outward appearance of interest in the enterprise and offer ready advice to the entrepreneur, but they are essentially not qualified to do so. In either case, the entrepreneur is surrounded by counsel that is unable to see the true issues and potential concerns of the business operations. It is very difficult for the entrepreneur to know who to trust. Some advisers might have a sincere motivation to assist the entrepreneur, but find that they are in over their heads in terms of knowledge and expertise. Other advisers may have more selfish interests in mind, but be equally out of their league in the area of advice they offer. Whatever the case, the entrepreneur must be careful in building the network and decide to what degree the advisers and referrals will contribute to the major decision making in the new venture.

# CHAPTER THREE

# *The Entrepreneur's Idea and Vision*

## The Conception of New Ideas

The process by which an individual entrepreneur conceives of a new idea and eventually turns that into an innovative product or service, process or technology, cannot be definitively outlined to describe all the subtle nuances of every entrepreneur's personal experience. And of course, there can be no such thing as a prescription for how to best do this in manner that affords the greatest potential for future success. But a few fundamental tenets will now be proposed that capture the general essence of the entrepreneurial new venture development process. Having already looked at the features of new ventures, and the characteristics of the entrepreneurs that drive them, the issues related to ethical behavior need one more component added to the mix, so as to establish a complete context for examining *how* values are established in small firms, and *what* situations are most susceptible to challenge moral judgments and business ethics. There is a good deal of evidence to suggest that, for the entrepreneur, simply having a long-term self interest is not enough to produce ethical behavior, because moral judgment and values can only be appreciated within the context of behavior and interaction with other individuals and organizations.[1] Even before the small firm is launched, the new venture development process is literally a series of tough choices that are made based on highly subjective perceptions about potential and value.[2] Successful entrepreneurial management of the venture development process is never based solely on overly intuitive decisions or quick problem solving, but on the ability to evaluate situations, analyze problems and issues, and choose solutions with calculated risk.[3]

There is no way to accurately predict the entrepreneur's potential for success in the formulating of a new idea, because most of the existing research is based on trait studies, whereas the most likely areas to focus on should deal with the behavioral aspects of the entrepreneur in creating the new organization.[4] There are numerous ethical considerations that are part of new venture origination, specifically the types of advice and resources drawn upon for input and direction,[5] the way that organizational emergence determines personal behavior,[6] the cognitive factors related to an individual's ability to persevere in the face of adversity,[7] and whether the smaller size of the new venture is more conducive to ethical compromise when compared to large firms, due to the lack of accountability and formal structure.[8] There are also questions to consider related to whether the personal values of men and women entrepreneurs are vastly different, as most organizational theories suggest.[9] The firm and the entrepreneur are the products of a three phase subjective sequence of new venture development. The direction and vitality of corporate America, it managers, and its entrepreneurs, cannot be fully understood without knowing and understanding more about the values and vision of the men and women who manage and direct it.[10] The new venture development process is essentially built upon an underlying philosophical basis that the ethical approach to business activities is a result of the priorities that values have in personal conduct, views of success, and matters of individual conscience.[11] The process of developing a new idea all the way to the point where it is transformed into a start-up venture is both a quantitative and qualitative procedure. There are certainly monetary costs and benefits, but also issues of values, judgments, rationales, and ethics.

There are three distinct stages in the origination of the entrepreneurial new venture. Figure 3.1 defines these as sequentially co-dependent, and cumulative in effectiveness. The horizontal axis represents time and the vertical axis shows the development of the venture concept with respect to its progress in being refined, better defined, and made increasingly tangible. The basis, the first stage prior to the successful launch of all new ventures, begins with the entrepreneur's original idea that spawns the process by which any new business is organized and introduced into the marketplace. This innovative idea is conceived and grounded in a highly subjective series of interpretations about something that the entrepreneur believes is missing within the present competitive environment. A rough sketch on the back of a paper place mat from a favorite lunch spot is one of the great vehicles of entrepreneurial folklore through which many new ventures come into being.

The entrepreneur believes very strongly that there is a gap of some sort between existing products and services in a certain market. There is a hole, a niche, within a market that has not yet been filled. There is a technology that would greatly improve the features and value of the present offerings available to end-users. There is a better way to do something, there is a process that will save time, there is a less expensive alternative to existing materials, there is a way to improve efficiency. The entrepreneur is consumed with the notion that there must be a way to improve upon the status quo. The targeted market and the existing product or service become a central focus of attention for the entrepreneur. Although there is not yet a tangible working prototype, the entrepreneur will conceive of an alternative to the present situation in the market, and then begin the process of turning the idea into a competitive offering.

Phase I contains some interesting dynamics that will have an eventual effect on the entrepreneur's ability to maintain ethical behavior and a solid commitment to inherent moral values. Figure 3.2 portrays the basic workings of how *entrepreneurial idea generation* takes place during Phase I of the venture origination process. The entrepreneur and the existing product or service are somehow linked to each other through various possible pre-existing circumstances. Perhaps the entrepreneur is already an active participant in the existing market and makes extensive use of the current products and services, technologies or processes, and is intrigued by the way these things work together. There could be personal links that are the result of the involvement of family or friends in that market, or an existing job description, or a current business associate at another firm. There could also be links based upon

## Figure 3.1
### Stages of Entrepreneurial Venture Origination

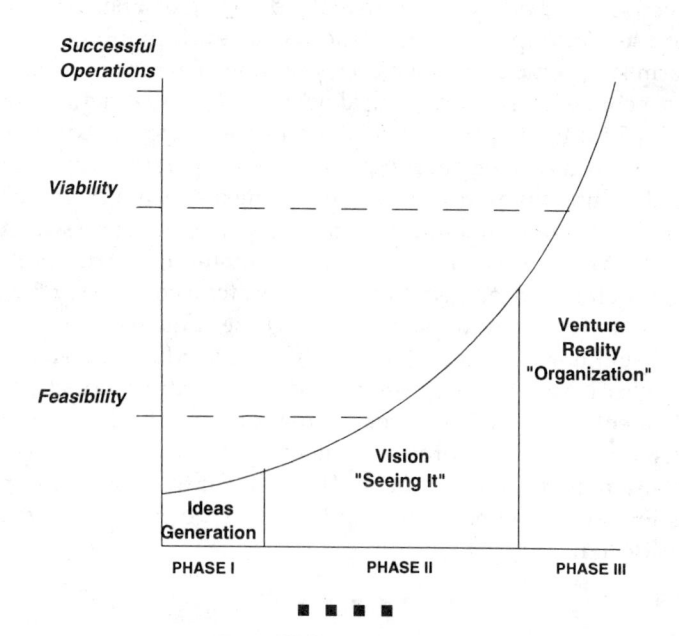

[Graph showing an exponential curve rising across three phases. Y-axis markers from bottom to top: Feasibility, Viability, Successful Operations. X-axis: PHASE I, PHASE II, PHASE III. Labels along the curve: "Ideas Generation" (Phase I), "Vision 'Seeing It'" (Phase II), "Venture Reality 'Organization'" (Phase III).]

individual interests or personal familiarity. Perhaps the budding entrepreneur has a hobby or recreational activity that is of special interest and related to the present market. The proximity links generally include some degree of emotional connection as well. The entrepreneur has personal feelings and vested interest in the market based on inherent individual moral bases and value judgments. These are often the primary source of the entrepreneur's passion for the new idea. The existing product, service, or process has been placed in close and subjective proximity to the entrepreneur through certain events and experiences.

Once the entrepreneur initiates a clear focus on the product or service, the technology or process, the market, its structure, the key players, and its organization, three things will happen. There first begins a process of evaluation (1). The existing features, the components, the materials, the costs and benefits, these are all weighed on a subjective scale within the entrepreneur's mind. An intuitive scoring system probably takes shape and an overall efficiency or utility rating is applied to various aspects of the existing product or service as the entrepreneur mulls over the present configuration and starts to ponders other possibilities. This begins the second endeavor (2), to identify the most likely areas or components for change. The features are casually delineated and the main characteristics are filed in order to focus in on that one key point that becomes the primary candidate for improvement. Not every idea is a landmark revolution for the market. Many ideas are continuous innovation, marginal improvements in existing products and services, the next "logical step" in the natural progress of a concept. A few ideas have the potential to revolutionize an entire industry, but they never get connected with the right entrepreneur.

The third exercise (3) involves taking the prior evaluation and identified area for change, and conceptualizing an initial form for the innovative idea. This is the first critical analysis and molding of the proposed alternative's features and benefits. It might be a flow chart for improving a process. It could be a rough schematic drawing of a new product. It might even be a description of a service improvement, or the way a new technology would function. This conceptualized form is to some degree a direct or indirect extension of the existing product, service, or process technology. But the "logical next step" is often neither logical, or the next step. This is completely subject to the personal biases and inferences drawn by the entrepreneur. What may be viewed as a logical progression to one person, may be seen as extremely insightful or radically different by someone else. The next step is a matter of opinion as well. One person thinks of a somewhat similar product, service, or process with some relatively minor adjustments to the features, functions, style, or materials used. Another person builds off the basic premise of the existing items, but incorporates a completely different design that departs from the original in many respects, handling the same functions and tasks, but providing additional benefits and effectiveness with greater efficiency. And still a third individual works off a clean slate, having disregarded the existing products, services, and processes in favor of an entirely new line of reason that does not build on anything that exists, but instead creates a whole new approach to meeting the market's needs, one that will, in effect, render the present technology obsolete. This is by far the most risky approach, because it brings into question both the effectiveness and value of the present school of thought based on an entirely new design.

■ ■ ■ ■

**Figure 3.2**
**Entrepreneurial Idea Generation**

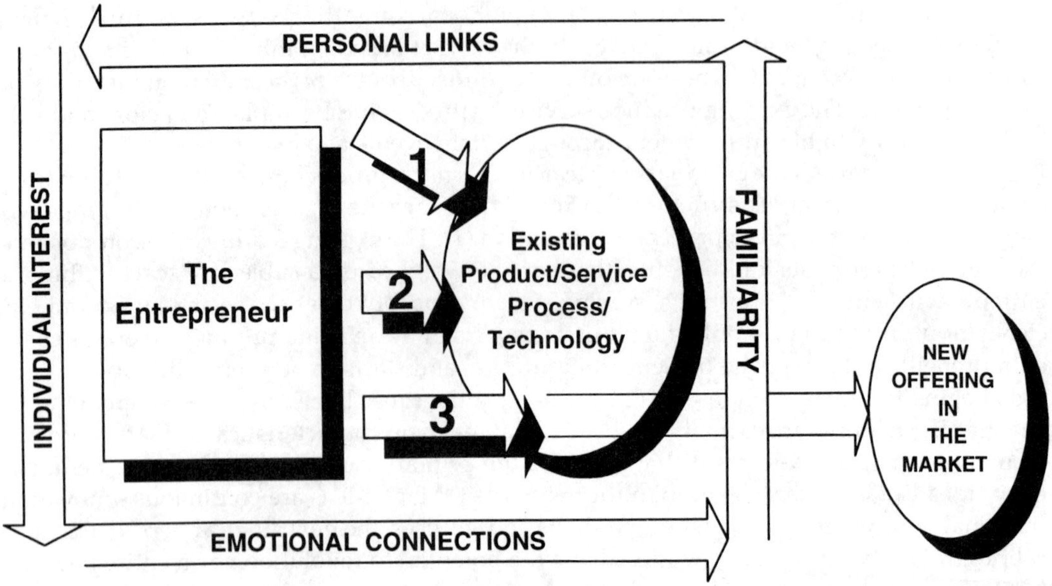

Once the entrepreneur completes this somewhat cursory review of the idea and declares it is worth pursuing, the new idea has now has a shape, maybe a name, and a preliminary identity. The first phase of entrepreneurial venture origination is now complete. But the idea must now prove that it is first feasible, that it *can* be produced as per the conceptualized design specifications, and it is viable, namely, it will be broadly accepted in a rapidly growing market that offers very large potential over the long term. There are many ideas that are feasible, meaning they *can* in fact be done as conceptualized by the entrepreneur. But they will never produce the wide range of adoptions in the market necessary to support a venture's worth of asset investment commitments. For example, a person could devise a software/hardware switching system that allows notebook computer users to share data over the airwaves translated into two or more languages simultaneously. But the fact remains, the identified market for such a product is so small, the annual sales would not be able to support even the most rudimentary marketing effort. Many ideas will probably be extremely viable, for instance an automobile that is fueled by water. However, the idea has not yet been made feasible, so the viability is voided with respect to launching a new venture. As feasibility is secured and viability appears promising, the idea begins the transition from Phase I into Phase II, defining the vision.

## Entrepreneurial Vision

The second phase of the venture origination process describes how the entrepreneur begins to literally see the product or service innovation being produced in a facility, with offices filled with various levels of support personnel, sales representatives in the field making presentations to potential buyers, and end-users putting the idea to work in their homes or businesses. The idea has proven to be *feasible* and there is a good deal of preliminary evidence mounting that the idea could be *viable* over the long-term. The next step is to take the idea off the drawing board by organizing the resources to bring the idea to the market in a tangible form. But many ideas never even get off the drawing board in the mind of an individual. Even though an idea is feasible and viable, the individual behind the innovation cannot muster the necessary support to begin the venture and bring the idea to the market successfully. The success of a new product or service is generally not a function of the inherent features, costs, or benefits that comprise the idea concept. Feasible ideas that offer strong potential for viability must be matched with entrepreneurial vision in order to make the transition from Phase I to Phase II. Every year, thousands of good ideas never get off the drawing board because there is no clear direction provided for the creation of a business entity to take the idea to the market. The entrepreneur, however, is able to successfully transfer what is conceptually on the drawing board to a clear picture of a firm, operating within the targeted market, producing the new idea in an efficient manner, and selling it to a rapidly growing sector of end-users at a reasonable profit.

The idea sparks the vision, and the vision makes the venture a reality in the marketplace. The entrepreneur is the generator of the ideas, the inclinations, the concepts, and the thoughts and perspectives that come together and define a new product, a new process, a new technology, or a new service. The entrepreneur then begins to translate all the components of the idea into a comprehensive view toward the future. The vision is the defining force in private enterprise through which the entrepreneur captures the imagination of other individuals with the resources that can bring the idea to fruition. Entrepreneurs are the initiators and implementors of vision. Their vision establishes a strategy for venture operations and market penetration. They then lead the entire scope of the implementation process by identifying the investment capital, managerial talent, technical expertise, and the appropriate marketing channels. Together, these resources must be configured into a cohesive entity with a clear focus on goals and objectives which will result in successful entry into the competitive marketplace.

But entrepreneurs are generally not interested in gaining power or security during the start-up phase of the enterprise development. These are more closely associated with the primary interests of corporate managers in large companies. The rationale that underpins the vision is the fuel for the fire that powers the new venture creation process. Power and security are risk averse factors, associated with a lack of risk taking and an eye toward stable business functions and no-going processes. The process by which a new idea is postulated is often the function of questions that take place outside the normal realm of accepted practices. Managers at large companies are focused on controlling their designated area of responsibility. They maintain basic functional procedures toward the goal of making certain sales or profit targets. They keep the operation flowing smoothly, and they try to motivate employees to stay on track with the sub components of the large scale strategy created by upper executive management. Any innovations or new ideas that come from the typical managerial structure and processes of the large firm are generally marginal in nature. There may be a new way to do a certain task that cuts down on time and saves two steps in the old process, while maintaining present levels of efficiency. This is a good thing for the manager's division, and it may contribute to an overall improvement in that division's performance, but it is probably not going to shake the industry or cause immediate concern among competitors. Now this is not to say that large firms cannot be the originators of new ideas and substantive innovation and improvement. Certainly there are scores of examples where the largest firms introduced radical innovations that reshape or redefined entire product lines and market structures. But typically, functional managers are motivated by the power that comes with managerial authority, and the security of having a salary, benefits, and access to large corporate resources for managing a singular business function within the firm. There may not be a great need for managers to originate, or even possess, a substantial vision of the organization due to the nature of their personal risk tolerance and values.

The typical process of gradual, continuous innovation is most closely associated with larger companies. The management component is generally directed at one functional area of responsibility, and performance is linked to meeting goals that were oftentimes passed down through the organization from senior executives. There may be some intra-departmental goals and objectives that originate with the manager, but the broad scope of the entire enterprise is in no way a concern of the functional manager. This individual is probably not a visionary. The manager does need to be good at executing directives and implementing company policy. But there is most likely little motivation to be thinking about brand new ideas and concepts that as yet do not exist. The manager's salary and bonus compensation is tied to target performance figures that are often the product of someone else's ideas about how the firm, and that department, should be performing in that particular market at a specific time. Vision is arguably not a primary characteristic of the functional managerial process. But a clear and captivating vision *is* a huge requirement for the entrepreneurial new venture development process.

Many entrepreneurs try to build a firm around a gradual, continuous innovation concept. The idea may have merit in terms of feasibility, but it lacks adequate viability, so it is probably not going to support the formation of a new business organization. Some gradual, continuous innovations may be perfect for new venture development because they will be placed in a huge market that should continue to experience tremendous growth for quite some time. The person with the idea does not have to be entrepreneurial. Many inventors are very risk averse and lack the organizational skills and vision to turn their idea into a successful new venture. But many inventors will partner with an entrepreneur who can organize the resources, make the contacts, conceive of the firm, identify the market channels, and effectively communicate the vision, and that can make for a great partnership. On the other hand, many entrepreneurial types cannot locate and define the right idea at the right time for the right market. As such, they are inclined to be involved in many ventures over the course of time, constantly searching for the next breakthrough around which to build the enterprise of their dreams. Vision is an interesting concept, because it is so extremely subjective in content and rationale, and yet it is, by far, the most necessary factor to motivate the organization of numerous business resources into a meaningful venture. This high degree of subjectivity and personal perspective makes vision a difficult characteristic to qualify relative to entrepreneurial types. But vision formation and effective communication is thoroughly enmeshed in the defining of entrepreneurial moral rationales, value judgments, and ethical behavior in the new venture, touching all aspects of firm representation, market expectations, financing, partnership arrangements, and firm culture.

Some research has recognized that both small business ventures and individual idealists are the predominant sources of useful innovations, and that large scale firms produce relatively few innovations.[12] Other empirical evidence suggests that smaller plants are significantly richer incubators for the birth of entrepreneurial ventures, when compared with larger plants, but that the entrepreneurial "level of expertise" is the primary causal factor in successful ventures, and not the size of the organization from which the entrepreneur emerges.[13] If objective and distinctive small business and individual entrepreneurship qualities could be transported upstream to large firms, persons could be schooled in the "science of entrepreneurship" and then set free to pursue innovative ideas and new venture concepts within larger firms. But large firms often possess minimal patience with new idea generation, and often lack sufficient freedom to allow risky business pursuits, both of which are necessary to innovators and entrepreneurs as they plan and manage new venture activity. Contrasted to this is the plain fact that most entrepreneurial innovators encounter significant hurdles and struggle a great deal in their attempts to transform ambiguous and uncertain prospects into clearly defined and specific business realities in a market.[14] Evidence exists that large firms are not particularly adaptive and often lack the necessary flexibility to adjust to a rapidly changing environment. It could be argued that the entrepreneurial element of vision is necessary to support sufficient innovation as a means of remaining a viable player in a market.[15]

A good deal of research also focuses on large firms trying to prepare environments that are particularly conducive to the growth, support, and on-going nurturing of an intracorporate form of entrepreneurship. But attempts to recreate these environments within the context of a large established company may not ever be truly capable of supporting true entrepreneurial innovation and vision.[16] The implementation of an innovative idea through the focused vision of the individual entrepreneur is paramount to the new venture development process. It would be quite difficult to try and replicate, or predetermine, the entire range of factors and conditions that come together in a unique manner to support new venture formation, including the individual's acceptance of risk transfer and the assignment vesting in the actual results of the endeavor.[17] The notion that there exists a formula that can create an ideal environment conducive to risk taking and innovative idea generation is perhaps pushing the limits of reasonable expectations. Granted, the large firm can allocate some funding to support a corporate new venture development business unit, much like they invest in research and development. And, yes, there is evidence to suggest that some large companies have been able to create new business opportunities through the internal corporate venturing strategy.[18] But, the spawning of a true start-up venture is an entirely unique phenomenon when compared with the many forms of intracorporate entrepreneurship programs at large firms. The process by which salaried managers sit down at the drawing board and devise new business opportunities for the large corporation is altogether different from the way the true Schumpeterian entrepreneur acts as the individual organizer of various financial, marketing, production, and managerial resources while bearing the risk for effectively turning the idea and the vision into a viable business entity. The managerial process of communicating ideas and vision to potential contributors to the new venture is tied directly to the entrepreneur's ability to effectively translate the opportunity into tangible actions. It is also a function of the entrepreneur's sincere efforts to convince other interested outsiders to believe in the idea and catch a glimpse of the vision for a profitable new organization in the competitive environment.[19] This passion and desire cannot be manufactured using discrete input variables and some sort of managerial bonus or profit-sharing compensation plan. The entrepreneur is literally consumed with the innovation product or service concept to the point where the profitability or remuneration schedule is no longer the driving force behind the pre-launch research and development, and the opening of the business. The new firm will literally be an extension of the entrepreneurs' dreams, and expectations, and hopes, and personal reputation that there was in fact a *real* opening in the fabric of the competitive landscape, and the idea was a good fit, and the entrepreneur was correct in seeing it before anyone else did. This speaks to the very heart of a defining entrepreneurial vision. It is woven into the passion that the entrepreneur brings to venture development. But, because it is so incredibly subjective in nature, and the product of a personal perspective of market viability, venture opportunity, and profit potential, it can be one of the best explanations for questionable ethical behavior and a lack of moral absolutes among individual entrepreneurs.

There may in fact be specific managerial structural environments that are more conducive to promoting certain styles and forms of systematic intracorporate entrepreneurship, but a significant percentage of chief executives in start-up firms recognize that one single and specific strategic turning point was instrumental in their ultimate success, rather than an environment of various objective stages.[20] The environment is often the focus of studies seeking to explain successful, versus unsuccessful, program implementation. But it is entrepreneurial activity that creates viable organizations, and functions as both innovator and catalyst in the design and support of new business directions. Many organizations do not function as catalysts and would find it difficult to support entrepreneurial activity.[21] Many argue that it is merely a matter of providing a conducive environment that supports goals and strategy formulation.[22] Certain firm environments support leadership, advising networks, individual sensitivity, decision flexibility, and clear communication.[23] It is unclear whether there is one specific firm environment that best supports intracorporate entrepreneurship.[24] Organizational innovation theory addresses factors within firms that are associated with, and perhaps causal to, types of innovation, and proposes that all firms go through distinct cycles of universally consistent and clearly defined stages of innovation. These include: the birth of a venture, followed by rapid growth, a settling or maturation period, a time of abbreviated revival, and then an eventual decline.[25] But an entrepreneurial organizational model seeks to explain the reasons and vision behind firm success, in that certain organizations display characteristics consistent with tenets of individual entrepreneurship as they engage in proactive, internally-generated risky and uncertain activities. This is the true distinguishing feature between the small, entrepreneurial venture and the large established firm, and individual vision is the basis for transforming a mere idea to the tangible business entity found in the third phase of the venture origination process.

## Ideas, Vision, and Venture Reality

The third and final phase of the venture origination process deals with the actual logistical arrangements and functional mechanics of launching the firm in the marketplace. This is the cumulative result of the prior two phases. The idea generation phase answers basic concerns about product or service concept feasibility, and begins to assess the potential for viability. At that point the entrepreneur introduces a clear vision of the business organization and starts to configure the investment capital, asset infrastructure, personnel, and marketing channels on the basis of articulating a company vision to all interested outsiders who might want to accept the risks associated with the perceived market opportunity. Although the launch of the venture is always an extremely exciting time for the entrepreneur, it can also be the most tenuous and anxious period as the venture hangs in the balance between whether the necessary complements of funding, technology, personnel, management, and production capabilities can be assembled together for the same target date in an organized fashion. This third phase can take months, and even years, for the entrepreneur to pull together.

The process of turning the idea and the vision into a real business entity is a particularly difficult period of time for entrepreneurial values exposure. The most ideal situation for the owner is that every piece of the business plan would fall neatly into place in a well-coordinated fashion, with nothing missing at the time of the launch. The business plan can be thought of as the "wish list," where the entrepreneur has outlined in detail all the funding, personnel, marketing, and operations issues deemed necessary for a successful introduction in the market. But short of this *ideal* situation, there are four distinct scenarios associated with Phase III that can test the owner's ethical behavior. Each of these scenarios opens the door to various challenges for the entrepreneur's personal value system. They are all very significant in the life of the new firm because the entrepreneur is placed in an "all-or-nothing" predicament with respect to the organization of resources and the timing of the launch. The new venture will either be open for business, or put on hold until another time. There is nothing in between. For example, in Phase III there is no gain in securing less than the full investment funding needed for the targeted launch of operations. The firm needs a specific amount of funding, anything short of that will place the success of the enterprise in greater jeopardy. There is no prize for merely opening negotiations with a *possible* buyer. The only thing that matters is when a buyer is under contract. The new venture cannot truly benefit from simply discussing key management positions with a highly qualified pool of applicants. Having interested people interview for these positions is not the same as having key managerial slots filled and operating. A new venture cannot use a machine part or equipment tool that is still being designed and tested. The only assets that matter are those installed in the facility that are operational. And it is never enough to be "working out the details" with various marketing channels. The only relevant issue is whether the product or service will fit the pricing, packaging, promotion, and merchandising specifications of the established distribution venues now, when the firm is ready to open for business. The anticipation of a certain deal, the expectations for specific arrangements, and the forecasts for planned results are all tied to the entrepreneur's vision. But at some point they must cease from being components of the new venture vision, and be transformed into new venture realities. The degree to which the entrepreneur is able to match the realized launch of the venture to the business plan vision will have a direct impact on the overall success of the enterprise.

### *The Early Departure*

The first scenario will be referred to as the "Early Departure." The entrepreneur will be tempted to leave too soon, ahead of the pace of other circumstances that are all required if the firm wants to have the best position relative to the identified business opportunity. This describes how the entrepreneur has been able to put together all the right pieces to the new venture launch. The funding is secured, the personnel is in place, and the operational business functions are ready to go. The problem here is that they came together earlier than previously planned. The whole package of capabilities fell in line ahead of the original "window," which will not come into complete view for several more periods of time. This leaves the entrepreneur in a difficult position of having to wait for the right timing when all the pieces are set in place. Granted, the good news is that the firm has everything it needs as per the original business plan. But the bad news is that, for specific reasons, it is presently not the best time to launch the firm. This could be based on the positioning of the competition in the market, the current macroeconomic situation, the status of a certain regulatory issue, or a seasonal time of the year for distributors and end-users.

### *The Missing Piece*

The second scenario will be called the "Missing a Piece." This described the new venture that has all but one of the required components of the business plan in place and ready to go. The firm looks great on several fronts, but one final piece of the puzzle is still missing. This item is just as necessary to the health and well-being of the enterprise as any other detail. For example, the entrepreneur may have five basic things that need to be in place prior to the launch. These include marketing, financial, personnel, legal, and production issues and capabilities. Everything is configured as planned, except for the final personnel requirements. The temptation for the entrepreneur will be to reason that the business is essentially four-fifths ready to go (and maybe even more than that because the final area should be worked out very shortly), so launch now and allow that last component to catch up at a later date. The problem with this situation is that it denies the interactive nature of the many components that come together to make a new business a reality. It would be disastrous to assume that the five functional areas just mentioned are autonomous and have no correlations or effects between each other. The entrepreneur has to decide long before this point whether launching the firm with anything less than the full business plan requirements is worth the risk of bringing the whole venture to a grinding halt because of capability gaps and insufficiencies. The owner needs to ask whether ninety percent funding is considered close enough to full funding to accomplish the tasks as planned. Or, does a smaller facility in a farther removed location have any negative effect on the business potential as outlined with a larger facility in closer proximity to the target market? Can the firm "get by" without a full time marketing director for the first few months while the search continues for the right person? Some segments of the new business might be considered secured "on paper," meaning there is a written agreement between the entrepreneur and certain outside suppliers, but the investment funds, or the manufacturing equipment, or the new facility has not yet been secured. Until an item is in place and ready for daily operations, it should still be considered outstanding.

### *In the Works*

The third scenario will be referred to as "In the Works." In this instance, the entrepreneur is presently engaged in numerous discussions with a whole host of outside providers of capital, supplies, personnel, and technology. Several pieces of the new venture puzzle have been documented and identified in the market, but are still waiting to be formally secured due to lengthy negotiations between the various providers and the entrepreneur. There is reason to believe that things should probably go as planned, but herein lies the problem. Three things can happen in this category of bringing the venture vision to reality. First, it might be that the final details of the arrangement have not yet been decided, and the negotiations that are in the works could stall for an indefinite period of time. This could slow down the venture launch even though everything else in place and ready to go. This creates a "missing piece" scenario. The second issue is that the owner could close a deal that secures something less than the originally desired level of commitment. It lacks the full level of substance deemed necessary, so it could be argued that the venture could either proceed with a decreased chance of success, or have to find another party to make up the gap that is missing in the current deal. The third problem is that the discussions could terminate without any deal being worked out, leaving the entrepreneur to either pursue other possibilities that could also be "in the works," or start all over again from scratch by approaching a new party. These three forms of potential arrangements are, from an ethical standpoint, essentially all the same, in that none of them are closed deals, and they each present the entrepreneur with a temptation to treat them as if they are.

### *Less Than Expected*

The last issue that impacts venture reality will be called "Less Than Expected." This is unique from the prior three situations. Here, the venture has secured final deals for every aspect of the business plan, so nothing is still "in the works" being negotiated. All the pieces to the business plan will be ready to go at the proper time for the planned window of opportunity. And, there is no component that was deemed necessary in the business plan that is missing from the launch plans. But there is an issue with the quality of the components that are secured and ready to go. The entrepreneur was, for various reasons, unable to secure the "best case" scenario from the business plan in one or more of the functional areas necessary for the launch. Because of this, the overall stature of the new venture posture is somewhat lessened. For example, the entrepreneur could have secured all the funding, but it is nearly all debt, rather than the sixty percent equity that was originally sought. Or, the venture secured key people for manufacturing and marketing operations, but the people hired are not the "first choice" of the entrepreneur, because the top candidates were recruited to a better deal elsewhere. The equipment might not be the brand or model originally sought, or the supplier might not be the nationally known firm that was targeted. Each of these can sway the entrepreneur's ability to accurately represent the status of the launch to capital providers, marketing channels, and end-users in the market.

## CHAPTER FOUR

# *The Entrepreneur's Personal Value System*

## Evidence of Entrepreneurial Values

All entrepreneurs incorporate some form of decision making guidelines into their own management style. The entrepreneur is faced with having to create guidelines for three separate areas of information regarding the firm that have ethical issues and moral implications, including technical and procedural, the organizational means of facilitating information flow, and the underlying approach to the value and integrity of information.[1] The final version will represent a unique and personal perspective of several issues related to the pursuit of enterprise and a methodology by which to assess situations and implement decisions. There are many characteristics that are somewhat common to the typical entrepreneur, yet these should not be confused with values and ethics. Evidence suggests that the entrepreneur is affected by stress, the challenge to the locus of control and responsibility, and even the social support system of the new venture in a very different manner when compared with managers at large companies.[2] And yet another Baylor University study by Justin Longenecker concluded that although individuals involved in running a small business are far more demanding in their work schedules, deadlines, and productivity output, they have a tendency to be more permissive (less absolute) in their ethical attitudes.[3] There are perhaps as many as six different schools of thought in the present field of entrepreneurship, and each has a different perspective of the entrepreneur's value system, capacity for ethical decision making, and ways of dealing with stress, risk, uncertainty, and firm management.[4] Many writers suggest that at some point, the entrepreneur is faced with having to try and manage a going concern that has far outgrown the founder's interests and abilities to effectively maintain a value structure and personal identity.[5]

The concept of *values* is many times defined in intangible, subjective terms. For the scope of this book, the concept of a value will be discussed as certain benefits received relative to the costs associated with the receipt. These costs can be both pecuniary and non pecuniary in content. Values are then first and foremost those specific *apriori* ideas and thoughts that comprise an individual's approach to what is deemed good and right, and what is viewed as adverse and wrong, as these relate to matters of living and participating in society. Values serve as the basis for all aspects that comprise personal and professional relationships, communication, all forms of transactions, and the allocation of resources such as time and money. An individual entrepreneur has assigned a certain value to the many aspects that define the endeavor of the new venture. Favorable benefits are positioned relative to the price (or cost) of acquisition, and in the same manner, unfavorable outcomes are also viewed as they relate to their respective costs. The favorable benefits are then weighed against the unfavorable outcomes based on the individual's personal assessment of what is considered right and wrong. Many contemporary writers in the field advocate that entrepreneurs transition back to the classic values of entrepreneurship that were present in the literature of work ethics, family values, personal integrity, customer service, employee loyalty, and treating others as one would like to be treated.[6]

Ethics are then a product of values. Ethics are the general and specific guidelines for action that an individual forms based on the process by which things are assigned a commensurate degree of value. One form of ethics is built on *absolutism*, namely, a predetermined set of guidelines that establish what is considered good and right and acceptable behavior. A second form is the product of *relativism*, or the assessment of each unique situation conditionally based on the immediate benefits and costs. Ethics serve as the parameters within which personal choices and activities function. An ethic serves the individual as the guideline for personal behavior. The manner in which an individual entrepreneur conducts business reflects the character of the person and communicates what is valued and what is not. Even by default, every person that pursues the activities of private enterprise will in some way, shape, or form display a manner, a style, a process, or an approach that is crafted from specific value judgments. And yet the entrepreneur's values basis and ethical results expressed in the firm are quite different when U.S. firm owners are compared with owners of similar small-to-medium size companies in Britain.[7] The basis for these value judgments are discussed later in this chapter, but all values have some form of a foundation (whether it is constructed objectively or subjectively) and the structure of a values system manifests itself in the ethics of how communication, transactions, relationships, and other interactive endeavors are pursued. There may be various degrees of ethical formality, but even at its most passive level of interest, each person will act so as to reflect some form of ethics, and this is the window that expresses the values system and its foundation. It is important to determine the types and sources of ethics that exist in entrepreneurial new ventures. There are literally a myriad of personal rationales and interpretations of business situations that dictate the format and style of ethical behavior among entrepreneurs.[8]

Remember, without clear and specific guidelines, many entrepreneurial firms risk significant exposure to economic loss due to lack of surety about the correct nature of decisions, employee inexperience in clear moral choices, and the lack of a professional ethic. If it is true that entrepreneurial satisfaction is the most fundamental measure of new venture success, how then do the entrepreneur's personal values interact with the firm's style of ethical decision making to contribute to success without compromise? Several empirical studies have shown that the ethics used with the business should be exactly the same as the ethical guidelines used by individuals in everyday relationships and personal communication.[9] In reality, most entrepreneurs may not want to deal with the ethical implications of their daily business operations, but it remains one of the most critical areas that pertain to effective management and company reputation in the market.[10] Numerous hypotheses have been raised over the last several years as to whether an entrepreneur's personal values have any impact on the relative success of the new venture. Some studies have even focused on whether an entrepreneur's personal religious affiliation has an impact on the style and success of ethical behavior,[11] or if a certain theological position is more conducive to moral standards within the firm.[12] There have recently been discussions as to the impact of the legal code and the propensity for entrepreneurs to act in an ethical manner.[13] Others have inquired whether the new venture's operations and success are direct reflections of the entrepreneur. The fact remains, it has been widely recognized by economists, historians, and sociologists alike that business ethics have a significant impact on economic activity.[14] But remember, it is very difficult to accurately measure ethical behavior, therefore a model for values-based decision making must be established.

It has been proposed that firms should develop and maintain a broad based moral and social responsibility to act ethically in the competitive environment.[15] In a similar manner, many have suggested that the sociological characteristics and contexts of the entrepreneurial new venture need to be formally incorporated into all aspects of the planning and decision making processes for all firms.[16] A good deal of empirical evidence has found that a greater degree of potential financial penalties that can impact the firm's performance are correlated with those businesses that tend to act in a more socially responsible manner, and that small entrepreneurial ventures are more likely to consider the idea that social responsibility must be included as part of the promotional marketing mix of the company, rather than just a negative cost of doing business.[17] Still, others have argued that a corporate ethics policy can literally transform the entire organization into an entity with *real* feelings and a company-wide conscience.[18] Some research into the ethical issues of smaller, entrepreneurial firms has concluded that the entire entrepreneurial development process is in reality a systematic manifestation of true organizational emergence, and that this requires a great deal of attention to the many levels and types of underlying values and ethical business principles that are essential to defining the character and position of the firm in the competitive market.[19] There has also been evidence to suggest that ethical behavior is in many ways, perhaps the greatest and most pressing challenge facing contemporary entrepreneurs in nearly every facet of the new venture development process.

The critical mass of big business in the United States experienced a renewed wave of interest in organizational ethics during the last three years of the past decade. The early 1980's were characterized by a sense of financial greed and a disregard for business ethics in the practical application of decision making with respect to corporate strategy and financing. By the beginning of Ronald Reagan's second term of office, America had already experienced several devastating ethical comprises in both the private sector and public policy decisions. On the heels of several years of seemingly bad judgment on the part of American business that included: the broad impact of the federal savings and loan crisis, a virtual plethora of successive high profile securities fraud cases, the Iran-Contra-BCCI money laundering fiasco, the PTL Broadcasting Network-Heritage USA investor misrepresentation, and the belief in no "downside" prior to the October 1987 collapse of the New York Stock Exchange, business and general news periodicals alike began to attract and review the very fabric of America's corporate ethic, and even called into question whether there was in fact any outward, measurable evidence of a moral code of conduct among private and public sector organizations and managers. Then, by mid-1988 and early 1989, business ethics and personal values began to slowly make a comeback as a concept worthy of inclusion in the modern business management portfolio, meriting some critical analysis with respect to its impact on firm performance.

Most commentaries presented a comprehensive outline of ethical behavior based upon both relative and absolute principles of personal conduct.[20] Within the realm of entrepreneurial ventures, ethics questions ranged from whether new venture development is inherently suspect with respect to moral choices and personal values in decision making,[21] to a wide range of issues that dealt with concerns over the intrinsic deservedness of profits to investors and entrepreneurs, and the significant potential for companies to engage in exploitation in the entrepreneurial process.[22] Recently, the *Economist* reported that more than three quarters of all American firms now have some form of systematic ethical codes of practice in place to serve as guidelines for decision makers at all levels within the organization.[23] Many researchers turned the nation's attention to the need for strongly advocating a new wave of business school curriculum requirements to provide students of commerce and finance with a wide range of classes that deal specifically, and in a practical manner, with ethical issues, value judgments, and moral choices within the corporate world.[24] Many business schools began to reevaluate their core courses and decided it was time to place extensive ethics course work at the heart of formal graduate business education so that future corporate managers and entrepreneurs would have a comprehensive exposure to various ethical situations that could involve the compromising of personal values and the relative worth of moral codes of conduct.[25] And yet, it turned out that the more entrenched the discipline of ethics and values has become in formal graduate business school curricula, the more bewildering and difficult to grasp it appears to the individuals who study it. Similar plans have been proposed and implemented to integrate clear, systematic approaches to managing ethics within the corporation as well.

It has been reported that senior management executives today are making unprecedented efforts to play by strict rules of fairness both internally and in the external market environment, and that this new interest is due in part to pressure not only from the consumer base, but from employees as well.[26] Big business has started once again to exhibit a somewhat renewed interest in, and commitment to, the corporate pursuit of rigorous ethical standards and guidelines to govern the fairness and outcomes of a wide range of commercial transactions. But concerns remain about the ethical conduct for owners of small-to-medium sized, privately-held, fast-growth entrepreneurial ventures. Certainly they are just as susceptible (if not more so) to incredulous daily business decision making and questionable procedural challenges. Many now advocate that successful new businesses are generally those that are built upon a foundation of ethical behavior, and that a common set of business values can speak to the very heart of every person within an organization and serve as a rallying point around which the new venture can gain momentum as a viable going concern.[27] And yet the smaller firm may be more apt to foster an environment that is not as strict in terms of its formal operating procedures, and as such, open the door for individuals to act in their own best interest. For example, an article in *INC. Magazine* recently reported that a small entrepreneurial firm was trying to promote employee trust, an openness to share information, and a commitment to allowing for broader decision parameters to increase employee responsibility for decisions; yet this increased individual freedom actually provided many high level employees with a perfect environment to systematically steal money over the course of several years before finally being caught. The lack of standard procedures along with clear checks and balances promoted an atmosphere that was more conducive to individual ethical choices, rather than a generally accepted moral code of conduct.[28]

Additional empirical findings by Baylor professor Justin Longenecker have also concluded that huge differences exist between the ways in which large and small firms approach the issues related to ethics, but that neither the large companies or the smaller entrepreneurial ventures had more successful results than the other in terms of the impact ethics and values had on performance.[29] Similar values-oriented studies have found that owners of small businesses generally tend to use essentially the same basic ethical dimensions in their decision making as are used by managers and senior executives in significantly larger companies.[30]

Some researchers have proposed a basic standardized framework through which small businesses can successfully implement a company-wide ethics program, and these are often founded on supporting an increased level of morale and heightened employee motivation due to involvement with all levels of the various decision making processes.[31] Some empirical evidence indicates that, for small entrepreneurial firms, ethical behavior (in practice) is often broader in scope than the black and white letter of the law requires, suggesting that individuals may have personal values that are even more stringent than the code of conduct found in general regulatory statutes.[32] Another research study found that entrepreneurs doing business in nonurban areas tended to have higher ethical standards than those business owners operating within distinctively urban areas, and that an individual's level of education was inversely related to the specific ethical values of honesty, integrity, and strict legal compliance.[33]

Significant questions still remain however, as to whether a renewed interest in ethics will be able to produce a measurable improvement in entrepreneurial and managerial decision making, as well as in firm performance. It has been suggested that ethical behavior can actually be rewarded by the market, although the venture and the external environment are often in direct conflict with each other.[34] Perhaps, when the economy hits a downturn and firms encounter decreases in sales and profitability, many small-to-medium enterprises may look for ways to cut corners and minimize their risk exposure due to increases in both business and market uncertainty. Some of the corners being cut range from somewhat questionable practices based on individual interpretation, all the way through to obvious criminal behavior.[35] It can be quite challenging for entrepreneurs to identify and implement a successful ethics program.

Much has been said about both the relative success and failure rates of firms that deliberately include a formal ethics program as part of their normal operations. In a recent speech given by the chief executive officer of *Levi Strauss and Company*, it was stated that ethics in the business environment is all about the character and courage of people, of individuals, and that doing the right thing is the most important practice in contemporary commerce, even it tends to cost the company more; and ethics and values in decision making should be placed above all other priorities in the company's long term strategic planning process.[36] One study even compared whether the American approach to business ethics is similar or unrelated to those values orientations displayed by companies from other countries, and found that ethics and values varied significantly with respect to what is considered the definition of inherently "right" versus what is inherently "wrong".[37] In a similar review of values and a moral code of business conduct, it was shown that ethical behaviors can tend to be somewhat consistent across different cultures, but that the basis for the type and content of moral reasoning varies significantly between different countries around the world.[38]

Many researchers believe that the core tenets of entrepreneurial ethics may be able to produce a values-based corporate culture that is embraced by both employees of the firm and other companies in the market. Some of these approaches have proposed that ethics should really be thought of as a somewhat simple mathematical formula that produces easily measurable results.[39] But many of these positions grossly oversimplify the nature of individual behavior and the many ways that moral compromise takes place in a business environment. Some writers would have firms believe that, although the focus on developing a clear corporate culture has begun to wane over the last decade, the revitalization of corporate culture and the nature of the internal decision making environment may now be the best response to dealing with values and ethics across all types of business conditions that any entrepreneur faces in building a new company from scratch. Some empirical evidence suggests that the benefits and costs to the firm that engages in company-wide ethical behavior are both literal and intangible. These included favorable literal effects such as profitability, sales growth, and market share, as well as intangible results like trust, loyalty, and confidence. However, there were also distinct negative effects including literal issues like bad debt, negative earnings, and bankruptcy, and intangible areas such as deceit, theft, and low morale.[40]

One very interesting study found that higher ethical standards can actually increase economic activity for the firm in the short run.[41] And, in a similar manner, many authors still argue that there does in fact exist a measurable, long-term cost to unethical behavior in the market. It has been documented that firms which stress business ethics actually experience increased profitability, and higher ethical standards increase economic activity in the short run. However, there are others who believe that ethical behavior will not be rewarded by the market, because such actions are in direct conflict with the very fabric of the competitive environment. It has been estimated that more than three quarters of American firms now operate with formal, ethical codes of practice. Yet, many individuals and companies are not sure of how to approach the issues of compromise and integrity, and remain perplexed as to how ethical standards are developed and ultimately implemented.

## The Tenets of a Personal Value System

Having laid some basic groundwork regarding the various hypotheses, positions, and interpretations of contemporary thought on ethics in the business community, the next logical step is to discuss the fundamental tenets that comprise a personal value system. The topic is at the same time very interesting and worthy of review, and yet quite difficult to formulate and elusive in its defining constructs. For the scope of this analysis of entrepreneurial ethics, the following outline will serve as the basis for all definitions pertaining to the many related terms, and any relationship between these concepts. Figure 4.1 shows an "entrepreneurial ethics wedge" and summarizes the three fundamental components that determine ethical behaviors in new ventures. The wedge is comprised of two parts, the *BASIS* and *VALUES*. The value system rests upon the formative *BASIS* that justifies the various actions that will

ultimately be displayed by the individual entrepreneur. The *BASIS* should be the strongest component of the entire
system because it supports and determines the structure of three levels of value judgments and it is the driving critical mass that directs the strength and form of ethical behavior implemented by the individual. The value system has three separate, but somewhat related, layers, and the shape of the these are dependent on the size of the basis. The thickest and broadest layer represents *CORE* values. These are the individual's most fundamental beliefs and perspectives. Core values come directly from a certain basis that is either objective or subjective in nature. The second layer depicts *MEDIAL* values. These are not as critical to the individual as core values, but they do form a narrowing extension of the core values. Relatively speaking, this layer is not as broad or as thick as the previous layer, but still touches on some aspects of the core values. These matters of right and wrong, benefits and costs, are less critical to the individual and may be subject to rethinking over time. The third layer describes *FRINGE* values. This area is quite thin and has the least breadth. Issues here are well removed from touching core values and are subject to impact from the various operating environments of the new enterprise. The strongest wedge configuration is not too narrow and not too tall. It creates a powerful driving force for behavior and has a thick and strong core layer that is not likely to tumble due to the force of impacts from outside influences in the environment in which it operates.

■ ■ ■ ■

**Figure 4.1**
**The Entrepreneurial Ethics Wedge:**
**A Basic Structure**

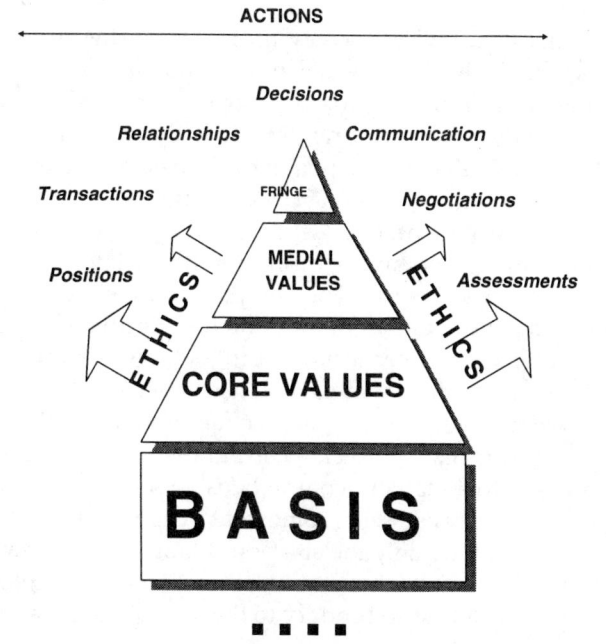

■ ■ ■ ■

Seven categories of actions have been selected as the primary activities that take place in both the internal and external commercial environments of operating the new venture. The first action involves the positions that the firm takes in matters of what is considered acceptable behavior and what is not, or the manner in which the firm "positions" itself with respect to business practices, customer relations, social policies, legal and regulatory practices, and prevailing community issues. The second action concerns the various levels and processes of discussions that take place with the external environment as well as with the internal matters that affect employees and company operations. The third area relates to the numerous categories and structures of internal and external transactions in which the firm engages, including financial, marketing, production, and human resources. The fourth area addresses the ways in that the company enters into and maintains various relationships with customers, suppliers, distributors, business partners, and government agencies. The fifth area involves the many types of communication the firm presents, both implicit and explicit, regarding the company's intentions, goals, and objectives. The sixth area covers the way decisions are made and the bases for those factors that comprise the decision making process. The last key area describes the way the enterprise makes assessments and analysis of situations and determines what is critical and what is not as it relates to company direction. It is important to take time at this juncture to explain in greater detail why these seven areas capture the full range of entrepreneurial firm activities that require the venture to act in a manner that reflects the heart of its very reason for existence. The organization will then move into these areas either with a predetermined sense of stability and purpose, or an open agenda that lacks purpose and fosters an unstable manner of carrying out the venture's competitive agenda.

## Entrepreneurial Positions

The entrepreneurial firm will ultimately find itself in the place where it will have to take a stance with respect to a host of internal and external issues. Some issues are relatively minor in terms of their significance to company operations and strategy. However, many issues that surface within the enterprise and outside in the market will *have* to be addressed in order to establish a defining company position. The issue may involve hiring and firing practices with respect to affirmative action. The firm may have to determine a position on both local and regional environmental issues. There may be a movement in the competitive market to provide some level of voluntary disclosure that relates to product components or service and maintenance track records. The company may have to state its position on a social issue that relates to children, under represented minorities, or the physically disabled. There may be a consumer call for censoring a product, an operating procedure, a certain group, or an individual and the firm will have to take a position in these matters.

The entrepreneurial new venture may be even more exposed to this because of the "newness" of its operations, and its lack of track record in the market. A distinct pressure can be placed on the entrepreneur to establish a comprehensive social and political platform for the enterprise, and yet these matters can seem somewhat insignificant (even trivial) with respect to the pressing issues at hand, namely the successful launch and growth of the firm. Often, the perception of the entrepreneur is that many of these issues are irrelevant to the success of the new venture, or they are at best, secondary to the core planning and decision making. At worst, these issues can appear to be annoying distractions that are taking up quality time of the entrepreneur to be diverted toward areas that are not high priorities in the overall scope of the business. It really hinges on whether the entrepreneur personally believes in the merit of the issue and then chooses to allocate time and resources to this area. The degree to which the firm takes seriously matters of positioning will be a direct function of the depth and breadth of the company's core value system and the foundational basis upon which it rests.

## Entrepreneurial Transactions

The second area that describes enterprise activities involves transactions. These are the contractual exchanges of goods, services, and funds between the firm and its employees, customers, and various intermediaries. These transactions can essentially take on one of two characteristics. They will either be somewhat rigid and closed-ended in structure and address those actions that are more or less *required* by firms engaged in commerce in a specific market, or they will be more flexible and open-ended in design due to the greater degree of *optionality* that underscores the rationale for the transaction. How a firm enters into transactions and then engages in completing the transaction will have very specific ethical considerations for the entrepreneur and all interested stake holders. In much the same way that company positions will have to be determined, so too, the firm will be defining itself through the style, structure, and directions of the transactions that it executes. These will directly reflect on the core values of the firm and provide a window into the foundational basis that guides the relative importance of the enterprise's operations.

As was just mentioned, some transactions are more standardized in content and structure because they are the elementary means of conducting the most basic form of business in a given market environment, or they are the first level of requirements for managing and directing company personnel. This first type can tend to be the transactions that are most likely to be devoid of any concerted ethical emphasis because they can be viewed as mandatory and are completed in essentially the same manner by literally every firm in the industry. They are so standardized that there appears to be no need to think through specific rationales or value orientations in their design or implementation. Examples include employment contracts, a basic package of employee benefits, banking services, production delivery schedules, certain warranties, and accounting payment terms. On the other hand, the second type of transactions are less standardized and more customized to the particular interests of the issue and the two parties involved in the related transfers. The transaction is not exactly like all others in the market and has a greater propensity to include specific rationales and value orientations in its composition and execution. The entrepreneur often perceives these not so much as transactions, but rather as "deals" that have been singularly conceived of for a special purpose, and the objective is aimed at a unique opportunity. This transaction includes a more personal approach to working with either internal or external constituents. Some examples include a unique joint venture, an employee stock ownership plan, the engineering of custom terms for innovative products and services by a financial intermediary, or a cooperative marketing plan with a consortia of complementary firms. Again, the firm has the opportunity to establish a defining perception among various "transactees," and either build or destroy a particular reputation among all internal and external constituencies.

## Entrepreneurial Relationships

The entrepreneurial firm will initiate, maintain, and eventually sever a wide range of internal and external relationships during the seed, launch, and on-going operations over time. These relationships, like the transactions related to them, can take on two distinct characteristics. A good number of relationships may appear to be required with its employees and outside stake holders. These may take on a superficial nature if the owner perceives that there is no choice in the matter with respect to dealing with certain people and organizations. Most entrepreneurs advocate a *laissez-faire* position regarding accountability and challenges to the progress of the venture. This attitude can pervade the related position that the firm takes on certain internal and external issues, and it can either negatively or positively affect the manner of designing and engaging in all types of transactions. So, relationships are actions that accompany positions and transactions, and they can be either required, standard, and somewhat formal, or they can be more optional, personally customized, and very informal based on the entrepreneur's personal perception of the other individual or group.

Some relationships just seem to happen because there is a natural link between firms in the marketing chain, or in the facilitation of accounting and financial matters. Many entrepreneurs are apt to express a lack of sincere interest in dealing with many internal and external constituencies because there exists a sense that this is *not* a relationship of choice, but rather one of dictated convenience. Examples may include the banker that handles the firm's normal working capital cash flow and mortgage loans, the firm that sold and now services the company's basic manufacturing equipment, the marketing representative from the new venture's main supplier, the employees that run the machinery on the shop floor, or the legal firm that counsels the entrepreneur in matters of regulatory requirements of the product or service. The entrepreneur may have a predisposition to back away from these type of relationships because they are interpreted as mundane interactions with boring individuals and companies that are only present because they have a monetary stake in the firm's performance, and who have no other qualitative links to the entrepreneur of the new venture.

On the other hand, entrepreneurs may exhibit a natural tendency to migrate toward more unique relationships that they believe are the result of their own initiation efforts. These relationships hold greater value for the entrepreneur because the interaction was probably the result of a specific idea or area of interest developed by the company founder, and there was a recognized match with other related parties that could participate with the new venture in a very deliberate manner. There may in fact be a greater sense of commonality and shared goals and objectives in these types of relationships, and this presents many ethical considerations for individual entrepreneurs to evaluate. For instance, there may be a tremendous sense of mutual interest between the owner of a new venture and the newly hired (and heavily recruited) director of information technology, while there may be significantly less attraction to the firm's receptionist, accounting staff, delivery truck drivers, or janitorial workers. The entrepreneur may have a special sense of accomplishment and admiration for the owners of a company that was specifically chosen to provide component parts for the new venture's product, but there is little inherent attraction to the owners of the firm that provides maintenance service for manufacturing equipment, or the banker that calls three times a year to simply "check in." The origin and rationale of relationships has a direct bearing on entrepreneurial ethical behavior.

## Entrepreneurial Decisions

Most entrepreneurs would probably divide their decision making into two clearly distinct categories. The first group of decisions are considered "average" or "everyday" in content. They deal with standard operating procedures and appear relatively typical in content and general in application. Many of these decisions are associated with the functional management of the enterprise and include such things as ordering parts, materials, and supplies, reviewing employee performance, hiring and training new employees, handling customer service inquiries, analyzing the relative strength of cash flow allocations, and monitoring a production schedule. The ethics involved in this first category of decisions may not be immediately evident because of the routine nature of the options presented and choices made. Entrepreneurs may create an *ethics decision realm* that tends to discriminate between decisions that exhibit obvious ethical implications, and alternatives that are perceived as not implying any outright moral judgments or values-oriented choices. But this is a poorly constructed paradigm for entrepreneurial decision making. All decisions draw upon some aspect of the individual's personal perspectives and biases, so they always contain an ethical component. Entrepreneurs think in this bifurcated mode because they either intentionally or unknowingly place a subjective level of importance to decisions based upon their own value judgments of what is deemed a pertinent ethical matter and what is not. This first group of decisions is somehow cast in the light of ethical insignificance due to the individual's belief that these "everyday" matters are not weighty with subjective implications of what constitutes right and wrong. They are merely viewed as "standard operating procedure" and even void of any values orientation.

The second group of entrepreneurial decisions is then characterized as ethically significant because these matters involve perceived issues of right and wrong. The entrepreneur has concluded that in certain instances a decision carries with it issues that could be either suitable or inappropriate in value content. Examples include the strategy chosen to court a new joint venture partner, the method by which to secure a new sale account, the method chosen to report certain accounting records for capital acquisitions, the degree with which to target performance relative to a regulatory compliance issue, or the time frame necessary to discharge a current employee or business associate. The discriminating point between these two groups is not a well-defined objective measure. It is in fact a personally constructed hedge based upon a personal world view and the interpretation of that world view in the context of the what is in the best interest of the entrepreneurial new venture. The subjective nature of personal decision making allows for a wide range of categorical placements for different decisions. But the truth of the matter is that *every* decision carries ethical implications. The morality of choice is even evident in the personal bias used to discriminate between these supposedly ethical and *non*ethical decisions in the firm. The full extent of this position with regard to decision making will be reviewed in detail in the subsequent chapters.

## Entrepreneurial Communication

Having described the positioning, the transactions, the corresponding relationships, and the categorical dividing of decisions, the next action that will require ethical consideration is that of communication. As in the cases of the prior actions, the entrepreneur is confronted with having to transfer and receive information with the various people and organizations present in the internal and external environments of the new venture. The manner in which communication takes place will actually communicate a great deal about the entrepreneur's personal attitudes toward the previously discussed actions, and the significance of the messages that go back and forth between the new venture and the respective persons or groups.

The quality of entrepreneurial communication is never a function the time allocated toward a person or organization in the internal or external environment. The key issue in communication is effectiveness and understanding the accurate impact of decisions on the firm. It is untenable to believe that the entrepreneur who spends more time communicating holds that situation in higher ethical position than those areas where less time is utilized. Many instances that require a good deal of time spent communicating may not reflect a higher values placed on the dialogue. Entrepreneurs often express disdain for the long, drawn out process of communicating in certain circles, and view favorably the short, concise, and direct dealing with an issue. Instead of trying to evaluate the relative worth of communications based on the time devoted to it, entrepreneurs once again use their individual perceptions and biases to structure preferences for certain types of communication strategies. Values will always play a part in effective dialogue within new ventures. The entrepreneur may , in the same morning, have to clearly address a matter of employee theft, and then speak with a supplier about a recent shipment. The lecture to the staff in the former case may take three hours, or it may take thirty minutes. The important issue is whether the message was received and does the entrepreneur place a good deal of core value to this matter. The phone call with the supplier could go for three hours, or thirty minutes, or even thirty seconds and yet have greater ethical implications than the former presentation. The important point is the weight assigned to the ethical value of the communication process and how it most effectively handled.

## Entrepreneurial Negotiations

The new venture is engaged in a tremendous amount of discussion pertaining to equipment acquisitions, equity capital investments, debt financing, employee recruitment, supplier procurement, orders from potential buyers, and joint operations with other firms. In every instance, the entrepreneur's positioning of the firm, perception of the transaction value, view toward to the relationship, category of the decision involved, and method of communication will together determine the ethical implications of the bargaining process. It is not enough to merely bid low and ask high. The ethics of negotiations integrate the entrepreneur's personal value system and the expected range of likely outcomes into a process that requires serious ethical thought. Some entrepreneurs see the negotiation process as having certain, predetermined ground rules that govern the interaction between supply and demand. Others view sitting down at the negotiation table as a unique experience each and every time a new deal is to be pursued. It is interesting to note that each of these ideas carries with it an entire range of ethical considerations. For instance, in the case of the former situation, the entrepreneur is convinced that all deals worth securing must flow through the same basic channels in order to reach an acceptable agreement. Regardless of the deal on the table, that approach to the negotiating table carries with it personal bias and expectations for how the process is to naturally progress. The latter situation reflects a distinctly opposite technique that does not utilize a format of objective rules of conduct, but that has as the rule that there is no prior plan for what is considered acceptable negotiation. Instead, the entrepreneur engages in offers and counter offers from the perspective that each deal is a separate potential conquest and the best strategy is to proceed on an *incremental discovery* basis, allowing the deal to unfold in its own random format, based solely on the circumstances at hand.

## Entrepreneurial Assessments

The seventh and final action that mandates an ethical response from the entrepreneur is the individual's manner of assessing and analyzing data and information that pertains to the factors of success or failure for the new venture. On the one hand, the entrepreneur can assess firm performance, direction, goals, and objectives based on a variety of computer-based information systems that each contain a tremendous amount of raw data pertaining to everything from accounting and finance, production and operations, management and human resources, to marketing research, promotions, and advertising, and even high technology applications and use. In addition, there are literally thousands of trade and industry journals that maintain databases on their member firms. Independent resources include providers ranging from the *Moody's Industrial Manual*, and *Standard and Poor's*, and *Value Line* to the *INC. 500*, the *Business Week 1000*, and the *Fortune 500*. And, on top of all this, most new ventures will also maintain their own in-house databases of customer profiles, sales trends, customer service parameters, and production output and efficiency. At the other end of the analysis spectrum, the entrepreneur has subjective instincts and perceptions about how to ascertain the firm's current and future situation. This type of assessment is often referred to as a "gut feeling," where the individual has a certain belief about actions and outcomes based on a wealth of prior experience and performance.

An ethical implication is raised at both ends of the assessment continuum. If the entrepreneur leans toward the supposedly "hard" data of the secondary outside sources and the primary in-house system, there may appear to be less opportunity for individual perspective and value judgments to be included in the assessment. In a similar manner, it may be presumed that assessing the firm's direction and actions based on the entrepreneur's individual experience and prior performance is a complete value judgment with greater ethical implications. The reality is that the very *process* of assessment is an ethical matter, not the ultimate choice of data input. There are interesting moral considerations to weigh when working with large data resources, and there are other issues to evaluate when assessments are made based upon a personal track-record. It is not that one method has ethical characteristics and the other does not, but rather that the procedure by which actions in the internal and external environments are assessed is completely dependent upon the entrepreneur's perceived value of whatever data is utilized. The very choice of what to refer to in assessing a situation speaks tremendously about the ethical perspective of the firm's senior executive. Subscriptions to every major database do not guarantee to improve the firm's ability to analyze situations. And "gut feeling" assessments do not open up more or less ethical problems than using secondary data sources. Regardless of what data is looked to and drawn upon, ethical considerations will always be a part of assessing firm status, and values will continue to form the basis for how data is incorporated into the individual's perspective.

## Values and Ethics Defined

Ethics describe the ways in which the individual approaches and executes these various actions both with the firm and in the outside competitive environment. Ethics are in reality the direct effect of the types of values that comprise and strengthen the individual entrepreneur's dealings with these seven actions. The unique personal perspective can be thought of as a wedge that makes a point of contact with the environment on initially peripheral issues, and then drives directly into the fabric with a sharp and forceful dividing of what is appropriate and what is not. But the wedge can take on other shapes as it tries to address the environment. It might be solid in some respects, but the base is too narrow and the wedge lacks sufficient breadth to cover the complete range of issues presented in the environment. As such, it lacks the lateral strength to clearly divide these related actions. It may also be broad enough to cover a seemingly wide range of issues, but it is lacking in depth of conviction and application to all scenarios equally, and so it never really makes an impact in the environment because it does not have the right shape for clearly dividing right from wrong. The wedge is strongest at its core values level, where the depth and breadth create a solid and definitive basis for actions in the firm and in the market. Ethical activities made nearest the core layer are more sure and most likely *not* to be second guessed by the individual. Actions that are more the function of medial values may be open to greater scrutiny and the process of periodic review. Ethics at this level are linked directly to core values, but they are one layer removed from direct contact with the basis and therefore lack the depth and breadth of force that exists at the core level. The ethical behaviors that are related to the fringe values have a somewhat minimal support base, and are once removed from the individual entrepreneur's core values. The outside surface makes direct contact with issues in the environment and is susceptible to wear and tear on its two exposed surfaces. There are no strong ethical actions at the tip of the wedge because the fringe values are still very much open to continuous interpretation and reevaluation as to their relative worth for interaction with the environment. The pointed fringe is the most vulnerable layer because it can easily be toppled due to its more narrow profile, and lack of depth.

The ethical *BASIS* is perhaps the most crucial component of the wedge because it provides the underlying rationale that supports the various types of ethical activities. An ethical basis can be either subjective or objective in its origin. A subjective basis is relative in its composition and is formulated to remain less broad in scope and not as deep in terms of the levels of issues that it directly touches. Because of this profile, a subjective basis does not provide the same degree of personal commitment in the environment and tends to operate based primarily on the current situation being faced, rather than on a fixed set of predetermined standards. An objective basis is absolute in is composition and is specifically formulated to be quite broad in scope and somewhat deep in terms of being applicable to various levels of issues that it encounters in the environment. This profile describes a higher degree of personal commitment and tends to operate more or less irrespective of the current situation being faced, but based on certain standards that are applied in all matters of actions in the environment.

This ethics wedge can also take on two other variant forms in terms of the three structural components. The differences will be present in either the *breadth* of the basis, and the subsequent layers, or in the *depth* of the basis and the way the layers are configured with regard to a thin structure. There are probably several different ways to configure the components of an ethics structure, but two types are the most important to this discussion of a personal value system. Figure 4.2 shows the first variation in the ethics wedge where the basis is quite limited in terms of its breadth of applications in the environment. As such, it can only support a limited critical mass of core values and this reduces the impact of ethical behaviors and activities in the environment. Some medial values rest on top of the smaller core area, but they are lacking a solid footing and their apparent reach, or penetration, into the area of actions is thin and increases the vulnerability to external impacts that threaten the individual entrepreneur's ethical resolve. At the pinnacle, the fringe extensions into the environment are even less resilient due to a minimal point of contact surface with the medial values and a thinning and increased exposure to positions, transactions, and the like. The entrepreneur has an identical surface area exposed to the various actions in the environment, but lacks the breadth of support for core, medial, and fringe values such that ethical positions are more likely to experience negative impacts that will alter the manner in which actions are carried out.

■ ■ ■ ■

**Figure 4.2**
**The Entrepreneurial Ethics Wedge:**
**A Lack of Breadth**

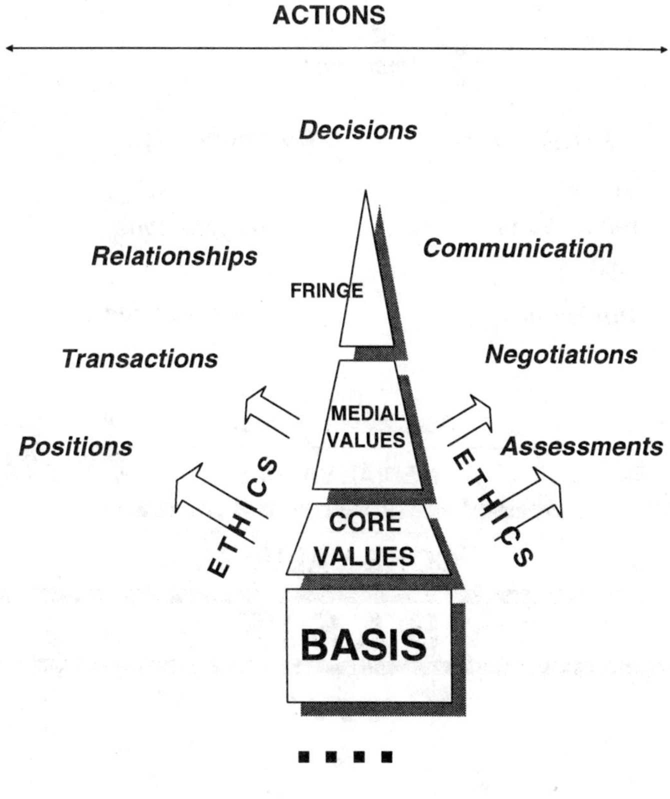

**ACTIONS**

Decisions

Relationships         Communication
              FRINGE

Transactions          Negotiations

                MEDIAL
                VALUES
Positions                    Assessments

                CORE
                VALUES

**BASIS**

■ ■ ■ ■

60 ■ Chapter Four

A second variation is represented in Figure 4.3 where the entrepreneur displays a broad range of expected applications in the foundational basis for the value system (similar to Figure 4.1), but this basis lacks depth of commitment. The core values also appear to be sufficiently broad in their scope as a function of the basis, but they too lack depth in terms of individual resolve to utilize these in a consistent manner. The subsequent medial and fringe layers of values continue the trend of thin obligations, and as such they greatly reduce the ethical reach of the individual's actions in the environment. The shortened version of the wedge lacks the structural integrity to consistently address transactions, decisions, and communications based on the objectivity of the support framework for the values basis. In this case, the entrepreneur does not significantly penetrate the environment, but instead the wedge makes only a surface indentation in terms of behavioral actions. It cannot be effective in all situations because its basis does not possess a sufficient depth of resolve and as such, the basis cannot generate enough force to make a noticeable impact in the environment.

■ ■ ■ ■

**Figure 4.3**
**The Entrepreneurial Ethics Wedge:**
**A Lack of Depth**

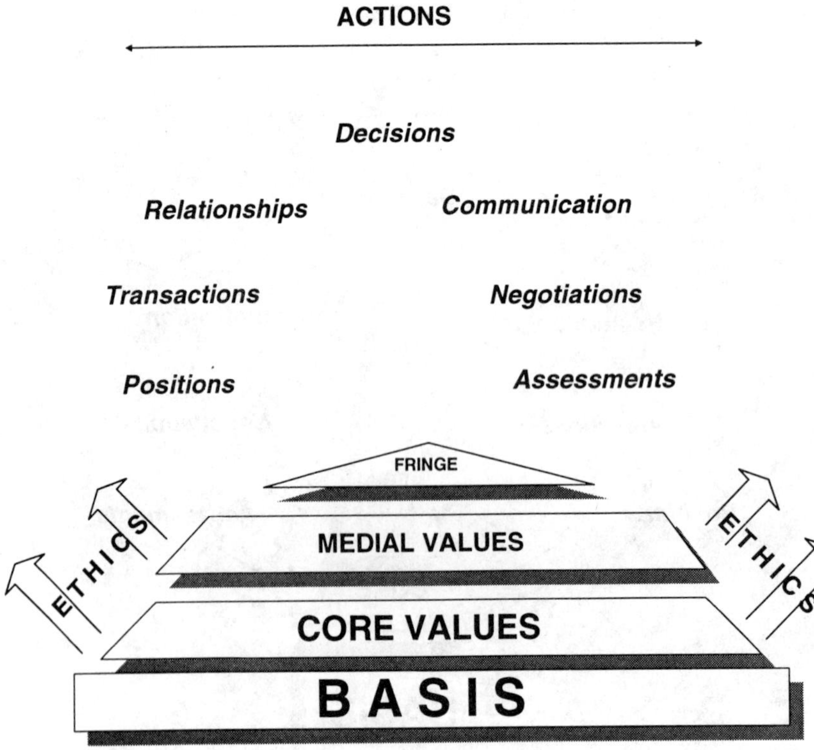

**ACTIONS**

Decisions

Relationships          Communication

Transactions           Negotiations

Positions              Assessments

FRINGE

MEDIAL VALUES

ETHICS          ETHICS

CORE VALUES

**B A S I S**

■ ■ ■ ■

Certainly, the discussion of a values system contains many other far reaching issues and implications. However, for the scope of this book, it is proposed that values exist as three distinct layers as a structure set upon a foundational basis, and ethics are the procedural and behavioral guidelines by which the individual engages in various forms of business related activities. These general areas include (but are not limited to): personal and business level discussions, all types of commercial, financial, and market transactions, qualitative positioning relative to the competition and issues in the market, personal and company relationships, the process and formulation of internal and external decisions, internal and external communication, and the procedures and criteria utilized in making assessments of business situations. This topical framework can be applied to both the individual as well as the new venture to the extent that it is a direct extension of the entrepreneur. The next area to explore involves the way a personal value system is implemented in a practical manner within an enterprise.

## The Personal Value System in Practice

As proposed, there are three basic manners by which an individual can implement a personal value system within the context of an emerging new venture. In the first technique, the entrepreneur exhibits a somewhat strict policy of absolute and very specific parameters within which to operate and execute actions (see Figure 4.1). The second style involves a plan to have numerous extensions of some form of a code of conduct that is supposed to deal with many interactions in the environment (see Figure 4.2). The third manner utilizes an apparently broad application of value constructs, but lacks sufficient operational capabilities to create a consistent pattern of use (see Figure 4.3). There are without a doubt numerous reasons to explain why an entrepreneur's personal value system would either be successful or not when put into practice in the functional operations of the new venture. Chapters six through ten will examine in detail the five most challenging venues for implementing ethics in the unique setting of the entrepreneurial firm. But at this time, it is important to discuss the *ethical facilitators* and detractors that contribute to three proposed manners that the ethics wedge takes shape in the practical aspects of managing the emerging enterprise.

Ethical facilitators define four component factors that can help to create an environment that is conducive to implementing consistent ethical practices in the functional areas of the business. These include the level of ethics awareness, the vested interest in the types of benefits available due to ethical actions, the network system to support ethical policies, and the identification of realistic expectations for the level of benefits accomplished in the process of ethical actions. The critical issue to making these facilitators work properly (in terms of practical implementation) is the degree of formality with which values and ethical actions are systematically initiated within the course of regular operations in the enterprise. If these four areas are presented within the context of a formal ethics plan, the likelihood of successful implementation increases significantly. The opposite effects of these four factors can also become *ethical detractors* due entirely to a lack of formality in the effort to put ethics into practice. Without a formal, systematic approach to the transfer of values into the fabric of the firm structure, either a lack of awareness, an inability to produce vested interest among employees, unrealistic expectations, or the lack of a well designed support system can each derail even the best of intentions on the part of the entrepreneur.

62 ■ Chapter Four

Figure 4.4 presents the relative positioning of a formal sequence of ethical facilitators. These are tactics utilized by the entrepreneur to improve the chances for the successful implementation of ethics with measurable results in firm performance for the activities described earlier in this chapter.

**Figure 4.4**
**Ethical Facilitators: A Formal Sequence**

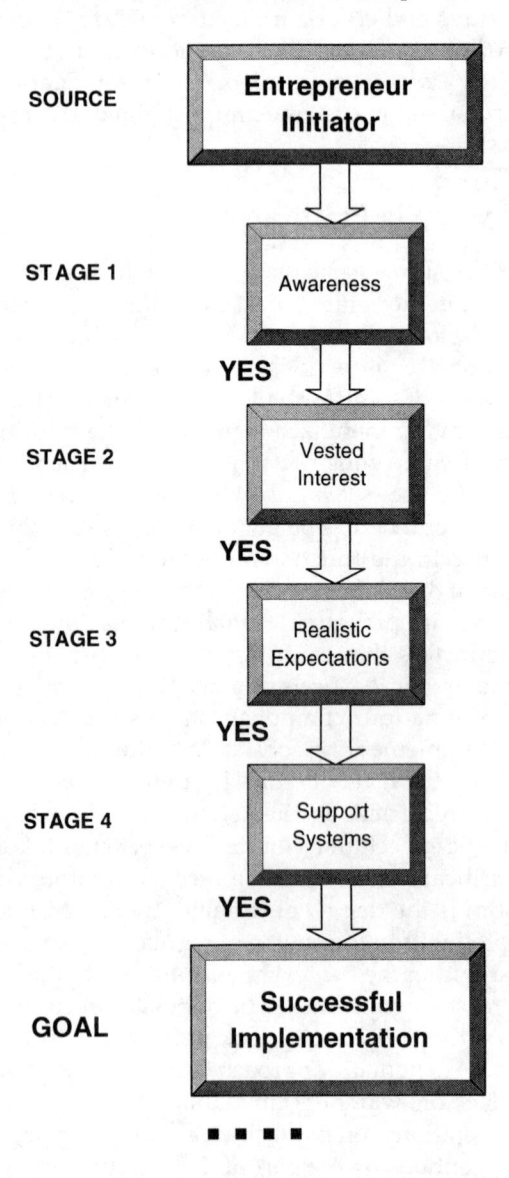

SOURCE — Entrepreneur Initiator

STAGE 1 — Awareness
YES

STAGE 2 — Vested Interest
YES

STAGE 3 — Realistic Expectations
YES

STAGE 4 — Support Systems
YES

GOAL — Successful Implementation

A formal ethics plan is able to effectively coordinate these four factors in order to gain measurable results in firm performance and reputation. The formal method should be a well designed and programmatic fit within the operational framework of the overall organizational structure of the firm, i.e. a formal, company-sponsored program. This represents the best case scenario where the entrepreneur initiates an awareness about CORE values among the various stake holders. A concerted effort is made to link the foundational basis of the entrepreneur's perspective to the personal ideas that employees have about values and ethical practices. Referring back to Figure 4.1 and the entrepreneurial wedge, the core values need to be both wide enough to cover all functional areas of the venture and deep enough to include all levels of actions in the firm environment. If awareness is brought to a sufficient position and the core values are successfully linked to the personal values of the employees, then the entrepreneur is responsible to effectively state the most realistic expectations for the enterprise as a result of formally implementing ethical practices. The last requirement to achieve success is to provide a well defined support system for ethics in the normal functions of the company. This sequence is most likely to gain acceptance and be successful if it is introduced as a formal requirement of all personnel.

The same sequence of these four stages can also be introduced in an informal manner. The lack of formality can take on either of two distinct characteristics in the entrepreneurial new venture. Figure 4.5 summarizes the problem of *conceptual ethical advocacy*, where the lack of awareness, the inability to create a vested interest among employees, or the lack of realistic expectations can detract the practical implementation of ethical behavior away from success and straight toward failure. This initial scenario describes the collapse of the entrepreneur's newly initiated ethics plan at one of the first three stages in the proposed sequence. The second problem due to informality is that of *operational ethical inability*, which describes the disintegration of a recently initiated ethics plan at the fourth stage in the proposed sequence. Figure 4.6 demonstrates that even though the entrepreneur was perhaps able to secure an introductory level of ethical awareness among employees, a minimum level of vested interest in pursuing ethical behavior, and realistic expectations among company personnel to practice values-based interactions, the new venture was unable to effectively introduce a clear program of systematic ethical behavior into the various functional areas of the enterprise because there were no support systems, no ethical infrastructure, designed and put in place to facilitate a successful implementation. Although the general idea of moral bases, core values, and ethical behavior may have gained some degree of conceptual momentum among employees, there was no way to operationalize ethics into the policies and procedures of the new venture.

The best opportunity for an entrepreneur's personal value system to be successfully put into practice becomes a function of the degree of formality with which the owner lobbies for the merits of ethical guidelines and a workable structure to facilitate a values-based code of conduct for all the functional areas of the firm's normal operations. Ethics cannot be perceived as something that is a transitional exercise or merely a temporary break from the mundane tasks of the daily office routine. Once the entrepreneur makes the decision to implement a base of parameters for firm conduct, there must be a formal program to define why ethics are important. If the entrepreneur can effectively communicate this, these moral bases must then gain the personal approval of every individual in the company, and be embraced as defining the enterprise and how it functions in transactions, relationships, decisions,

**Figure 4.5
Ethical Facilitators: An Informal Sequence
"Conceptual Failure"**

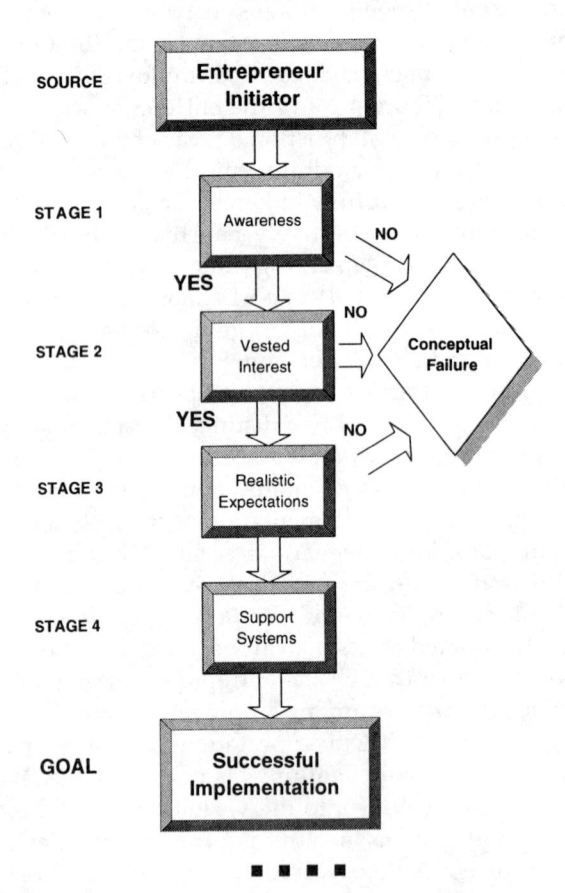

- SOURCE: Entrepreneur Initiator
- STAGE 1: Awareness — YES ↓ / NO → Conceptual Failure
- STAGE 2: Vested Interest — YES ↓ / NO → Conceptual Failure
- STAGE 3: Realistic Expectations — NO → Conceptual Failure
- STAGE 4: Support Systems
- GOAL: Successful Implementation

communication, positions, negotiations, and assessments. But many of the entrepreneur's interpretations of the venture may not translate well into each of these normal business activities. For example, one of the most prevailing perceptions among owners of new ventures is that business risk can be effectively hedged through a corporate form of legal organization. This *limited liability myth* can tend to create a false sense of security that there is somehow a comprehensive financial hedge protecting the owner from negative economic consequences or even bankruptcy. Firm conduct and moral bases must be substantive and customized to the unique nature of the people and strategies that comprise the core operations of the enterprise.

## Individual Values and Firm Values

The final piece of the initial format for reviewing the entrepreneurial ethics puzzle is the manner in which the firm represents the owner's personal value system. This will be referred to

## Figure 4.6
## Ethical Facilitators: An Informal Sequence
## "Operational Failure"

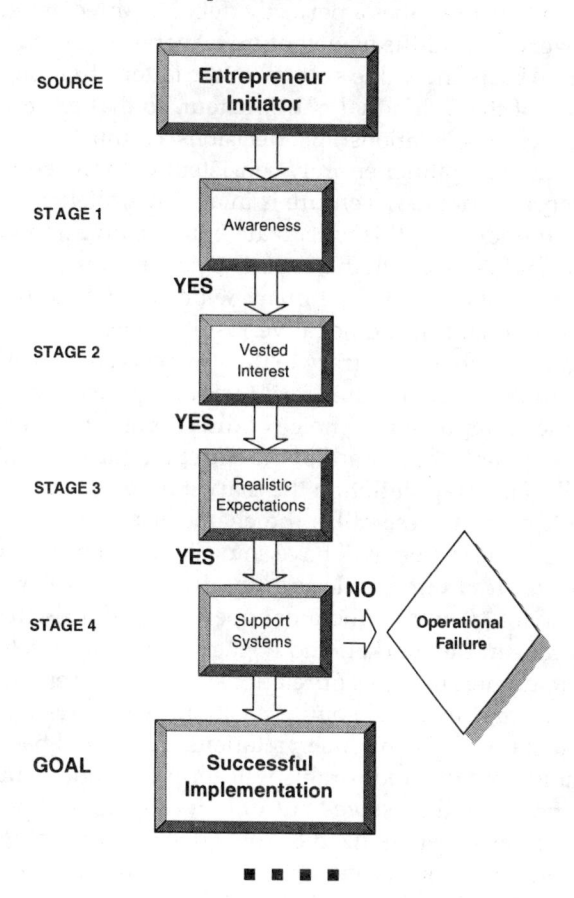

| | | |
|---|---|---|
| SOURCE | Entrepreneur Initiator | |
| STAGE 1 | Awareness | |
| | YES | |
| STAGE 2 | Vested Interest | |
| | YES | |
| STAGE 3 | Realistic Expectations | |
| | YES → NO | Operational Failure |
| STAGE 4 | Support Systems | |
| GOAL | Successful Implementation | |

as the *values reflection factor*. This describes the degree to which the actions and attitudes of the new venture are a function of the moral basis and ethical behavior of the entrepreneur. Evidence will be presented in the coming chapters to support this concept and reveal two distinct patterns of reflection. The first pattern describes a vague likeness of the entrepreneur that is not so much a direct reflection as it is a general profile of a few basic components. In the same way that a police department artist creates a rendering of a criminal based on verbally communicated descriptions of the suspect, many firms may reflect a basic image of the founder, but this is limited to one or two general guidelines that are more like a mission statement. The entrepreneur may promote a certain "rule of thumb" or a latent business motto that provides only cursory ideas about personal values and ethical behavior, and lacks any specific calling to detailed policies and procedures based on moral rationales. As such, the new venture firm culture is more a composite of the numerous and diverse personalities and experiences represented in the management and staff. The internal climate of the enterprise is actually multifaceted based on the composition of the various departments. The entrepreneur has been relegated to the position of figurative influencer, rather than the true leader and implementor of company values. Ethics become the result of many individuals who decide when certain behaviors are appropriate or not.

The second pattern type describes a perfectly detailed, direct reflection of the entrepreneur and captures in every level of the new venture's operations, each specific feature of the founder's personal moral basis and value system. In the latter situation, the firm has become, in essence, an extension of the individual entrepreneur, so that all facets of the firm's handling of positions, transactions, relationships, decisions, communication, negotiations, and assessments are achieved in a manner entirely consistent with the entrepreneur's own ethical behavior. The entrepreneurial new venture is in an unparalleled situation to take on the ethical character of the founder, but this will create both positive and negative effects for all levels of stake holders that interact with the firm. The positive results of this can be a smooth and seamless management style, and a company-wide sense of pride in the work accomplished, and how it gets done. But the negative results could be that the work force feels pressured to act a certain way that is contrary to their own personal beliefs. Many employees may simply "go through the motions" in regard to ethical policies and behavior in order to appear supportive of the entrepreneur's choice of direction for the company.

The firm may never be able to fully adopt the entrepreneur's ethical positions and moral bases, but the firm will stake a reputation in the market based on its degree of reflectivity in defining how well the company resembles the character and integrity of the owner. The entrepreneur's personal value system will have some degree of impact on how the new venture is organized, because it is impossible to fully divest the owner's biases, moral judgments, and ethical behavior from the functional operations of the enterprise. The company will have to take positions in the market, and engage in various levels of transactions. The firm will be involved in numerous types of relationships, and be engaged in negotiations at various levels of internal and external communication. A wide range of decisions will be made based on assessment policies and interpretations. The moral basis or rationale for distinguishing the desirable from the undesirable will support fundamental core values. These may remain private and work themselves out only in the entrepreneur's personal ethical behavior, or they may become systematized to some degree in defining the company's policies in the seven business activities. The entrepreneur, the driver of the new venture, is also in a position to drive (or park) core values and ethics for the firm.

**CHAPTER FIVE**

# *A New Model of Entrepreneurial Ethics*

## A Unique Approach

This book presents the study of values-based decision making and approaches to ethical situations in business from the unique perspective of the relatively new and fast-growth entrepreneurial venture. Chapter One highlighted six specific characteristics of these types of firms that included: a direct relationship between risk and return, the presence of some degree of business uncertainty, the role of business innovation, the prospects for realizing significant market opportunity, the less formal internal environment of these smaller firms, and the organizational structure that supports a highly concentrated core of managerial responsibility. It was argued that these function together and create an ethical compounding effect that predisposes smaller enterprises to a significant exposure to ethical concerns. Chapter Two then examined how the individual entrepreneur exhibits six personal characteristics that are directly related to the primary features of new ventures, and that these open the door to a range of ethical considerations. These six respective personal characteristics included the inclination to manage business risk with an eye toward a commensurate *expected* return, the problem of invited (and accepted) business uncertainty, the trap that can occur in formulating innovation, a potential flaw in recognizing and pursuing what appears to be significant market opportunity, the concerns about the entrepreneur desiring complete control of the firm's operations, and the potential negative effects of the entrepreneur utilizing a network of referrals and professional contacts.

Chapter Three then discussed the intricate process through which new ideas are conceived and how the entrepreneur originates a comprehensive vision for the venture that will facilitate taking the new idea to the market. It concluded with the problems that arise when the idea and the vision meet with the complete range of potential outcomes that comprise venture reality. Chapter Four continued that the entrepreneur brings a personal value system to the new venture and the tenets of this arrangement are expressed in seven actions, or activities, that will require some form of values-based perspective from the entrepreneur. These actions will take place in both the internal environment within the enterprise and in the external environment of the competitive market, and were identified as: taking positions, executing transactions, dealing with numerous individual and company relationships, formulating decisions, effectively communicating, engaging in many types of personal and business negotiations, and making assessments of situations that affect the long-term viability of the firm. A basic model was presented that defined the relationship and differences between values and ethics, and how a personal value system and ethical behavior is put in practice given the unique interaction of the individual entrepreneur and the new venture.

It is generally agreed that entrepreneurs introduce newly designed products and services, launch new companies, and create new markets through innovation and the ability to recognize opportunity, often when others do not notice such openings in the competitive market. They maintain control of the venture and tend to operate with a less formal internal environment. The tremendous amount of uncertainty surrounding an entrepreneurial venture may contribute to this lack of rigidity with respect to policies and procedures. How then are entrepreneurs, the ideas they conceive, the vision they articulate, the formation of their markets, and the structure and organization of the new ventures they launch uniquely exposed to the potential for ethical compromise? The recent focus of the National Conference on Business Ethics dealt with the impact that mergers, takeovers, and corporate restructuring have on ethical behavior as firms are suddenly transformed into different organizations almost overnight, complete with new rules for success and failure. There are distinctly unique bases from which ethics can be formulated as well, including Judeo-Christian and biblical foundations, humanistic approaches, and basic tenets of situational relativism.[1] And even within the Judeo-Christian principles there are various schools of thought (including Summists, Jesuits, evangelical philosophers, and a wide range of naturalists) concerning what constitutes a moral absolute and the basis for value judgments.[2] Moral theories also have roots in Darwinian evolution and theories of natural selection, socialism, Marxism, Buddhism, Hinduism, and the writings of Freud.[3] Much of the contemporary discussion of business ethics and values is interpreted through a decidedly *post-modern* perspective, which tends to classify morals as subjective and the product of rational experience, observation, and convenience.

It is not imperative that this book address each of the many philosophical bases for moral reasoning and ethical behavior. There are numerous excellent works that trace the history and development of modern ethics through the many schools of thought.[4,5,6,7] It is important to continuously review the status of ethical practices and to make formal recommendations as to how individuals and firms can improve their behavior in the future. And even once the questions about origins and foundations have been addressed, individual entrepreneurs will still have to make decisions about the practical matters of *how* to apply ethical beliefs, and *when* certain behaviors are most appropriate for use within the setting of the firm.[8] However, the research findings available on business ethics today is overwhelmingly aimed at large corporations. Literally all of the published works dealing with small, entrepreneurial ventures offer either anecdotal situations about employee fraud[9], difficulties within family-owned firms,[10] issues about personnel hiring and firing practices,[11] or advice from senior executives about how to do ethics in other firms.[12] Many empirical studies make recommendations about how ethics can enhance a company's profile in the market,[13] or report on correlations between ethical behavior and various demographic data about the entrepreneurs, such as sex, age, education, income, religious commitments, and profit motive.[14]

The following model is designed specifically to examine how this incredibly unique situation of new ventures and individual entrepreneurs is positioned with respect to values and ethical behavior. The model recognizes that the entrepreneur's individual characteristics first comprise a foundational component that cultivates and supports the following six core personal factors of influence on the new venture:

1 - *the degree of risk tolerance,*
2 - *the openness to business uncertainty,*
3 - *the creation of a product or service idea innovation,*
4 - *the view toward significant market opportunity,*
5 - *the informality of the organizational structure,* and
6 - *the need to concentrate entrepreneurial responsibility.*

Together, these will ultimately translate into a specific type of values system that will form the defining vision for the venture's direction. Each particular configuration of the entrepreneur's personal factors and the venture's characteristics is then likely to produce a unique vision and business ethic, and translate into a venture-level perspective for how company actions are implemented both within the firm and in the external market. Figure 5.1 summarizes the detailed relationships within this model of entrepreneurial ethics. Notice that the entrepreneurial characteristics layer of the values and ethics wedge (previously defined in chapter four) has been further clarified to specifically identify the six designated tenets of the individual entrepreneur (described in chapter two) that correspond to the fundamental features of new firms (summarized in chapter one). It is proposed that entrepreneurial core values are a function of both moral rationale and the six primary tenets.

This uniquely entrepreneurial layer of individual characteristics is combined with an underlying moral rationale and defines what is right and wrong, or acceptable versus unacceptable, behavior. The individual's *BASIS* and entrepreneurial propensities together define a vision for the new venture.

The innovative idea has been conceived of, the risk and uncertainty have been ascertained, the entrepreneur has glimpsed the market opportunity, the network of contacts and resources has been assembled, and the informal organization has been established with the managerial responsibilities of the firm deliberately configured to allow the founder maximum control over the ventures pursuits. Core entrepreneurial values are formulated and business ethics policies are articulated with respect to the seven actions that describe literally all internal and external operations. It is then proposed that entrepreneurial ethical behavior will experience a continuous process of confrontations and challenges across five separate domains of new venture business operations that are the most susceptible to ethical dilemmas and the potential for moral compromise. These include:

1 - *Representation,*
2 - *Market Expectations,*
3 - *Financial Requirements,*
4 - *Partnering Agreements,* and
5 - *Firm culture.*

## Figure 5.1
### The Entrepreneurial Ethics Wedge

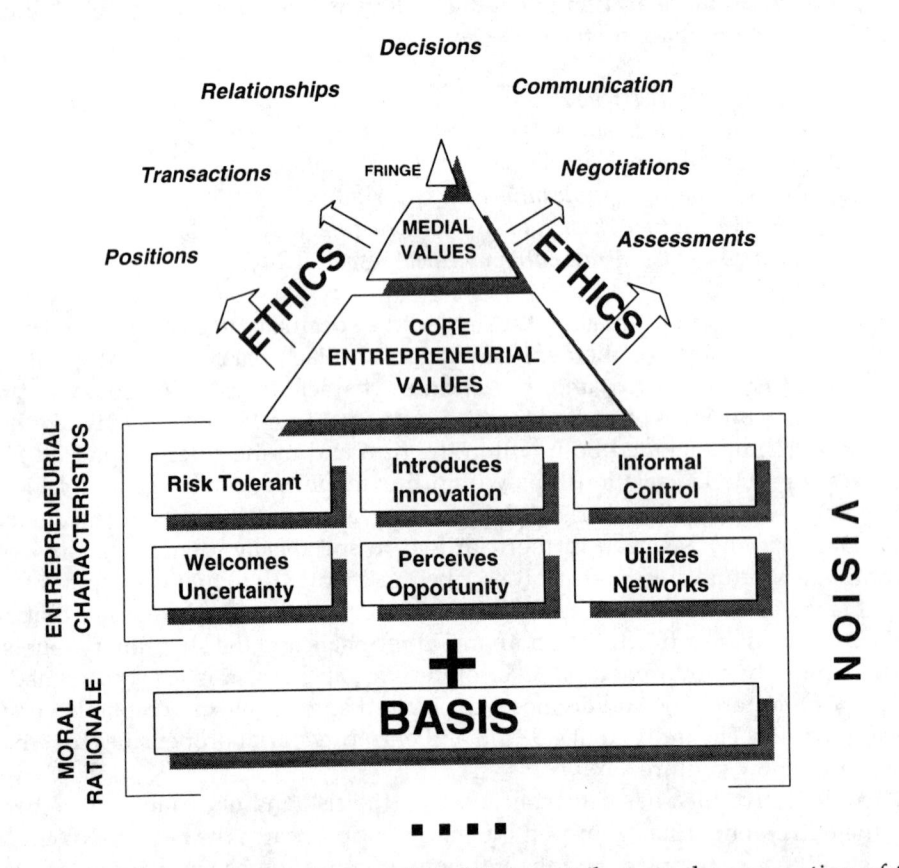

*Decisions*

*Relationships*   *Communication*

*Transactions*   FRINGE   *Negotiations*

MEDIAL VALUES

*Positions*   ETHICS   ETHICS   *Assessments*

CORE ENTREPRENEURIAL VALUES

**ENTREPRENEURIAL CHARACTERISTICS**

| Risk Tolerant | Introduces Innovation | Informal Control |
| Welcomes Uncertainty | Perceives Opportunity | Utilizes Networks |

**VISION**

**+**

**BASIS**

**MORAL RATIONALE**

The entrepreneur's unique personal qualities contribute to the conception of the new venture, a display of certain individual values, and support for some optimum level of risk tolerance. The combined interaction of the factors at the personal level produces the defining vision for the enterprise. As the entrepreneur's ethical wedge is formulated over time, it takes on a certain shape and configuration in terms of the relative breadth and depth of core, medial, and fringe values. The seven generic "actions" are then behavioral extensions of the foundational vision of the individual, and this may even be successfully transferred throughout the entire organization in the form of company-stipulated ethical policies and procedures.

Figure 5.2 is a proposed values and ethics interaction matrix. This is essentially an individual and company scorecard to determine the cross correlation between the six factors that uniquely expose the entrepreneur and the new venture to ethical considerations, and the seven types of actions that comprise effective management in the enterprise. The entrepreneur is in a unique position to either transfer values and ethics to the business entity on the "firm" level through a clear and defining vision, or relegate firm behavior to the personal perspectives of individual employees in the firm. It is at the venture level, that these seven generic actions are expressed across five separate *ethical domains*. These domains are the five critical areas unique to the new venture that subject the entrepreneur to the an increased exposure to ethical choices, and a greater propensity for ethical compromise. These will be examined in detail because they constitute the forefront of ethical dilemmas and managerial value judgments in the entrepreneurial new venture. After they have been briefly introduced, a summary of the database of recent primary empirical data will be presented. The numerous evidences of representation, expectations, financial requirements, partnering, and firm culture reveal insights into the issues of contemporary entrepreneurial ethics.

■ ■ ■ ■

**Figure 5.2**
**Ethics and Values Interaction Matrix**

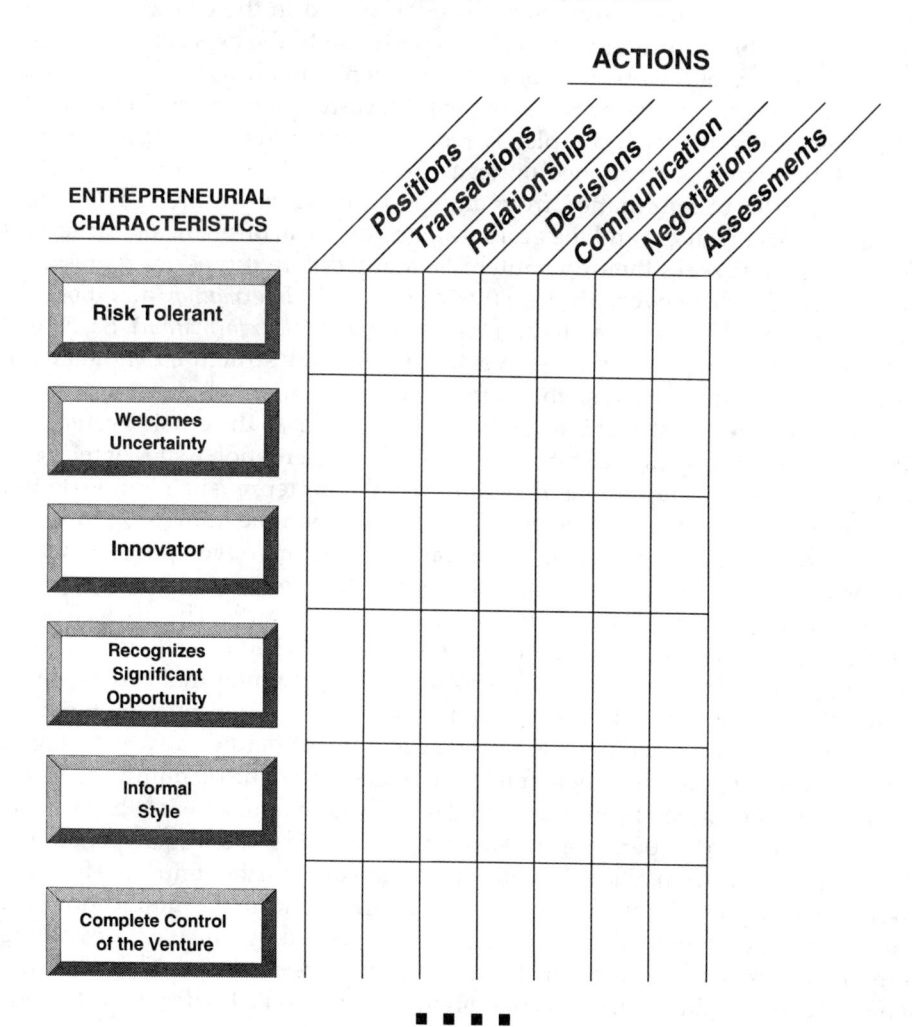

ACTIONS: Positions, Transactions, Relationships, Decisions, Communication, Negotiations, Assessments

ENTREPRENEURIAL CHARACTERISTICS:
- Risk Tolerant
- Welcomes Uncertainty
- Innovator
- Recognizes Significant Opportunity
- Informal Style
- Complete Control of the Venture

■ ■ ■ ■

## Entrepreneurial Representation

The first *ethical domain* involves entrepreneurial representation. Within the first few years of operations, the entrepreneurial firm will make numerous representations about its prospects for new product and service innovations, financial performance, and competitive positioning. There are three primary constituencies that should expect to receive these various types of representations. The first group is comprised of the capital providers who supply the financial resources for the seed and launch of the new venture. The second constituency is made up of the various partners in the vertical marketing chain. These include suppliers, transporters, wholesale and retail distributors, and equipment manufacturers. The third area involves the ultimate end-users of the firm's products or services. These can be other firms who purchase items at the wholesale level for use in other forms of production and operations, or consumers who purchase at the retail level for use in their homes or offices. The new venture, and specifically the entrepreneur, is often placed in the position of being the primary originator of the information flow that is pertinent to the expectations about the relative success or failure of the business operations. There will always exist a pressure to construct an image of *star quality* for the new venture, casting the enterprise as the next truly substantial revolution that will completely redefine the marketplace. The three constituencies often find themselves positioned opposite the firm as the receptors of this information release. The transfer of information from entrepreneur-insider to the stake holders can be quite a complex arrangement and the grounds for a good deal of suspicion, strife, and heated dialogue as each side seeks their own interests. Many different types of representation, are then sent back and forth between the firm (which has *insider information*) and the three groups previously mentioned (which may have a form of *asymmetric information*). Based on the previous chapters, the entrepreneurial new venture is uniquely structured and motivated with respect to ethical considerations so that numerous values-oriented questions need to be addressed regarding the transfer of information from the firm to the outside constituents.

Perhaps the best way to understand the ethical representation issues of the new venture is to examine the three dimensions that comprise the entrepreneur's rationale to disclose information. There are several interesting facets based upon the dimensions of new venture *representation disclosure content*, the timing or stage of the firm's development when the representation is made, and the source of the information flow, either voluntarily offered by the entrepreneur or requested of the founder by outside stake holders. The disclosure dimension defines the objective content of the information transferred. This can either be a *full disclosure* (an entirely truthful representation), a *partial disclosure* (anything that contains elements of truth but falls short of a full disclosure), or a *nondisclosure* (a transmission that is untrue, a misrepresentation). The timing of the firm's development defines at which stage the new venture is presently operating, whether it is in the seed stage (the planning and research time prior to launch), the launch itself (normally lasting less than one year), the fast-growth period where the company experiences rapid sales growth and market share penetration, or the fourth stage of stabilization. These first two factors are then further impacted by the source of the information request. There are both subtle nuances and major implications for ethical behavior based upon whether the information is requested by outsiders or volunteered by the entrepreneur. When information is solicited from outside the company, it can either be courteously requested in a spirit of cooperation between stake holders and the senior management, or it can be bluntly demanded in a manner that tends to create a relatively adversarial situation. These three dimensions of representation offer a mechanism that can be used to locate the greatest propensity for questionable and outright unethical representation for either of the three previously mentioned associates of the new venture that have a stake in the firm's business operations, namely the capital providers, the marketing channels, and the end-users. The exposure to ethical compromise relative to these three groups will take on very different configurations due to the nature and status of their stakes in the firm, and the arrangement of the content, timing, and initiation source of the representation. These variations and issues will be explored in detail in Chapter Six.

The information provided by the entrepreneur is the primary form of communication available for outside stake holders, yet investors, marketing channels, and customers may often discount the credibility of entrepreneurial representation for two possible reasons. First, they believe the information is *false positive representation*, where the entrepreneur deliberately amplifies the news that is released in order to secure a favorable perception of the firm in the market. On the other hand, the information may be *false negative representation*, where bad news about the company's performance or prospects is downplayed in order to create the appearance that things are not really that bad. This overemphasis of the positive information, or the de-emphasis of the negative content may in many instances not be considered as misrepresentation, but is sometimes referred to as "white lies." These partial disclosures can be either *voluntary omissions*, where the entrepreneur excludes information that should have been included in the representation, or *interpretive perspectives*, where the entrepreneur acts like a commentator providing a personal editorial viewpoint that is highly subjective in content and based on the unique biases of the individual's interpretation and values with respect to the issue. The ramifications of these representation issues are discussed more fully in the following chapter.

## Entrepreneurial Market Expectations

The second *ethical domain* is the entrepreneur's market expectations. The new venture generally seeks to be strategically positioned in order to exploit a newly emerging opportunity in either a well-defined or vaguely-defined target niche in the competitive market. Empirical evidence has suggested that entrepreneurs are characterized as being able to spot new opportunities at the very earliest stages of emerging product or market trends. They then rally and coordinate the necessary resources to execute a deliberate move into the market so as to create and capture the initial demand for a product or service innovation. The prospects for uncovering the next revolutionary product, or the future process in a service industry, or the manufacturing or process technology that will redefine an entire industry presents a formidable goal to be set before an individual. The end results are often forecasted based upon a series of qualitative and quantitative assumptions about the feasibility of the proposed introduction, the long-term viability for this innovation to produce sustained demand by the market, the timing and volume of competitors arriving in the market, the sensitivity of the concept to price fluctuations, the compatibility with existing products and services that are of similar function, and the possibilities for government-imposed regulations that could severely restrict or even prevent the free market movement of the product or service.

The entrepreneur progresses through three distinct stages related to the market expectations for the new venture. The opportunity is first identified, then the resources and logistical issues are configured so that as the opportunity comes into focus, and then the entrepreneur defines the full scope of the endeavor. Then at some point, the venture is launched and the market expectations are realized to some degree. It cannot be overemphasized that the most significant underlying issue within the realm of perceiving market opportunity and establishing market expectations is the entrepreneur's firm belief that a gold mine exists in a poorly-defined or yet undefined market, and it is just waiting to be uncovered and tapped into by the right person with the best business strategy. It is plain and simply a huge prize that has moved from the identification phase to the point where it is now literally within the grasp of the entrepreneur. This opportunity carries with it tremendous financial reward (and maybe even personal fame) and a loosely defined window is set before the entrepreneur and the potential results draw the individual in and serve as the catalyst to move the opportunity from the realm of expectations to the region of realization. But even the grasp of opportunity occurs in many different ways and comes with a variety of ethical dilemmas that directly impact the entrepreneur's values and choices.

The most important contributing factors that are related to the entrepreneur's approaching these market expectations are the types, or the bases, of assumptions employed in defining a market that, as of yet, does not exist in the growing, mature, and profitable fashion of the entrepreneur's expectations. There are two fundamental types of assumptions employed by the entrepreneurial new venture, and both of these present various ethical implications for decision making and the firm's actions in the market. The first type involves qualitative ideas that deal with questions like, "What does the market really want in this kind of service," or "What features are really most important for this kind of product?" Other areas will address color, shape, ease of use, perceived benefits, time savings, prestige, image, and value. The ethical focus will deal with how the entrepreneur plans to convince the market to embrace the new venture's definitions of these areas. On the other hand quantitative assumptions can appear to be somewhat objective in style because they generally involve market and sales forecasts, *pro forma* income statements and targeted break-even output quantities, and present value cash flow analysis. But these types of assumptions present equally significant ethical issues for the entrepreneur because they remain, as always, *assumptions*, and are therefore subject to the same personal biases and perspectives of their qualitative counterparts.

The two types of assumptions are then directed toward several key issues that will come together and clarify the magnitude of the market expectations and the likelihood of realizing the opportunity. The first issue that impacts expectations is that of *feasibility*. This defines whether the product or service can actually be produced from the proposed design, and a firm can be effectively organized to manage the logistics of establishing a foothold in the competitive market. The next question then addresses the complex issue of firm *viability*, as to whether the company and its product or service will be able to demonstrate sustained sales growth, a definitive and substantial market presence, and strong profitability over the long-term. Many expectations have clear feasibility (the entrepreneur can truly establish the venture), but they lack viability. And, yet some prospects may identify a viable market, but the technology or natural resources, or the costs of production, still lack logistical feasibility. Some new ventures may lack both, and some may exhibit strengths in both areas. The focus for this discussion however, will deal with the ethical ramifications concerning the representation of these matters. Other issues about assumptions will address the expectations for product or service price sensitivity in the market, the compatibility of the idea or concept with other products or services in the present market system, and the probability that government regulations may significantly affect both the market's perception of the venture, and the firm's plans for manufacture and distribution.

These five issues are then generally related to the type of product or service innovation presented by the entrepreneur. Some market entrants will employ a form of *continuous change* that modifies an existing product or service. William Hall championed the notion that this type of strategic introduction is either a similar type to those already in the market but with a lower price, or it is a superior type to the present offerings in the market but at an equivalent price. The new idea has in essence built the next logical progression onto the existing product or service (e.g. a second sliding door on a mini van). On the other hand, *discontinuous change* offers a complete departure from the existing products or services that is radical in design and redefines the market (e.g. personal computers in the typewriter market). How these are represented to capital providers, market channels, and end- users carries the potential for ethical concerns and value judgments. These matters of representation will be thoroughly reviewed in Chapter Seven.

## Entrepreneurial Financial Requirements

The third *ethical domain* that presents the greatest challenges to the entrepreneur deals with the entrepreneur's financial requirements for the new venture. This impacts values-oriented decision making at several levels. One of the most frustrating aspects of feasibility and viability is the financial implications of limited resources or funds that carry prohibitive restrictions. The entrepreneur is confronted with an exhaustive list of potential sources of funding, but for each positive aspect these bring to the venture, they all have particular drawbacks as well. The fact that there are so many sources to approach for funding increases the entrepreneur's exposure to numerous ethical concerns related to what has to be given up in order to secure certain types of capitalization. Issues deal with managerial control and direction of the firm, as well as *expected* returns on investment. The dilemma of capitalization requires the entrepreneur to examine the costs and benefits of the open-ended ownership positions of equity capital versus the fixed obligations of debt financing. And once the optimum capital structure is targeted, the owner must navigate the trade-offs between long-term commitments as opposed to near-term relationships with investors and creditors. Often, the entrepreneur's personal preference for financial resources exists in one form on paper during the planing stages of the new venture, but this "ideal" wish-list is generally altered significantly during the various rounds of talks with potential funders as negotiations introduce competing agendas for returns on investment, exit strategies, percentage ownership in the company, and the scope and degree of managerial decision making input (or advice) that accompanies outside investors and creditors. And of course, these deliberations involve significant opportunity for personal moral judgments and ethical trade-offs based on fundamental values about money, disclosure, and direction of the enterprise.

The underlying factor that dictates much of the terms and interactions in the decision making for the financial requirements of new ventures concerns the stage of the enterprise development process. Five distinct stages describe the majority of entrepreneurial firms. The first is the *Seed* phase, where financial requirements focus on what is referred to as "front-money," or seed money. These funds are used for two purposes: to do testing and research related to the feasibility of the venture, and to make relatively minor asset acquisitions. Equipment purchases are generally limited when compared with the final asset configuration that will ultimately be necessary to operate the venture on a full time basis. There are difficult ethical matters related to either having outside investors or the entrepreneur's own funds support the testing and research of an idea that may never produce a feasible or viable going concern. The second phase, or *Launch*, presents three critical ethical areas dealing with *underfunded adjustments*, where the entrepreneur must decide if it is worthwhile to press ahead depending on whether adequate launch funds are raised to support a full scale operation, or a somewhat limited production function. Investors will want to know the probability for success without full funding, and the owner can be tempted to modify capital requirements simply to get the firm going, even if it decreases the chances for success. Many values-oriented questions will be addressed concerning the size of the initial operation relative to what the entrepreneur perceives to be the future prospects and timing for expansion and growth.

Once the venture is up and running, the entrepreneur will need to have a plan in place that provides accounts receivable-accounts payable timing gap financing, also known as a bridge loan. However, the funding of mismatched cash flows is a very different investment proposition than capital used for asset purchases. The sources of funds and questions pertaining to the previous matters of return on investment, debt versus equity, and percentage stake in managerial decision making will introduce numerous moral issues dealing with disclosure and the pecuniary and non pecuniary costs of raising capital. In addition to short term working capital, another group of ethical issues will confront the entrepreneur after the firm has been successfully launched. The new venture often reaches a point where it is profitable and no longer in need of bridge financing, but the positive cash that is generated is entirely inadequate to support the pace of sales growth that is happening in the market. Again, the enterprise is faced with having to weigh what has to be given up in exchange for the funds that are necessary to facilitate the anticipated growth curve. Many new ventures are preoccupied with the prospects of making an initial public offer of common stock to investors in the broader equity capital market. "Going public" can produce a form of tunnel vision that becomes a huge distraction from the strategic and operational concerns of the firm. The entrepreneur must carefully weigh the relative benefits and costs associated with the need for a major infusion of outside funding and the issue of control and direction of the business. And finally, new ventures that experience hyper-growth experience a rate of increased sales that challenges the production capacity of the start-up asset base and produces significant diseconomies of scale, often characterized by severely decreasing marginal revenues and rapidly increasing marginal costs. Each stage of new venture development brings to the entrepreneur a different set of ethical financial issues and the need to make values-based decisions regarding ownership structure and outside commitments. These will be dealt with in detail in Chapter Eight.

## Entrepreneurial Partnering

The fourth *ethical domain* is entrepreneurial partnering. The new venture must deal with the contractual partnership arrangements that tend to be widely utilized by smaller, start-up firms. The entrepreneur is one who is able to muster the resources necessary to provide a product or service to a market in a timely and profitable manner. The entrepreneur tends to utilize extensive networks of personal, professional, and organizational contacts and referrals in order to accomplish this task of launching a new venture toward a perceived market opportunity. There is both skill and a degree of chance involved in the formation of this network. There are four basic structures of partnership deals, and each of these brings with it a unique set of ethical factors and value perspectives. The first type is a joint venture, where two firms partner in a business effort that has a well-defined, predetermined time frame for operations. On the opposite end of the continuum, there are on-going, open-ended arrangements for both suppliers (backward up the marketing chain) and distributors (forward down the marketing chain). But even the supplier deals will vary from component parts, raw materials, or finished goods, and each of these must be evaluated as to the degree of exclusivity that the other party commands with respect to the entrepreneur's options for alternative arrangements with others in the same market. Distributor partnerships will also vary across transportation deals, as opposed to wholesale or retail buyers. The fourth partnership that will be examined is the consortium, where several firms work together on one business function, or they share a designated resource such as an office facility, a warehouse, a manufacturing area, or a research laboratory. This has many perceived benefits for the smaller venture to diversify certain risks, but it also raises many values-based issues that could potentially place the entrepreneur's ethical basis in direct opposition to another individual or member firm. And again, the degree of formality will have a direct bearing on the performance of the partnership and the relative level of satisfaction that all partners will experience once the deal is agreed to and implemented.

The most fundamental ethical concept related to the entire range of partnering arrangements is that of negotiation. This is similar in many ways to the process of firm representation covered previously. But it is also very different for two reasons. First, the process of negotiation is as much an art as it is an objective technique. And second, the rules that govern partnering contract negotiations are based on the premise that all deals with other individuals and companies are the result of formal and informal compromise. *Formal compromise* is the procedural agreement whereby the entrepreneur willingly gives up certain prior requests or demands in exchange for the counterparty giving ground to a similar degree on issues that were important on the other side of the negotiating table. *Informal compromise* happens when certain components of the proposed deal are never "officially" codified in the documentation of the forthcoming agreement and specific actions are not particularly designated. The ethics of such partnering are quite interesting for the new venture. The entrepreneur can either be the target of an implied condition or target the counterparty with one or more implications that in various ways directly and indirectly pertain to the partnership.

The partnering ethic is also concerned with the continuous jockeying for an advantageous position that characterizes negotiated arrangements between two or more individuals or firms. This is a constant movement that has impact on both the formal and informal aspects of the partnership. It often remains as an underlying dynamic that vacillates between various degrees of advantage for the parties in negotiations. Much of the partnership ethical controversies are a functions of which counter party initiates the discussion as the proposer, and which is then placed in the initial position of respondent. And finally, the focus of the partnership arrangement will also have a bearing on the relative positions and final terms of the deal. The focus can be either a marketing endeavor, a production-manufacturing deal, a financial co-investment, a plan to share personnel, or a research and development project.

There are distinctions in these five categories with respect to the clarity of the defined outcome proposed. The entire scope of ethics and new venture partnering will be examined in detail in Chapter Nine.

## Entrepreneurial Firm Culture

The fifth and final *ethical domain* that will be examined with regard to the entrepreneur's increased exposure to ethical issues is that of entrepreneurial firm culture, also referred to as corporate culture. The enterprise will ultimately take on a defining personality in terms of how personal communication happens among various levels of employees, how decisions are evaluated and then made, how customers and suppliers interact with the firm, and how various types of information are shared and distributed. Also, the firm will eventually establish a practical application of its mission for daily functional operations within the company. To some degree, the corporate mission statement will capture some general values and perhaps evoke a certain set of ethical standards or guidelines for behavior. There may or may not be a clearly articulated expectation for business transactions, and the firm will also have to decide whether the mission and values should remain general in their definitions and applications, or whether they should take on a specific nature to impact the venture's code of conduct. The mission and any accompanying values must be evaluated regarding the moral rationale or basis for the various policies and procedures that define the firm's culture. This basis can be either a function of a moral absolute, or it may be the result of a relative approach to dealing with issues in a case-by-case manner.

The most important question associated with firm culture deals with whether the company environment is deliberately designed to reflect the individual entrepreneur's personal value system, and if so, to what degree is that accomplished in a practical setting. Many ethical concerns come to mind when firm culture is defined as a direct function of the entrepreneur's perspective on all matters related to business operations. The most notable extension of entrepreneurial new venture internal culture is the passion with which the owner seeks to transfer these personal values and ethics, and inculcate a personal sense of acceptable and unacceptable conduct to company personnel, and the resultant degree of receptivity that the various levels of employees demonstrate in response to the owner's initiative (or lack thereof). Entrepreneurs will be confronted with company employees who either truly embrace the same (or similar) personal values position and actively work hard at finding the most effective means of implementing these values throughout the workplace, or those who merely pay lip service to the founder's initiative, but personally tend to disagree to some extent with this specifically advocated position. There are a host ethical of implications that must be identified and analyzed in the area of "value transfers" and the relationship between their delivery and their reception.

The new venture must decide how the company will attain this corporate level personality. Some entrepreneurs will simply try to copy what has worked elsewhere, believing that if a certain method was successful in one company, it can be transferred to the new venture and embraced as part of the firm's mission. Other entrepreneurs shy away from what others are doing in favor of seeing the firm reflect their own personal positions and policies regarding values and ethical behavior. A third method simply lets the firm develop a culture on its own based on the diverse perspectives of the personnel that make up the company work force, and the required ways of transacting business in the outside market. This three-way choice will be very interesting to examine in terms of the entrepreneur's intentions for the firm and the relative effectiveness of the method utilized. Once the firm has established a form of corporate culture, the real issues may just be getting underway. There is a tremendous need to effectively manage firm culture on a regular basis. The entrepreneur cannot be expected to monitor the success or failure of new venture firm culture. The firm is not in business to foster a certain culture, but a certain culture will soon become evident in literally all levels of the enterprise whether the entrepreneur takes an active interest in this matter or not. Some breakdowns can occur when the responsibility for corporate culture is delegated to a human resources specialist, or worse, when it is relegated to a less than prominent position in the firm and it loses its priority in terms of personnel awareness, decision planning, and resource allocations.

The last area of concern that will be dealt with is the concept of entrepreneurial traits and the expectation that entrepreneurial characteristics can be successfully transferred to employees throughout an organization. Of course, even if this could happen due to an organized, deliberate, and systematic plan of attack, concerns will have to be evaluated as to whether it is really the best thing for the firm to have layers of entrepreneurial behavior. Ethical implications will be raised regarding the reality of transforming the firm into an entrepreneurial breeding ground, and the rationale behind that attempt. Perhaps it is not best that everyone think and act like the firm's owner, because the company needs well-trained, responsible men and women to operate and manage the functional areas of the going concern. Yet, the opposite might be equally disastrous for the firm, namely to have a internal firm culture devoid of entrepreneurial tendencies. These ethical matters about the venture's environment will be discussed in Chapter Ten.

## Empirical Evidence: The INC. 500 Survey

It was decided very early on, in this research project's planning and feasibility stage, that it would be best to provide two complementary components in addressing ethics from the distinct position of the entrepreneur operating the relatively new company. The first component would be my own personal interpretation, ideas, and commentary on ethics and values in the specific context of the growing and successful entrepreneurial new venture. The second ingredient would be to compile a source of primary and contemporary empirical data containing the results of a survey of widely recognized, successful entrepreneurs. An initial pool was compiled of nearly three thousand five hundred entrepreneurs whose firms were listed on the *INC. Magazine* "500 Fastest Growing Privately Held Companies" covering the 1990 through 1996 listings. Approximately five hundred individuals were randomly pre-approached by telephone and asked if they would complete a confidential survey containing both general demographic items and forty business situation questions. About three hundred entrepreneurs (over sixty percent of those contacted) agreed to participate in the study. Surveys were returned between September, 1996 and early January, 1997. The final database contains two hundred and fourteen (214) usable surveys which represents over forty percent of those contacted, and more than seventy percent of those that agreed to participate.

A survey questionnaire was specifically engineered to obtain personal preference responses for eight separate categories of ethical situations and value judgments. Questions were strategically placed in an apparent non random order to try and avoid patterns in the mix of inquiry responses. Many ethical items were built into seemingly unrelated questions in order to gain a degree of confirmatory results from the individual respondents. Each group of responses targeted the five previously summarized business capabilities plus three other related areas with a number of questions about each topic, including: *representation* (nine questions), *market expectations* (eight), *financial requirements* (eight), *partnering* (five), and *firm culture* (eight), as well as *personal ethics/values* (sixteen), *vision* (three), and *business experience* (three). Some of the forty questions were intentionally worded to yield data for more than one of the eight prior categories.

## Qualitative Data Validity

The "intentions" of how individual questions are structured and interpreted by each respondent, and whether responses do in fact specifically address the targeted issue of each question, are always concerns in a qualitative primary survey. Entrepreneurial decision making behavior and ethical implications can certainly be misinterpreted due to question comprehension error in the wording of the survey items. Rigorous pretesting and great care were taken to ensure that questions would be clear, direct and concise, and that responses to different *ethical domains* would be distinguishable from one another. Several layers of confidentiality were designed to provide an assurance that the unique responses of any one individual entrepreneur would only be published as part of an aggregate study, and this would increase the likelihood that respondents would answer in a forthright manner, rather than answer based on how they would like to be individually perceived. The survey items were intentionally structured as either dichotomous variables, or as three-point Likert scales (based on agreement, disagreement, or neutral responses). Many variables were designed to be complementary as well as confirmatory with respect to the five *ethical domains*. All of the forty questions reflect the personal bias and intuitive preconceptions of this author with respect to this type of research, but they also were designed as short situations so as to avoid ambiguity on the part of the respondents regarding specific constructs in the fields of values, ethics, and entrepreneurship.

The final database contains two hundred and fourteen responses, divided into three levels of evaluation. The first level includes demographic summary data for each respondent, including industry, the entrepreneur's age and sex, the number of employees, the year the firm was started, and the founder's level of formal education. The second level included basic summary statistics and frequency distributions for the forty decision situations. The third level is comprised of descriptive and predictive regression functions, canonical correlations, and analyses of variance based on numerous hypotheses, to provide inferences concerning entrepreneurial values and ethical decision making issues in the context presented in this work.

## Entrepreneur Profiles

The vast majority of the respondents were male (93%). Table 5.1 summarizes the age of the entrepreneurs, ranging from 30 to 73 years, with an average of just over 45 years. Table 5.2 presents the level of education for each respondent. Over eighty percent (80%) of the entrepreneurs had at least a four-year college education (B.S., B.A.), and about three out of every ten (28%) had masters degrees (M.A., M.S., M.B.A.), and one in twelve (8%) had doctorate degrees (Ph.D., M.D., D.B.A., Ed.D.). Table 5.3 summarizes the industries of the companies and Table 5.4 reports firm employment. About forty percent of the firms employed less than fifty people, while nearly two-thirds employed less than one hundred people. Only about one in twelve firms (8%) had more than five hundred employees.

Table 5.5 shows how long the ventures have been in business. About seventy percent of the companies are ten years old or younger, and less than five percent have been in business more than fifteen years. Some of the more typical profiles represented were a forty-five year old male with a B.A. and a seven year old manufacturing firm with about ninety employees; a forty year old male with an M.B.A. and a nine year old computer hardware/software business with around fifty-five employees, and a forty-one year old female with a B.S. and a five year old marketing company with thirty employees.

## The Model in Practice

It was previously stated that the values and ethics interaction matrix presented in Figure 5.2 can be thought of as the new venture's scorecard. In chapters six through ten, this matrix will be applied and analyzed in detail for each of the five areas that have been deemed as critical to the consideration of entrepreneurial ethics in practice. The scorecard works in two ways. It is first an *ex ante* managerial tool to highlight the anticipated relative degree of exposure that entrepreneurs and new ventures will experience within that ethical domain, specifically with values and ethics situations. It is also an *ex post* instrument for evaluating individual and firm performance in these five fundamental areas of business dealings. Within the contest of this book, the matrix will be used primarily as a forecasting tool to propose the potential problem areas that the entrepreneur should be looking out for in the most basic daily business functions. As with nearly all of the material presented in this work, the proposed interactions and effects on the entrepreneur's ethical behavior are the product of both quantitative analysis from the empirical research, as well as personal intuition and subjective biases based on the author's experience in the field. The scorecard is by no means a perfect science, where forecasted areas are highlighted and then objectively measured after the fact. The entire premise of this study is that ethics will be a significant part of each and every aspect of the entrepreneurial new venture development process. The firm owner cannot be divested from the personal perspectives and moral bases that define right and wrong on the individual level. The questions are focused on the degree to which the entrepreneur's personal positions and interpretations become those of the new firm, and identifying the more prominent areas within the new venture that are most susceptible to ethical challenges for compromise.

The matrix model is proposed to serve both the thinking of, and planning for, ethical considerations, as well as the effectiveness of the entrepreneur and the enterprise in dealing with the planned exposures to ethical scenarios. The *INC. 500* survey data will be thoroughly integrated into the discussions on two levels, to provide empirical evidence for the conceptual framework that is proposed in this book. The first level involves the implicit suggestions that the survey uncovered in various combinations of survey items. These find their way into the book in the form of inferences that guided the design and development of the numerous

### Table 5.1
### The Entrepreneur's Age

| Age Range | Frequency | Percent |
|---|---|---|
| 30-39 | 63 | 31.0% |
| 40-49 | 83 | 40.9% |
| 50-59 | 45 | 22.2% |
| 60-69 | 11 | 5.4% |
| 70 and over | 1 | 0.5% |

### Table 5.2
### The Entrepreneur's Education

| Degree | Frequency | Percent |
|---|---|---|
| High School | 42 | 20.7% |
| BA or BS | 86 | 42.4% |
| MA or MS | 26 | 12.8% |
| MBA | 33 | 16.3% |
| Doctorate | 16 | 7.9% |

### Table 5.3
### New Venture Industries

| Type | Frequency | Percent |
|---|---|---|
| Manufacturing | 42 | 20.1% |
| Construction | 10 | 4.8% |
| Engineering | 10 | 4.8% |
| Financial | 15 | 7.2% |
| Computer Hardware | 9 | 4.3% |
| Computer Software | 31 | 14.8% |
| Marketing | 14 | 6.7% |
| Publishing | 9 | 4.3% |
| Wholesale | 12 | 5.7% |
| Retail | 10 | 4.8% |
| Other | 47 | 22.5% |

**Table 5.4**
**New Venture Employment**

| Employees | Frequency | Percent |
|---|---|---|
| Less than 50 | 86 | 40.2% |
| 50 to 99 | 50 | 23.4% |
| 100 to 500 | 61 | 28.5% |
| 501 to 1000 | 13 | 6.1% |
| More than 1000 | 4 | 1.9% |

**Table 5.5**
**New Venture Operations**

| Year Started | Years in Business | Frequency | Percent |
|---|---|---|---|
| 1970 to 1980 | Over 15 years | 10 Firms | 4.8% |
| 1981 to 1985 | 11-15 years | 45 Firms | 21.6% |
| 1986 to 1990 | 6-10 years | 128 Firms | 61.5% |
| 1991 to 1996 | 0-5 years | 25 Firms | 12.0% |

■ ■ ■ ■

topical areas and subsections regarding ethics in the small firm. The second level deals with reporting the raw data responses at the close of each chapter, and then the effects and interactions of many combinations of variables that are explored in detail in the final chapter. It would be difficult to try and document each and every subjective inference from the survey material and how it impacted the structure of the chapters and the ideas for identifying problem areas in entrepreneurial ethics. Again, the goal of the book has never been to recommend, or even suggest, *how* best to do ethics, or to somehow determine *what* works best, or propose *when* ethics are most applicable. The data will be used in support of various proposals to identify and address the potential for a wide range of ethical difficulties in the key activities of fast-growth, entrepreneurial firms.

There are also obvious limitations that can be placed on what the *INC. 500* survey database can, and cannot, do in making summary statements about the ethics and values in new ventures. But, the information gleaned from these two hundred and fourteen entrepreneurs is certainly valid in its ability to help point inquiry in certain directions, even if it cannot absolutely define all matters of ethical behavior and values integration within the entrepreneurial new venture development process. The data is very rich in content and opens up numerous windows through which to view the firm owner making decisions in these various categories of daily business activities. The seminal research work on new venture characteristics and entrepreneur profiles provides a solid foundation for defining those qualities and attributes that contribute to the unique propensity for entrepreneurs to meet ethical challenges in the distinctive internal and external environments of the fast-growth new venture.

# CHAPTER SIX

# *Entrepreneurial Representation*

## Introduction

The new venture will be examined by numerous contingents of outsiders with various interests in the prospects for successful operations. The entrepreneur will be the primary source of information to these parties, both during the period prior to the launch, and in the various stages of growth once the firm is up and running in the market. Many would argue that the entrepreneur is really engaged in matters of ethics within the context of full time public relations.[1] The owner is also the point person responsible for the ethical issues related to influencing consumer opinion about products or services.[2] The entrepreneur will have to decide between the extent of legal obligations and ethical responsibilities in all matters of representing the new venture to outsiders.[3] Unlike the investment industry that is policed by the *Securities and Exchange Commission*, entrepreneurs must develop awareness and a sense of responsibility for standards in matters of representation and information released.[4] The new venture must be able to establish credibility with all outside stake holders in order to nurture trust and accountability in the way information is presented to the market.[5] Entrepreneurs can easily lose the public's trust through poor and deceptive communication, an inability to monitor the flow of information, and a lack of follow through with rapport in the external environment of the enterprise.[6] Many would advocate a formal, written code of ethics be adopted by all new firms as a way to clearly define responsibilities in matters of communication and representation.[7] Many entrepreneurs have found that an open approach to sharing information and a forthright disclosure in representing the firm to outside stake holders encourages others to adopt similar policies and paves the way for greater trust and credibility among new ventures and investors.[8]

There appears to exist a sometimes vague and negotiable perimeter set between the internal operations of the newly launched venture and the various constituencies that comprise the external marketplace within which it functions. This figurative boundary is characterized as the conduit for a two-way flow of information between the entrepreneur and the stake holders who are interested in the outcome of the business over various portions of the firm's life cycle. Within the first few years of operations, the entrepreneur and more generally speaking, the enterprise, will make numerous representations about many different aspects of the firm, including prospects for new product and service innovations, the status of on-going research and development projects, a wide range of financial performance measures, the company's competitive positioning, and even the relationship with consumers and other end-users. Business periodicals provide editorial commentary about the financial and marketing health of private enterprise, and trade journals normally present volumes of secondary data pertaining to firm performance in certain industries. The *Securities and Exchange Commission* makes 10-Q and 10-K reports from publicly traded companies available for the asking, and most companies internally publish one or more forms of marketing view books, product and service catalogs, stockholder reports, financial summaries, or employee policies and procedures handbooks, all of which represent the enterprise to the outside world. The founder may speak to investors, give a speech to a local, regional, or national association, or even conduct a press conference to announce new company plans or to respond to concerns about performance due to some recent even that has occurred in the external market. The various ways in which the entrepreneur decides to represent the venture's pertinent information is the first of five ethical domains that comprise choices based on moral rationales and value judgments. It sets the tone for the other four areas because it deals with the fundamental value of information and the means through which it is controlled, communicated, and deciphered by interested parties. The entrepreneur does possess certain personal motivating factors that will impact what information is released, how it is represented, to whom it is targeted, and the underlying rationale for why it is delivered.

The focus of this chapter will initially deal with both the personal and firm reputation that is formulated and conveyed within the realm of representation, and then it will examine the three principal stake holders and their interest as receivers of entrepreneurial representations about the firm. These three groups will then be examined in terms of the proposed facets that together define entrepreneurial representation. The last portion of this chapter will then apply the *Ethics and Values Interaction* (EVI) matrix model introduced in chapter five to both a forecast of ethical entrepreneurial representation positions, and then the empirical inferences derived from the *INC. 500* survey data.

## Personal Reputation

The representation of information provided by the entrepreneur is the primary form of venture communication available for outside stake holders, yet those who hear and interpret this information may often discount the credibility of entrepreneurial representation. The heart of the ethical issue is first and foremost tied to the personal reputation of the entrepreneur. There will always be a sense of questioning the truthfulness of representations made because of personal value assessments and biases about the nature of the enterprise, its market, the industry, and either the perceived status or notoriety of the company founder. Many entrepreneurs spend a great deal of time and money to create a certain "public" image and a strategy to effectively promote that impression to the targeted stake holders (both present and future). There are some entrepreneurs that demonstrate a good deal of personal charisma and have a few well-defined, unique, and easily recognized traits that establish awareness among the outside public about their background, values, vision, or work ethic. Other business owners are content to keep a low profile and remain relatively removed from the public eye, desiring instead to stay somewhat personally anonymous within the financial and marketing communities, while their company gains the public recognition. Faces like *Microsoft*'s Bill Gates, *Apple*'s Steven Jobs, or *Wendy*'s Dave Thomas are almost instantly recognizable due to magazine and newspaper articles, or television advertisements. The public will become more aware of entrepreneurs like *Netscape*'s Marc Andreeson and *QAD*'s Pam Lopker, who recently joined the *Fortune 400* as the "richest self-made woman in America." But a high degree of public recognition is not necessarily the best method by which to define personal reputation. Many consumers cannot forget the ubiquitous *ZZZZ Best* carpet cleaning television commercials that made Barry Minkow an almost household name in southern California during the mid-1980's, as his firm's stock went public at $2 per share and increased six fold within a few months. Yet, his elaborate scheme of product and service contracts fraud and financial misrepresentation soon came to be public information, after which the firm folded and he landed in federal prison. The primary ethical consideration rests with both the crafting of the entrepreneur's public image and the ability of the stake holders to differentiate promotion and publicity from substance and content.

## Firm Reputation

The new venture is generally perceived to some degree as an extension of the individual founder-entrepreneur. There is no clear evidence to suggest that this will always be the case, but there are various levels of reflection that the enterprise can display relative to the personal values system and ethical behavior of the entrepreneur. This will be discussed in greater detail within the issues of entrepreneurial firm culture in Chapter Ten. But the venture will also be assigned various labels and descriptors by the outside market that will supposedly express the impressions that various groups have of the business as it operates in specific financial and marketing circles, and the broader society in general. Questions will surface as to whether the public's perceptions of the firm are direct reflections of the entrepreneur or the result of a number of factors dictated by the posture of the competitive market. It has often been said that "honesty is the best policy," and certainly there are many firms that implement that creed to some extent on a daily basis. But the focus of this chapter is not intended to coin phrases or examine loosely configured mottoes for doing business. The objective is to define the various aspects of representation and then highlight the most pressing ethical and moral implications of certain activities as they relate to the values basis within the unique setting of the entrepreneurial new venture.

There are several reasons why many new businesses may find difficulty in establishing a company reputation. The process of representation is a critical component of the strategic viability of the new venture. There are certainly numerous types of information that are routinely passed along to the public through various media. There is carefully guarded information, and information intentionally leaked in a cumulative sequential format to slowly reveal the firm's intentions or observations regarding some new marketing or financial maneuvers. Third, there is information that is closely guarded but is leaked to the public unintentionally, and this creates a near panic situation for the enterprise with regard to trade secrets, patents, research and development projects, financial transactions, or matters pertaining to the recruiting and valuation of intellectual capital. A finally there is information that involves the strategically planned transfer of information that is deliberately represented as critical and of great importance to the firm's future prospects, but is in fact nothing more than a decoy to either move other firms away from the true trail the company is pursuing, or to point stake holders in a certain direction with specific expectations and then surprise them with superior results from the same direction, or similar results from a different direction. Corporate communication is comprised of these four primary information release tactics that all have significant bearings on the ethical behavior of the entrepreneur and the reputation that the firm will cultivate among it peers and onlookers in the competitive market. A well crafted and consistent firm reputation is the result of a comprehensive approach to representation and information, and these are the responsibility of the entrepreneur, and carry with them the direct and indirect impacts of the founder's individual values systems and moral rationales for action.

The personal and company reputation are important factors in the process of new venture entrepreneurial representation for several reasons. Primarily, the various outside groups will often find themselves positioned opposite the firm as the receptors of the information released in one of the previously mentioned modes. This transfer of information from the insiders to the stake holders is a complex arrangement and provides a rationale for outsiders to interpret entrepreneurial representation with a good deal of suspicion, strife, and heated dialogue as each side seeks the best relative position to guard their own interests. Many different types of representation are then sent back and forth between the firm (which has *insider information*) and outside stake holders (who probably have a form of *asymmetric information*). The entrepreneurial new venture is uniquely structured and motivated with respect to ethical considerations so that numerous values-oriented questions need to be addressed regarding the transfer of information from the firm to the outside constituents. First, stake holders may believe the information is *false positive representation*, where the entrepreneur deliberately amplifies the news that is released in order to secure a favorable perception of the firm in the market, a form of *touting*. On the other hand, the information may be *false negative representation*, where bad news about the company's performance or prospects is downplayed in order to create the appearance that things are not really that bad. This overemphasis of the positive information, or the *de*-emphasis of the negative content is often viewed not as misrepresentation, but as a "corporate white lie." Many individuals justify forms of less than entirely truthful representation on the basis of personal values and moral interpretations. The different forms of representation will then have a tremendous impact on the firm's ability to effectively dialogue with the market.

## Three Representation Groups

There are three primary outside constituencies that are positioned to receive these different types of representations: debt and equity capital providers, those at various levels within the marketing channels, and product or service end-users, such as consumers or wholesale buyers. The new venture must learn to deal with these groups in many different ways and for numerous purposes. First and foremost, the entrepreneurial representation will be affected by the type of stake the outsider has in the firm's operations and prospects. Second, the company also interacts based on the particular stage of development in which the enterprise is presently functioning. New ventures, and individual entrepreneurs in particular, attract different crowds at different stages in the firm's life cycle. There is also evidence to suggest that entrepreneurs perceive each of these groups uniquely because of the anticipated degree of vested interest each has in the firm's relative success or failure. For example, literally all forms of stakes fall into one of two categories. The first category includes clearly financial implications. This includes those private individuals and institutional parties that provide debt financing for the new venture, either on the short term basis in the form of working capital, lines of credit, trade credit, inventory financing, and receivables factoring, or long term basis in the form of promissory notes, equipment financing and leasing, commercial facility mortgages, and in some instances bonds. Other financial stakes include equity shares in the ownership of the firm. These can be either in the form of general partner or common stock positions that come with an element of active participation in the management of the firm, or in the form of silent partner or preferred stock stakes where fixed dividend payments are made in exchange for having no managerial input in company decision making policies and procedures. And remember, not every financial stake is automatically an "investor" or "creditor" position. There are other companies that have various financial oriented stakes in the venture, but these are through a primarily marketing or production based relationship.

The new venture is caught in an awkward position of having to represent itself to these groups and yet the style of representation that is expected or required by these separate interests may be quite different from each other. For instance, some groups may want to have periodic written communication dealing with their pertinent information. This may come to them in the form of a quarterly or semi-annual report, a production schedule, a marketing plan, or a strategic plan. The firm may provide some basic and somewhat generic information, but hold back on the primary decision variables or the exact process by which the final direction of the firm will be implemented. Other groups may expect regularly scheduled presentations from the founder and the key executives on the senior management team. This could come in the form of an evening round table session, a press conference style forum with questions and answers, or a more formal meeting that resembles a typical shareholders meeting for a publicly traded corporation. The entrepreneur is the point person that must walk the fine line between making available various levels of disclosure and at the same time protecting the fundamental precepts of firm strategy that are strictly proprietary in nature. It is the same situation that most firms find themselves in when they compile their company prospectus for their initial public offering of common stock. A balance is supposedly maintained between open access to certain information and restrictions placed on other types of information. There are many ethical areas of concern in this delicate game of "open and close." The issue of core values issue involves the level of comparative knowledge between insiders and outsiders, and the basis or rationale for the *intentions* behind the plan for entrepreneurial representation.

## *Capital Providers*

The first group is comprised of the investors and creditors who provide the equity and debt financial resources for the seed and launch of the new venture. These capital providers have very different interests in the firm's risk and return expectations, as well as its exposure to various categories of business uncertainty. It is very interesting to realize that while both groups want the new venture to experience a significant degree of success, the way in which the entrepreneur arrives at that place is perceived in contrasting reasons. So although the motive remains very similar (they both want the firm to experience tremendous sales grow and demonstrate strong positive cash flow), the underlying principle for this to happen is unique for providers of equity and debt capital. Equity providers understand that a relatively high level of managed risk will be tolerated by the entrepreneur and that certain exposures to uncertainty cannot be avoided when launching a new venture. As such, these investors have generally abdicated current fixed payments from the firm in exchange for a clear percentage share in the open-ended actual results of the business performance. If the company loses money, these investors will also lose money. But if the firm is incredibly profitable, these equity stake holders will experience very significant returns on their original investments. Debt providers are plain and simply creditors of the firm, and as such they have an entirely opposite view of risk management and exposure to uncertainty. They are much more risk averse, and so would rather see the company be more prudent in its approach to the marketing effort and spending in general. Their agenda is built around a desire to preserve the capital base and generate more reliable before-tax, periodic cash flow. This is because they are concerned with the term and safety of the borrowed principal, and the reliability of the stream of interest payments made from the gross profits after operating expenses. Sales growth and market penetration are admirable goals, but never at the expense of the venture's near-term capability to make timely fixed payments.

The reality is that the entrepreneur is placed in between these two somewhat opposing constituencies. The process of engaging in various levels of representation calls the entrepreneur to a place where a strategy for balancing these two groups must be formulated and utilized in a tactful manner. There are many ethical ramifications from trying to play both sides of the capital provider fence. On the one hand, certain representation plans may be a big hit with the shareholders, while the bondholders feel that the current strategy presents too great a risk to their planned cash flow receipts. On the other hand, representation can seek to satisfy and assure the creditors that the firm is on solid financial ground and that most risks are clearly hedged in order to insure the steady interest paying ability of the firm, but the equity partners in the company want the firm to be more aggressive in terms of pursuing growth in the net worth of the enterprise as a risk premium compensation for their ownership stake. These two groups of capital providers are not merely interested in exclusively *financial* issues either. They want to hear the entire scope of every qualitative production, marketing, research, and technology management issue as well.

## *Market Channels*

The second constituency is made up of the various partners in the vertical marketing chain. These include suppliers, transporters, wholesale and retail distributors, service providers, and equipment manufacturers. The vertical marketing chain is actually a series of interlocking vested interests in each other. This network has risks on both the top end and at the bottom end where the products and services make their way to the ultimate end-users. Each separate company that occupies a link niche has the opportunity to hedge its risk dependence on firms in both directions by maintaining various degrees of contingency relationships and alternative plans for replacing any lost value due to the inadequacy of another company link to meet its contractual obligations. This complex network of different suppliers and producers can tend to be incredibly interdependent.

The entrepreneurial new venture is no different. In fact, many recent start-up firms experience exposure to an *over-dependency risk factor* due to the more limited number of links utilized in the vertical marketing channel. This describes the situation where the start-up company has built perhaps as few as just one or two supply and distribution connections due primarily to its limited production capacity, lack of significant capitalization, or minor market penetration. The enterprise depends almost exclusively on this small number of outside firms for component parts, raw materials, or other supplies and the timely distribution of its product or service. However, from the perspective of these firms, the entrepreneurial new venture is an extremely insignificant component in their overall marketing mix. This can create a tendency for the entrepreneur to embellish representation about market share, production capacity, labor requirements, or shipping schedules in order to appear like a more formidable "player" in the industry. The small firm has grown so locked in to these one or two supporting companies, it cannot afford to lose its present position in their facilities scheduling. As the entrepreneur deals with these market channels, there are real pressures to create an image that the new venture is doing very well, growing at a great rate, a dependable business associate, and has other options with a wide range of alternative firms in the marketing channels if the present situation does not work out favorably. The enterprise must try to represent itself as a source of significant future business for the right marketing channel that has the vision to see what the entrepreneur sees as the long-term prospects for growth and profitability. Many times marketing channels experience a draw toward smaller new ventures because there appears to be a reasonable chance for this company to bring in a large amount of business once the new venture firmly establishes its presence in the competitive market.

But market channels can also have direct financial stakes in the new venture as well. It is quite common for established channels to extend various degrees of short-term trade credit to smaller entrepreneurial ventures or to even take a cash stake in certain deals based on the lack of traditional outside financing or investment available to the new venture. The entrepreneur may feel compelled to represent the firm as a tremendous opportunity for an equity position by a larger company that already has complementary supply of distribution products and services that the newer firm needs. The entrepreneur may not actually be looking for a marketing relationship, as much as a partner with somewhat "deep pockets" that can carry the small firm's credit and maybe even provide a capital infusion as a means of protecting its interests in the new venture. The basic objective is that the entrepreneur's representation to these channels is: "you need us more than we need you," hoping that the right combination of professional appearances, current business transactions, and future potential growth will together create a basis for continuous interaction in the existing channels, and open doors for a widening of influence in the entire vertical network.

### *End-Users*

The third group for representation includes the ultimate end-users of the firm's products or services. These can be other firms who purchase items at the wholesale level for use in other forms of production and operations, or consumers who purchase at the retail level for use in their homes or offices. The new venture, and specifically the entrepreneur, is often placed in the position of being the primary originator of the information flow that is pertinent to the expectations about the relative success or failure of the business operations. But with this group, the entrepreneur is required to represent the new venture's products and services to the target market that purchases these items based on the interpretation of necessary benefits, the particular price level, and the resultant perceived value in the benefit-to-cost ratio. This group may at first look upon the new venture with a degree of skepticism, due to the firm's lack of an established track record and the novelty of the innovation offered, or the initial evaluation of the products or services by the broader market. Traditional marketing textbooks often describe the market as comprised of innovators, early adopters, late adopters, and laggards. This is perhaps the best general description of the intentions and interests of the wholesale and consumer end-users. It is to these categories that the entrepreneur is required to make a formal representation about the new venture, its offerings to the market, and its prospects for the future.

The end-user *innovators* may actually be the best match for the small enterprise because they tend to identify with the representation that the new firm offers a cutting edge product or service that will revolutionize the market and their early recognition of this places them in a prestigious position. The other three groups of end-users are, to varying degrees, a bit more skeptical about being the first ones buy in to the entrepreneur's sales pitch. The early adopters are content to allow the innovators to serve as the trial group that pays the highest price for the yet untested product or service. If all goes well with the first group, they will adopt at a later time. If the initial marketing results are somewhat negative due to inadequate features or lack of compatibility relative to the price, there may not even be an early adoption second phase in the marketing life cycle. With these first two groups, the entrepreneur's representation can appeal to the market's sense of pioneering and desire to be in the vanguard of technology. There can be a very significant opportunity for the entrepreneur to engage in compromising representation due to embellishing the truth about features and benefits, *touting* the present and future status of the market for this product or service, or making promises about subsequent product versions and models that are in development and are soon to be released, when in fact they are barely in the concept phase or have not even been proposed at that time.

The entrepreneur's focus and representation tactic can shift dramatically when dealing with the late adopters and the laggards in the marketing mix. The plan is no longer an appeal to a sense of adventure, innovation, and prestige with being first, but is now built around the steady, reliable, and time tested features that have already been recognized by a significant portion of the market, the mature nature of the firm, and the products and services. The appeal is now centered on the end-users to not be left out of the current innovation wave. The entrepreneur's representation may shift to matters of incredible value due to discounted prices, and unconditional warranties due to the established track record in the prior phase of the introduction. Whatever the group or time period in the marketing mix cycle, the entrepreneurial new venture is confronted with numerous scenarios that will require an ethical decision making capability and a values basis for dealing with the subtle nuances of perceived product and service innovations.

## The Facets of Representation

The three targeted groups present numerous ethical challenges for the entrepreneur within the context of product, service, and company reputation through certain representation strategies. The entrepreneurial perspective of moral bases related to representation is proposed as a function of three separate and distinct facets that comprise an individual's rationale to disclose certain types of both pertinent and nonessential company information. There are several interesting and significant ethical issues that are a direct result of the firm-specific configurations these three facets of entrepreneurial information transfer. The first involves *representation disclosure content*. This describes the type or level of plain and truthful information that is included in the representation, measured as either a *full* disclosure, a *partial* disclosure, or a form of *non*disclosure. This is a very important component in the representation process because individuals can develop a wide variance in defining what constitutes "full" in terms of disclosure. There is a major ethical concern due to the subjective nature of how different individuals perceive what others *need* to know and what they *ought* to know. The second facet captures the timing or stage of the enterprise development during the representation. The intuitive basis for this is that disclosure type will interact with whether the firm is in the seed stage, the launch stage, the fast-growth stage, or the stabilized stage of development. There can be many reasons why an entrepreneur makes a certain form of representation in the early launch stage of enterprise development, yet that same rationale could be modified significantly once the firm begins to experience growth in sales and profitability. Again, it remains a highly subjective perception that is prone to individual interpretive biases on the part of the entrepreneur. The third facet addresses the source of the information flow. The representation is either offered voluntarily by the entrepreneur or is requested by the outside stake holders. Many entrepreneurs will offer different interpretations of what constitutes normally *expected* disclosure volunteered by the owner, compared with specifically *requested* information that is out of the ordinary flow of representation. The entrepreneur may press the advantage to be the sole means of determining what can be considered "normal" and "regular" periodic information release to outside stake holders. The outsiders may not be pleased with how the entrepreneur manages the flow of information, and this could contribute to a greater sense of ethical challenge to the control and direction of the venture. Figure 6.1 presents this three-faceted representation cube as a means of locating the most common areas of ethical problems and the configurations that are least likely to be of ethical concern.

    The left vertical axis defines the form of disclosure content for the information being transferred. This facet of entrepreneurial representation ranges from a *full disclosure* (an entirely truthful representation), to a *partial disclosure* (anything that contains elements of truth but falls short of a full disclosure), to a *nondisclosure* (an untruthful, misrepresentation). The left horizontal axis examines the firm's development stages and defines at which point the new venture is presently operating, whether it is in the seed, the launch, the fast-growth period, or the fourth stage of stabilization. These first two factors are then further impacted by the source of the information request, namely did it originate with the entrepreneur or was it requested by the outsiders. There are both subtle nuances and major implications for ethical behavior based upon whether the information is requested by outsiders or made available by the entrepreneur. Just because the entrepreneur volunteers information does not mean that the content is desirable or even appropriate for the given issues associated with the firm's development stage. When information is solicited from outside the company, it can either be somewhat courteously requested in a spirit of cooperation between stake holders and the senior management, or it can be bluntly demanded in a manner that tends to create a relatively adversarial situation.

**Figure 6.1
The Representation Cube**

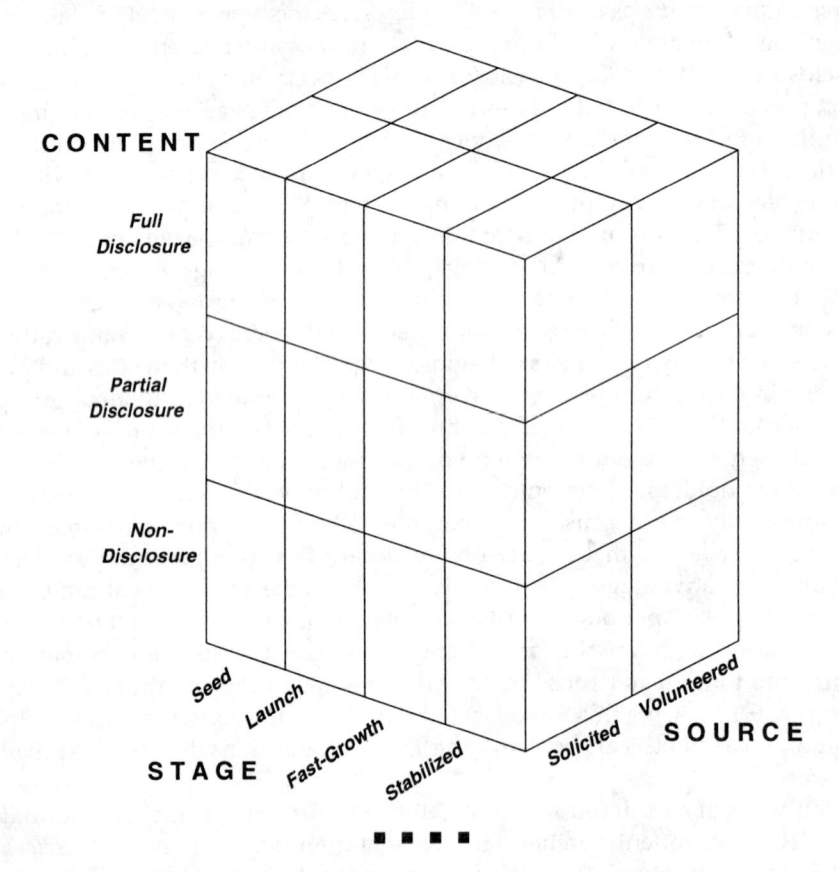

*CONTENT*: Full Disclosure, Partial Disclosure, Non-Disclosure

*STAGE*: Seed, Launch, Fast-Growth, Stabilized

*SOURCE*: Solicited, Volunteered

## Types of Disclosure

There are various ethical rationales that will have an impact on whether the entrepreneur makes a full, partial, or non disclosure to the outside stake holders. There are two clear motivations for the entrepreneur to make a full disclosure. First, the complete scope of the truthful information is very advantageous to the support of favorable perceptions about the firm's future prospects, so it obviously follows that the entrepreneur will want to represent the enterprise in light of this content. The second reason for a full disclosure is that, although the information is not altogether favorable to the overall perception of the firm, it is not entirely devastating either, and a full disclosure will hopefully build bridges of openness, trust, and cooperation between the new venture and the outside constituencies. There are then two primary bases that contribute to the entrepreneur making either a partial or a non disclosure in terms of representation content. On the one hand, the entrepreneur possesses information deemed somewhat detrimental to the venture's prospects, so there is a temptation to either minimize its inclusion in the representation or remove it altogether. The other factor could be that there does not yet exist the specific kind of positive information that is vital to supporting the favorable prospects of the new venture, but the entrepreneur believes it is critical to make an apparently favorable representation, so some degree of the missing information is then included in the information transfer process. This calls into question the entrepreneur's basis and core values structure, and whether ethical guidelines already exist for decision making.

The ethical implications of representation are not always clearly defined for many entrepreneurs. An interesting level of representation content is that of partial disclosures. The first type is called a *voluntary omission*, and deals with the situation where the entrepreneur knowingly excludes information that should have been included in the representation. The second type is called an *interpretive perspective*, where the entrepreneur acts like a commentator providing a personal editorial viewpoint that is highly subjective in content and subject to the personal values and biases of the individual's interpretation of the issue. For instance, the owner of the firm could be engaged in confidential talks with either capital providers or certain outsiders in the market channels regarding a proposed deal that, once it is completed, will tremendously improve the firm's long-term viability in the industry. Although the final agreement has not yet been reached, the entrepreneur may find it difficult to withhold this information and represent it to the outside stake holders in one of two forms. It could either be included in the dialogue, but truthfully represented as nothing more than a possible deal that remains very much undetermined at that point. Or, the entrepreneur could make a nondisclosure (because it is not yet a done deal) and then be accused later of not making a partial disclosure about the deal that was in the works. Every one of these disclosure contents comes with a range of corresponding rationales for how to make the representation. The underlying critical issues are based on the personal values of the entrepreneur, and the decision ethic that is utilized versus the desire to protect the firm's perceived position.

### *Stages of Venture Development*

The entrepreneur also makes representations as a function of the firm's development stage. There are generally four successive stages that describe new ventures. The *Seed stage*, followed by the *Launch*, which is followed by a period of *Fast-growth*, which eventually stabilizes to what is called *Competitive Equilibrium*. The initial move toward the market is the seed stage, and includes the primary processes of examining the fundamental feasibility of a prototype for the proposed business organization. It does not involve any systematic manufacturing or sales, but is focused on determining what components must be in place prior to the initiating of regular business operations. The launch phase of establishing a viable entrepreneurial new venture is often characterized by relatively slow sales growth, high expenses for initial production, promotion, and distribution, and negative cash flow. During this period, the venture requires a reliable source of working capital to support daily operations until adequate sales are generated. The entrepreneur has cleared the basic hurdle of venture feasibility (the venture is up and running), but it is yet to be seen whether the market will catch the same vision and provide the necessary demand for the product or service. The third phase is characterized by a rapidly expanding customer base and average sales growth generally in excess of five percent per month. After the firm is successfully seeded and launched, there exists an approachment process between buyers and the business that must gain momentum. Many new ventures experience a near-term (between twelve and eighteen months) or intermediate term (two or three years) period where a large and accepting market is readily adopting the new product or service at several levels. Most firms begin to show a profit during this phase. The fourth phase, *Stabilization*, occurs when the business experiences a leveling off in both sales and market share growth, accompanied by good profitability and an established presence in the competitive market. During this period of *competitive equilibrium*, the firm must establish reliable procedures, consistent managerial policies, and highly efficient and standardized functional capabilities in order to support a smooth running enterprise. Many firms will require a new round of innovation in order to once again initiate growth in sales and market share. A fifth stage *hyper growth* (actually a modified version of the third stage) can also occur, but this is more directly related to the ethics and values of financial operations, and will be dealt with in detail in Chapter Eight. The entrepreneur is uniquely exposed to value judgments and ethical dilemmas based on these stages of firm development, so that venture representation to the three stake holder groups will present both personal inducements, as well as disincentives, for the entrepreneur to implement certain tactics in the information release process.

### Sources of Disclosure

The third facet of representation address two distinct origins, or sources, for the information transfer. The first is called a *solicited* transfer. This happens when one of the outside stake holder groups initiates contact with the entrepreneur and desires that information be provided. This form of representation has two forms, *requested* and *demanded*. These capture the difference between a cordial outside inquiry regarding pertinent information about the new venture, and a belligerent demand that the entrepreneur make an immediate and complete representation because of some concerns expressed by the outsiders. For example, there may already be a close working relationship between capital providers and the founder of the firm. If the creditors normally contact the entrepreneur periodically and submit requests for financial information, production output figures, or market share data, the entrepreneur does not perceive any threatening tone or concerned motivation behind the solicitation. On the other hand, a market channel supplier may not have a very friendly relationship with the entrepreneur, and is quite concerned with the status of a particular order that appears to be behind schedule. In this case the supplier contacts the owner and demands that specific information be provided by a certain time. This solicitation may include direct or implied threats that there will be negative consequences to the entrepreneur if the response does not come in a timely manner, or if it does not contain the full scope of information sought by the outsider.

The second category of origin deals with the entrepreneur's voluntary offer to make information available to the outside stake holders. In this instance, the stake holders are first contacted by the owner and a representation is made about some form of information pertaining to the enterprise. There are two types of volunteered sources. In the first case, the entrepreneur has an established, regular practice of making normal periodic representations to the outsiders. The current information released is part of that typical routine. The stake holders expect the entrepreneur to maintain this practice and they tend to rely on the firm to initiate any contact. The second case is called a *preemptive release* because the owner does not have a normal pattern of releasing information, but initiates the release to appear open and create a sense of rapport, even though it may be lacking in disclosure content, or be inappropriate for the given stage of the venture's development. The preemptive move can also be a very positive strategy designed to offer an immediate full disclosure representation about positive news, and is tied directly to the current stage of the firm's life cycle.

The representation "source-stage-content cube" can provide interesting insights into the propensity for various forms of entrepreneurial ethical conduct within several configurations of these facets. Figure 6.2 highlights the primary combinations that may help to define representation motivations and intentions from both the entrepreneurial and stake holder perspective. The section of the cube marked *E1+* describes the most likely (and easiest) form of favorable ethical action, as the entrepreneur voluntarily offers a full disclosure of the positive information about the venture's rapid increases in sales, market share, and profitability. The section marked *E2+* is another favorable area where stake holders request relevant information amidst the uncertainty of the seed stage and the entrepreneur provides a full disclosure. Sections *E1-*, *E2-*, *E3-*, and *E4-* are most likely to create ethical problems for entrepreneurial representation because of the pressure to make less than a full disclosure based on the source at certain stages in the company's life.

■ ■ ■ ■

**Figure 6.2**
**The Representation Cube: Key Ethical Locales**

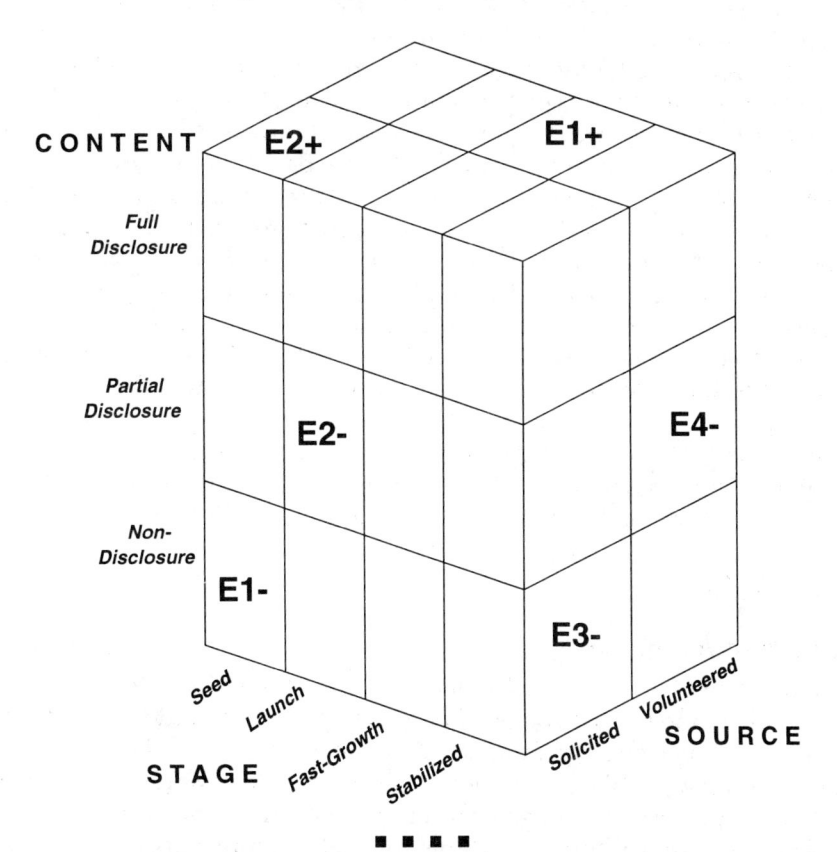

■ ■ ■ ■

## The Ethics Model and Representation

The likelihood of the entrepreneur engaging in questionable ethical areas, such as those that were just highlighted in the representation cube, will now be examined within the broader context of the proposed entrepreneurial ethics model and the *Ethics and Values Interaction* (EVI) matrix that were introduced in Chapter Five. The model proposed that individual entrepreneurs possess a moral basis or rationale that is coupled with six specific entrepreneurial characteristics to form core values for the venture, as well as other medial and fringe values. The breadth and depth of these values support certain ethical behaviors within the internal and external venture environment with respect to seven fundamental business actions. The entrepreneurial characteristics have differing impacts on these seven actions based on the five *ethical domain* areas of interaction in which the entrepreneur operates on a regular basis. The EVI matrix will first be used to provide an intuitive forecast of the proposed locations that have the greatest propensity for questionable ethical *representation* for capital providers, market channels, and end-users. Exposure to ethical compromise relative to these three groups will take on very different configurations due to the nature and status of their stakes in the firm, and the arrangement of the content, timing, and initiation source of the representation.

Figure 6.3 presents the proposed ethical "problem areas" associated with entrepreneurial representation. The owner's penchant for a high degree of risk tolerance and an open welcome to business uncertainty are each expected to have an effect on how situations and information are *assessed* and then *communicated* to the three groups of stake holders. Because the new venture is a vehicle to disseminate a particular form of innovation, the entrepreneur will exhibit a tendency to make assessments that are based on the firm experiencing a tremendous gain in reputation due to the new product or service introduced. This will be a contributing factor to the owner's ability to accurately represent the firm and the innovation due to a personal bias and value judgment about the scope of the innovation's eventual impact in the competitive market, and the "ripple effect" it might be able to produce for various stake holders. Because the entrepreneur perceives a significant market opportunity, the firm's policies and procedures may experience an ethical challenge in how they are positioned and communicated to interested outsiders. There will likely be some form of bias due to the entrepreneur's vested interest. Also, the individual's informal style will be subject to ethical issues related to both the relationships and the negotiation posturing that comes with representation. Finally, it is anticipated that the entrepreneur's desire for complete control of the firm will have an impact on the dynamics of relationships with stake holders.

## Empirical Results

### Representation Focus

The entrepreneurs were asked to characterize their most basic focus for the venture in terms of their own individual managerial perspective of the operations and direction for the firm. About seventy percent (68%) stated they are most focused on the longer-term strategic issues of their company, while one in four (27%) said that they were focused on nearer-term matters of daily operational management for the enterprise. Five percent stated they focus on both. This appears to confirm the assumption that entrepreneurs in fast-growth ventures

■ ■ ■ ■
**Figure 6.3**
**Forecasted EVI Matrix: Representation**

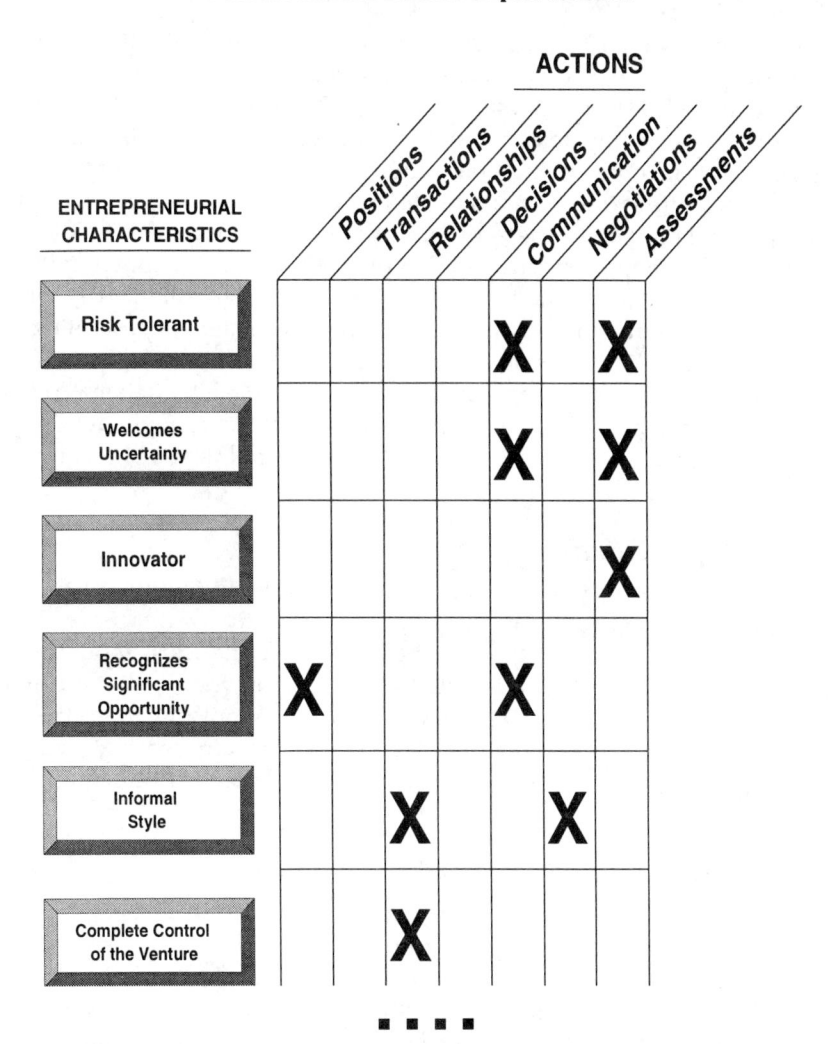

ACTIONS: Positions, Transactions, Relationships, Decisions, Communication, Negotiations, Assessments

| ENTREPRENEURIAL CHARACTERISTICS | Positions | Transactions | Relationships | Decisions | Communication | Negotiations | Assessments |
|---|---|---|---|---|---|---|---|
| Risk Tolerant | | | | X | X | | |
| Welcomes Uncertainty | | | | X | X | | |
| Innovator | | | | | | | X |
| Recognizes Significant Opportunity | X | | | X | | | |
| Informal Style | | | X | | X | | |
| Complete Control of the Venture | | X | | | | | |

■ ■ ■ ■

are generally disinterested in the managerial functions associated with the short-term horizon of normal business operations.

## *Launch Representation*

When asked how information about the firm's products or services was communicated to the outsiders in the market during the critical period of the new venture launch, approximately seven out of eight entrepreneurs (88%) said that the founding owners of the company were the primary means of representing the enterprise to the outside market, while the remaining one in eight stated that formal programs and systems of promotional marketing and advertising were the main methods used to transfer information about the firm to the market. This appears to be what is generally expected of the classic entrepreneurial mind set.

### *Unbiased Representation*

The entrepreneurs were also asked about the type of information that is represented to the marketplace as part of the promotion of the new venture with respect to other firms, and competing products and services. About one in five (21%) agreed that their personal belief was that it is best to present only objective, unbiased information about the venture, and then allow the market to make up its own mind, rather than to present their own personal interpretation of various features and benefits related to the firm's products, services, and position in the competitive market. It was very interesting that more than half (51%) completely disagreed with this position, stating instead that they felt the market should not be the entity involved in the interpretation of the firm's performance, but that the entrepreneur should present a personal interpretation of the business within the context of promoting the venture to outside stake holders. The remaining one quarter of the individuals (26%) were not sure about this and did not have a preference on this matter, but instead felt that the responsibility for subjective interpretation in this area of venture representation should depend on the specific circumstances related to the nature of the information and the outsiders involved in the information transfer.

### *Awareness Representation*

Although the vast majority of the entrepreneurs attributed the success of their venture to their on personal values system, they appeared to be relatively indecisive with regard to representing how to make the market aware of their venture and learn about the firm's business operations. Just over half (54%) attributed the level of awareness that the market has to their own personal reputation as owner-founders. It is very interesting to see that the remaining (46%) entrepreneurs stated that the primary method for representing the firm to create awareness was the sales promotion of the company's brand name or trademark for products and services.

### *Investor Representation*

A significant majority of four out of five entrepreneurs (81%) believed that they should present both negative and positive aspects of firm performance when speaking with prospective investors who are interested in providing funding for the new venture. But it is very interesting to note that the other one in five (19%) felt that the representation should generally stay focused only on the positive aspects of the firm. A second scenario was posed regarding the entrepreneur's representation of negative news about the firm's financial performance to existing investors, as opposed to prospective investors. Less than forty percent (38%) of the entrepreneurs believed that it was *never* acceptable to not volunteer negative information about the company. The remaining individuals agreed that it was either "sometimes" acceptable to not volunteer negative news (50% of those surveyed), or it was "always" an acceptable policy (12%). This is very much a concern for the entrepreneur controlling the flow of information to the outside.

## Personal Representation Style

The entrepreneurs were also asked to characterize their own personal management style with respect to the decision making associated with firm representation. A significant majority of seven out of ten individuals (70%) stated they had no distinctions between their "public" manner that is seen by everyone outside the company, and their "private" style, which was seen only by the insiders working for the new venture. But it is very provocative to see that three in ten entrepreneurs do in fact make use of a separate "public" and "private" managerial decision style in running their companies.

## Forecast Representation

New ventures are based on many different forecasts of *expected* future results. The basis for constructing such forecasts will have an impact on how to represent various numbers to the stake holders who have various levels of vested interest in these outcomes. Roughly two-thirds (65%) of the entrepreneurs surveyed said they only use the "most realistic" expectations when formulating financial projections for the new venture. The other two groups provide some insight into the tendency to deliberately misrepresent forecasts due to the uncertainty of future prospects. About one quarter of the entrepreneurs (23%) believed it is best to intentionally discount expectations lower, while one in eight went the other direction and stated that it is best to mark-up expectations higher than realistic numbers. In each case, the entrepreneurs believed that the strategy of discounting or marking up was an appropriate means of covering the risks of the unknown decision factors.

## Information Release

When the entrepreneurs were given a basic scenario regarding the company's general procedure for publicly acknowledging and releasing reports about the firm's performance, almost two-thirds (64%) stated that they would acknowledge and release both negative and positive assessments of the venture's results. But it is most disturbing that more than a third (36%) stated that their fundamental policy is to acknowledge and release *only* positive assessments of firm performance.

## Representation Responsibility

There is always a great deal of discussion as to whether the entrepreneur insider or the outside stake holders are ultimately responsible for the timely release of accurate information. About three quarters of the entrepreneurs (76%) did agree that it was their responsibility to "offer" pertinent information so that investors could ascertain the financial strength of the company. But one in five said that the responsibility falls on the investors to "request" pertinent information in order to ascertain the financial health of the firm, and another five percent felt that it was a mutual responsibility.

## Financial Reporting

A final representation scenario was presented, where their firm was compiling financial statements and reports in the process of applying for a business loan. The entrepreneurs were asked about the importance of presenting the most positive image of the company's assets, sales, profits, and capital position. Literally all of the owners agreed that the representation of the firm in a positive light was extremely important in securing debt financing, and they were almost completely united (96%) that it is never acceptable to alter accounting figures to better fit the loan request. But four percent did admit that the positive representation was important enough that it could be acceptable to alter accounting figures to construct a better fit for the company to receive the business loan.

## Conclusions

The basic responses from the entrepreneurs regarding firm representation are interesting starting points from which to engage in inquiry about the potential situations for ethical compromise in the owner's portrayal of the enterprise to various outside constituencies. Many researchers automatically assume that the only way for owners to achieve significant success in smaller, entrepreneurial new ventures is to be looking out to the long-term horizon, searching for new opportunities, and essentially delegating the near-term functional concerns to a managerial support staff, or production and operations personnel. This appears to be what is generally expected of the entrepreneurial mind set. The most pressing concern about ethics and representation in the new venture is whether entrepreneurs are so engaged in strategic issues and long-term planning that they are somewhat detached from the daily routine of policies and procedures. As such, the owner could become generally disinterested in the moral implications of how the enterprise functions with, or without, values on a daily basis. Questions remain as to whether the near-term oriented entrepreneur is more or less inclined to promote ethical behaviors and the systematic development of company values. This will be examined in Chapter Twelve.

The firm owner is usually considered to be the number one spokesperson for the firm's introduction of a product or service innovation in the market. The personal presentation about marketing objectives, financial plans, and business strategy that comes directly from the mouth of the firm's founder is normally perceived as the most likely form of external communicating that entrepreneurs utilize. Internal representation was not specifically singled out in the survey data, but the entrepreneur's portrayal of the firm's prospects and performance are readily available to be interpreted by the employees as well as the outside stake holders. Although the majority of entrepreneurs seemed to feel that negative information about the firm is either never to be omitted, or is sometimes negotiable in representation, it is worth noting that about one in eight believed that because they controlled the information flow and would never volunteer negative news about the company.

And even though seven out of eight owners took the responsibility to be the primary conduit for information transfer to outsiders, about twelve percent gave up that lead position, choosing instead to rely on the more traditional media of advertising to send the message about the firm to the outside market. Granted, over half of the entrepreneurs appeared to feel that the control of information was in their jurisdiction. But almost an equal number did not state this outright as their position. Of these, half were not sure about which is the best position for the entrepreneur in the chain of interpreting data for outsiders. This is very interesting and appears to be somewhat out of character for the typical expectation of the owner. As the primary conduit for information about the venture, entrepreneurs can exact a great deal of sway on outsider opinions and feelings about the firm's prospects. This can range from various ways of creating *systematic optimism* in the enterprise, to amplified *fatal-*

*ism*, depending on whether the entrepreneur wants to stir up positive anticipation among potential investors, or negative impressions about firm prospects to buy some time with creditors. In its worst forms, the entrepreneur can be involved in either *touting* (embellishing) the firm's prospects to investors, market channels, or end-users, or go so far as to instill suggestions of *guaranteeism* to outsiders, such that certain results are essentially promised first-hand by the entrepreneur, even though the outcome is subject to numerous competitive factors. As a privately-held company, literally all of the evaluations made by outsiders is based to some degree on personal contact with the entrepreneur, such that firm representation becomes a crucial ethical concern in the new venture development process.

Of course the new venture *does* want to create a high level of awareness and build a clear reputation in the market. The entrepreneur is intuitively the best positioned to do this effectively, and yet herein lies a common place of potential ethical compromise, because the owner has complete control over the content and regularity of the flow of information. The entrepreneur can impact the content and scope of representation through subjective interpretations about the meaning of certain data. And the owner can also decide on the frequency with which disclosure is provided. This holds true for all levels of representation to capital providers, market channels, and either wholesale or retail end-users. But almost half of the entrepreneurs perceived that this happens through traditional business channels related to the marketing mix and promotional strategies, rather than their own personal influence. So questions are still pending as to how they make their influence work in the various scenarios of new venture representation. Later on, in Chapter Twelve, It will be interesting to note how this interacts with the timing of representation in the life cycle of the new venture. Outsiders should always be wary of any form of e*ntrepreneur-dependent assessment*, because the owner of the new venture has a tremendous level of vested interest in every aspect of the company's market and financial prospects which can easily cloud the interpretation of what constitutes both good and bad news for the enterprise.

The first look at the data appears to point to the entrepreneur's ethical leaning somewhat toward full disclosure. But remember, because over half of the entrepreneurs felt that their own personal interpretation of the information released was the preferred position in terms of disclosure, they do introduce personal biases and prejudicial perspectives about what constitutes favorable and unfavorable information release in that "full" disclosure. Perhaps firm owners feel that they are the best judge as to what constitutes positive and negative information, subject to their own personal biases and interpretations on behalf of the outside stake holders. But when more than six out of ten firm owners believe it is either sometimes, or always, acceptable to hold back negative information about the firm's financial performance, it becomes clear that personal biases and subjective interpretations will have a huge influence regarding what is considered negative news versus what is deemed positive news. The entrepreneur's desire, and ability, to make that determination could be the key to understanding the many ethical issues and scenarios involving firm representation. The entrepreneurs who tended to be discounters of information appear to think that it is important not to anticipate something too high because the end results will most probably be much lower than originally expected. This can be viewed as an inherently risk averse position, and out of character with the typical entrepreneur. But even the very definitions of discounting will vary with each individual's personal approach to handling the downside risk of making projections available to outsiders. Those who tended to mark-up forecasts probably did so in order to aim for a higher goal and are then willing to fall a bit short, rather than aim to an apparently low target and not make it at all. It certainly is interesting to note how the entrepreneurs feel about this issue of representation and control of the information flow. The interaction effects of these representation issues will be examined in greater detail, and in the broader context of all the ethical domains, in the last chapter.

# CHAPTER SEVEN

# *Entrepreneurial Market Expectations*

## Introduction

Entrepreneurs find themselves pursuing several types of primary markets in the quest to realize the personal dream of seeing the new venture operating successfully and growing in value and influence. The entrepreneur has been characterized as an individual who can spot opportunity in the marketplace at a time when no one else is even looking in that direction, or in a manner that is unique to others who are also examining possibilities in the same market area. The founder of the new venture is actually involved in a process of scanning the innovation horizon of the external business environment in search of some form of product or service inadequacy, or a much needed process technology that, as yet, is not feasible in its design specifications. The market is not a respecter of personal perceptions. Many budding entrepreneurs believe they have uncovered the next great product, service, or technology revolution in the marketplace, when in fact they have only found a small niche that is seeking a new pricing structure on existing products, or they find a widely applicable product concept that still lacks the necessary consumer awareness and compatibility to gain broad acceptance.

There are distinct ethical limitations in the market, and these are usually grounded in the social values of the general population.[1] Many researchers have sought to find a link between the process of building a business on wide open market opportunity combined with a solid values base.[2] The issue of ethics seems, in many ways, to be unrelated to the process of capitalizing on a broad market opportunity. This speaks to the questions about whether there really is such a thing as "overnight success," or whether the successful entrepreneurial new venture is really a product of perseverance and hard work that paid off in the long run.[3] Many entrepreneurs will tend to approach new market expectations based on their "gut feelings," believing that their prior business experience served as a deciding factor with respect to pursuing a new opportunity that may or may not ever materialize.[4] The market is such an abstract entity, that entrepreneurs must decide if expectations are realistic or *idealistic*, and this is often the result of personal biases and value judgments about which behaviors are most appropriate in a newly emerging market, and which are not.[5] The focus of a new market strategy may be based on personal perception, or it could be based on what appears to be a more solid basis of interpreting existing data and research in that field. Many entrepreneurs involved in the attempt to penetrate a newly emerging market will employ a formal advisory group in order to access the most current and reliable information about the probability for a significant market opportunity to come to fruition.[6] But a wealth of research findings show that small business owners essentially believe that they do not have the time or the resources to wait for the complete information from the market that they perceive is essential to creating the proper strategy, so they often rely on personal ingenuity, spontaneity, and plain old individual hustle and effort.[7] On top of these many competing positions, the entrepreneur is often still not sure whether formal business ethics will coincide with the overly subjective issues of "gut feelings," their own ingenuity, personal perception of opportunity, and being spontaneous with respect to market expectations. There is a good deal of contemporary commentary that advocates the integration of social responsibility, or *cause-related marketing*, as the foundational component of the marketing mix.[8] This chapter will examine the intricate workings of personal values and entrepreneurial ethics as they pertain to the process of deciphering the emergence of a newly founded market and the formation of specific expectations for venture success versus failure as a result of various approaches to this uncertain opportunity.

## The Market Scanning Process

The strategic assessment of the external environment is a very similar process to the scanning and detection of emerging opportunities and the entrepreneur's subsequent market expectations. United States International University professor H. Igor Ansoff, in his explanation of *strategic issue management*, likens this scanning of the competitive horizon to the operation of a radar and sonar screen found on Navy vessels.[9] Having personally listened to, and benefited from, his countless insights through articles, texts, and lectures that so accurately capture the essence of spotting *expected* changes in the external competitive environment, it seemed quite appropriate to apply these tenets to the topic of spotting opportunity and assessing market expectations. This most fitting analogy will clarify several key ethical issues at the heart of the process whereby the entrepreneur detects, correctly identifies, and chooses a response in the face of the lure and attraction of new market expectations. Consider a naval technician perusing the layers of concentric circles on the radar screen that denote progressively further distances out from the ship's present location to gain any visual signals that there may be something detected out there in the vast environment surrounding the ship. This attendant also wears headphones connected to the ship's sonar to listen for any slight sounds that may be intercepted revealing some type of significant movement in the external areas. This model underscores both the sophisticated attention, and yet the subjective difficulty in assessing what is out there beyond the scope of the view with the naked eye. A blip on the screen might be something worth further investigation and clarification, or it may just be a densely clustered school of fish. The very faint sound that is picked up on the sonar may actually be a significant event, but it also might be nothing more than the natural flow and activities of the regular currents.

Figure 7.1 depicts what Ansoff refers to as the level of knowledge about the approaching event in the environment on the Y axis, and the timing between the initial detection of the outside reception and the when the event will be known in full by everyone in the market.

The signals are described as somewhere between *weak* and *strong* in composition quality. A weak signal describes a faint initial point of contact that may only be a one-time event or intermittent in frequency of occurrence. It embodies a relatively low level of knowledge about the approaching event, but the complete information will unfold rapidly over a very short duration of time. On the other hand, a strong signal appears on the horizon, and remains there emitting a relatively steady frequency of signal. The level of knowledge builds in a more predictable fashion over a longer period of time and full knowledge becomes a function of the dependable rate of information unfolding over this longer time duration. This captures several key applications related to entrepreneurial market expectations. Many opportunities are extremely difficult to perceive and do not provide a steady, dependable unfolding of the new trend. Other strong signal opportunities cease to be true "opportunities" at a certain point in time because nearly everyone interested in that market segment has already gained significant knowledge about the event and the market is no longer wide open, but has begun to fill up with numerous first time entrants.

■ ■ ■ ■

**Figure 7.1**
**Opportunity Signal Reception**
**in the External Environment**

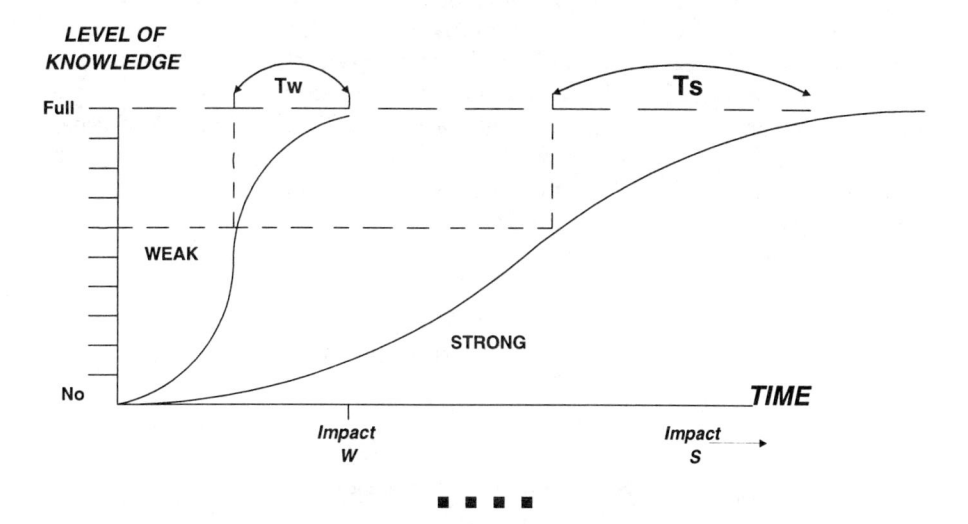

■ ■ ■ ■

There is no specific way, or operational plan, to guarantee an entirely accurate interpretation of various levels of market indicators. It is not a management science, but perhaps more of an art, a skill, or an experiential intuition. The entrepreneur is that attendant looking at the scope and wearing the headphones. The art, the skill, the *pure chance* of spotting distinct market opportunity and formulating some type of entrepreneurial expectations is quite difficult to describe in objective terms. First, the entrepreneur must be able to differentiate meaningless, random "noise" in the market from meaningful, non random intentional "signal." Second, the entrepreneur must determine the appropriate timing of *when* to make a move in response to the perceived "signal." And third, the entrepreneur must decide on the level of response to implement in order to purposefully address the types of resources that must be allocated and assigned to the perceived opportunity. At any of these three levels, the entrepreneur could subscribe to a wrong view or interpretation of the data and therefore act in an inappropriate fashion in terms of response. Determining entrepreneurial market expectations is generally tied to "weak signals" from the environment, because these describe the greatest probability to capture a significant window of opportunity. There are two possible configurations of opportunity signals for entrepreneurial expectations. In the first instance, the individual engages in various types of responses to a *False Weak Signal*. In the second, the entrepreneur implements responses to a *True Weak Signal*. In the former case, ethical questions will be introduced because of the problems involved with perceiving and responding to what is essentially a non-issue in the market. The latter case opens up ethical questions related to incorrectly interpreting and not responding to a truly significant window of opportunity.

Figure 7.2 examines the entrepreneur's possible reactions to a false signal, based on the timing of the response and the level of the resources committed to the pursuit of a perceived market expectation. Notice that the entrepreneur might use one of two types of responses. The first type of responses will be referred to as *Prudent Market Expectations*. These include actions BD and AD (which is best). In the first action (BD), there was a slight temptation to begin allocating resources in view of the possible opportunity, but in time, the firm cut way back to no response in light of the greater level of accrued knowledge. In the second action (AD), the entrepreneur correctly made no substantive response and this remained the strategy as full knowledge was disclosed over time. The other types will be referred to as *Excessive Market Expectations*. These include actions CE and CF (which is the worst case). In the first action (CE), the entrepreneur grossly overestimated the possibilities that might transpire and made a full-blown commitment, but was at least able to cut back a bit and minimize some of the venture's losses. In the second action (CF), the entrepreneur made significant commitments, but was unable to cut back sufficiently over the ensuing time period as the market opportunity never materialized.

■ ■ ■ ■

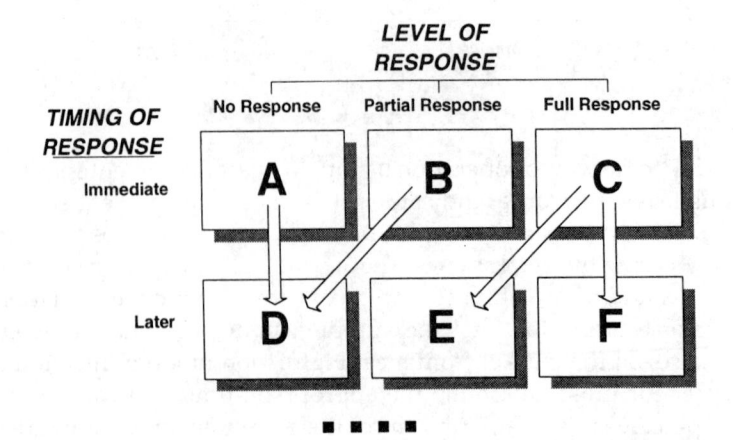

**Figure 7.2
False Weak-Signal Response**

## Figure 7.3
## True Weak-Signal Response

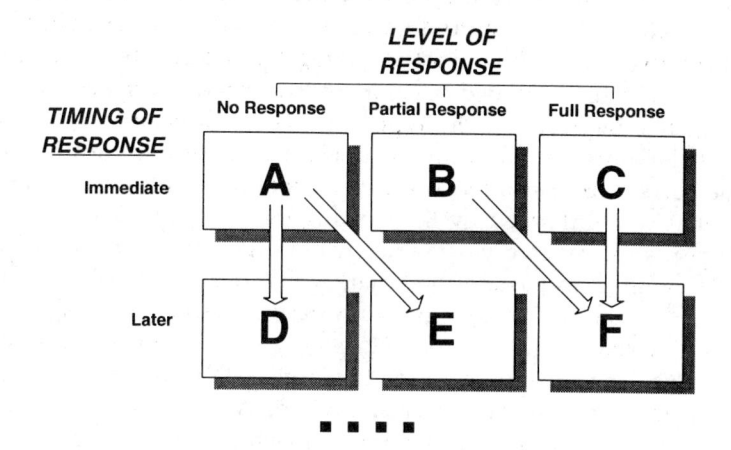

```
                        LEVEL OF
                        RESPONSE
  TIMING OF      No Response   Partial Response   Full Response
  RESPONSE
     Immediate       A               B                 C

        Later        D               E                 F
```

In a similar manner, Figure 7.3 illustrates the entrepreneur's possible responses to a true signal (a *real* window of market opportunity). At the first detection of the market potential, there are again two types of responses. The first group will be referred to as *Captured Market Expectations*. These include actions BF and CF (which is best). In the first action (BF), the entrepreneur was a bit too cautious in responding to the opportunity, but was able to increase the firm to a full commitment sometime after. In the second action (CF), the entrepreneur made a complete move toward the newly emerging market and was perfectly positioned to take advantage of the opportunity, and maintained that level of commitment. The other types will be referred to as *Missed Market Expectations*. These include actions AE and AD (which is the worst case). In the first case the entrepreneur completely missed the coming market opportunity, but was able to muster a partial commitment at a later time. In the second instance, the entrepreneur not only missed the initial signal and chance to gain a primary foothold in the market, but was unable to generate any resources at a later time, either due to a lack of internal capabilities, or the fact that the market had already become saturated with competitors by the time the firm was ready to enter.

## Types of Market Opportunities

The prospect of opening a new market opportunity is a very subjective issue that is often a direct function of the entrepreneur's personal perspectives and biases regarding the interpretation of some recent external environment data that has been detected and deciphered concerning a product concept, a service innovation, or a technology innovation that has a forecasted "fit" with the existing channels and end-users in a particular market. Harvard professor William Hall described four possible ways in which this generally happens.[10] Figure 7.4 summarizes the various matched pairs of product or service innovation type and target market. In the first type of market entry, the entrepreneur approaches an already existing and active market with a newly designed and innovative product or service. In the second form of entry, the entrepreneur takes an existing product or service to an entirely new market. The third type describes the entrepreneur introducing a newly designed innovation to a brand new emerging market that previously did not exist. The new venture's product or service offering literally establishes this new market for the very first time. And finally, the entrepreneur may offer an existing product or service within an established market. Hall concluded that the two most advantageous strategic positions are either the new venture that can attain the most differentiated position, or the firm that can achieve the lowest cost. This perspective generally describes the Type B and Type C scenarios. For example, a Type B strategy involves the entrepreneur who has devised a slight modification to a product or service from the current market offerings, but has found an entirely new application for a group of users that was untapped by the existing market. This describes a differentiated position. The Type C strategy involves a radically redesigned new product or service innovation introduced to a large and established market that has previously purchased the prior generation product or service. This also generally describes some form of differentiated position. In the Type D scenario, the entrepreneur's only strategy for success is to achieve the lowest cost and compete head-to-head with the large, established market. However, many entrepreneurs dream endlessly about securing a Type A innovation, completely differentiated from anything else, creating rapid growth of an entirely new market for this product or service. These four scenarios can be thought of as different types of *perception connections* between the entrepreneur and the external market, similar to the acceptance of market innovation previously shown in Figure 2.1. Each of these expose the entrepreneur to a unique form of market expectations for the newly launched enterprise, and ethical considerations for the entrepreneur and the firm's stake holders.

■ ■ ■ ■

**Figure 7.4**
**Innovation-Target Market Matrix**

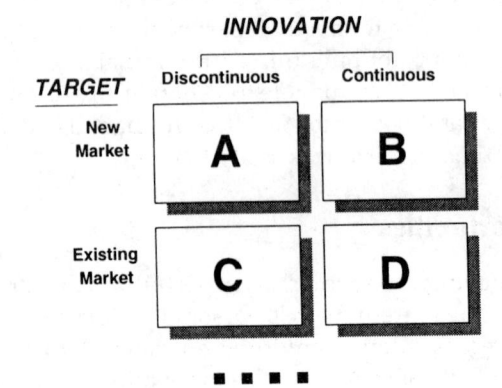

|  | INNOVATION | |
| --- | --- | --- |
| TARGET | Discontinuous | Continuous |
| New Market | A | B |
| Existing Market | C | D |

■ ■ ■ ■

## Market Expectations

It is proposed that the entrepreneur's market expectations are a direct function of the perceived market opportunity. The planned level of innovation introduced, combined with an assessment of the market's ability and capacity to absorb this new entry, together create a volatile combination of inputs that form the basis of the new venture's prospects. The most fundamental direct output of the innovation-market capacity trade-off is a series of four separate expectations that often define the initial image of the new venture, and its longer-term attraction for prospective investors, suppliers, distributors, buyers, and partners. The definition of the entrepreneurial new venture's market prospects are the product of *assumption-based model building*, the construction of a simulated representation of reality that incorporates one or more inferences about the various implied relationships between specifically chosen variables that are involved in the outcome for the proposed decision.

## Assumptions and Market Expectations

Figure 7.5 summarizes the four stages of the assumption-based model where each stage is sequentially dependent (a direct output from) the immediate predecessor stage. They are in their entirety, normally based on a prevailing underlying series of core assumptions which are a functional representation of the entrepreneur's personal biases and value perspectives.

**Figure 7.5
The Expectations Sequence**

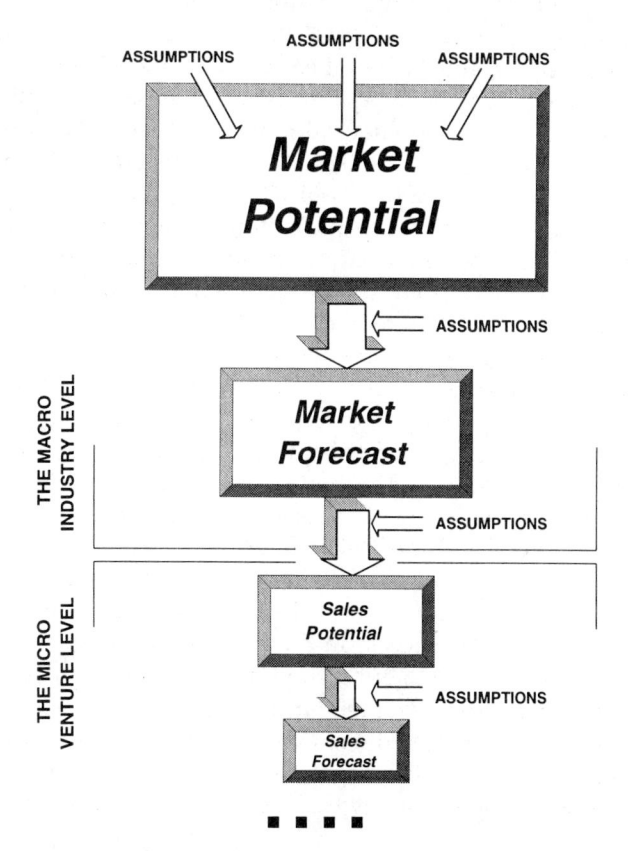

The entire process begins with the entrepreneur's personal view and assumptions about the *market potential*. This is the most liberal aggregate expectation for combined annual sales in this targeted market based on the underlying assumption that every possible end-user that meets the buyer profile were to purchase their respective allocation of the product or service. It represents the highest prospective saturation of the market. The second stage derives the *market forecast* as a sub component of the market's potential. It is the reasonable aggregate expectation of how many potential end-users will actually enter the market and purchase the product or service, and represents the total sales figures for *all* sellers in a market. Market potential yields the market forecast. The third stage, *sales potential* is the resultant sub component of the aggregate market forecast. This represents the highest possible sales that the new venture believes it can capture based on the maximum saturation level of their own product or service in the competitive market. The final stage is the firm's individual *sales forecast*. This is supposed to be some reasonable component derived from the company's overall potential. It is around this sales forecast that the entrepreneur builds the new venture's marketing plan, production schedule, pro forma income statement and balance sheet, and personnel requirements.

There can be, however, a huge difference between an assumptions-based model of the firm's annual sales and the actual results of the marketing effort during the first year. The entrepreneur has first produced a crisp and clean laser-printed spreadsheet with a personally interpreted version of the size of the potential market for this new entry. Based on the innovation-target matrix presented in Figure 7.4, three market expectation attitudes can be exhibited by the entrepreneur, and each of these presents their own versions of ethical considerations with regard to personal values. And, each of these has implications for affecting the process and content of the entrepreneurial representation to the three outside groups of stake holders (this was discussed in detail in the previous chapter). The first expectations attitude will be referred to as *venture paroxysm*. The entrepreneur experiences a sudden but sustained sense of euphoria that the company is literally going to explode on the scene of the competitive landscape. This expectations attitude is tied to the perception that a Type A innovation-target scenario will result from the company's marketing efforts and strategy based upon superior product or service differentiation. If the founder truly believes that the firm's introduction is the next version of total market revolution, this will have a tremendous ethical impact on the relative degree of objectivity for all matters of personal decisions and representation. There will exist a high level of entrepreneurial bias positioned directly opposite a wide range of stake holder questions and skepticism. The ethical concerns will have to deal with questions about the founder's susceptibility to clouded vision during the seed and launch phases due to a values base that is not sufficiently open to outsider input and feedback.

The second expectations attitude will be referred to as *venture enthusiasm* tied to either the Type B or Type C innovation-target mix. The entrepreneur is thoroughly convinced that either the new product has great potential to claim some of the existing market, or the existing product will meet with great success in the newly devised application for another untapped market. There is no euphoria, but a good deal of optimism pervades each and every conversation and forecast that the entrepreneur formulates and transfers throughout the seed and launch phases of the new venture development. This is also probably based on a form of differentiation strategy, but not to the degree of the Type A offering. The third attitude is called *guarded optimism* and is most likely built on a strategy aimed at exploiting the lowest cost position, because the new venture is offering a very similar version of the existing product in the same market. These three attitudes open up a great deal of ethical concern about entrepreneurial perspective, objectivity, and decision making capabilities. The entrepreneur's attitude will be both a *result* of a personal values bias and interpretation, and a then one of the contributing factors in the process of formulating market expectations and representation for the new venture.

This raises two fundamental ethical concerns right from the start. First, the basic choice as to which assumptions are incorporated and which ones are disregarded is the direct product of the entrepreneur's personal feelings and interpretation of the situation concerning which factors are deemed pertinent and which are considered immaterial. Second, once the choice of assumptions is made, the entrepreneur further complicates the process by then deciding the content and the proposed degree of impact that these included assumptions will have on the marketing strategy. The main ethical ramifications of these two choices is the level of sensitivity that the decision outcomes will have based on even slight changes in which assumptions are utilized, and the relative weights assigned to the variables that comprise those assumptions.

## Five Core Assumptions

Rather than trying to outline and discuss the full range of entrepreneurial *expected* rates of return, or return on investment, it is more important to examine the underlying rationale behind the financial return requirements. It is proposed that there are only five core assumptions that the entrepreneur deals with in the process of formulating market expectations. These include: 1) the *feasibility* of the product, service, and venture formation, 2) the degree of *compatibility* that the product or service demonstrates with the attitudes and perceptions of the present market structure, 3) the *viability* of the product, service, and venture over the long term, 4) the *price sensitivity* that the product or service and firm operations will experience relative to supply and demand in the competitive market, and 5) the *possibility* of future government regulations on the manufacture, pricing, distribution, competition, or use of the product or service innovation. The entrepreneur must assign a personal value judgment about this particular sequence of assumptions in order to establish a process of seed-inquiry, a launch point, a marketing plan, an operations agenda, a production schedule, financial projections, and a network of contacts and referrals throughout the competitive environment

### *Feasibility*

The very first (and most obvious) hurdle that all entrepreneurial new ventures must clear is the issue of feasibility. This identifies and clarifies the relative degree with which the entrepreneur's business idea can actually be translated into a real, marketable product or service. It deals only with the ability for venture operations to get started and does not address the issue of whether the firm will experience success in the market. Many new ideas never even get off the ground and out of the seed stage because they cannot establish a critical mass of feasibility due to conceptual, technological, or logistical impracticalities. For example, the entrepreneur envisions a new device that would improve the speed of a certain telecommunications reception, but the venture never materializes because the technology cannot be manufactured in an efficient and profitable manner, or the design renders the item impractical for the target market. The entrepreneur has to be very careful about preaching the merits of a supposedly great idea when the prototype does not yet even exist in a marketable and profitable fashion. This can create ethical challenges that affect both the entrepreneur's representation of the idea, and forecasted market expectations in discussions with capital providers, market channels, and potential end-users.

### *Compatibility*

If the entrepreneur is convinced of the feasibility, the second concern must address the compatibility that this new product or service offering will have with all forms of complementary, dependent, and tangential associated products and services. There may be interesting features, a sleek design, or significant operating efficiencies in the new product or service, but the market may not be able to connect with the entrepreneur's perception of these benefits because it has little or no ability to work within the established product or service parameters for cost, ease of operations, or complementary characteristics. And, unless the new idea is a true landmark innovation, there may be a somewhat apathetic reception from the many individuals and companies in the existing marketing network. The entrepreneur can overly estimate the impact and review process in the market's final assessment of the applications for the new product concept. This will once again challenge the owner's ability to be objective and unbiased in determining the life cycle and market expectations for penetration and growth.

### *Viability*

The third hurdle that all entrepreneurial new ventures must clear, is that of viability. Once the feasibility issues have been addressed and the compatibility has been examined, the entrepreneur then determines the ability of the product or service innovation and the sponsoring new venture to maintain a strong competitive position in a continuously growing market over the long term. This addresses the issues related to the size of the market potential, the expectations for the market forecast of adoption, the firm's sales potential, and the ultimate sales forecast around which the venture is constructed. It defines whether the market will grow sufficiently over many years and not exhaust the pool of potential users in a short time period. It also speaks to the "staying power" of the firm relative to existing and future competitors, and the market's continued demand for the product or service. There are many ideas that could exhibit a tremendous level of viability but they are not yet feasible. There are many feasible ideas that are targeted to such a small market niche that there is not sufficient opportunity to motivate the entrepreneur and the financial resources in this endeavor. There are also some very feasible ideas that would remain viable for the long term, but the lack of compatibility creates a difficult obstacle with respect to suppliers and customers alike. The entrepreneur can be subject to numerous personal biases regarding these assumptions, and as such the market expectations are considered tremendously unrealistic by most outside onlookers. Just because the owner is thoroughly convinced, it may not be enough to win over the broad support necessary to pursue the venture.

### *Price Sensitivity*

Having determined the feasibility, compatibility, and viability of the idea, the entrepreneur must then address the degree to which the product or service offering and the new venture's operations are sensitive to any changes in the anticipated pricing structure of the market. If a new idea appears to be feasible, compatible, and viable at a certain price, the entrepreneur needs to determine how these positions change due to small upward and downward adjustments in price. For example, if a product will sell a certain critical mass and show some basic profitability at one price, but would forfeit its profitable position if the firm was forced by increased competition to match a slightly lower price, that reduces its viability. On the other hand, if the firm had to raise its prices to establish profits at a later time but found that demand for the product was highly elastic, the venture would again be placed in an awkward position of being viable "only if" certain variables (price in this case) can remain constant. The entrepreneur may have difficulty accepting and representing this price sensitivity, feeling that it is an unfair perception by the market. But the entrepreneur's perception may be in direct opposition to the outsiders and create a difficult situation for entirely ethical actions and values-based decisions, especially if the firm's life is on the line based on this one assumption.

### *Regulatory Potential*

The fifth core assumption must ascertain the possibility that the use of product or service, the production process, the pricing, or the distribution will one day be subject to local, state, or federal regulations as the market matures and the volatility of the external environment stabilizes over time. Many times when a start-up company introduces a new, discontinuous innovation (and even certain forms of continuous innovation), the market is often poorly defined, and the external environment is quite volatile, as many firms and individuals jockey for position to try and gain a competitive advantage. It may take various regulatory agencies several months, if not years, to enter in to the market and examine product disclosure, the accuracy of benefits and proposed features, the pricing policies, and the production process. The brand new market is not yet settled into its regular courses, the networks have not been clearly defined, market share is still very much up for grabs, and the end-users have not yet had enough time to determine the strength of the innovation's features and warranties. If the entire fate of the firm rests in the assumption that the market will remain turbulent, the entrepreneur had better examine the consequences under alternative assumptions. For instance, the firm may look very profitable and viable with little or no competition and unencumbered production methods. But the venture may look very different if the courts stepped into the center of the pricing or fairness of the competition arrangements, or they could impose environmental regulations on suppliers and producers that radically changed the cost structures and overall profit potential of the venture. This assumption, like all others, cannot be perfectly known during the planing stages, but entrepreneurial market expectations will continue to be highly subjective and conditional decision outputs as long as the individual values, perceptions, and ethical considerations of the entrepreneur remain the basis for assumption-based model building in new ventures.

## The Qualitative Quandary

The process of constructing market expectations has a very interesting ethical misconception associated with it due to the nature and perceptions of the form of supporting information used to make these decisions. The entrepreneur must generate market expectations and represent these within the context of the various planning phases, primarily throughout the seed and launch stages. The entrepreneur will face a difficult ethical issue pertaining to the value placed on prior business experience, intuition, motivation, ingenuity, and personal feelings. Although these are all highly subjective inputs to the market expectations process, there can be a tendency for the entrepreneur to overly rely on these items due to their supposed strength of experience and applications. The qualitative issues are sometimes given too much input when evaluated opposite the many quantitative models and formal mathematical decision hierarchies available for use in establishing clear market expectations for the new venture. The entrepreneur may not feel very mathematically inclined or believe that models do not accurately capture the true essence of the firm's peculiarities. Many owners conclude that they must somehow choose between these two mutually exclusive options. This latter format of decision making using database figures, and various columns and rows of spreadsheet numbers could actually improve greatly the overall perspective and quality of the initial personal perceptions, individual beliefs, and interpretations of the entrepreneur. But the discounting of the quantitative models in light of a personal sense, or "gut feeling," of the company is a juxtaposition that creates a *qualitative quandary* that impacts the ethical bases of the owner's ability to make decisions.

The quandary describes the individual's inherent capability to always be more inclined to trust (and therefore *use*) personal instincts and common sense before using a quantitative decision tree or matrix. This experiential component may have more credibility for inclusion in the formation of market expectations, but that does not mean that there can be no value gained in utilizing a library's three-ring binder of industry facts and figures, or a downloaded electronic financial database. So the entrepreneur must make a values-based decision whether to include quantitative formulas and figures in the decision mix, or to somehow discount these models and rely instead on the greater perceived value of personal instincts. It really comes down to a moral judgment about trust and perceived truth on the part of the entrepreneur. The decision may later be judged as lacking in substance if it is built too heavily on formulas and models, but it may also be considered too "soft" if it is leaning entirely on the personal experience bias of the owner. This quandary exposes the entrepreneur to ethical considerations about reliability, truthfulness, and trust in the formulation of market expectations.

## The Quantitative Legend

On the other side of the table, an argument can be made for the solid footing that is supposedly available to the entrepreneur who builds the firm's market expectations on objective models, reliable secondary data, and highly logical process flows of goals, objectives, and contingencies. Business schools are champions of developing high level quantitative competencies in budding entrepreneurs and future corporate managers alike. Decision trees, Markov transition matrices, Bayesian probability analysis, linear programming, and multivariate econometric models are designed to sift and sort all the assumptions and contingencies and provide the perfect risk-weighted expected value for all the possible outcomes. However, it is proposed that this image of formality regarding these methods and formulas supports a *quantitative legend*, in which the black and white input and output variables of modern decision theory are overly relied upon as superior to the subjective areas of intuition, individual experience, personal values, and "gut feelings." Many entrepreneurs get caught in the trap that believes that the most reliable and accurate information about the venture must come from a computer model and be reviewed in a formal laser-printed report. This legend is just that, a legend. There is no substitute for the entrepreneur's common sense and a strong business acumen based on previous experience. Quantitative models are only as good as the numbers that go into them and the assumptions that direct the interaction of the independent decision variables. It is just as easy to produce "garbage out" from highly sophisticated, quantitative computer-based decision software as it is to utilize a poor rationale and unrelated assumptions in a qualitative heuristic. The key point is that the entrepreneur should be aware of both the *quandary* and the *legend*, but that each of these processes utilize numerous assumptions to arrive at a decision direction. The entrepreneur will have to examine many moral bases and value judgments in constructing market expectations, because it is at the same time both a science and an art.

## The Problem of Realistic Expectations

Market expectations are certainly the product of considerable debate among both originators of the forecast (generally the entrepreneur) and the outside stake holders who receive and evaluate the relative merits of these projections of the future. The anticipation of certain sales due to the impact of the firm's innovative activities is never guaranteed, and should never be thought of as a distinct point in time. Instead, market expectations are the product of the entrepreneur's specific alignment of opportunity type, the various assumptions from which the forecast is derived, and the capability to accurately scan the approaching environment in order to acquire clear and reliable indicators about the most likely coming events. Even if the firm has established a formal mechanism for "listening" to and monitoring the external horizon for emerging issues and signs of volatility and new trends, the entrepreneur is still in the driver's seat concerning what interpretation to make based on this incoming information flow. One form of underlying ethic that is directly related to market opportunity and projected sales is for the entrepreneur to use only the most *realistic* expectations. This sounds great in theory, but it is altogether difficult to define in practical terms.

Realistic expectations are supposedly the "most likely" outcome that can be anticipated, based on the entrepreneur's various assumptions about the market's reception of the new product or service, the possible positioning of the competition's share, the pricing and demand dynamics, and some sort of risk factor to capture the impact of variability in these issues. But what does *realistic* truly mean? The concept is completely a function of each individual entrepreneur's interpretation of what constitutes a highly probable result. And this is not to say that an "average" result is always the most probable. True, a mathematical mean (*expected value*) is a functional outcome of the weighted probabilities for all of the most likely results and should well express the relative placement of the high end, the low end, and all the options in between. But such an average expectation may not accurately reflect all the qualitative issues as perceived by the entrepreneur. And the entrepreneur draws an approach to the expectations from a moral rationale and core values about what is acceptable and what is undesirable. The problem with speaking of *realistic* expectations is that there may not be such a thing in reality. For if "realistic" is implied to be some sort of general consensus, then the personal biases, moral judgments, and values-based ethics of the delegation that comprises this polled reference group has become the subjective collective rationale for the enterprise. This is every bit as precarious as trying to label the entrepreneur's view of what is considered too optimistic or too pessimistic in arriving at the construct of *realistic*. Values comprise the very heart of assessing degrees of significance, and are therefore fundamental to an entrepreneur's understanding that this forecast is really an ethical issue, with considerations for representation as well.

## The Caution of Conservative Expectations

It is very popular to hear entrepreneurs speak of utilizing a *conservative* approach to formulating market expectations. On the surface, this appears to be a reasonable approach to placing a value on the new venture's future prospects. However, as was the case with the prior construct of *realistic* expectations, there does not appear to be a generally accepted, subjective definition of what constitutes a *conservative* position, so the entire notion of arriving at a firm figure that is somehow inherently more reserved than others is equally a matter of applying personal value judgments and the entrepreneur's prevailing business ethic to the assumptions and variables that are used to formulate the expectation of the market's value and, more specifically, the new venture's prospects for sales and eventual profits. The notion of a conservative forecast carries with it some connotations about risk and uncertainty, as well as the implied prudence or moderation of the individual that supports this position. But the truth is that there is again really no such thing as an absolute conservative forecast of the market, only a position that is relatively more modest in its expectations and generates a lower dollar value than a less conservative approach.

The concept of a conservative market expectation does not translate into a better forecast, or a more reliable opportunity in the market. No special premium should be placed on the firm that formulates a conservative market expectation versus a supposedly realistic goal. It is possible to be overly conservative in constructing projections for the new venture. But even that is another function of the personal bias that decides what is an acceptable conservative position versus an unacceptable stance. Maybe the most realistic market expectation is in fact a forecast based on the most conservative assumptions available to the entrepreneur. Maybe it is based on liberal expectations. This underscores the need to define market expectations as an ethical issue and a direct extension of the entrepreneur's personal values and prejudicial perspectives about the numerous variables and assumptions that create the forecast in the first place.

## The Temptation of Liberal Expectations

The third area that should be examined involves the lure of being recklessly optimistic about what the new venture can anticipate in terms of market share penetration, sales growth, and profitability. Outside stake holders will be especially wary of market expectations that are based on the top end of the market potential. Personal judgment will once again be used to decide what is "too liberal" or overly optimistic. There is no firm definition for *liberal*, only a relative positioning at some level higher than "realistic" and significantly far above the "conservative" approach. Warren Briggs, senior professor with the Sawyer School of Management at Boston's Suffolk University described the subjective nature of market expectations in the context of the following analogy. New venture development is actually an expedition referred to as *entrepreneurial pioneering*, regarded by many observer's as a personal journey into the great unknown and untamed wilderness, where savage beasts, harsh weather, and lack of adequate resources are combined with unknown factors to make the trek quite treacherous and highly questionable. But entrepreneurs view the new venture market landscape as wide open with opportunity and full of huge potential rewards for those willing to persevere and lay hold of the opportunity set before them. Few (if any) predecessors have gone on ahead into the new region. Uncertainty abounds due to extremely limited information about the environment, and any information that is available is generally not current or reliable with regard to its source. Entrepreneurs are pioneers who are either extremely visionary and incredibly opportunistic because they believe in the possibilities that eventually may come to fruition, or they are ill-prepared and lacking in common sense because they seem to disregard the high level of risks and uncertainty. The final verdict will be based completely on hindsight gained some time after the uncertainty has passed away and the new market environment comes into clear focus. Some pioneers are never seen or heard from again. Others return from the expedition with fabulous tales of opportunities that are still out there waiting for someone to come along and lay claim to them. But some entrepreneurial pioneers stake out a large section of the once unknown territory and turn it into a profitable venture with little (if any) competition, and no challengers arriving on the immediate horizon.

## The Ethics Model and Market Expectations

The likelihood that the entrepreneur will engage in questionable ethical activities, such as those summarized in the various assumption issues related to market expectations, will again be examined within the broader context of the proposed entrepreneurial ethics model and the *Ethics and Values Interaction* (EVI) matrix that were discussed in Chapter Five. This model proposes that entrepreneurs possess a moral rationale coupled with six entrepreneurial characteristics to form core values, whose breadth and depth support types of ethical behavior in seven fundamental actions. The entrepreneurial characteristics impact these seven actions within five distinct *ethical domains* of new ventures. Figure 7.6 presents the proposed ethical "problem areas" of the EVI matrix associated with entrepreneurial market expectations. The owner's propensity for a high degree of risk tolerance and business uncertainty are each expected to affect the judgments related to the various transactions of evaluating data and constructing models to forecast the future market. As an innovator who spots opportunity, the entrepreneur's personal values will have an effect on the positions that are taken regarding the emerging market's potential and forecasted value. The opportunistic-innovator will also be faced with having to sort through ethical positions of both assessing the value of input information, and the decision outputs of the market forecast. Decision processes will likely be impacted by the choice to maintain control of the firm's plans and directions as they are based on the personal perspectives, positions, and assessments of the entrepreneur's predisposition to optimism about the future prospects of the venture. The informal style will have a direct impact on the entrepreneur's ability to discuss the market's composition and communicate an advocacy for generous expectations, while arguing against any feedback that would discount future expectations to lower levels. The entrepreneur is most likely to face objections and the outside "voice of reason" in the process of establishing the profile of the target market. Yet the owner will have great difficulty in detaching these

120 ■ Chapter Seven

personal characteristics from the forecasting process and will be exposed to ethical concerns about truthfulness, accuracy, reliability of the numbers, the relative values of assumptions, the objectivity of perspective, and the personal advocacy for a specific view.

■ ■ ■ ■

**Figure 7.6**
**Forecasted EVI Matrix: Market Expectations**

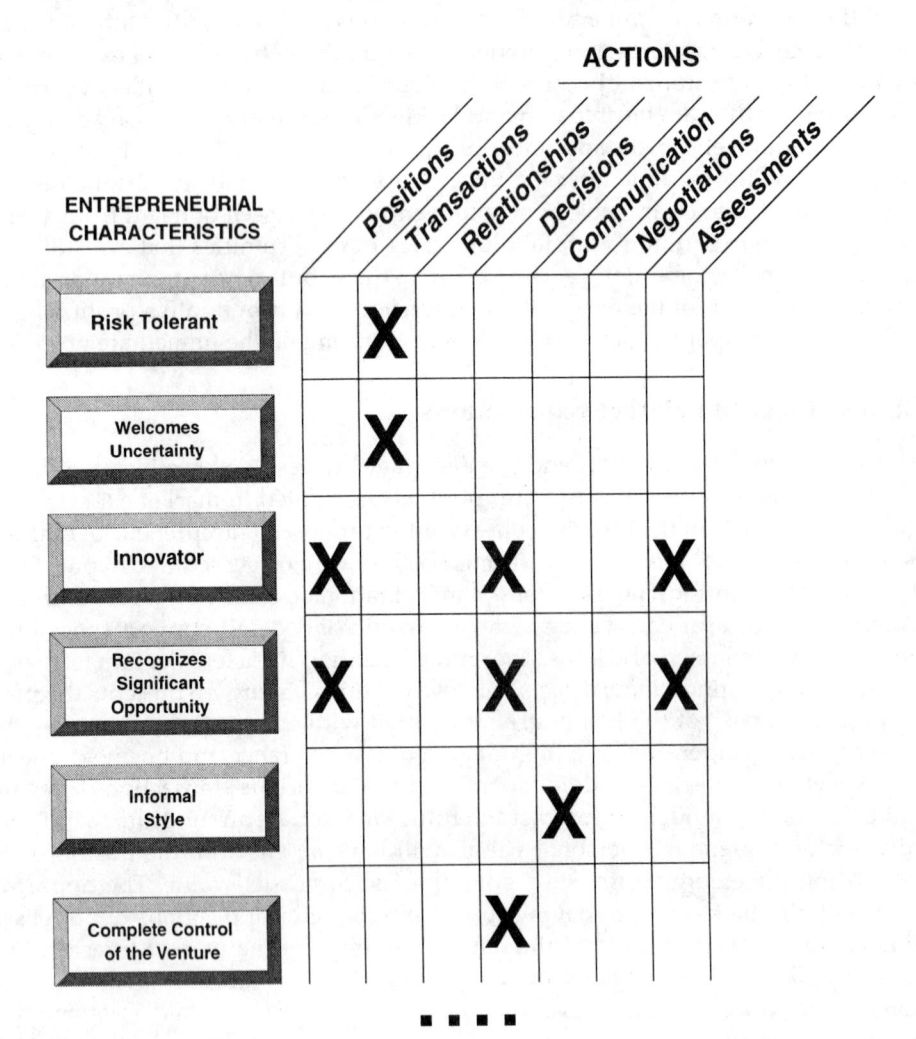

| ENTREPRENEURIAL CHARACTERISTICS | Positions | Transactions | Relationships | Decisions | Communication | Negotiations | Assessments |
|---|---|---|---|---|---|---|---|
| Risk Tolerant | X | | | | | | |
| Welcomes Uncertainty | X | | | | | | |
| Innovator | X | | X | | X | | |
| Recognizes Significant Opportunity | X | | X | | X | | |
| Informal Style | | | | X | | | |
| Complete Control of the Venture | | | X | | | | |

(ACTIONS)

■ ■ ■ ■

## Empirical Results

### *Qualitative Basis for Growth*

The entrepreneurs were asked to assess the source of the underlying initial position of the new venture in the market. One quarter of them (26%) felt that their idea was a completely brand new concept, product, or service that was unique compared to the existing market offerings. It was interesting to find that the remaining entrepreneurs (74%) recognized that their idea was either a replica or a further extension of an existing idea, concept, product or service. This starting point appears to have an impact on the entrepreneur's primary value basis as a true innovator in the market.

They were also asked about the cause of the significant growth that landed them among the *INC.* magazine top five hundred entrepreneurial firms. More than one quarter (29%) of these entrepreneurs felt that their growth was primarily due to a unique and superior product that was in very high demand in the new market. But the vast majority of the owners (71%) felt very strongly that their growth was the result of a company-wide emphasis on superior customer service.

### *Sales and Profit Forecasts*

The entrepreneurs were also asked about the relative degree of difficulty involved in formulating company expectations in the form of financial projections. More than two-thirds of the owners (68%) stated that it was either very difficult or almost impossible to forecast accurately due to market uncertainty. The remaining (32%) entrepreneurs stated that financial projections were not difficult or were actually somewhat easy to forecast due to their knowledge of the market. But when they were asked about market expectations for a new product or service, more than nine out of every ten entrepreneurs (92%) felt that it was entirely unacceptable to overestimate their company's sales expectations in the context of trying to gain interest from potential outside investors. Only a small percentage (8%) of owners expressed the opinion that it was acceptable to overestimate sales forecasts.

### *Accuracy of Expectations*

The interesting issue was that the entrepreneurs were somewhat split in half as to the overall accuracy of their firm's original financial projections. Just over half (54%) believed that their expectations were generally accurate when compared with the actual results, while the other group (46%) felt that their original projections were inaccurate. This tends to lend support to the notion that the new venture does contain a tremendous amount of risk and uncertainty about future prospects.

### *Formulating Projections*

At this point, it is appropriate to review data from the prior chapter. The entrepreneurs typically felt (65%) that when formulating a projection it is best to use only the most realistic numbers, while about one quarter of them (23%) said that they would choose to discount expectations lower in order to compensate for the risks of the unknown decision factors. The remaining group was somewhat smaller (12%) but chose to utilize a strategy of marking expectations higher as a means of covering uncertainty. Together, about one third of the owners do not use "realistic" expectations.

### *Promotions and Advertising Expectations*

The last segment dealing with expectations involved the entrepreneur's perception about whether the new venture was engaged in a marketing push strategy, or responding to a marketing pull phenomenon. About one quarter of the owners (27%) said that when they formulate their marketing promotion and advertising in the marketplace, they primarily focus on creating a new need for their product or service, while exactly two-thirds (66%) stated that they focus on meeting an existing need in the market. It was interesting to see that only a small number (7%) felt it was a combination of both effects.

## Conclusions

The entrepreneurs generally believed (by about a three-to-one ratio) that their market expectations were tied to demand for a product or service that was similar to the existing products or services in the market. This is interesting in light of the common perception that entrepreneurs are product or service innovators. Perhaps the innovation is the *manner* in which they bring their wares to the market. The entrepreneur might bring a values-based interpretation about a distinctive competency versus some form of continuous innovation. Many products and services could be quite similar to the existing market offerings, and yet the entrepreneurs believe that their idea or concept is truly unique from the competition. Or, the owners might perceive that theirs is a replica of the existing market offerings, when in fact it is really different in terms of features and cost.

The entrepreneurs bring various backgrounds and prior experiences to the new venture development process as well. In Chapter Twelve, the links between past experience and innovation will be examined in light of personal values and ethical behavior. One notable interaction deals with the groupings of entrepreneurs into very similar proportions across several different measurement items. For example, over two-thirds of the owners said that their previous business experience prior to the launch of the venture was in a similar or complementary field. An almost equal proportion also stated that their product or service was a replica. There are many intuitive connections between prior business experience and the personal evaluation of the product or service concept relative to the existing market. Also, the entrepreneurs tended to base their company's projections on the most "realistic" numbers, which could continue as a function of their background and belief in the market penetration potential for their product or service. And finally, once again, two-thirds of the entrepreneurs said that they were generally meeting an existing market need for the product or service, rather than creating a need for something that does not yet exist. And the combined interaction of these personal perspectives could very well define the degree of difficulty that is perceived in making various types of market expectations. It is fascinating to see that about two-thirds believed that it was very difficult, or nearly impossible, to make an accurate forecast due to the uncertainty present in the market.

The entrepreneur's ability to remain entirely objective in assessing market potential could be called into question due to the effects of prior experience and the nature and composition of the product or service offering in the market. Also, a *monotony fallacy* can exist once the firm has cleared the launch and appears to be sailing along, seemingly unaffected by any form of change. It is during this period of apparent stabilization that the entrepreneur can be lulled into a false sense of security about the venture's prospects for continued success. Perhaps there are inevitable and unavoidable ethical complications in formulating market expectations simply because the assumption-based models are products of personal perspectives and moral judgments about the factors that affect market performance, and the extent of the impact that various conditions bring to the final analysis. Or it might be that there cannot exist a truly absolute ethical criteria for assumption-based model building due to the inability to separate personal values from the process. Information is one of the key components to the assessment and expectations process. Both the degrees of timeliness and access that outsiders have to the owner-insiders pertinent information define the form of *market efficiency* that exists between these two parties and their related levels of vested interest. If the entrepreneur controls the requisite information, market expectations can be viewed by many outsiders as numbers that simply fall out of the sky with no visible justification for their formulation or accuracy.

The entrepreneur's prior experience, the product or service type, the formulation of the forecast with respect to conservative or liberal numbers, and the perceived difficulty of making accurate assessments, together provide insight into the entrepreneur's profile for making highly ethical representations of the firm to outside stake holders. This is not to say that in each of these four situations the same two-thirds of the owners are responding in a consistent manner. But it does raise the concern about how the entrepreneur chooses to represent the business in the face of risk and uncertainty, past experience, and the market's familiarity with the firm's offering. It might be that the most likely candidates to compromise firm representation are the entrepreneurs who perceive that they are creating a new market need by introducing a distinctively new innovation, and yet have previous experience in other unrelated areas. How they handle market expectations could tend to be overly optimistic because of pre-existing inclinations to accept higher levels of risk and uncertainty in approaching what appears to be a wide open market segment. Later on, in Chapter Twelve, it will be interesting to see how entrepreneurs with different forms of product introductions handle uncertainty and accuracy of expectations. And it will be shown which of the entrepreneurial types is most likely to mark-up or discount projections, and whether there are specific market scenarios and firm types that are more likely to cause the entrepreneur to overestimate the prospects of the new venture, and how that is represented to outsiders.

## CHAPTER EIGHT

# *Entrepreneurial Financial Requirements*

## Introduction

Entrepreneurs of newly launched ventures are presented with a host of ethical issues directly related to the various financial requirements necessary to both initiate operations and maintain successful performance of the new company. The notable issues surrounding these financial considerations are the relative degrees of risk exposure and business uncertainty inherent in the entrepreneurial enterprise process. Many would argue that the ability to fund the development of a new product or service innovation idea is by far the greatest weight on the shoulders of the company founder(s). There has been a good deal of research supporting the notion that the "best" configuration and most appropriate amount of start-up financing to raise is always in excess of the true targeted figure necessary to get the venture into operations and a successful launch.[1] But many view financing as secondary to the qualitative issues of strong content, mature skills and behavior areas, the proper mentality to operate and persevere with the small business, and the right personality to deal with the many risky and uncertain issues that comprise the first several years of making the new company a viable reality in the market.[2] For some entrepreneurs, the ethical issues related to financial matters does not move beyond the perceptions of whether the funding can adequately support the growth of the firm or the risk and impacts of employee theft.[3] There is even the emphasis on making sure that qualitative issues like customer service and truth in advertising will have positive impacts on the new venture's short-term cash flow, because happy customers are more likely to pay on time and in full.[4]

However, the entrepreneur is often not all that interested in the financial details of cash flow and marginal revenue analysis, but is instead focused on sales growth, marketing strategies, and smooth production operations. Many entrepreneurs, even those with accounting and financial backgrounds, tend to discount the financing aspects and may not keep track of the numbers the way they should, and then lose control of the firm's ability to maintain a clear direction.[5] The inability to keep a pulse on the company's external financial transactions and internal flow of funds has been called the cash flow quagmire, because the entrepreneur can easily get the company bogged down in a seemingly endless stream of bills going out with automated regularity while cash receipts from sales lack relative dependability.[6]

The increase of shareholder wealth has often been quoted as the primary objective of the managers in a corporation. However, many smaller start-up companies are beginning to reexamine tangible earnings per share in light of the true *value* that is really worth building into an enterprise, namely reputation, firm culture, ethical behavior, fair and sound policies and procedures, and a clear moral basis for decision making rationales.[7] The financial support of the venture may in fact be tied to the entrepreneur's ability to create a truly ethical organizational atmosphere that is receptive to working hard on ethical issues and dealing with tough problems related to production, distribution, and financing matters.[8] Too often the founder believes that the only ethics associated with the financial aspects of the venture must deal with topics like insider stock trading, securities fraud, company takeovers and manipulation, and that the small firm is unlikely to deal with these at any time prior to going public.[9] Much of the research about financial ethics tries to focus the small firm on the same type of securities mismanagement or fraud issues that face the largest capitalized, public companies,[10] when the real heart of values and ethics in entrepreneurial financial decision making has closer ties to the subjective aspects of risk and *expected* future return, and dealing with uncertainty in light of market opportunity and the value of information. The popular *Templeton Plan* for ethics and firm success proposed that "accuracy" is the absolute key in financial forecasts, budget preparations, cash flow analysis, and equity offers to generate strong ties of goodwill between firm owners and the various financial stake holders in the company.[11]

Perhaps the number one concept borrowed from the financial academy that has application and direct impact on entrepreneurial ethics behavior in the management of the small firm is the *"value of information."* If buyers and sellers in a new venture market have equal access to, and content understanding of, the same quality and timeliness of pertinent information, the dealings for pricing transactions and appropriate returns on investment are said to be efficient.[12] The outside marketplace is very interested in gaining insights to the entrepreneurial mind, the firm's plans and prospects, and the expectations in the market. One ethical concern deals with how outsiders obtain their pertinent entrepreneurial information and whether these tactics are altogether ethical with respect to the small firm's right to privacy and proprietary information.[13] The sales forecast and other market expectations discussed in Chapter Seven, are then tied to the entrepreneur's means and strategy of representation as outlined in Chapter Six. Together, the transmission or protection of the information flow in the small firm is a critical ethical matter of privacy and protection of access. Financial institutions can also contribute a range of ethical problems for small entrepreneurial ventures due to the level of values-oriented behavior displayed in their dealings with new businesses in matters of financial services, reporting, funds management, capital access, and debt and equity financing alternatives.[14] For many smaller, privately-held firms, internal data such as return on investment is not always associated with increased sales volume or the level of market share a firm holds.[15] The outside stake holders have numerous levels of vested financial interests, but the small firm itself is not always the best provider of an unencumbered information flow.

## *The Dilemma of Capitalization*

Several ethical issues of choice will affect the entrepreneur's decisions about how best to capitalize the new venture, based on personal perceptions and interpretations of various subjective trade-offs associated with debt and equity financing. The finance community has for quite a few decades debated the appropriate mix between equity and liabilities in formulating a capital structure to support the asset base. Empirical evidence has been presented from both sides of the argument concerning topics such as optimal capital structure, various agency issues related to creditor and stockholder interests in the firm's risky operations, and ultimately the calculation of the appropriate costs of capital. About thirty years ago, Franco Modigliani and Merton Miller captured the fundamental basis for the capital structure discussions by dismissing cost of capital as a function of the company's mix between debt and equity, and instead turned attention to the perceived risk class in which capital providers classify the firm's operations.[16] Their work laid the basis for this book's premise that financial requirements, like capital structure and cost of capital analysis, are in fact entrepreneurial ethical issues of new ventures because they are drawn from the individual's subjective biases and an interpretive rationale about risk tolerance, business uncertainty, the interpretation of the window of opportunity, and market expectations. It is crucial to view financial requirements as one of the five primary *ethical domains* in the new venture development process. The entrepreneur's decisions about how to best capitalize the firm, what rate to use in discounting future expectations, and the firm's applicable risk class are all tied to personal values and a unique perspective of the firm's prospects. These also relate to the manner of representation the entrepreneur utilizes in dialogue with outside stake holders.

The first point of ethical decisions is whether capitalization should lean on the debt or equity side of the balance sheet. A new venture looks very different as an all-equity organization versus an all-debt concern. The entrepreneur will make values-oriented decisions about whether the firm's stock ownership structure should be spread beyond the owner-managers to outside shareholders, or whether the owners should retain tighter controls over the common stock voting rights and instead deal with a large creditor segment of outsiders. Company communication and rapport happens in a very different manner with these two distinct groups of capital providers. Shareholders have a different agenda than bond holders or other long-term creditors. The firm's cash flow has different obligations placed on it based on the majority position of the equity versus debt. The shareholders may have a somewhat separate set of values and target goals than the entrepreneur, even though they each have vested interest in the company's after-tax earnings, cash flow, and dividend policy. The agenda of the creditors is focused on the firm's ability to generate dependable pre-tax cash flow used to make timely interest payments on principal. These are fundamentally exclusive positions in the venture.

Although they both hold common stock in the company, the entrepreneur is often unique from the outside investor because of the ability to maintain a longer-term position in the firm, even when dividends are not paid and earnings are not growing at a steady and strong pace. The entrepreneur has an additional link to the venture based on value factors such as wanting to see the dream become a reality, and giving the company an almost unlimited and open-ended time-frame within which to achieve significant market penetration with the product or service innovation. Outside shareholders, on the other hand, may forego the periodic interest payments of creditors in exchange for open-ended growth prospects of the firm's net worth, but they also see the company as an investment, a place to park funds for a specified investment horizon, and a view toward a profitable, and opportune *exit strategy*. The equity outsider may support the more risky tolerances of the entrepreneur early on in the life of the seed and launch stages, but shareholders may then have a tendency to want the firm to "settle down" and build profitability in order to set the stage for cashing out in a stock sale (rather than continue to reinvest funds into further research and expansion).

Conversely, the creditors are looking for some forward movement into the market, but nothing "too risky," based on their perceptions and tolerances for certain types of exposure. They certainly want the venture to be successful, but they are concerned about guarding the integrity of the principal on the loans. Any ill-advised capital investments or poorly managed fund allocations could weaken the asset base and erode the face value of mortgages, bonds, promissory notes, and working capital lines of credit. The entrepreneur's personal values and ethical considerations about the firm's future prospects will often be, in some ways, very similar to the shareholders' desire to forge ahead with company plans and objectives in a more subjective (instinctual) or risk-prone manner, but they will generally not have the same level of patience for expectations to materialize. Their time frame may be tied to a separate investment portfolio horizon related to other equity positions held for an overall diversification strategy. The entrepreneur, on the other hand, has placed all the resource "eggs in the same basket" and does not perceive the venture merely as one of several investments in an overall portfolio plan. The creditors are then advocating the move forward but in a more cautious manner, not wishing to have the shareholders gain at their expense. Creditors simply want to get paid on a regular basis, and for that interest payment they have accepted a risk transfer position, giving up a vote in the management of the firm in exchange for periodic interest payments, the risk premium paid by the entrepreneur. There are then tremendous values confrontations that take place between the various stake holders, as conflicting perspectives and financial agendas compete for the leading voice in directing the company's strategy. The entrepreneur will have to confront this *dilemma of capitalization* and choose an equity or debt basis for the venture's financial foundation.

## The Struggle to Seed

The entrepreneur's first round of financial requirements for the venture are tied to the seed stage, in order to fund certain research and development projects, the design and testing of prototype products and services, and the market surveys to determine the feasibility, compatibility, and viability of the firm's concepts and ideas. It is extremely difficult to obtain outside financing at the seed stage because outsiders realize that funds could be appropriated for these preliminary investigations and evaluations by the entrepreneur, but in the end they could result in one of three possible outcome scenarios. Each of these prospects places ethical pressures on the entrepreneur to provide timely accurate disclosure of the venture's progress, but they also impact the manner with which the founder chooses to represent initial results and the possibilities for performance improvement over time. And, it certainly interacts with the entrepreneur's judgment about what constitutes acceptable progress in the seed stage, and the core values associated with taking risks in such an early phase of firm development. Any outside stake holder would certainly want to maintain an extremely close and watchful eye on every aspect of the research process, because after all, the entrepreneur is using someone else's money to test the credibility of an untried idea. So while the entrepreneur may have a moral rationale linked with vision, opportunity, and a personal tolerance for risk and uncertainty, the capital provider at this early stage realizes that their pecuniary vested interest is competing with the founder's non pecuniary stakes in the exploration of the firm's prospects for being able to deliver the product to a real market at the designated price level. The entrepreneur must surely be looking for someone who shares the vision, sees the same potential, recognized the same market opportunity, and is willing to risk funds in the pursuit of establishing the logistical bases for the venture's introduction. The struggle to seed describes the hard work involved in locating, courting, and convincing a capital provider to join the fledgling enterprise at a time when few onlookers are persuaded that the entrepreneur is capable of "pulling off" this endeavor.

The first of the three types of outcomes that can result from funding at the seed phase in the development process is referred to as *trampled seed money*. The funds never really got to a chance to take hold due to problems with the practicality of the design, or logistical difficulties in the production process, or the lack of an adequate "working" technology for this particular application. Accountants will refer to these funds as *sunk costs*, because although they helped establish the likelihood of potential success, or the overwhelming shortcomings of the new idea, they do not generate sales dollars that can be used as a return on investment for these original capital providers. In the case of trampled seed money, the entrepreneur will either have to admit defeat or look for another course of funding, while the investor loses everything and has little if any assets against which to seek recourse for reimbursement purposes. Many times, entrepreneurs fall back on various forms of *bootstrapping* strategies to try and salvage the enterprise. This describes the process by which an entrepreneur supports business operations without the influence or resources of any outside assistance, even though it may appear that the internal capabilities of the enterprise cannot provide an adequate foundation. It is derived from the nineteenth century western American literature where an individual could rescue himself from rising waters if he picked himself up by his own bootstraps. Obviously, with less than stellar initial results, the founder is left in an awkward position to try and assemble some form of resources for the venture. However, ethical concerns will surface about whether the entrepreneur is now throwing good money toward a bad idea.

The second outcome is called *incremental seed money*. This describes the way in which these initial funds brought the research and testing procedures forward to a level of limited success. The venture is still alive and breathing at this point. These are not trampled funds. The sunk costs in this scenario have produced a few qualitative paybacks due to promising and favorable results. But herein lies the difficulty. The venture has cleared one or two of the initial hurdles toward producing a working prototype, or a feasible process. The venture is not ready to fail, but it does need more funds in order to go to the next level of knowledge about the technology features, or commercial applications for the new idea. This is a highly subjective crossroads in the life of the venture. Based on some limited success, the entrepreneur once again becomes a lobbyist on behalf of the venture, and in this second round, there will be even greater tendencies to personally filter the representation of the firm's prospects and future market expectations. The idea is once again a candidate for financing, and it could be even easier to persuade an investor at this point because there are already some measurable "results" from the first round of financing. But, the this scenario can place the entrepreneur against the investor's personal perspectives and interpretations of the initial performance results, and the firm itself actually gets involved because it is in jeopardy of being terminated unless it can secure an infusion of a second round of funding. The entrepreneur will obviously have to deal with the temptation for *touting* the initial positive results, or downplay the original negative results in the context of trying to convince an outsider to "join the cause" and "catch the vision."

The third outcome involves obtaining very promising results with the first round of seed funds, and now there are plenty of individuals and sources of capital investment literally lining up for the chance to make a presentation of their own to the entrepreneur about why their funds, personal perspective, and values-based rationales are such a great match with those of the entrepreneur. This is called *free-agency seed money*. These funds were not available prior to the first round of funding, but now that there are clear and tangible positive company results, the world is literally beating a path to the entrepreneur's front door. The entrepreneur is like the athlete who, after just one season of relatively decent performance, has become a hot commodity in the free-agent market as several teams bid for services based on a subjective perceptions of increase in market worth. Now the ethical issues will center on the founder's ability to remain objective while dealing with various unsolicited offers. Remember, many of these suitors would not give the time of day when the entrepreneur originally came calling. Now that the venture has apparent value, the capital providers will now agree with the entrepreneur's assessment and communication of market expectations, and want to be sure and join the company for the next round of potential positive results. But even more importantly, these late-interest capital providers have their sights set on being the primary stake holder when the seeding is complete and it is time for a launch of full-time commercial operations.

The entrepreneur may experience feeling a sense of duty to stay with the first round provider. But that may not really be the best purely "financial" decision for the future of the venture. Questions of loyalty will surface when the entrepreneur must decide on staying with a potentially limiting and smaller first round financial provider, or making the switch to a perhaps much larger and reputable funding company that also has other managerial and technical assets and personnel resources that would be available to the entrepreneur during the second round of the seed phase, and could greatly increase the propensity for continued success. Ethical behavior will be challenged as the proliferation of various monetary funding options begins to attract the entrepreneur. Vision can become tainted if the entrepreneur feels it is necessary to compromise some core values in order to secure the best possible funding offer from the outside sources that have assembled to bid on the firm's free agency. Future direction and control of the firm may be challenged by outsiders who have swayed the entrepreneur to accept their offer of funding for the next leg of the venture development process. This third outcome opens up many doors to values and moral choices related to the upcoming topic of partnering, which will be dealt with in the next chapter.

## The Labor of the Launch

Once the new venture establishes obvious logistical feasibility, market compatibility, and a reasonable degree of perceived viability, the entrepreneur must wade through the many ethical issues dealing with how to transition the "good idea" into a company that can truly deliver the product or service innovation to market in a timely and efficient manner, and eventually do this at a profit. The most glaring differences between the launch and the seed stages come from two fronts. The first noticeable contrast concerns the huge increase in the scope of the operations at the launch versus the more narrow focus of testing and research at the seed phase. The second distinction is the major increase in the funds necessary to launch as compared to the seeding activities. The firm must get set up to mass produce, move efficiently through the right marketing channels, engage in significant promotions and advertising to effectively communicate the relevant message to the market, and then organize and train a coordinated managerial and laborer work force to meet demand and show a profit. On the surface, it can be an exciting time in the life of the firm. But the reality is that everything about production costs and sales revenues prior to launch has been nothing more than projections based on the entrepreneur's highly subjective qualitative instincts and equally subjective assumptions built into quantitative models and functions. The launch is seen by most entrepreneurs as the one of the few chances to make a good impression on the three groups of stake holders regarding the reality of the venture's long-term viability, and accuracy of assumptions. The venture is no longer a conceptual idea that only exists on the drawing board of the entrepreneur's mind, during which time there are many moral concerns about how the vision and target market are represented. The venture will begin to generate tangible results, but several new ethical issues now come forward.

### *The "Catch-22" of Bridge Loans*

Most new firms will experience a very unique period in their life cycle that presents several difficult ethical situations for the entrepreneur. The company secures a facility, purchases supplies and equipment, hires and trains employees, executes marketing transactions, establishes a banking relationship, and begins production operations. Initially, the company will have relatively high fixed overhead expenses compared to quantity output. Bills will be due almost immediately for rent, mortgages, equipment leases, loan installments, all types of inventory, utility costs, and payroll. But the initial sales volume will not be comparable to the scope of the firm's asset configuration and optimum production function. Also, even if sales volume does grow quickly, many newly secured invoices will have extended credit terms to buyers of between sixty and ninety days or more. The business will need cash to pay current bills, but sales receipts will not come in at a commensurate pace until a later time. During this period in between paying current bills and waiting on customers to pay, the firm will have an obvious cash shortage. New ventures can utilize several working capital credit strategies to secure immediate cash flow to pay current liabilities. But this situation creates a credit "catch-22" for the entrepreneur. Financial institutions generally want to see strong sales and receivables before they approve a working capital line of credit. However, the firm cannot establish strong sales and receivables until it has credit to cover the negative cash flow gap. This credit process also presents the entrepreneur with an ethical "catch-22," a second issue that challenges qualitative perspectives.

Any form of covering this negative gap is normally referred to as a *bridge loan*, because, like a bridge, it transports the new venture across this relatively short time period of insufficient cash flow. The difficulty comes in trying to assess how long that period will be prior to the launch and making arrangements for working capital to bridge the span. If the entrepreneur estimates the need for funding far in excess of the actual figure, it will provide a cushion for bill paying, but send overly optimistic signals about market expectations and opportunity, and could call into question the authenticity of the owner's representation of the firm's forecast assumptions. If the entrepreneur estimates too low, the firm will be caught short and continued business operations could be jeopardized. The firm's credit rating will also be adversely impacted by an inability to pay bills on time. This presents a "catch-22" for the entrepreneur. Ethical questions must be dealt with concerning the appropriateness of pro form cash flow budgets relative to the firm's market expectations and assumptions about the depth and breadth of the opportunity. Also, because this forecast is an assumption-based model, the entrepreneur's personal reputation will be directly impacted by the accuracy of the proposed amount of bridge financing. This brings to full circle the issues of personal perspectives, individual value judgments on firm projections, and the need for credibility and decisions about liberal, realistic, and conservative biases. This decision leaves the entrepreneur caught between appearing either overly cautious with a conservative high-end need for bridge financing, or too liberal and confident in the firm's sales prospects and maybe short of funds once bill paying begins with actual sales levels.

### *Lack of Internal Security*

Having made arrangements for the bridge financing, the entrepreneur must now address a second potential scenario of the launch phase. Once the firm hits its stride and is able to pay current liabilities from receivables, positive cash flow must be assessed in terms of its ability to fuel continued company growth. Granted, the entrepreneur is pleased to be at a point where sales volume is adequate to pay bills. But the more important issue is whether this growth rate in new sales is sufficient enough to produce the necessary positive cash flow for funding increased production, a wider marketing campaign, larger stocks of inventory, a higher payroll, and periodic upgrades to office equipment, transportation infrastructure, and other fixed assets. For many entrepreneurs, arriving at positive cash flow appears at first to be a blessing, but it can actually be a very difficult decision point in the life of the new venture because the company's internally generated source of funds cannot sustain the owner's forecasted market expectations. When a company outstrips its inherent funding capabilities, an outside source of capital must be located and persuaded to join the asset mix, and this creates several values-oriented hurdles for the entrepreneur.

The company must have an additional round of capitalization in order to secure the assets that will increase the firm's capacity to meet the projected growth in demand. Without this infusion of funds, other competitors in the market will seize the opportunity to make these necessary investments and capture a significant share of both the existing and anticipated customer base. Even if the intrusion of competitors is not immediately substantial, the new venture may be extremely sensitive to both price changes that could occur due to competitive pressures, and slight decreases in sales due to overcrowding in the market structure. The most pressing moral questions are, "How far will the entrepreneur go to ensure the protection of the existing customer base?," and "Will newly acquired funding be accompanied by adverse influences on the managerial decision making perspectives of the entrepreneur?" Many entrepreneurs will wrestle with the thought of having to concede a portion of ownership control in order to secure the capital that is necessary to maintain a competitive position in the market. No owner wants to see the venture slowly come to a halt because the internal growth rate of profits was less than the growth rate of sales in the external environment. But, the entrepreneur probably does not want to sacrifice certain personal guidelines and complete responsibility for managing firm direction, transactions, and communication. The lack of *internal security* that often accompanies the move into venture profitability, can dampen the overall prospects of the company because of numerous qualitative factors pertaining to the entrepreneur's fear of compromising the individual vision for the firm, a sense of mission and purpose, and a certain style of firm operations.

This crossroad is similar to the scenario where a motorist must cross a vast expanse of dry desert. The driver has half a tank of gasoline, and based upon anticipated driving conditions, trip length, and the car's *expected* fuel consumption, the trip should go smoothly. But the weather changes, there are more cars on the road than were anticipated, and a required detour is diverting traffic away from the original route. The driver now has concerns about running out of gas and being stranded. At the next stop the driver asks for directions and is told of another route that has a gas station several miles down the road. As a less traveled road, the driver would also avoid the existing slow traffic. The driver is faced with a moral decision about whether to accept outside input and new risks, balanced against potential benefits. These are subject to the driver's personal interpretation about what is the best thing to do. Entrepreneurs are often put in the same position of having to decide between outside influences, the continued success of the venture, and a personal values basis that either excludes certain actions at all times, or evaluates each situation as it arises. The driver could stay on the marked detour route and run out of gas and be stranded, or find that the traffic pace eventually picks up shortly ahead and the car just makes it to the destination. But the driver could also try the other route, and refuel at the gas station, and make even better time than originally anticipated, or find the new route to be full of potholes and slow going, and the gas station closed because the owner went fishing. Many entrepreneurs put tremendous faith in their vehicle, the new venture. But external factors may require adjustments to the original plan and these carry ethical implications for the owner.

## *The IPO Mirage*

Many new ventures find some sort of a plan to fill the working capital gap and they can even hurdle the initial lack of *internal security* with some form of stop-gap financing. But perhaps the greatest ethical issue to deal with during a successful launch involves the temptation to begin thinking about making an *initial public offer* of the company's common stock in order to generate substantial outside funds that are often perceived to be the savior of the small firm. The entrepreneur will have to sift through both the benefits of tapping into a large source of equity capital, and the potentially devastating change in direction that can accompany the admission of new voting shares to the managerial mix of the venture. An *initial public offer (IPO)*, "going public," is the first sale of a corporate firm's common stock to investors in the formal equity market, exclusively represented in a formal written prospectus filed with the *Securities and Exchange Commission*. The sale is generally underwritten by an investment bank that accepts the risk of disseminating the shares, creating a ready liquid market for the stock on either a regional or national market basis. This source of funds can be much like a mirage sitting out on the firm's horizon. It appears so good and can draw the entrepreneur toward it because it promises huge financial gain for the firm and personally for the owner as well. But as a mirage, it can also have a devastating effect on the entrepreneur's values and decision making, and adversely alter the course of the new venture's direction.

Many entrepreneurial firms experience both internal and external pressures to make an IPO, believing that an IPO sends the industry very positive signals about the firm's future. But that qualitative recognition can never, by itself, provide the only rationale to go public. The IPO mirage effect is that the firm will no longer have any financial troubles once the stock is publicly traded and investors have poured in. But the entrepreneur must understand that the company will have to make a formal, written full disclosure of the firm's entire operating history in the prospectus to potential investors. The entrepreneur will also be accepting new voting owners to as much as forty, fifty, or even sixty percent of the company's common stock holdings. And the entrepreneur will now be required by securities regulations to make regular, periodic public disclosure of the venture's operations and financial performance. The primary ethical issue for the entrepreneur involves not only ultimate control of the firm's direction, but a competing focus away from the competitive product and service market toward the daily price fluctuations of the stock market. The decision to go public places the founder in a partnership position with outside investors who will challenge the entrepreneur's personal perspectives, market expectations, and the process of interpreting and representing insider information to outside stake holders.

## *Complications of Hyper-Growth*

The entrepreneur can also experience another round of financial ethical issues once the new venture has been successfully launched. If the company experiences fantastic increases in sales of three or four times the original market expectations, this is called *hyper-growth*. This generally occurs in the near-term period of the first twelve-to-eighteen months after the launch, and can decimate the firm as its internal capabilities experience a distorted amplification of immediate demand for the newly introduced product or service that completely eclipses the company's ability to keep up with production supply. It is characterized by exponentially expanding sales and market share penetration, but generally does not include increasing profitability. Rates of monthly increases in sales are usually double-digit and supply cannot keep pace with market demand. The firm experiences rising negative working capital cash flow because current production costs are payable now, but receipts from growing sales are due in future weeks and months. Production facilities approach capacity while marginal costs can increase dramatically due to asset inefficiencies of scale.

When *hyper-growth* first begins, the entrepreneur is often elated. Most observers would initially assume that this is a good thing and worthy of recognition for the managerial proficiency of the founder(s). A newly launched firm has been capitalized based on specific assessments about the ability to deliver a product or service to a developing market area. But if that market begins to expand at a pace far beyond the forecasted levels, the new venture will actually be placed in a very awkward financial, operational, and ethical position. There are two primary values-oriented complications of this hyper-growth. The first impacts the representation of the firm's true ability to fill these rapidly incoming new orders. The second deals with whether the entrepreneur is prepared to reevaluate, and then reestablish, completely new market expectations and parameters for continued firm growth. Both of these will be based solely on the individual perceptions and interpretations of the recently adjusted data. The entrepreneur could deem the increases nothing more than a short-term anomaly and choose to not make a major readjustment in the firm's assets and financial base, but run the risk of burying the company for good if the *hyper-growth* is sustained. The owner could also decide that this rapid increase in demand is a significant shift in the market's long-term trend and begin to accumulate additional assets and financial resources only to find that sales eventually slow down considerably and the company is left with higher overhead costs and excess inventory. So much of the continued health of the venture depends upon the entrepreneur's keen senses and accurate assessment of what is required in the market. These matters at the seed and launch stages have ethical concerns rooted in the nature of the values-oriented relationships between the entrepreneur and the two primary types of outside capital providers.

## The Difficulty of Equity Relationships

The entrepreneur has a significant values-based interaction with both the insider (employees, managers, partners) and outsider equity holders. This is described across three separate dimensions: *voice*, *time*, and *return*. The *voice* dimension deals with the managerial implications of the dialogue between the company's founder and the stake holders. The *time* aspect captures an implied level of commitment between the entrepreneur and the equity stake holders. And the *return* facet serves as the underlying rationale for the lines of communication with respect to the voice and the time areas. It works in this manner. Equity holders can be either silent partners, who have a vested stake in the firm's net worth but no participation in the decision making for the company's direction, or they be general partners (share holders) whose vested stake carries with it a vote in the policies and direction of the venture. The equity holder is generally positioned in the firm for the longer-term, wanting to take advantage of the open-ended opportunities to share proportionately in the profits of the venture, and the building of wealth (share value) over time, rather than accept immediate fixed installments in exchange for giving up an assignment stake in the actual financial results. The voice and time together determine the equity cost of capital, which is the required rate of return necessary to satisfy a shareholder for the risks associated with certain managerial input and a specific time horizon.

Figure 8.1 depicts the various relative positions of equity holders in the new venture. The entrepreneur's position (*E*) is somewhat fixed with respect to these three dimensions, with arguably the most significant voice in choosing the direction of the firm, a fundamental commitment to remain with the venture through favorable and unfavorable times, and a relatively high cost of capital to compensate for the risks of formulating and organizing the strategy for the new idea in the competitive market. Some of the leading insider managers (*M*) are positioned in near proximity to the entrepreneur. The limited partners (*LP*) and preferred stock holders (*P*) have different stakes in the firm based primarily on their own personal investment time horizons. Stockholders (*S*) have return expectations based largely on their time horizons and the degree to which they believe their voting stake can have a significant impact on managerial policies for the company's direction. Some are in nearly complete agreement with the entrepreneur's position and they offer little difficulty, but others may have a shorter-term agenda or different "outsider" perception of the impact of their voting rights and create opposition for the entrepreneur and other insider perspectives.

There exists a good deal of variance in the relative positions for every equity holder other than the founding entrepreneur due to the level of overall commitment they make with respect to their individual risk tolerances, personal agendas, and interpretation of the firm's

### Figure 8.1
### New Venture Equity Positions

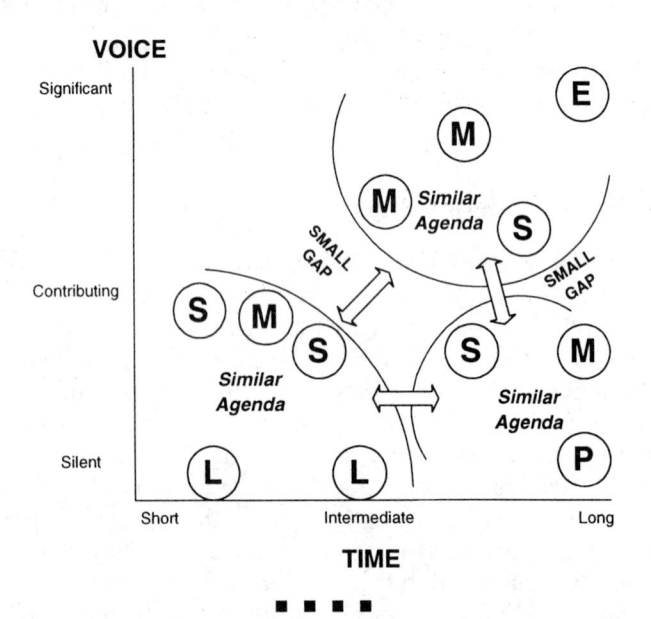

**VOICE**

(Y-axis: Significant, Contributing, Silent)
(X-axis: Short, Intermediate, Long)

**TIME**

expected future outcomes. Some tend to be closely related to the entrepreneur's subjective stake in the company, while others are less likely to line up in full agreement with all the ideas, vision, and direction that the entrepreneur supports. The placement in this context will have a direct bearing on the entrepreneur's ability to hold to certain values and make ethical decisions based upon personal views and interpretations of what is most important to the overall health of the firm. The difficulty will manifest itself in how shares are voted in major policy decisions, and how the entrepreneur and insider-managers assess and represent the company's performance among owners with other levels of commitment. These different individual positions for risk tolerance and expected return based on various configurations of *voice* and *time* parameters, are all products of personal, intuitive assumptions about what are the most significant factors that affect the firm's capabilities to effectively address demand in the competitive market. These in turn create unique views of what is considered an "adequate" rate of return as compensation for the equity position. When contrasting agendas meet head-on, the entrepreneur is placed in the difficult role of being a corporate politician that must have open ears to hear from the various stake holder contingents, and yet balance that with a personal sense of what is considered "right" and "best" for the business at that time. It can present some very difficult situations when equity holders appear to be similarly positioned to the entrepreneur, yet they have distinctly different opinions about what is most appropriate for the firm's direction, or they interpret the market opportunity in a more or less optimistic fashion. The entrepreneur is more likely to encounter subtle nuances and more subjective dialogue with equity holders versus debt holders.

## The Difficulty of Debt Relationships

The same basic premise exists for the entrepreneur's relationship with the various creditors of the new venture. Figure 8.2 shows how the entrepreneur has a much more "distanced" relationship with respect to the various creditors to the firm. The bond holders (B) may have included some protective provisions within the indenture agreement of the debt issue that allows them to have some minor voice in certain policy decisions that affect future debt levels or how loan installments are managed, but for the most part they have a very different agenda than the entrepreneur. Their view of the risk-return trade off is probably unique as well, in that they were willing to accept fixed periodic interest payments in exchange for relinquishing voting rights in the management of the venture. They could be in for the long-term or not, based on the perspective they have of how the company's debt fits into their overall portfolio investment horizon with other fixed income securities. Other creditors (C) like banks, finance companies, and factors may have minor influence in dealing with the entrepreneur on financing terms and use of funds, but again, like all debt holders, they have a unique perspective about market expectations, risk tolerance, and expected return. Dialogue with creditors may tend to be more forthright, with less disparity because of the discrete positions they occupy relative to the entrepreneur.

■ ■ ■ ■

Figure 8.2
New Venture Debt Positions

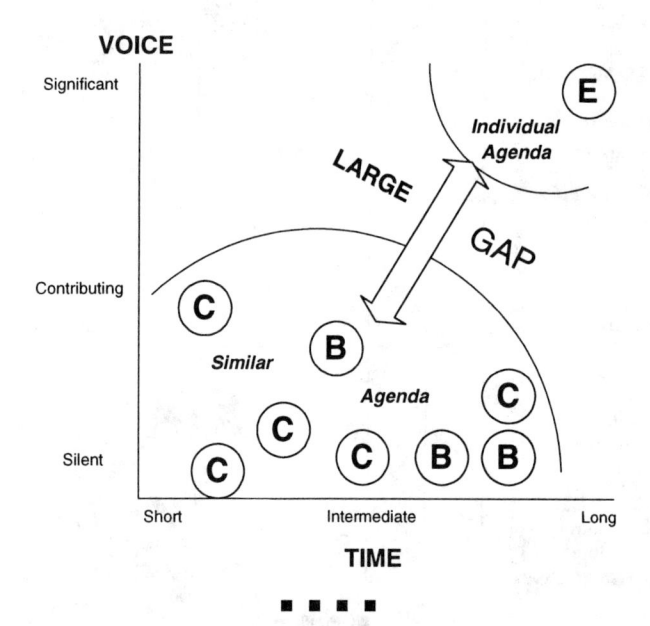

■ ■ ■ ■

## The Ethics Model and Financial Requirements

The entrepreneur's propensity to engage in questionable ethical activities related to financial requirements will be examined within the context of the entrepreneurial ethics model

138 ■ Chapter Eight

and the *EVI* matrix. The entrepreneur's moral rationale is coupled with six entrepreneurial characteristics to form core values which support certain types of ethical behavior across seven business functions. The entrepreneurial characteristics impact these actions within distinct *ethical domains* of new ventures. Figure 8.3 summarizes ethical "problem areas" from the EVI matrix associated with financial requirements.

■ ■ ■ ■

**Figure 8.3**
**Forecasted EVI Matrix: Financial Requirements**

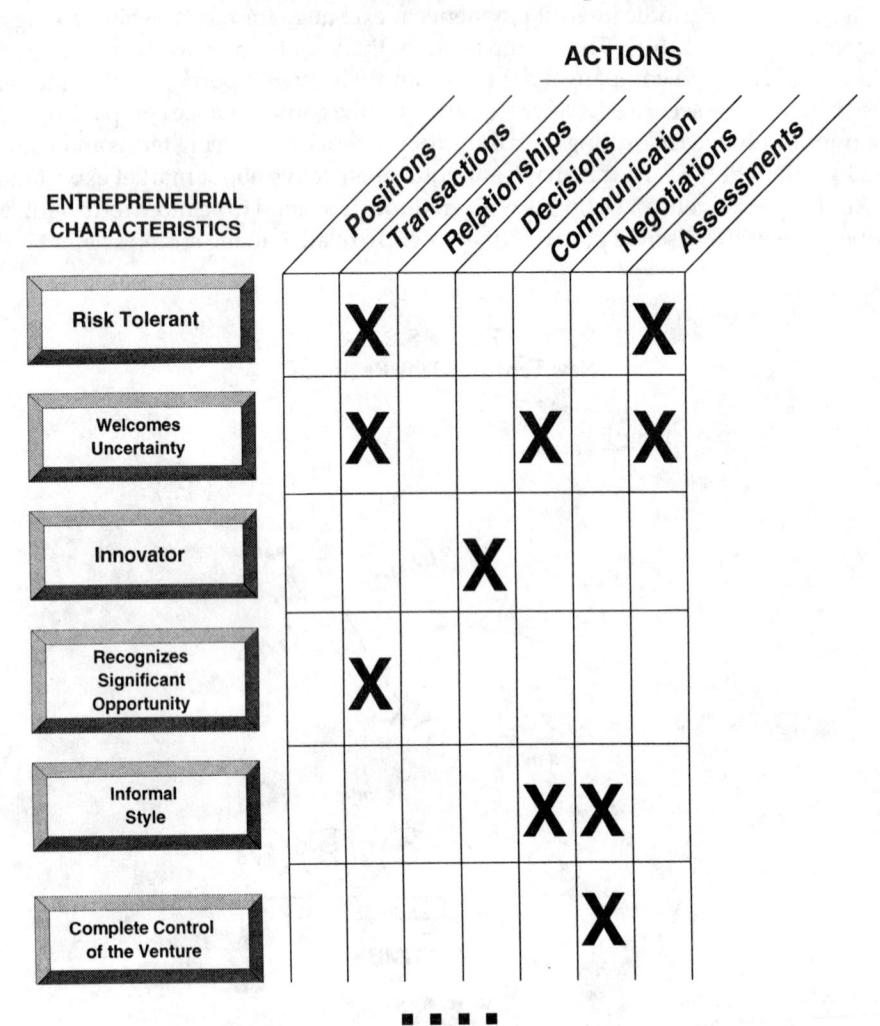

**ACTIONS**

| ENTREPRENEURIAL CHARACTERISTICS | Positions | Transactions | Relationships | Decisions | Communication | Negotiations | Assessments |
|---|---|---|---|---|---|---|---|
| Risk Tolerant | X | | | | | X | |
| Welcomes Uncertainty | X | | | X | | X | |
| Innovator | | | | X | | | |
| Recognizes Significant Opportunity | X | | | | | | |
| Informal Style | | | | | X | X | |
| Complete Control of the Venture | | | | | X | | |

■ ■ ■ ■

## Empirical Results

### Financial Projections

The entrepreneurs were asked about the relative degree of difficulty that was involved in developing expectations in the form of financial projections for the first two or three years of sales, cash flow, assets, and profit. Over two-thirds (68%) stated that it was either very difficult or almost impossible to forecast accurately due to the high degree of market uncertainty. The rest of the entrepreneurs (32%) said that financial projections were actually not difficult, or were somewhat easy, to forecast due to their personal knowledge and understanding of the market.

### Funding Requirements

The process of securing capital is very difficult in the pre-launch stage of the venture's life, and can be even more complex later on when the company is searching for second and third rounds of outside funding, or even contemplating an initial public offer of common stock. When the owners were asked about raising financial support for the venture, more than three out of four (79%) believe that it is best to secure funding in excess of the amount required based on their business planning. The others (21%) stated that it is best to secure the exact amount of funding required, no more and no less. This is interesting because it opens up the prospects that entrepreneurs do in fact have a good idea about how much funding they need to satisfy their capital requirements, yet they may want to provide a hedge to their risk exposure of possibly being caught short of funds at a later date, so they try and raise funds in excess of their targeted figure.

### Potential Investors

The prospects of securing outside capital providers as either debt or equity investors in the new venture are subject to numerous factors. But the most basic condition that defines this process is the meeting of the minds between the entrepreneur and the investor. About one in five (19%) owners stated that when speaking with potential investors about their providing funding for the enterprise, they would generally stay focused on only the positive aspects of the firm and its operations. The remaining four out of five entrepreneurs (81%) disagreed with that tactic, and said that they would present both the negative and positive aspects of the firm to potential investors. This has some overlap with the ethical issues surrounding firm representation. But it is interesting to note that the exclusion of negative information is recognized and well utilized in raising capital for small firms.

### Existing Investors

Having looked at the entrepreneur and the prospective capital provider, the owners were also asked about their financial dealings with the current investors in the venture. About one in eight (12%) said that it was "always" acceptable to not volunteer negative information about the company's financial performance to the outside investors. But the remaining owners did not all agree to that it was "never" acceptable to withhold negative information. Just over one-third (38%) agreed with this notion that they had an obligation to readily make available any negative news about the firm. But exactly half of the entrepreneurs (50%) were not strongly committed to making full disclosures regarding negative news, believing that it was "sometimes" acceptable to knowingly withhold negative news about financial performance from the investors. Many entrepreneurs believe in a *weathering capability* based on a "wait and see" approach to dealing with risk and the potential for financial difficulty. But owners cannot simply hope that, if given enough time, negative news will just blow over and give way to clear skies.

Many of the entrepreneurs seem comfortable leaving the responsibility for the flow of information in the lap of the investors. This seems to connote that they expect the investors to accept some of the obligation and initiative for obtaining financial news about the company. The entrepreneur is once again the main conduit through which the information will be released, but the type of information and how it is transferred, either by investor request or by managerial offer, are subject to the personal interpretations and perspectives of the individual owner. About one in five (19%) entrepreneurs felt that it is the responsibility of the investors to request pertinent information in order to ascertain the financial health of the firm, and another five percent (5%) said that it was a joint responsibility of both the investors and the owner to provide access to the pertinent financial information. But a very solid three quarters (76%) of the venture owners viewed this responsibility as theirs to offer pertinent information to the investors.

### *Accounting Data Integrity*

The overwhelming majority of the entrepreneurs (nearly 97%) believed that, when applying for a business loan, although it is very important to present the most positive financial picture of the company's assets, sales, profits, and capital position, they would never go so far as to knowingly alter accounting figures to have them better fit the loan request. This appears to be heartening at first glance, but there can still exist some potential for ethical compromise based on the entrepreneur's personal definition and interpretation of what exactly constitutes "altering" accounting figures. The most likely scenario involves the outright changing of financial figures to suit the loan provisions. But, accounting data could be purposefully consolidated in order to create a more general (less specific) overview of the firm's financial performance, where no data was actually changed or altered in the sense of using erroneous and fictitious numbers, but the "packaging" that took place was crafted to draw attention away from obvious problem areas and focus attention toward positive results. Of course, although it is a very small proportion, three percent (3%) of the entrepreneurs stated very openly that if the most positive image is necessary to secure business financing, then it was acceptable to alter some accounting figures.

## Conclusions

The entrepreneurs are obviously very concerned about the firm's financial performance, how the financial information is disseminated, who has control over the content of the release, and where the process of information transfer originates. Some might point to the strong showing with regards to whether firm owners would engage in the outright altering of accounting figures as a strong sign of highly ethical behavior. But the rest of the responses, taken in their entirety, illustrate that the entrepreneur is not always interested in offering financial information to the existing investors, and is apt to knowingly withhold negative financial news either all the time, or at least on an "as necessary" basis. And potential investors are also somewhat likely to hear only the good news about the firm's financial performance. These attitudes are indicative of a classic "don't ask, don't tell" policy for information release.

Chapter Twelve will examine the patterns of financial disclosure in the new venture across the various types of personal values characteristics displayed by the entrepreneurs. The individual ethical determinations are highly subject to the nature of the firm's particular situation, and the interaction of the entrepreneur's stance on firm representation and the formulation of future expectations. The financial situation of first attracting capital providers, and then keeping them happy in their investment positions, will challenge the owner's ability to remain clear and objective about the venture's assets, sales, profits, and capital positions. But if the new venture's performance begins to wane, the entrepreneur may begin to believe that everything can be solved simple by raising more capital. This *quantum effect* tends to reduce everything down to a financial issue, when in fact throwing more money at a poorly managed firm, with a marginally sound idea, in a fixed or shrinking market is not going to produce positive results. After all, the long term viability of the enterprise depends largely on the entrepreneur being able to present a sound financial picture of a rapidly growing company.

# CHAPTER NINE

# *Entrepreneurial Partnering*

## Introduction

Entrepreneurs typically formulate a network of personal and organizational contacts and referrals from which they draw advice, ideas, and counsel about company direction and other logistical applications for the enterprise. Their start-up ventures will generally make extensive use of a wide range of cooperative agreements with various suppliers, manufacturers, vendors, and distributors in order to take advantage of changing opportunities throughout the marketplace. These arrangements afford the entrepreneur greater flexibility in dealing with newly opened markets, and often are less expensive and less capital-intensive than traditional in-house operating strategies. However, these partnerships can create several difficult ethical situations for new ventures. Harvard Business School professor Michael Porter identified four forces that impact the new venture and contribute to the formulation of the company's competitive strategy, two of which, *bargaining power of new customers* and *bargaining power of suppliers*,[1] are directly related to the fourth ethical domain of entrepreneurial partnering. The new venture has set forth on what is essentially a very radical journey into the competitive market environment. Many aspects that mold and shape the firm's position come from within the internal organizational capabilities and structure of the enterprise. However, the company must also deal with outside parties, many of whom will not have a direct ownership or creditor stake in the firm's prospects, but rather a *procedural contribution* arrangement in either development, functional support, production processes, or the distribution flow of effectively bringing innovative ideas to the market.

There are now more than ever numerous ethical challenges to firms in the newly emerging era of extensive partnership arrangements as enterprise becomes more specialized and focused on primary competencies, rather than on a broad diversification of every aspect in the production and marketing channels.[2] Some of the newest moral and ethical controversies affecting firms come from the need to arrange a wide support framework of subcontracted suppliers, shippers, manufacturers, distributors, promoters, advertisers, and support functions within a corporate strategy that is increasingly specialized in one key area of the private enterprise process.³ The various arrangements that make these types of distinctive competencies and specific functional qualifications work are increasingly more and more subject to a wide range of value judgments on the part of the organizations that utilize them. The prospects for a partnership come hand-in-hand with the potential for initial and in-process disputes over the satisfaction of contractual terms and conditions, and the personal interpretation biases that guide deal structures.⁴ The entrepreneurial new venture will be faced with having to sort through differing opinions about status, implicit and explicit meanings and definitions, and various forms of pecuniary and non pecuniary consideration. Verbal agreements may turn into formal written contracts, but other deals may rest on oral representation, and the entrepreneur will be subject to an increased exposure to risk management, and opportunities for personal perspectives to determine the meanings and conditions of contractual fulfillment and the bases for forfeiture.

There will also be a subtle, but expressly required, pressure for the entrepreneur to own up to responsibilities and obligations outside the firm that may change over time with respect to the venture's strategy and market experiences. Nevertheless, the owner is still bound to abide by previously negotiated conditions and terms regardless of whether these provisions remain applicable to the current issues that constitute the immediate needs and expectations of the company. For instance, decisions to lay-off workers can be based on a recent downturn in the company's performance, but that may in fact contain various implied or detailed contractual representations made at a former time, but these are now deemed inconsequential in light of the firm's present predicament. Questions must address the scope and impact of lay-offs with the overall company strategy of the competitive market and the entrepreneur's personal benefits and gains.⁵ Or think about the numerous sweatshop scandals that utilize illegal immigrants, or children, for manufacturing and the impact it has on the entrepreneur's ability to provide a truthful representation of the venture's operations, and the ethical issues these raise over the moral basis and control of the enterprise.⁶ The owner-entrepreneur also faces increasing pressure to represent the firm within discussions of corporate policy, commitments, and longevity pertaining to the recent waves of organizational transformation and downsizing brought about by mergers, acquisitions, hostile takeovers, and company restructuring.⁷

Many companies often stand accused of being able to think only of the profit implications of partnership arrangements, and the effects on the senior managerial compensation packages that will occur if the firm does not trim operating budgets.⁸ Some would even argue that the most obvious ethical negotiation may actually be the entrepreneur's ability to keep promises made to customers.⁹ There are also potential ethical problems when former business partners each want to make use of jointly developed resources with different applications or different market strategies in competition with each other, and the original conditions and terms of written and oral agreements must be reviewed in order to establish clear rights of authority.¹⁰ Contract negotiations can also deal with the ethics of predatory pricing policies in a marketing agreement as a direct function of the entrepreneur's personal interpretation of what constitutes acceptable business practices and what does not.¹¹ The new venture CEO brings personal characteristics and values to the negotiation bases of all venture partnering deals, and this has a direct impact on the strategy process and, more importantly, the strategy content of contracts.¹² And the entrepreneur is often in a unique ethical position as the one individual who originates much of the contacts, referrals, and joint arrangements for the new venture during the seed and launch phases when most, if not all, of the company's performance bases are nothing more than market expectations, forecasts, potential plans, and contingencies.

## New Venture Partnering Focus

There are five different areas of focus for new ventures to partner with other individuals or organizations, and the type of emphasis will have an impact on both the nature of the ethical issues facing the entrepreneur, and the basis for the where certain value judgments are most likely to unfold. The research does not support the notion that the partnering focus is tied in any way to a particular stage of enterprise development. For instance, marketing arrangements are not more characteristic of the launch process than are production or financial deals. But the type of focus does open up unique matters of inherent values and enterprise perspective for the various parties that engage in deal-making with the entrepreneur. Table 9.1 presents the five distinct categories of venture focus for entrepreneurial partnering:

■ ■ ■ ■

**Table 9.1**
**The Focus of Entrepreneurial Partnering**

1. *Marketing/Promotions*
2. *Production/Manufacturing*
3. *Financial/Accounting*
4. *Personnel/Human Resources*
5. *Research/Development*

■ ■ ■ ■

The entrepreneur will be engaged in a cooperative effort in a single functional area that, in its partnership form, will not have the same degree of overlap with the normal comprehensive scope of internal operations due to the other firm's business presence and perceived stakes in the resulting benefits. There will be strict adherence to the observance of territorial lines of influence and jurisdiction. Although the two firms are "partners," that does not always connote the presence of a truly seamless operating strategy. Much of the procedural components of the deal may be carried out through somewhat formal and discrete channels in order for each partner to maintain a sense of individuality and identity, and to avoid all possible appearances of dependency on the contract specifications or the other firm.

Most contractual arrangements tend to be influenced by four separate factors that define the give-and-take dynamics of typical partnership deals. The first factor involves the way in which the firms share information, the second factor measures the degree to which the firms provide managerial support, the third factor addresses the various core physical infrastructures of the partners, and the fourth defines how funds are allocated for related capital expenditures. These four parameters provide a general means for defining the majority of ethical problem areas for new venture partnerships. Figure 9.1 provides a framework by which, before hand, the entrepreneur can assess and rank both the primary *(1)* and secondary *(2)* contractual implications for effects on personal perspectives, value judgments, and ethical decision priorities that might exist based on the focus of the partnership arrangement. The five directions of the partnering focus are on the horizontal axis, and the four influence factors are across the horizontal plane. *Information* deals with shared knowledge, ideas, or intelligence about external situations. *Managerial Support* involves top level executive decision input, strategy, and direction from the firm. *Infrastructure* includes fixed assets like physical plant, equipment, supplies, technical facilities, and communication links. *Funds allocation* covers financial resources to be allocated in support of the deal. Each cell is ranked as either a primary or secondary concern from the entrepreneur's perspective. The research basis for this matrix is to identify the two most pressing issues in each category of partnership type. These are the factors that have the greatest influence in the entrepreneur's decision process for partnerships and are therefore most likely to create exposure to ethical issues of disclosure and positioning in all phases of the process used to establish contractual partnership agreements.

For example, primary issues for a production deal (*infrastructure* and *funds allocation*) are somewhat different from marketing focus (*information* and *funds allocations*), but completely unique when compared to a personnel focus (*information* and *managerial support*). The entrepreneur's perception of the counter party's most important contribution to the partnership is critical in describing the values-oriented priorities and rationales that guide the negotiations and eventual workings of the agreement. But the entrepreneur is most likely to pay attention to just one or two areas perceived to be core factors and leave the other two out of the formative stages of discussions. The primary areas (*1*) vary based upon the entrepreneur's

■ ■ ■ ■

**Figure 9.1**
**Partnership Focus and Influence**

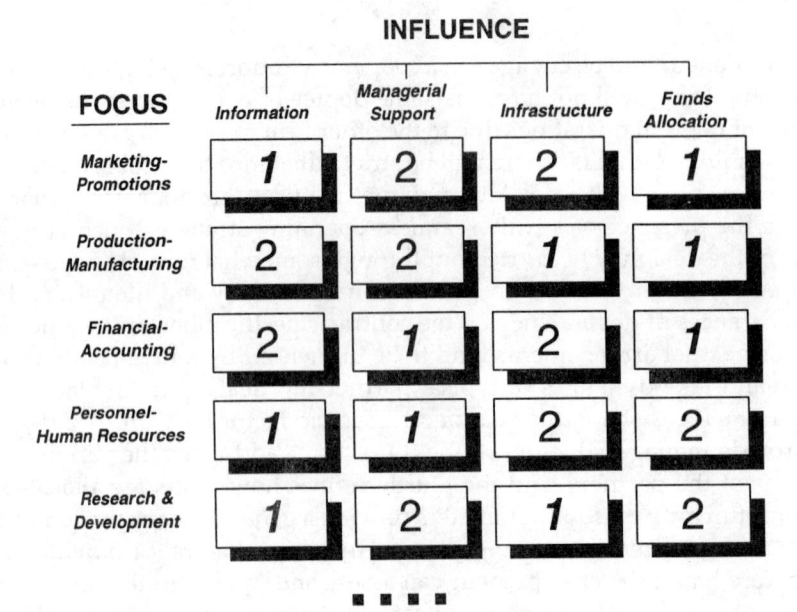

| FOCUS | Information | Managerial Support | Infrastructure | Funds Allocation |
|---|---|---|---|---|
| Marketing-Promotions | 1 | 2 | 2 | 1 |
| Production-Manufacturing | 2 | 2 | 1 | 1 |
| Financial-Accounting | 2 | 1 | 2 | 1 |
| Personnel-Human Resources | 1 | 1 | 2 | 2 |
| Research & Development | 1 | 2 | 1 | 2 |

INFLUENCE

■ ■ ■ ■

interpretation of the core focus. In each of the first three focus areas, *funds allocation* is a big concern to the entrepreneur's partnership arrangement. But it is joined by a separate factor of influence in all three cases. In the last two areas, *funds* are secondary and *information* is primary. This matrix can provide the entrepreneur with an *ex ante* planning tool from which to locate qualitative and quantitative influences that dominate the partnership plan, and open up a clear delineation of the cells most likely to create ethical concerns.

## Concerns about Arrangements

The entrepreneur can enter into five types of partnership arrangements. These structures have some common areas of objectively defined positioning for the new venture and the outside party. But, more importantly, they have other components that create subjective differences between the underlying rationales for pursuing the arrangement, and can contribute to subtle shifts in the factors that most influence the partnership contract terms. They also help to raise the awareness of agreement inputs, as well as the range of output expectations that affect each party's positioning throughout the term of the relationship. Table 9.2 lists these five categories of partnership types.

■ ■ ■ ■

### Table 9.2
### Partnership Types

1. *Joint Venture*
2. *Strategic Alliance*
3. *Consortium*
4. *Supplier Accord*
5. *Distributor Accord*

■ ■ ■ ■

Granted, fundamentally these are all partnerships. But they also have unique components directly linked to the subjective aspects of perceived outcomes, mutual benefits, and underlying basis or rationale. They are all subject to the inherent difficulty that partners may ultimately want to obtain an advantageous position relative to the other party. Although the deal is supposed to benefit both firms, there is always a tendency to want to gain a slightly improved benefit-to-cost (BC) ratio. Initially, there may be a *seniority position* (relatively stronger negotiating stance coming into the deal) and a *minority position* (relatively weaker stance at the outset). The entrepreneur is often placed in the minority negotiating role perhaps due to the shorter track record of the company, a more limited asset base, a less experienced work force, and fewer financial resources. The entrepreneur will want to coordinate the perceived outcomes, mutual benefits, and underlying basis or rationale into a certain configuration called *tactical positioning*, which describes the goal of achieving the most favored stance or location that each counter party desires to attain relative to the outside partners in the agreement's terms and conditions. The entrepreneur targets one or two different positions that are each similarly acceptable with respect to the goals and objectives of the partnership as individually interpreted and determined by using the enterprise focus and influence parameters previously reviewed (see Figure 9.1). Prior to starting the contractual process, the entrepreneur determines what issues are open to discussion and what issues are not, based on the primary and secondary labels given to the factors of influence. Subjective value assessments are then made regarding the costs and benefits for each primary and secondary issue and the specific terms that would accompany each item during the entire partnership process. The entrepreneur establishes personal judgments on the worth of each potential contractual area and the process of negotiation gets under way. The entrepreneur eventually hopes to successfully manipulate a final consent that gives up less than what is obtained to create a net gain position.

These general rules of positioning form the critical subjective decisions and analysis of the partnering structure, so they present the most obvious impact to the entrepreneur's ethical considerations. There are clearly identifiable differences between the five entrepreneurial partnering types however. The form of *tactical positioning* employed will be, to some extent, a function of the entrepreneur's moral rationale and core values, as well as the type of partnership pursued. The following sections overview these different partnership arrangements, first from their structural tenets, and second from their potential ethical implications.

## *Joint Venture*

The entrepreneurial new venture can enter into an agreement to pursue a specific business project together with one other firm (or several firms). If this deal is tied solely to this one project, and describes how each company will have jurisdiction to handle certain aspects based on the agreed upon functional capabilities that each recognizes in the other, then this constitutes general joint venture. The structure of the joint venture is based on a formal demarcation of decision making authority and responsibility for specifically designated components of the functional operations necessary to accomplish a certain project within a required time period to meet a target completion date. The key issue is the structure. There is now a new entity formed between the two firms that is a deliberate composite of two sets of resources designated for the very purpose of starting a new third venture. There are many forms of subjective interpretations between the two companies in the agreement, as well as an underlying dependence on each other. The joint venture will not be successful based only on the achievements of one firm. For example, two auto makers can enter into a joint venture to produce a new sport truck. The final product will be comprised of technologies and features from both firms, and the new sport truck cannot be introduced into the market unless both firms each meet their deadlines, and hold up their own end of the deal. If one company falls behind schedule, or is unable to deliver a certain component, the entire venture is placed in jeopardy.

The primary ethical considerations rest in how well the firms were able to successfully define each company's span of control and areas of expertise. If their are too many implied responsibilities, the venture will have difficulty in trying to decide these once the venture is in full operation. Also, the term "joint" connotes a sense of equal inputs into the venture. However, the entrepreneur may have a sense that the small firm is providing tangible resources like facilities, personnel, or capital funds, while the other company is "only" providing intangible items like technical, managerial, or marketing expertise. It is crucial that the firms each agree in advance that there is equal *value* placed on their respective contributions to the venture. But again, this value is subject to the personal moral rationales and qualitative biases of interpretation and perspective of the individuals who pull the deal together. Agreement in these areas can be difficult to achieve, and there is always the risk that one party may feel that the final offering of the venture may be perceived by the market as reflecting one firm more than the other.

## *Strategic Alliance*

If the entrepreneurial firm makes an agreement to share information, or swap personnel, or support another company's complementary products and services in the same market, and this will be an on-going relationship, the companies have entered into a strategic alliance. The defining component is in the structure. The entrepreneur's enterprise will remain distinct and separate from the corporate ally in all aspects of decision making responsibility and authority for functional areas of operations (as will the other company). This structural separation effect means that the entrepreneur will probably not have the same direct access to the other firm's resources as would be the case in a distinct joint venture. Because of this clear boundary between separate operations, and because there is not third entity comprised of the two, there are far more opportunities for the entrepreneur and the other firm's senior management to engage in subjective interpretations of whether there is truly any measurable gain to be realized in this cooperation between the firms. For example, the entrepreneurial venture could add certain features to its product that make it entirely compatible with the larger company's leading product in the market. The big company will allow the entrepreneur to show the two products together in its advertisements, and list the large firm's name in its promotional specifications. The alliance is supposed to let the entrepreneur piggyback on the main product in the market, while the large firm has access to the entrepreneur's customer listings to generate prospects for product upgrades and a wide range of technical services. A very good chance exists that the entrepreneur may "feel" that sales are not actually growing as anticipated, but the large firm is securing major new accounts through the small firm's customer database of referral business. Or, the entrepreneur may be hard pressed to convince the larger firm that the customer referral business is commensurate with the new venture's sales growth due to the compatibility effort. The entrepreneur could even begin to believe that sales might actually be doing very well without the alliance to the market leader, and that in fact, the partnership arrangement might be limiting its scope of applications due to an increasing market interpretation that its products are not designed for a wide range of alternative models made by other firms. The on-going nature of the strategic alliance can also produce a difficult ethical decision for how to best terminate the arrangement based on the subjective, personal interpretations of the entrepreneur.

## *Consortium*

The entrepreneur can also enter into an agreement to share information, technical and managerial expertise, or research and development designs with one or more companies, but this arrangement will not create a new entity (like the joint venture), and will not involve complementary applications of final product or service support in the same market. Although structured to insure a clear separation of the two companies (like an alliance), the emphasis is generally placed on functional areas prior to the end market, in matters of research and development, production and manufacturing, or technology designs. The consortium members recognize that they should all continue to pursue their own agendas in these areas, but that a formal agreement is necessary to share pertinent information or expertise in functions that will have tremendous benefits for everyone involved. For example, the entrepreneur might join a consortium in order to insure that as the emerging market for this new innovation progresses and matures, the final version of the product will incorporate the contributions of the consortium in a style that insures greater standardization and compatibility, and complementarity between the different firms.

The fundamental subjective moral basis that supports the consortium is an eye toward a true "win-win" situation for all firms involved. The rationale is first that there are negative effects if all the competing firms work concurrently on identical ideas, process, or technologies. And second, that no one wins if everyone comes to the market with several unique versions of virtually the same concept. The market expectations must be such that there will be sufficient volume and share to support all the firms, and that a more standardized and complementary market has a better chance of sustaining growth over the long term. The greatest ethical concern lies in the subjective interpretation of what the final market will really look like. Concerns will be raised over who might end up better positioned in the long run. Also, the entrepreneur will experience a tendency to want to leave the consortium behind and develop the idea or process alone and perhaps capture the entire new market for the new venture. But that will be balanced by the rationale that if that optimistic scenario does not happen as hoped, and if the other consortium firms arrive to the market first with a process, product, or technology that is not complementary with the new venture, the entrepreneur will be on the outside looking in, excluded from the potential market. The key issue is tied to the interpretation of what constitutes proprietary information, and the perceived value in one firm's individual knowledge with respect to the other companies in the industry.

Of course, as with the alliance, another difficult ethical problem will be how and when the entrepreneur determines it is best to terminate participation in the consortium. There are many implied issues of confidentiality, as well as reciprocity that must be dealt with. For example, the entrepreneur may try to raid specific information from the consortium and then make a quick exit, believing that this is the missing piece to the puzzle that unlocks the market's true potential. But it can also happen in reverse to the entrepreneur's firm, when others have their sights set on the new venture's core competencies. The decision on the timing of an exit also carries ethical questions about the value of inputs versus outcomes during membership, and whether there are any areas still left to share based on research or technology momentum that will carry past the "official" date of exit.

### *Supplier Accord*

Many entrepreneurial new ventures will establish partnership agreements with materials and parts suppliers on the back side of the marketing channel. These can range from formal, closed-ended deals that are then renegotiated, to informal, open-ended arrangements that are periodically updated based on the entrepreneur's, or the supplier's, perception that the terms have begun to shift benefits in a manner that is no longer considered equal for both partners. There is no new entity created, and the firms stay completely separate in functional operations. Even pertinent information about the product, services, technology, or processes does not have to be shared. The relationship is often built more out of convenience, rather than some underlying moral rationale or personal connection between the entrepreneur and the supplier. This is also the basis for the ethical problems that can arise. The entrepreneur and the supplier can treat each other as relatively expendable, and easily substituted in the case that situations change in the future market. The entrepreneur needs these supply resources, and the supplier needs to move product, so they may enter into the agreement based on convenience and functional utility, rather than a qualitative relationship.

## *Distributor Accord*

The same can be said for the entrepreneur's partnerships with various distributors on the front side of the market channel. The new venture wants to find reliable outlets to move its products and services, and an agreement based on convenience may be formed with one or more distribution centers on the wholesale or retail level. Ethical concerns here are similar to supplier accords. There may exist a lack of qualitative rationale to the deal, and there may not really be anything more than a professional relationship based solely on proximity, price, costs, or financial terms. The entrepreneur is viewed as a distributor by suppliers, and as a supplier to other distributors, so the positioning in the market channel is not the factor worth noting here. The ethics of doing business with another party touch on matters of *how* to deal with problems or concerns that arise, *who* takes responsibility for these, and *why* there should be a defined basis for the arrangement and its continuance. The entrepreneur is either faced with having to try and make a qualitative, moral basis for the partnership, or tighten and formalize a very loosely defined arrangement that lacks adequate clarification and objectivity.

## Problems in the Partnering Process

The entrepreneurial partnering process is comprised of five sequential stages that are involved in every business deal that the new venture enters. At each level of dialogue and relationship, the entrepreneur is presented with unique situations that will challenge personal values, motivation, moral judgments, and expected outcomes. These five stages also address the degree of formality with which the entrepreneur engages in communicating and defining the new venture's *tactical positioning* for the relative trade-offs between perceived costs and expected benefits. Figure 9.2 summarizes the five basic stages of the partnering process: the *approach* of the two parties, the *assessment* of the benefits and costs, the *negotiation* of the terms and conditions, the *closing* of a contractual agreement, and the *maintenance* of the on-going arrangement by the partners. Each of these stages presents unique ethical considerations for the entrepreneur due to way they impact the eventual new venture positioning in the market.

Starting at the bottom of the diagram, the entrepreneur either approaches or is approached by an outside firm and opens up discussions about a potential deal. Both parties assess the relative prospects of the proposed partnership, and the approaching party tenders an initial offer of terms, called the bid. The most important aspect of the process involves the content, accessibility, and perceived value of the *information* directly pertaining to the benefits and costs involved for each party. Negotiations ensue and move toward possibly closing a deal. During this segment, two very interesting phenomena are present: the *manipulation enigma* and the *jockeying principle* (each of which will be discussed in detail in the next sections). The factors surrounding information, and the level of manipulation and jockeying, together define the negotiation process and the eventual close of the agreement. The maintenance of the partnership is a joint responsibility and presents the difficult ethical issues of

**Figure 9.2**
**The Partnership Process**

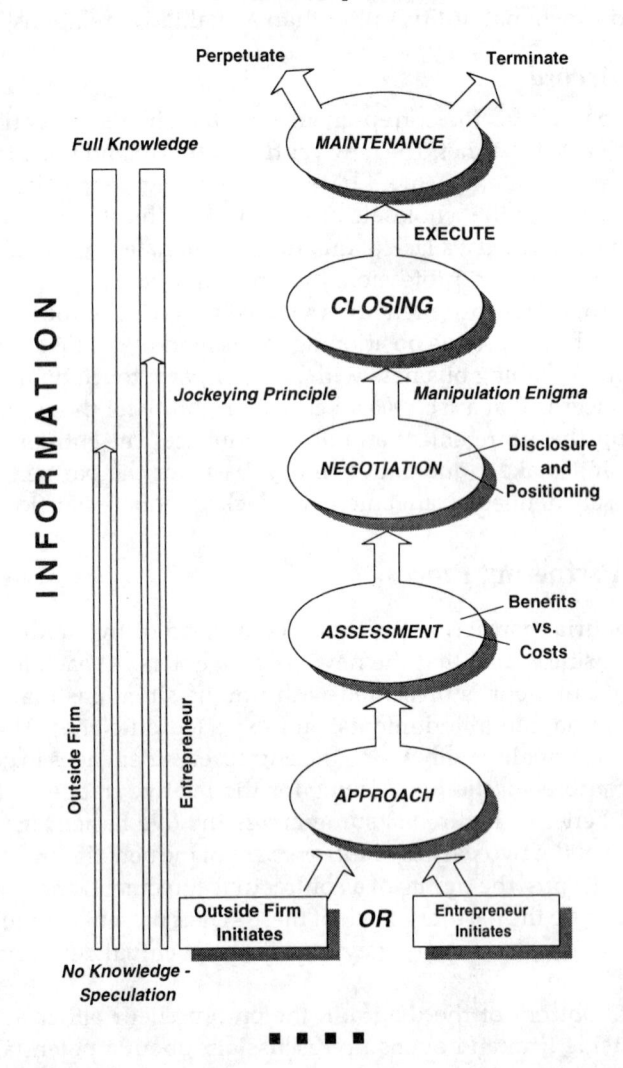

first executing the terms of the partnership, and then later on, either perpetuating or terminating the deal. The entrepreneur and the outside firm will each possess some degree of basis information that defines the initial approach and the opening of dialogue. As the assessment begins, the information levels will rise as the two parties begin to analyze each other's perceived positions with respect to the potential benefits and costs. The two information channels that measure the level of knowledge at each successive stage will either run somewhat equal to each other, or one party may lag behind the other with the potential of creating a relative advantage for the more informed. These levels may adjust back and forth as the deal aims toward closure. It is at the critical third stage of negotiation that the two issues of manipulation and jockeying are most prominent. If the information conduits and infrastructure are efficient, then the two parties should have essentially the same knowledge of the proposed deal and its tenets. However, should an inefficiency exist, one party could hold a distinct advantage in directing the course of perceived benefits and costs, and the final terms of the agreement. Because both the entrepreneur and the outside party understand the *value* of information, there will be significant ethical concerns about representation, expectations, and anticipated financial requirements related to the deal.

## The Manipulation Enigma

The entrepreneur engaged in the partnering process must clear several subjective and interpretive hurdles that impact ethics and personal values, as well as the final positioning of the partners and the ability to make future adjustments to the agreement. The firms will normally be placed in initial *minority* and *seniority* positions based on the origin of the approach. If the entrepreneur initiates, then the outside firm listens to the approach and may accept the first proposal. But the greatest "need" rests at this time with the new venture, which seemingly places the outside firm in the seniority position. But the trick at this stage of the process is that the most crucial information probably rests with the entrepreneur who made the approach. It is crucial to understand that although the outside firm did not have any apparent need of the new venture prior to the approach, the entrepreneur is in a position to "package" the offer in a way that could suggest a tremendous value to the outside firm, and this does not mean that it is deceptive. It could be completely true. But if the information were not entirely beneficial to the outside firm, the entrepreneur can experience a temptation to amplify or *tout* the initial offer as a means of attracting the outside firm's attention to some potential rewards. Once the entrepreneur represents the initial level of information, the progressive negotiation strategy is often aimed at reversing the original positioning, and gaining the seniority stance based on possessing superior knowledge value versus the outside firm. The burden of proof rests with the entrepreneur at this first half of the manipulation enigma.

The other side of the manipulation enigma involves the period of time immediately after the outside party has received the entrepreneur's offer. The outside firm wishes to maintain the seniority position and must decide what level of credibility to assign to the offer, and what type of reaction to display upon receiving the partnership proposal. The outside firm must make a decision regarding the veracity of the entrepreneur's offer and determine if the conditions and terms as presented do in fact create enough curiosity in the benefits and costs to justify serious dialogue. The outside party can either respond to the initial offer with interest, or dismiss the approach outright. But the implied rules of negotiation assume that the first offer is generally quite lower than the final position the offerer is ultimately willing to accept. So now the honesty of the outside firm's response must be evaluated by the entrepreneur. If the outside party truly believes that there is significant value in the initial offer, there is a temptation to respond in a manner that appears relatively unimpressed with the proposed partnership benefits, in order to try and maintain the seniority position. The outside firm does not wish to find itself in the minority position of "needing" the entrepreneur's offer (even though that may be the case). But remembering Chapter Five, the outside firm could also move the discussions toward a realistic agreement based on partial representation, or a complete misrepresentation by the entrepreneur. This dynamic can continue back-and-forth for several volleys, and at each round the receiving party must decide on the true *value* of the information presented and herein lies the heart of the *manipulation enigma*. The entrepreneur could use truthful representation to attract a seniority partner, but be misinterpreted due to skepticism, and be dismissed. On the other hand, the firm owner could make a less than truthful representation and gain a preliminary position of advantage, only to be unable to deliver the results at the first reckoning. Each partnership process exposes the entrepreneur to this spectacle, and the perceived value of information appears to be a most important factor in how the entrepreneur deals with this.

## The Jockeying Principle

Another phenomenon can occur at the negotiation stage of the partnership process. The entrepreneur can either make an approach, or be approached, but also concurrently seek other possible outside parties as insurance against either being dismissed by the approached firm, or showing no interest in an initial bid proposal received from another firm. The core value involved in this tactic is one of "covering all the bases" by establishing various layers of contingency plans in an overall design to diversify the risks of rejection. The ethical problem is created either when the entrepreneur approaches more than one outside firm at a time, or when the new venture receives an offer and believes it is the only firm being approached, when in fact it is one of several companies approached. In both of these cases, an ethical problem is apparent, because the possibility exists that at some point in the purposed partnership process, more than one firm could accept the offer and there would then be a direct conflict between two competing firms for one partnership opening. The attempt to keep two or more offers alive at the same time, without letting the other firm(s) know about the ploy is called the *jockeying principle*, because the company that made the offer will have to constantly keep moving between negotiations to balance the probabilities of acceptance by each firm relative to the other firm(s) in a manner that brings into question the issues of representation and future expectations. This is generally due to the likelihood of having to make conspicuous portrayals based upon varying forecasts, each customized for the unique areas of interest and motivating factors of the different firms approached.

The jockeying principle also creates ethical problems related to both the seniority and minority positions in the *negotiation, closing,* and *maintenance* stages of the partnership process. It is primarily tied to the period of time where negotiations move toward a closed deal. The entrepreneur wishes to hedge the possibility that a final deal will not work out with the firm that was first approached. The temptation is to contact other companies and make the same representation about the potential partnership, but without alerting different outside firms that there are other negotiations happening concurrently. This creates an ethical showdown as the entrepreneur balances two or more parallel rounds of negotiating, all of which could turn into a completed agreement at any time. The biggest problem is not even so much the process of maintaining concurrent negotiations, but the tactics used to close a deal with just one outside firm at a point where perhaps two or three firms are all poised to enter into a partnership agreement. The level of disclosure during the approach and assessment phases lays the groundwork for this questionable activity. Now, there is nothing wrong with initially sending out opening approaches to a series of potential partners, and then waiting to hear back from any that are interested in opening formal negotiations and pursuing a deal. If each firm clearly understands that the entrepreneur is actively soliciting many companies to determine the level of interest in the market, then they all have the same information as the new venture insiders and there is no question of the genuineness of the approach representation. But the pressure to keep all the options open could cause the entrepreneur to conceal the scope of this multiple approach tactic that has turned into parallel negotiations and misrepresentation. Questions also arise regarding the degree of commitment that is associated with an oral approach and assessment combined with a parallel negotiation tactic. The entrepreneur could casually approach several firms and maintain a somewhat informal contact process while assessing all the alternatives. Some outside firms could construe certain discussions within the approach as serious moves toward closing a good-faith partnership agreement, when in reality the entrepreneur's perspective is that nothing is substantively communicated or agreed to until a formal written contract is signed. Again, the ethical situation is a function of personal moral bases, individual value judgments about right and wrong, and subjective interpretations about what constitutes acceptable or inappropriate behavior.

## Commitments from Compromise

The entire partnership process is in reality a perplexing configuration of positioning based on individual perceptions. And the negotiation sequence of the entrepreneur making a bid value, the outside firm countering with an asking value, then the continued volley of resubmitting bid and ask values until a common ground is established is founded entirely on the need for each party to recognize and adopt various tactics of compromise. This will determined the regularity and content adjustments during each round of the exchanges between the offering firm and the approached firm. But this is all supposed to ultimately result in a partnership agreement. Once finalized, the necessity to effectively utilize continued compromise is greatly diminished, if not abandoned altogether. It seems very ironic that what will ultimately be a deal that involves mutual benefits, common goals, and a unified objective starts out on the one hand as a competitive process of positioning with tactics aimed at protecting proprietary information, while on the other hand offering various forms of pecuniary and non pecuniary remuneration to serve as incentives for reaching an agreement. And the final terms and conditions are very rarely "ideal." Instead, a settlement is just that—a position that the entrepreneur *settles* for after weighing all the benefits and costs of securing the deal, after which the two firms put aside their singular agendas and agree to work together and support each other in a common cause and agenda.

## The Ethics Model and Partnering

The entrepreneur is again faced with the opportunity to possibly engage in dubious ethical behavior related to actions involved in business partnering. The values associated with these deals will be examined within the context of the entrepreneurial ethics model and the *EVI* matrix. The entrepreneur's moral rationale for pursuing joint ventures, strategic alliances, and consortia is an expression of many entrepreneurial characteristics and ethics. Together, these form core business values which support unique ethical behavior across seven functions within the venture. These characteristics impact the entrepreneur's perspective and approach to these actions within the *ethical domain* of partnering. Figure 9.3 outlines the proposed "problem areas" associated with entrepreneurial partnership arrangements.

## Empirical Results

### *Use of Partnerships*

The seminal literature in the field and a good deal of contemporary empirical research has found that entrepreneurs tend to make extensive use of networks, contact referrals, and a wide range of business partnerships in coordinating the many functional areas of the new venture. The owners in the survey group were first asked about their firm's use of partnership deals such as joint ventures, cooperatives, and different forms of alliances. It was very interesting to find that for these fast-growth new ventures, only about three out of every five owners (59%) stated that they make extensive use of these arrangements. The remaining entrepreneurs responded that they make "little or no use" of business partnerships in their firm. They obviously work with traditional market channel arrangements, but forty percent of the companies are likely to not utilize formal contractual deals in joint ventures, consortia, or alliances.

### *Positioning Tactics*

The process of discussing partnership alternatives and negotiating a final deal offers many intriguing dynamics that touch in some ways on prior issues of representation and expectations. Most business deals are the culmination of a lengthy procedure involving offers and counter offers back and forth for several volleys until an acceptable point of compromise is attained for each party. The entrepreneurs were asked whether it is a perfectly acceptable partnership tactic to enter into negotiations with an initial offer that is far in excess of their expectations and goals in order to provide a means of eventually settling at an acceptable position. About one third of the owners (31%) agreed with this tactic, but an almost equal number (29%) disagreed with this approach to the partnership negotiation process. The largest group (40%) were not sure and felt that it would depend on the unique circumstances of the proposed deal as to whether to use this tactic or not.

Once the negotiation tactic is chosen, the issues of compromise and what ground to settle for must be decided. The entrepreneurs were asked whether a joint venture, partnership, professional consortium, or business alliance should be structured in a manner that provides the maximum value to their firm when compared with the value to the other parties involved. It was very interesting to see that roughly six out of ten entrepreneurs (59%) disagreed with this concept, and only about one in every eight (12%) agreed with this basic approach to settlement compromise. But well over a quarter of the respondents (28%) stated that they were not sure about this strategy and felt that the approach needs to be based on a personal interpretation of the unique circumstances inherent in the proposed deal, and the two parties' positions with respect to the costs and benefits.

### *Oral Agreements*

There are certainly many types of situations that could be proposed to the entrepreneurs involving ethical issues related to the process and content of oral arrangements made between two companies. The scenario that was chosen for this item asked the owners wheth-

## Figure 9.3
### Forecasted EVI Matrix: Entrepreneurial Partnering

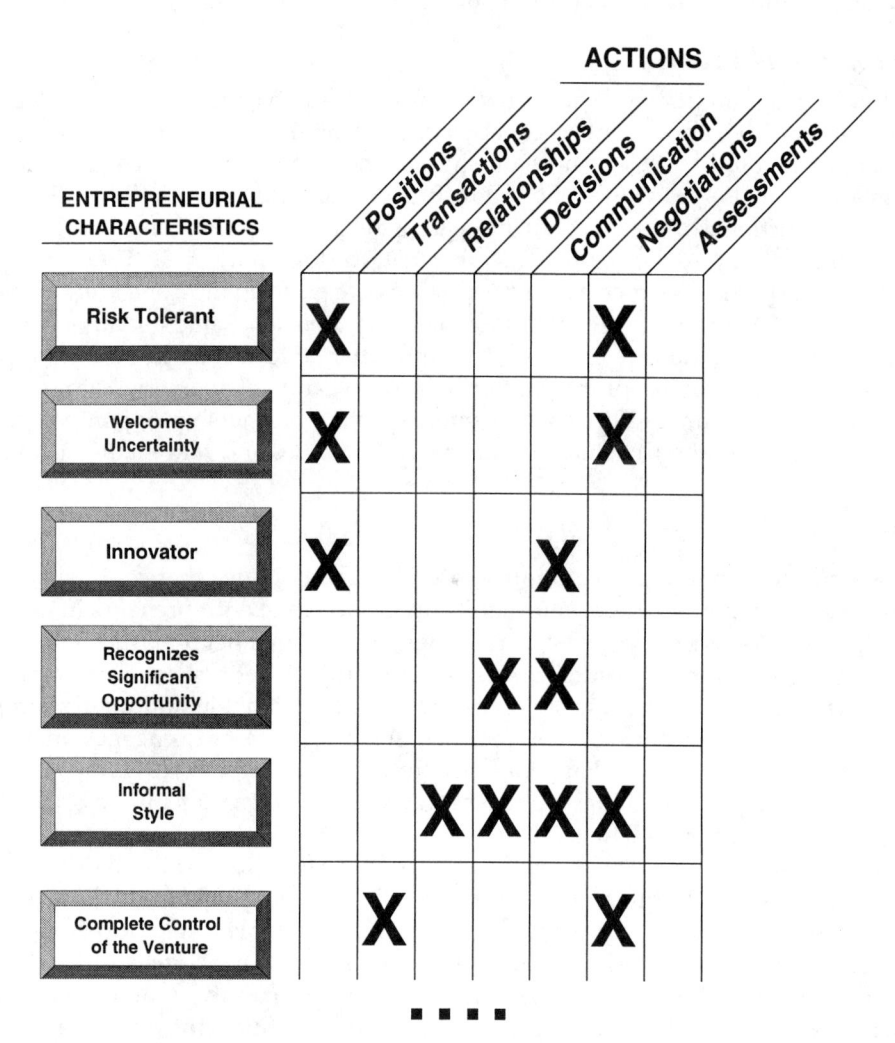

**ACTIONS**: Positions, Transactions, Relationships, Decisions, Communication, Negotiations, Assessments

| ENTREPRENEURIAL CHARACTERISTICS | Positions | Transactions | Relationships | Decisions | Communication | Negotiations | Assessments |
|---|---|---|---|---|---|---|---|
| Risk Tolerant | X | | | | X | | |
| Welcomes Uncertainty | X | | | | X | | |
| Innovator | X | | | X | | | |
| Recognizes Significant Opportunity | | | X | X | | | |
| Informal Style | | X | X | X | X | | |
| Complete Control of the Venture | X | | | | X | | |

er they viewed an oral arrangement made during the negotiation process as final and binding, or merely a segment of the normal give and take from which they could walk away or proceed further. Two thirds (66%) of the entrepreneurs stated that if they had recently made an oral agreement to enter into a joint venture or business partnership with one firm, and then a significantly better deal came along with another company, they would accept the original arrangement with the first firm. But surprisingly, one third (33%) of the owners would try to get the first firm to back out so they could pursue a new deal with the second firm. The remaining one percent said it would depend on the nature of the situation as to whether they would honor the oral agreement or not. There is always the possibility that any oral arrangement could invite problems dealing with both *explicit forfeiture* and *implicit forfeiture* issues. These involve various forms of expectations that are not fulfilled, even though one party considers the deal finished. Clarity on the front end of the negotiation process is the best way to avoid hassles and disappointments later on.

## *Partners and Values*

Entrepreneurs can pursue deals in several ways. It can be strictly a "functional fit" between two firms with complementary capabilities, such as an agribusiness with a food packaging plant, or it could be based more on sharing the same subjective conditions such as mutual interests, goals, and values about how business should be carried out. There would obviously be a functional connection, but the heart of the deal might be common moral ground. But entrepreneurs may use *suggestive interpretation*, to downplay their firms' strengths in order to lower the partner's expectations for new venture performance; or *touting*, and embellish their capabilities to secure a contract; or *voluntary omission* while initially representing the venture's resources and capabilities. These and other styles of *tactical positioning* involve questionable ethical behavior for the partnering process, and yet an overwhelming majority (92%) of the entrepreneurs said that when entering into a partnership or joint venture, it is important that they other party share in their personal values and sense of business ethics.

## Conclusions

New venture partnering is certainly exposed to many issues that could create ethical concerns for entrepreneurs. There were significant numbers of entrepreneurs in most of the partnership survey areas that opted in a very straightforward manner for tactics and approaches to the deals that call into question the issues of mutual benefit, shared information, and honoring certain personal positions. Perhaps the most questionable underlying component related to new venture partnering involves the tendency for owners to engage in many forms of *entrepreneurial fraternizing*. This happens when the entrepreneur seeks to establish numerous business contacts and professional references into either a formal or informal network for securing advice, favors, and all manners of assistance for the venture. It can happen through memberships in social organizations, civic groups, and affiliations with other local and regional business owners. But the motivation and rationale for many, if not all, of these contacts is *opportunism*, in order to get help for the firm and be able to tap into a pool of individual and corporate counsel. The entrepreneur is not so much concerned with maintaining solid business relationships as much as staying in close proximity to numerous resources with the potential to assist the new venture in the future with financing, production logistics, or technical support. Entrepreneurial partnering can be tied to the owner's need to feel "connected" to solid companies that might serve the interests of the new enterprise, creating a *reciprocity illusion*, whereby they garner significant benefits from other firms while providing an appearance of (but no substantive) consideration in return.

# CHAPTER TEN

# *Entrepreneurial Firm Culture*

## Introduction

New ventures can display a wide range of organizational environments and numerous types of atmospheres for nurturing challenges to ethical managerial decision making. This corporate firm culture plays a huge role in the defining of personal and business-level reputation in the market. Even companies that do not intentionally formulate and support a target firm culture will have, by default, a certain style based simply on the way in which the entity functions in both operational and managerial policies and procedures. But the biggest issue, and most pertinent to this book, deals with whether the start-up company is a direct representation and function of the entrepreneur's personal values, moral judgments, and ethical management style or more of an aggregate blending of the numerous individual techniques and approaches of all the firm's employees. If there are measurable similarities, the next issue deals with determining to what degree are the entrepreneur and the venture similarly tied to certain moral bases and ethical behavior, and whether this is intentional or merely a matter of due process over time.

Much of the current focus in research related to firm culture is anticipating a significant managerial revolution that will place its focus primarily on the company's horizontal procedures rather than on the vertical structures of the organization.[1] The entrepreneurial new venture is no different, but in fact may be more likely to be defined by these lateral lines of communication flow and dialogue, as opposed to the adoption of a certain framework. Some empirical evidence suggests that the particular characteristics of the firm's social style for interaction are the most useful framework for helping individual entrepreneurs understand themselves, employees, and others with whom they work.[2] Many argue that this social parlance is actually a direct function of the new venture's goals and objectives, and that the firm culture must always be viewed as linked to some form of social responsibility for actions within the market.[3] The trick to the ethical perspectives of firm culture is often expressed as whether the entrepreneur and the outside investors together perceive that there is a clear increase in economic activity due to the firm adhering to a form of moral posture in its functional activities.[4] Because there are numerous underlying personal rationales to motivate an entrepreneur to implement an ethics program, many of these reasons are not based on moral ground, but rather purely economic considerations,[5] such as increased market share, improved recognition by end-users, and greater external visibility through various means of publicity. Certainly, it appears that the way a firm conducts business will directly impact its normal decision making processes, and create an identity relative to other companies in the industry.[6] But the truth remains that, with respect to increased business activity and profitability, no two managerial or economic philosophies are exactly alike,[7] and each layer of rationale that underlies the firm's motivation for ethical practices is the result of a personal interpretation about what constitutes right and wrong. The economic impact of justice, inequality, and other normative criteria will remain subject to the various interpretations and inferences of individual entrepreneurs,[8] rather than an objective formula where profits are a function of discrete behavioral inputs.

Beyond the scope of the personal moral bases for ethical decision making in new ventures, the firm itself will display a certain character and style that places the organization as a responsible agent within the larger framework of society in general. Whether or not the entrepreneur is ready to accept this form of evaluation, the enterprise will be held accountable for specific actions and their effects on people, other firms, and the formation of societal norms.[9] There are certainly numerous layers of expectations placed on the entrepreneur, and at the macro level the firm, to act in a manner that exhibits some generally accepted rules or procedures based on what society as a whole has determined is appropriate, whether that be in hiring practices, core business values, consumption of resources, or even the nature of the work environment.[10] But this is a very tenuous exercise at best. The prospects for clarifying some type of universal code of conduct and organizational culture to promote this is subject to a wide range of personal biases and moral interpretations, as are any proposed economic links or effects.[11] This can often become nothing more than a promotional ploy to create an image of social concern and values-based company policies, when in fact the insider information about daily procedures, decision making criteria, and the representation of the venture's goals and objectives tell a very different story about functional and operational efficiency.[12]

The entrepreneurial new venture is placed in a very interesting position relative to the formulation of firm culture and company-wide ethical procedures and policies. The reality is that individuals make up the company's personnel force and they are the ones who actually *do* the work. The entrepreneur's ability to effectively legislate a firm culture and morality might be an inverse relationship with the size and scope of the company's operations. For instance, similar firm culture types are less informative about ethical behavior when compared to diverse personal characteristics of employees and individual interpretations of what the firm culture means in practical applications of daily business operations.[13] The *American Management Association* published a classic work containing three dozen anecdotal rules for personal survival within the firm culture of formal business organizations, and highlighted several universal implications of certain activities in the most general situations.[14] But these, like many collections of case studies and "war stories" fail to effectively inculcate a company-wide values system for the interpretation of different situations, and instead draw attention to the various ways in which individuals within similar environments respond differently to the same ethical situations and decisions. Books focused on some experience-based list of rules, or procedures that can supposedly be transferred from a successful organization to all firms, do little to address the core issues of firm culture and ethical behavior in business.

Several attempts to codify the "way to do ethics" have been presented over the years as if the moral corporation is somehow a function of the right number of managerial sessions, focus groups, accountability schedules, or value input memoranda.[15] The ethics focus within the five domains proposed in this book is based entirely on the level of commitment to values based on an underlying, individual moral basis or rationale as to what constitutes right and wrong. It remains the position of this author that the domain of firm culture is therefore an extension of the entrepreneurial profile and the degree to which formal and intentional efforts of time and money are committed to developing common factors for operating the company. It has been argued that there can be no separation of the entrepreneur from the process of incorporating business ethics into the new venture development process, because the firm and the founder are already united in terms of human morals, friendships and other relationships, and perspectives of what constitutes value. This "bureaucratization of ethics"[16] is essentially an attempt to delegate morality compliance throughout the firm culture as if it is nothing more than a formal procedure that can be looked up in a company policy manual. But many corporate "whistle blowers" have testified that the presence of supposedly ethical guidelines does not necessarily translate into greater ethical behavior or a heightened awareness of moral absolutes.[17]

There are also those who believe that personal managerial testimonials and case studies, about what worked and what did not in certain sized firms from particular industries, will enlighten entrepreneurs to adopt a similar framework for the new venture firm culture.[18] But moral bases and ethical behavior must be far much more than simply choosing results from a menu of those already tried and tested. Ethical firm culture must move beyond the transfer of reports and research, or the alterations of someone else's plan for success in this area,[19] and get to the heart of identifying what is valued by the entrepreneur, whether the employees share those core values and beliefs, and the commitment of resources to create an effective structure to serve as a mechanism for mutual accountability in the implementation of these values into literally every aspect of the firm's normal operations. Perhaps the best way to approach the formation of firm culture in the new venture is to clearly identify the most likely areas for potential problems to surface, define the overall nature of these areas within an ethics context, and discuss the ways in which these areas are connected to other areas that create extensions of the personal moral basis in the firm.[20] This makes much more sense given the numerous individual accounts of why "bureaucratized" ethics are generally not very successful when compared to clear, personal choices in moral areas of decision making.[21] There are many examples of companies who preached a message of trust, open information, and employee empowerment, only to have certain employees see that framework as the perfect vehicle within which to shield theft, deceit, and shirking.[22]

The new venture firm culture will be intimately linked to the effectiveness of the company in developing timely and appropriate policies for everything from minority recruitment, to compliance with disability legislation, and policy representation on environmental and consumer protection issues.[23] The internal environment can either be a formal and objective collection of what are considered the top ten ethical managerial principles, or it can reflect a personally lobbied example of attention to values and moral judgments on the part of the entrepreneur. The recruitment, selection, and training of employees should be more a function of matching personal perspectives and experiences, rather than trying to modify the behavior of persons who might possess certain functional capabilities.[24] The entrepreneur must recognize that the development of an ethical firm culture will in many ways go directly against the grain of many potential employees, market channels, capital providers, and even customers. The likelihood of a firm owner refusing to do a certain deal or engage in a specific activity due to personal moral bases is often argued as being inversely related to the level of *expected* economic gain that the firm will realize as a result of this proposed decision.[25] This pessimism speaks right to the very heart of what a firm culture is really supposed to be in the first place. The internal environment of the new venture cannot merely be a set of rules and regulations with rewards made available to those who comply and penalties assessed to those who do not. The firm culture should reflect an attitude about *why* the enterprise exists and operates in that market, in the same way that corporate vision and mission cannot merely state a few claims about some ideal commercial arrangement in the market. Entrepreneurial firm culture must be shared personal values, beliefs, and moral judgments about dealing with people and organizations.

## Entrepreneurial Values and Firm culture

The process by which a new organization codifies and implements a specific firm culture should not be perceived as the result of some sort of managerial planning exercise or corporate weekend retreat at the start of the fiscal year. Firm culture must start with the entrepreneur. The individual ethical behavior of the entrepreneur begins with core values defined by a clear moral basis. This explicit moral rationale is then the result of years of individual experiences, a unique background in executing decisions, and a lifetime of assessing the value of various types of behavior in numerous commercial and personal relationships. The entrepreneur's business ethics are a function of a wide range of inputs, including successes and failures. These positive and negative experiences, together with any adherence to certain philosophical moral absolutes, comprise the basis or rationale upon which values are founded (Figure 5.1). Core values are those most likely to remain constant with respect to the changing external business environment. Medial values are somewhat important to the entrepreneur, but they can be subject to interpretation based on the unique nature of certain situations. Fringe values are noncritical in nature and operate, in effect, like basic "rules of thumb" to gauge general circumstances that are often not related to specific aspects of the new venture's primary business thrust.

The entrepreneur is uniquely positioned to either be an effective *champion* or *sponsor* of personal values, an *influencer* in matters of ethical questions, or a *neutral observer* as far as initiating attention to potential "problem" situations and appropriate behavioral standards. These three levels of commitment or involvement will be referred to as *ethical patronage*. This defines the degree to which the entrepreneur chooses to sponsor awareness and adherence to precise moral standards for the firm as it engages in the seven previously defined actions of positioning, transactions, relationships, decisions, communications, negotiations, and assessments. The owner can choose to come out very strong in favor of specific actions and definitions of what is considered right and wrong. If this is the case, the entrepreneur must make a deliberate decision to be more than just an influence on certain ethical behavior. The employees will have to view the owner as the defining vision for ethics in the firm. If the entrepreneur chooses instead to merely influence the behavior of other individuals, then policies and actions may carry an implied statement that the final decision still rests with the individual employee involved in a particular situation. Firm culture will probably not be able to make strong connections to this form of "advocated" ethical behavior if it connotes that this manner of business is, to some degree, optional based on each person's individual interpretation of a given business situation. The other form of ethical patronage, a *neutral observer*, means the entrepreneur has abdicated the forceful presence and passionate convictions of personally embraced moral absolutes in favor of a "wait-and-see" style that allows the firm culture to come into focus gradually over time, as employees settle into the routines and expectations of company operations. This approach to firm culture is often the easiest form for the entrepreneur to utilize in the early stages of the venture's development because so many other concerns about sales, costs, profitability, marketing, and production logistics are viewed as "tangible" and mandatory issues, while business ethics may be perceived as "intangible" and discretionary.

Figure 10.1 summarizes the basic factors that define firm culture in the context of entrepreneurial ethics. These two dimensions are the *definition* of the values basis, and the *determinant* of ethics applied to a given business situation. There are four possible combinations that provide insight to the defining of entrepreneurial firm culture. Each type contains inherent aspects that are favorable and unfavorable with respect to two key managerial concerns: the ease of implementation and the consistency of results. The style of the *neutral observer* entrepreneur is depicted in the upper left quadrant, a generally defined ethic founded upon a relativistic basis or rationale. The entrepreneur is comfortable taking a "back-seat" approach

**Figure 10.1**
**Firm Culture Definitions and Determinants**

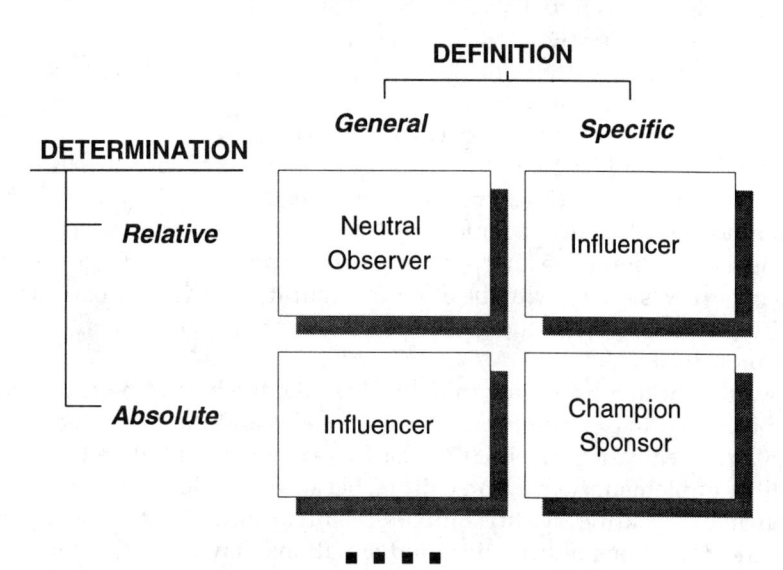

|  | **DEFINITION** | |
| --- | --- | --- |
| **DETERMINATION** | *General* | *Specific* |
| *Relative* | Neutral Observer | Influencer |
| *Absolute* | Influencer | Champion Sponsor |

to values-based policies and procedures, allowing the firm to operate under some general guidelines based on the employees' individual abilities to recognize the benefits and costs in each decision circumstance. This is by far the easiest firm culture to develop in a new venture because it allows the internal environment to come into focus on a gradual basis as the firm matures over time. However, it can also create the greatest levels of confusion regarding the appropriateness of decisions and actions because each person is operating independent of each other and subject only to their own interpretation of certain trade-offs between benefits and costs to the company. The results of decisions that are made in this manner can be very frustrating for the entrepreneur because it is often impossible to maintain any level of consistency in dealing with capital providers, marketing channels, and end-users. Granted, some decisions may work out for the best due to the individual interpretation and choice of a certain employee, but that relativistic basis can also result in many poor decisions because the entrepreneur feels that the choice was inappropriate.

The entrepreneur-influencer of firm culture could be characterized by either the upper right or lower left quadrants. In the first case, the owner would have to classify some very specific definitions about certain situations, but these would be based only on unique prior experiences. These explicit details would be more anecdotal than substantive in content, and could again leave employees with the impression that the specific aspects of the policy are tied to just those cases that are nearly similar in to those past experiences in terms of the decision factors. But if the present situation does not appear aligned with the narrow profile of the prior cases, then employees must use their own judgment of the situation and perhaps make a decision that is only a modified application of the specific principle. It could be argued that there really is no such thing as a "specific-relative" influencer in practical terms because specific definitions of behavior could not be based upon relativism. A comparable scenario describes the opposite diagonal, where the entrepreneur has built a firm culture based on clear absolute moral standards for decision making, but the standard is too ambiguous with respect to all of the various ethical situations that can arise in the operation of the firm. Although the approach to a given decision is rooted in a clear rationale, the means of implementing it can be somewhat vague due to very general and broad interpretations. It might be very easy to introduce prior experiences and then leave new situations to be interpreted relative to the current facts about benefits and costs, but as with the *neutral observer*, the results could vary based upon the ways in which employees make value determinations. On the other hand, it could also be easy to implement several core absolute values into the firm culture, but leave these as general principles for decision making and operations. The broader definition leaves some room for the entrepreneur to define a basic position, but allows for some level of employee interpretation with respect to how the general principle is to be used in a given decision. As with the other configurations, there still exists a possibility for frustration by the entrepreneur due to the application of the general definition (even though it has an absolute basis).

The lower right quadrant may initially look like the best of both worlds because the firm culture is rooted in clear and consistent rationales and the mechanics for applying the ethics is very specifically defined. But this also has several potential problems. First, it can be very difficult to implement such a firm culture, because it could be construed as ethical cloning based on an overbearing rigidity. Employees might function with clear moral absolutes, but the specific definitions of behaviors and situations may not allow for any slight variations that could occur. In the case of such a discrepancy, the employee may once again be forced to make a personal interpretation of what is deemed "best" in the given situation. But the hope is that there is a firm foundation of underlying shared values to provide a consistent basis for this new decision. This quadrant describes the entrepreneur who champions the cause of ethical behavior and strong moral bases for the firm culture. Some would argue that this type of internal environment might be too stifling or rigid, and not allow for any breathing room for employees to function intelligently. Or it is criticized because the specific definitions must be viewed as overly detailed procedures that confine creativity and initiative, which could be true if taken to the extreme position.

## *The Problem of Reflectivity*

The degree with which the new venture's firm culture expresses the personal values and ethics of the entrepreneur is called reflectivity. As previously mentioned, there are three basic ways that the company's founder can be involved in the development of the internal environment for the firm. But these three levels of involvement each create distinct ethical problems for both the entrepreneur and the employees within the new venture. The difficulty is generally a result of the focus for the entrepreneurial ethic image. The image, like that on a lens, can be either sharply focused to a crisp and well-defined resemblance, or it can be a generally good likeness, but with some ethical "fuzziness" around some of the edges. The image is recognizable enough, but it lacks the clarity of the original. There is basically an image that, after careful study, can be discerned and identified as resembling the entrepreneur, but the colors, expressions, and details are not quite comparable to the original. And, finally, the image can be somewhat out of focus, to the point where observers know that there is something up on the screen, they can see the motion and some basic forms, but these are essentially indiscernible, and cannot be recognized, even after several attempts to interpret the actions and general contours of the image.

The first case of reflectivity may on the surface appear to have no ethical problems associated with it, because, after all, it is essentially a perfect likeness of the firm owner. But the degree of focus necessary to create such a sharp and clearly distinct image as this can be a source of frustration for both the entrepreneur and the employees in the company. On the one hand, the entrepreneur is faced with the task of trying to clone assessment and decision making behavior. This can be quite a formidable task just from the position of whether it is even feasible to effectively transfer entrepreneurial characteristics within a moral rationale and certain ethical perspectives. And even if it was possible to accomplish this task, the process would certainly require a huge commitment of managerial time and funding to follow a strategy that would delineate the entire spectrum of actions in each of the five primary ethical domains for the new venture. The training and review procedures would also require a significant commitment of the firm's resources, and this would be in direct competition with the more pressing issues of marketing, production, and basic operations. The entrepreneur could begin to resent the time and money being allocated to this task, and reevaluate the resources being committed versus competing investments.

It can also place employees in an awkward position with respect to their functional duties within the enterprise, and their working relationship with the founder. First, the personnel mix was assembled to accomplish various levels of tasks, many of which are "operational" in terms of content and the impact on the firm's capabilities. These include functional areas of accounting, shipping and receiving, order processing, customer service, data processing, and general office procedures. The entrepreneur could become the source of a good deal of frustration if every employee is suddenly asked to think about very specific moral issues and ethical behavior from the perspective of the entrepreneur, when in fact most of them work in limited scope functional operations that do not deal with interdepartmental decisions and ethical issues linked to the strategic "big picture" of the company's prospects and future direction. The entrepreneur's scope could be too broad in its perspective and not have a good fit with the more limited range of decisions and issues at the departmental level. For example, the customer service representative who answers telephone inquiries from buyers has been trained to listen to the concerns of purchasers, and offer one of a few previously defined remedies as per the basic functional policies of that area. Any attempts by the entrepreneur to instill and nurture a highly sophisticated and sharp focus of ethical reflectivity within the limited range of business decisions and assessments for this type of employee could ultimately result in distracting the worker from the main concentration of the job tasks, and foster some confusion as to when it is appropriate for this ethical behavior to be applied and how to handle situations that are not a perfect match with some narrowly interpreted situation. The resources and time spent in training for specific ethical situations could send mixed signals about job descriptions and lines of authority within the organization. This could develop a sense among employees that the entrepreneur is trying to do their job for them because they are not capable of working on their own. The entrepreneur must be careful not to turn employees away from the goal of developing a values-orientation and ethical behavior due to the overbearing nature of the delivery and the process for implementation.

And finally, it can also be counter-productive in some aspects, if the employees are being deliberately molded and shaped to think exactly like the entrepreneur thinks, assess all situations within the same structural heuristic, and respond with decisions that include the entrepreneur's sense of vision and company mission, as well as personal values and moral bases. The counter-productive results to the firm are that there could become too many entrepreneurial minded people in the enterprise, and the need for procedure and policy to be implemented in the functional areas on a daily basis could be burdened with too many thoughts about the "big picture" for every possible decision. An entrepreneur does not ever really want to be surrounded with a company full of entrepreneurial-oriented employees because the firm needs personnel who can accomplish specific tasks within the framework of a larger firm strategy without a constant review process at every level of delegation. Two entrepreneurial partners in one company can often be a difficult experience to manage as they each have a personal perspective and vision about the firm's directions, competitive positioning, sense of mission, and scope of ethical implications for managing the firm. A great deal of compromise must take place within the firm between two partners, even those that tend to see things the same way and share a common set of basic values and expectations. To turn every employee into an entrepreneur based on an "ethics" direction, could backfire and instead create employees who are going to play the game of entrepreneurial "want-to-be" and suddenly look for ways to have input at all levels of decision making. Too many different views and interpretations of processes and policies could slow down the efficiency with which the very basic functional areas of accounting, office management, shipping, receiving, and customer service are handled on a daily basis. The owner must think carefully about creating a firm culture that is so entrepreneurial it loses functional efficiency.

The next case of reflectivity is at the opposite end of the continuum from the sharply defined focus previously discussed. This involves the firm culture where the entrepreneur takes no active role in training employees in ethical behavior and company core values. The culture's image of the entrepreneur is essentially out of focus. Outside observers know that there are activity and decisions going on within the organization, but these actions lack any cohesiveness or consistency from one situation to the next. The firm's mannerisms are often a direct function of the individual who happens to handle a particular situation, and this may be handled in a way that is quite different than the entrepreneur's interpretation of the circumstances. The messages and reputation being presented by the new venture can become indiscernible to outsiders. The entrepreneur has virtually abdicated the role of leadership in the area of ethics and company values to the individual ideas and positions of the separate employees responsible for each point of contact with the capital providers, marketing channels, and end-users. This is often the easiest approach to take. It defers a great deal of planning and attention away from the supposedly intangible aspects of value judgments and moral responsibilities toward the more apparently tangible issues of sales, finance, production, and corporate development.

It is very wishful thinking on the part of the entrepreneur to surmise that each employee will be capable of assessing all the decision parameters for ethical concerns and moral rationales at their particular level of the firm structure without some form of direction and training communicated by the entrepreneur. Ethical behavior cannot just happen sporadically throughout the firm on a chance basis due to a certain employee's interest in this issue and a personal interpretation of the benefits and costs associated with a decision. The entrepreneur who elects to allow the firm culture to slowly develop through random processes without an intentional plan to define and transfer basic core values will probably find a wide range of both success and failure in dealing with outsiders and insiders, because it will literally be a "hit-or-miss" tactic whose effectiveness is completely subject to the individual employee's personal values and rationale for ethical behavior.

Somewhere between the two extremes, the entrepreneur should be able to find a balanced approach to establishing firm culture. The employees need clearly stated goals and parameters for subjective behavior. The firm must commit funds, time, and managerial resources to the planning and practice of defining the firm's core values, its moral rationale and basis within the market, and its level of commitment to distinct ethical behavior. But it must not go so far as to try and breed entrepreneurial clones that look and think and act in the exact same manner as the firm's owner. The key is to provide a fairly wide range of general guidelines that are determined by clear moral absolutes such that the general definitions have a solid basis that can allow for consistent applications even in areas that are not specifically delineated. Referring back to Figure 10.1, the lower left corner describes the entrepreneur as an influencer that builds a solid basis for generating ethical behavior, but avoids the potential for monitoring behavior in an overbearing manner that tries to anticipate every moral judgment that could occur or specific action necessary in the areas of positioning, decisions, transactions, communications and the like.

### *Concerns of Structural Formality*

Many new ventures tend to exhibit a firm culture that is casual and thrives on the flexibility of informal lines of communication and a somewhat flat organizational structure. Entrepreneurs often laud the ability for individuals to easily adapt to rapidly changing market factors, and many times they demand that all of their employees display this form of rapid response in business management and communications. Numerous attempts have been made to systematize intracorporate entrepreneurship programs through the training of employees in objective processes and characteristics to translate entrepreneurial behavior and activities into large organizations.[26] Many argue that *intrapreneurship* is a necessary process in order to avoid the oversized and inefficient enterprise.[27] This may be very effective for certain aspects of funding research ideas or generating new market concepts within large firms, but many argue that true Schumpeterian entrepreneurship does not share the risk shelter and certainty of funding provisions that are evident in corporate venturing programs. The structural integrity of the small firm is very different than the highly sophisticated and often elaborate framework of organization at larger firms. The process of bringing values and ethical behavior to the entrepreneurial firm culture is never simply a matter of setting up the right structural mechanism to make it happen.

The new venture is still a product of the entrepreneur, and the founder has inherent characteristics for dealing with risk, uncertainty, and expectations that serve as the driving force behind the venture's push for success. The firm and the entrepreneur are often times inseparable and indistinguishable to the outsider. But the firm culture could take on a distinct personality of its own due to the entrepreneur's level of involvement in formulating and implementing the internal environment based on individual values and ethics. Figure 10.2 compares the possible outcomes that could occur in the new venture based upon the entrepreneur's personal character preference for either a formal or informal organizational and managerial style, and the type of internal firm culture that develops in the company. Many would argue that it would be impossible to have anything other than a Type I or Type II blend because the entrepreneur must match the firm's style. But that statement assumes that the entrepreneur has taken a strong position of influence in defining the firm culture, and that is not always the case. Granted, if an entrepreneur with a very formal style took an active role in establishing the new venture's moral basis and core values, the firm would be likely to reflect that higher level of formality and be perhaps more structured in its lines of communication, policies, and procedures. And, if the informal entrepreneur were to deliberately instill a basis for firm culture and employee behavior it would be reasonable to assume that the company would have a more casual manner of doing business. These are the expected results of an *influencer* or even a champion who sponsors a comprehensive company code of ethics.

The concerns about structure are focused on the entrepreneur who acts as a *neutral observer*, who provides no deliberate strategy for defining moral rationales and ethical business practices, but allows the firm culture to take on a composite character that reflects a wide range of perspectives and ideas about assessing situations and what constitutes appropriate decisions. An entrepreneur with an informal style might end up working in a firm culture that has become very structured and highly organized because the employees have generally migrated toward formal lines of authority and communication, and clearly defined managerial roles and decision making responsibilities. This could become a tremendous source of frustration for the entrepreneur who wishes to operate in a more spontaneous and flexible manner, because the firm has adopted a definitive and programmatic style of operations, and the owner is now viewed as the "maverick" or the "loose cannon" that is normally at odds

## Figure 10.2
## Entrepreneurial Type and Firm Culture

**FIRM CULTURE**

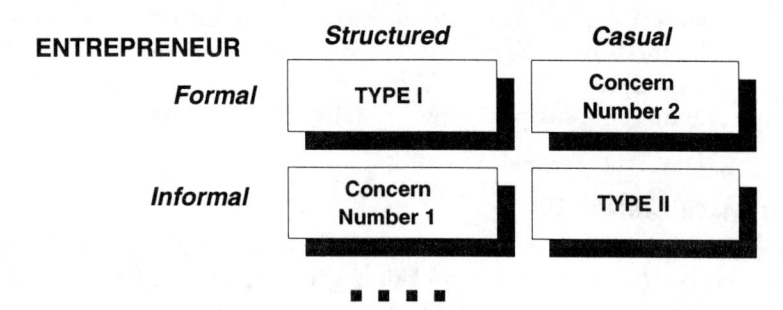

|  | Structured | Casual |
|---|---|---|
| **Formal** | TYPE I | Concern Number 2 |
| **Informal** | Concern Number 1 | TYPE II |

ENTREPRENEUR

with the fixed policies and procedures that have been developed over time. The ethical implications are interesting because the firm could move toward various forms of established policies, while the entrepreneur wants to deal with situations on a case-by-case basis relative to a personal interpretation of the perceived benefits and costs.

On the other hand, the second area of concern could position a formal decision making and ethical style from the entrepreneur against a firm culture that has become quite casual over time. Again, the *neutral observer* owner has, for various reasons, backed away from defining ethical behavior and values for the company and now finds that the company has developed a firm culture that is somewhat resistant to firm policies and procedures in these supposedly subjective areas of behavior and *situation ethics*. In both areas of concern the firm culture can become mismatched with the owner's personal style because the entrepreneur has decided to take a passive role in addressing issues pertaining to company core values and forms of ethical behavior. This proved to be a very common occurrence in the field study as entrepreneurs expressed frustration in wanting employees to operate in certain manner, and yet they often did not take an active role in defining these behavioral expectations and offered no mechanism to facilitate awareness and training for how ethics in the business should be handled.

## Personal Choice and Firm Culture

Inherent in the two types of firm culture *influencer* positions, as well as the *champion sponsor*, the entrepreneur has made the choice to take on some form of an active role in defining and determining the new venture's reputation and character. As was just discussed, the *neutral observer* has taken a very different position, allowing the company to work out behaviors and values through the collective interaction of the employees and the individual interpretation of situations as they arise. For the owner who wishes to be actively involved in the process of formulating a distinctive firm culture there are three basic ways this happens. Firm culture can either be the result of copying someone else's plan, a direct transfer of the entrepreneur's personal values system, or a combination of the first two. The venture will either directly reflect the entrepreneur, another firm's cultural norms, or a hybrid model based on the best of both. There are several ethical issues dealing with values assessment and ethical choice that must be addressed within this context of raising a commitment to a certain form of internal environment. Each method has implicit and explicit benefits for new venture development. But they might also create difficulty, both in establishing the firm culture and operating within it on a consistent basis. The choices made by the entrepreneur will have a direct impact on the overall success of the policies and procedures due to several factors. Each of these three methods must be examined across two criteria for success. The first measures the degree of employee vesting in the firm culture and the second examines the degree of accountability among company personnel in matters of value judgments and ethical decision making.

### *The Borrowed Culture*

The first method develops the internal environment by copying, what has been interpreted as, a very successful format that is working well in another organizational setting. The entrepreneur initiates a formal discussion about moral bases, core values, and ethical conduct in order to develop a clearly defined firm culture. During the initial process, the owner invites both input and feedback about the proposed expectations for ethical behavior and fundamental guidelines for the venture's business operations. A company-wide dialogue is created and the employees work with the owner to clarify procedures and policies in light of shared ethical interpretations across the entire firm. This generally takes a good deal of effort on the part of the entrepreneur, and may require a significant commitment of time and financial resources to make it truly work. The secret is to instill a vested interest for employees to embrace the moral basis and core values as their own. But this can bring about difficult problems as well. What worked in one company may not always be easily transferred with the same positive results to another firm. There were qualities and circumstances inherent in the formation of the model culture that might be quite dissimilar to the new venture. The most general provisions of communication dynamics, personal relationships, and sense of company mission and purpose could form a template for a basic internal environment, but this might lack the ownership and vested interest of a specific culture that reflects the personal morals, core values, and ethical behavior of the unique personnel in the new venture.

### *The Replicate Culture*

The second method is to simply allow the entrepreneur's personal moral basis and core values be transferred directly to the inner workings of the new venture's business structure. The owner could define a critical hub of actions, perspectives, attitudes, and behaviors that are personally important, have inherent value for organizing and operating the enterprise, and then introduce a model for the firm based on individual values and moral bases. These would have to be modified to fit the various functional departments within the new venture as company policies and guidelines for procedures. The entrepreneur would have to devote a good deal of time and funding to operationalize individual traits into corporate applications and directions for doing business on a daily basis. Employees would need to be trained and nurtured in the entrepreneur's sense of company mission, core values, and business ethics. This can only be successful if there are strong links established between employee effectiveness and positive company performance, and the underlying subjective rationales and perspectives that support the framework. The image of the entrepreneur's ideas about right and wrong will then be figuratively imprinted upon the new venture's internal functional capabilities and external actions in the market.

But there can be one significant hitch in this plan. The employees cannot feel as though they are being systematically cloned into the very likeness of the entrepreneur. This perception could undermine the whole basis for the firm culture from the very outset of the training and implementation because it is perceived as either imposed indoctrination, or coercion that might affect a person's job security, compensation, and prospects for advancement. If the work force views the attempt to create a replicate firm culture as a master plan to somehow brainwash employees into various forms of submission to strict ethical mandates, the entrepreneur will be ineffective due to resentment and a lack of interest within all levels of the personnel ranks. The only way to make a replicate culture work is to keep the initial ethical principles sufficiently broad enough to allow each employee some degree of personal application in finding ways to make ethics work in their functional area of the firm. Once general guidelines have established vested interests with the work force, new ideas for other applications or more specific uses can develop through regular dialogue, continuous training, and follow-up with the entrepreneur and other employees. The entrepreneur may not want to be completely replicated throughout the work force because there are many advantages to having alternate opinions and variant interpretations of the many different business situations that the new venture will encounter. The firm might do well to grasp and adopt the owner's general vision for moral principles, and then allow specific ethical behaviors to flow from that basis.

## *The Hybrid Culture*

The third manner is a combination of the first two, and is referred to as a *hybrid culture*. This captures the situation where the entrepreneur mixes together what is believed to be the "best of the best" in order to arrive at a firm culture that contains both personal values and ethics, as well as tried and true principles that have stood the test of time and various situations in other firms. At first glance, this might appear to be a rather desirable balance between what has worked well elsewhere, and what the owner hopes to see from an individual perspective. However, the hybrid culture can have just as many problems as the previous examples for supporting ethical behavior. The borrowed culture may lack definitive links with the unique composition of the new venture, and the replicate culture could tend to become too confining of actions and overbearing in its specificity. The hybrid culture could very well become a worst case scenario by incorporating both nonapplicable issues from other firms and overly explicit instructions to handle every aspect of the company with the same attention to details as the entrepreneur. The internal firm culture could become nothing more than a mixed bag of imported standards that do not fit the organization, combined with the owner's compulsion to have everyone behave in a uniform manner. For ethics to work effectively in the formulation of new venture firm culture, there must be regular, periodic time set aside to accomplish the task of nurturing core values and ethical behavior. And there must be funding allocated to support the on-going process of training and implementing a moral basis and a sense of purpose and mission for company operations. The entrepreneur must lead by example in placing a high priority on developing firm culture in a manner that allows all employees to embrace ethical principles as their own.

## Complications of Managed Morality

The new venture encounters a huge risk in tackling the process of formulating a distinctive firm culture. Perhaps the most difficult issue in making firm culture work for the small firm involves complications in ethical behavior due to the entrepreneur's attempt to manage morality throughout the firm. It is one thing for the firm owner to have individual core values, and strong personal convictions about what is right and wrong based on personal moral standards. But it is altogether a different matter when the entrepreneur seeks to systematically integrate these beliefs and perceptions into every aspect of the new venture. When the owner attempts to weave ethics into the fabric of the enterprise, there are two primary areas for potential trouble. The first deals with the underlying philosophy that could create a somewhat managed morality, and the second deals with the process by which the entrepreneur introduces values and ethics into the company. These can dismantle the structural integrity of new venture firm culture on several fronts. The most likely point of contact is whether the employees are really practicing ethics, or merely "going through the motions" as if it was just another item on their list of job requirements.

In the area of philosophy of firm culture, the entrepreneur can either impose ethics on employees, or develop an ethical awareness. In the area of firm culture process, the owner can either make ethics training a mandate from the top of the organization, or a desired activity in which all employees choose to participate. If the overall objective is to see values reflected in the attitudes and work habits of employees, then ethics must be something that includes all levels of personnel in the formation of firm culture. The entrepreneur should want to make the work force accountable to each other and to themselves individually. Employees should want to formulate and practice ethical behavior because they believe in its merits and they recognize the positive impact it can have on the firm's performance. If company personnel perceive an ethical firm culture in a negative light, they will either find ways to create an outward impression of adhering to company values and ethical behavior, or they will outright rebel against the entrepreneur's mandate for certain actions and conduct. Because the new venture is relatively small in size, the entrepreneur can make that work to the advantage of an ethical firm culture by working with smaller groups of employees to identify how core values could be implemented into daily business functions. But because the firm is small, the entrepreneur also faces the possibility that an informal organizational structure and overlapping lines of communication could derail plans to make core values and ethics a formal component of the firm culture. If ethics is viewed too casually, the firm culture may not accept core values as an important part of business policy.

## The Ethics Model and Firm Culture

The entrepreneur is once again faced with an increased propensity to engage in questionable ethical activities, this time due to the nature and composition of the new venture's internal firm culture. The potential trouble spots will be reviewed within the context of the entrepreneurial ethics model and the *EVI* matrix. The owner's underlying moral rationale is tied to six unique entrepreneurial characteristics to form core values which support certain types of ethical behavior across seven basic business actions. The entrepreneurial characteristics are then expected to impact these actions within the distinct *ethical domain* of new venture firm culture. Figure 10.3 summarizes the proposed ethical "problem areas" from the EVI matrix associated with entrepreneurial internal firm culture.

■ ■ ■ ■

**Figure 10.3**
**Forecasted EVI Matrix: Financial Requirements**

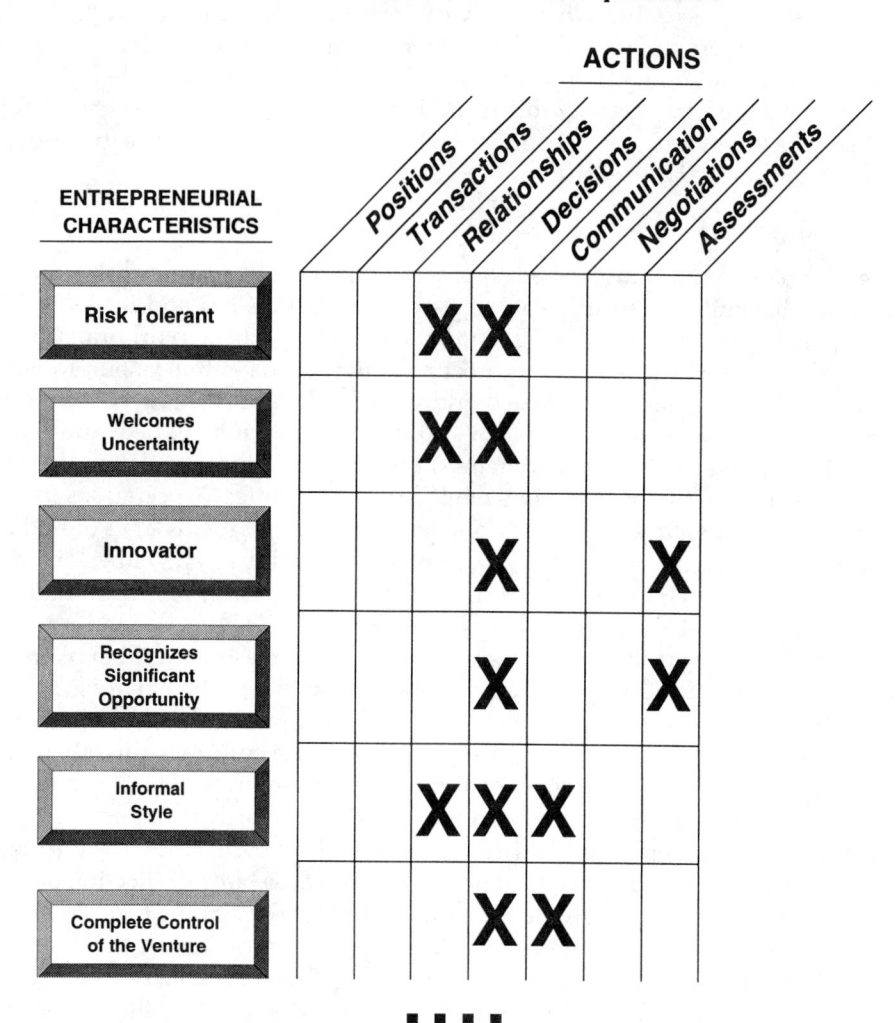

ACTIONS

| ENTREPRENEURIAL CHARACTERISTICS | Positions | Transactions | Relationships | Decisions | Communication | Negotiations | Assessments |
|---|---|---|---|---|---|---|---|
| Risk Tolerant | | X | X | | | | |
| Welcomes Uncertainty | | X | X | | | | |
| Innovator | | | X | | | X | |
| Recognizes Significant Opportunity | | | X | | | X | |
| Informal Style | | X | X | X | | | |
| Complete Control of the Venture | | | X | X | | | |

■ ■ ■ ■

## Empirical Evidence

### Firm Culture and Venture Success

The entrepreneurs were provided with a situation and asked whether their firm's success was due primarily to the strength of their product or service as opposed to the entrepreneur and the employees adhering to a moral code of business conduct or developing a certain corporate culture. The context was how accurately the entrepreneur's interpreted the perceptions that the outsiders had about the firm's culture with respect to the success of the enterprise. Only about one fourth (24%) of the owners agreed that their firm's culture and company-wide code of conduct were more responsible for success than the perceived strength of the product or service in the competitive market. Over half (56.5%) disagreed with this idea about firm culture and placed the success of the company due primarily to the strength of their products or services. But what was very interesting was that about one out of five entrepreneurs (19%) were not sure about whether success was due to their intangible firm culture or their tangible products and services. They stated that success depended on particular circumstances of firm activity in the market, that it was sometimes the firm culture and the adherence to a moral code of conduct, but it was equally likely to be the leadership of the company's products and services.

## *Reflectivity*

The entrepreneurs were also asked to describe the most important factor that defines their firm's internal culture and the way employees work together and interact with each other. Exactly six out of every ten owners (60%) stated that their firm's corporate culture was generally very unified and was really a direct reflection of the entrepreneur's personality, expectations for the enterprise, and sense of individual values. Essentially all of the remaining entrepreneurs (40%) described their firm's culture as being quite varied, and rather than reflecting just one person's (the entrepreneur's) positions on ethical behavior, the company reflected a wide range of many individual employee personalities, expectations for the venture, and definitions of values. Just under one percent said that it was a bit of both. This is very interesting because the entrepreneurs seemed to view this as an "either-or" situation, believing that firm culture is clearly a product of the entrepreneur, or a compilation of the many views and ideas of the employees.

A second scenario was then presented regarding what reasons could explain why the new venture conducts business in a certain manner and with a particular style. Once again, about six out of ten entrepreneurs (62%) stated that the manner and style of the company's conduct were primarily due to an intentional plan for the firm culture to directly reflect their own personal values and beliefs. More than one third of the owners (37%) stated that the company's manner and style of business conduct was due primarily to a unique composition of many individuals who represent the firm in the outside market. And only one percent of the owners said that the venture's style of doing business was both a reflection of the entrepreneur and the wide range of individual employees that represent the firm.

Another situation was presented regarding to what degree the venture's defining vision was synonymous with the vision of the company founder. Exactly two-thirds of the entrepreneurs (66%) stated that this was the case, but it was interesting that one-third (33%) believed that the venture's vision was formulated for the company due to the nature of the competitive market. The remaining one percent felt that it was a little of both. The notion that the vision for the enterprise is established outside the firm by market forces is a troubling perspective about the entrepreneur's contribution to the direction of the venture's firm culture.

## *Commitment to Firm Culture*

Previously in this chapter, the issues related to the tangible commitments of the owner in formulating a clearly defined firm culture were discussed in detail. The surveyed entrepreneurs were asked about their individual level of commitment to developing a distinctive firm culture. About six out of ten entrepreneurs (61%) agreed that their company regularly devoted planning time to a company-wide systematic development of a common managerial philosophy and distinctive ethical guidelines for both personal decision making, and group decisions as well. Only about one in six (16%) disagreed and said that they do not devote time specifically to develop a unique, ethical-oriented firm culture. The remaining entrepreneurs, about one quarter of those surveyed (23%) stated that although they did not devote time to this on a regular basis, they tended to do some planning as needed based entirely on the specific circumstances they were facing.

## Conclusions

The most interesting concept in the study of entrepreneurial ethics is the extent to which the new venture takes on an identity that is similar to that of the founder. Numerous research findings have sought to link the start-up firm with the entrepreneur across several dimensions, including risk position, the openness to uncertainty, opportunism, and distinctive competencies. As was mentioned earlier in the book, most entrepreneurial trait studies have proven to be inconclusive in establishing sub groups of entrepreneurial profiles and their respective tendencies toward certain new venture types. However, there does appear to be some potential for linking small firm culture with the entrepreneur's managerial style, personal values system, and sense of moral basis for behavior. Just under half of those surveyed were willing to say they believed their corporate culture was responsible for their firm's success, or were willing to say that it *might* be the reason for positive performance. A significant majority also believed that their corporate culture was a direct reflection of their personality, expectations, and sense of individual values. This infers that as many as one-third, to as high as forty percent, of the entrepreneurs believe that their personality, values, and business ethics are the primary reasons for the success of the new venture. And when nearly the same proportions of entrepreneurs said that their firm's style of management is a direct reflection of their own values, and that the venture's defining vision is also a reflection of their own view to the future, a strong case begins to take shape in support of new venture reflectivity.

The main interest for entrepreneurial ethics in this context is then this. To what extent are these reflections due to a deliberate and systematic approach for transferring vales and ethics to the organizational structure of the firm, and how much of this "just happens" as a natural result of proximity? Again, a nearly identical two-thirds proportion of the owners stated that they devoted specific planning time on a regular basis to the development of a systematic, company-wide philosophy and distinctive ethical guidelines for doing business. Without a strong commitment from the owner, the new venture is susceptible to developing a *values vacuum*, where employee ethical relativity and ambiguity reign supreme due to the lack of a clear values focus initiated by the entrepreneur. The owner might shy away from trying to mandate a corporate morality, and yet end up doing nothing, which allows the firm to be devoid of any form of absolute ethics or values identity. Suddenly, the company begins to exhibit *negotiable standards* that really hold no weight in the context of ethical decision making, because they exist in name only. These can also be thought of as *optional commitments*, because they appear to be firm policy, but are always used subject to the present circumstances. The greatest challenge for those entrepreneurs who do engage in the deliberate process of reflectivity is how to avoid the complications of managed morality and the negative impacts of informality in firm culture. The business functions of the new venture are characteristically positioned in very close proximity to the typical business management profile of the entrepreneur. There is now some tangible evidence and interest as to the extent that new venture firm culture is also positioned close to the owner's personal values and individual business ethics.

# CHAPTER ELEVEN

# *Change and New Venture Momentum*

## Introduction

The most difficult issue involved in navigating the moral rationales, core values, and ethical behavior of newly launched companies is directly related to the perpetual conflict that exists between the impact of change on the firm, and the entrepreneur's need to maintain new venture momentum. The entrepreneur is often pressured to address change with prompt and vigorous actions to grow the business in response to the shifts in the market and transitions in innovation with a high level of competence, even though the firm may have recently experienced poor prior performance.[1] But the reality is that the market and the competition do not wait, or make allowances, for anyone at anytime. Inherent in the free market system are degrees of risk and uncertainty based almost entirely on the prospects for encountering change, and this actuality can contribute very significantly to an attitude among entrepreneurs that there are in fact no rules on how to do good business.[2] The effects of change bring about either opportunities or threats to the long-term viability of the new venture. Information about the cause, the source, the degree of impact, and the probable effects of change will always be at a premium in the market. The entrepreneur is very interested in finding and maintaining reliable sources of pertinent information because it can literally be the difference between continued success or complete failure of the enterprise. But there will be huge challenges to the core values of the entrepreneur with respect to where the information is located, who has access to it, how it is obtained, and in what ways is it used in the competitive market.[3] Information about the external environment will be a very valuable commodity in light of impending changes and their effects on the venture. There will be temptations for the entrepreneur to gain control over the flow of information in order to regulate its potential impacts among competitors. In some instances it may appear beneficial to leak false information, or in other cases to withhold truthful information, and each of these tactics are based on personal interpretations, individual choice, and managerial style.[4]

Changes in the regulatory environment can have either positive effects, or devastating consequences, on the new venture's prospects. For instance the deregulation of the airlines opened up huge new markets to competition and price wars. The entrepreneur may actually be in a position to change the rules or redirect new opportunities through legal challenges and the introduction of radical innovation.[5] For example, in the early 1980's, the personal computer market was unfolding with the introduction of the "PC" by *international Business Machines*, using a generic central processing unit, a microchip from *Intel*, and a primitive disk operating system from a nascent Seattle-based software company. *Eagle Computer* challenged in the courts a claim by *IBM* that this computer was proprietary in design and function. Dozens of software and hardware manufacturers watched with eagerness during numerous months of legal haggling. By the time the ruling came out in favor of *Eagle*'s right to copy the generic design, more than ten companies were ready to offer a "clone" of the personal computer. Although *Eagle* never recovered from the time and financial drain on resources, an entirely new and huge market was open for direct competition. The legal change devastated *Eagle* (they went bankrupt), severely reduced *IBM*'s long-term hold on market share (their stock value began a six year nose dive), and provided a competitive kick-start for scores of new ventures across a wide range of computer hardware market niches.

The entrepreneurial new venture is also not immune to changes that are born out of general shifts in societal norms, cultural interaction, and new expectations for population trends. Change can be forced upon the entrepreneur by society's decisions about what is important. The doctrine of social responsibility for business recognizes that companies cannot operate independent of the greater social system in which they are located. Business actually depends quite heavily on social systems for its very existence.[6] Many significant issues can come to the forefront of society's questions and concerns about safety, employment, poverty, taxes, health care, housing, and transportation. A solid moral rationale and well defined core values should be able to support entrepreneurial ethics in all matters associated with the five business domains, as well as in change that results through issues that come from the greater social conscience. Tom Peters reminded all entrepreneurs that ethical guidelines for the "little stuff" should be wholly consistent with the ethics necessary to deal with the "big stuff" that comes with societal changes, and that "capitalism and democracy in society are messy."[7] He applied this to the crucial issues about consumer safety in almost every food and drug product, brought to the social front as a result of the Tylenol tampering that killed several people. A major set-back for one company fueled an entirely new industry for tamper-resistant packaging. This change came swiftly, and the response from most companies was almost immediate. But other firms waited and debated the increased costs of production, negative impacts on gross profit margins, and the perceived need to refocus advertising and promotional efforts. The entrepreneurial firm has accepted numerous implied commitments in it dealings with the larger society in general, including truth in representation, product safety, and critical information disclosure. But each of these issues, and many others as well, are all subject to the entrepreneur's interpretation of what constitutes "truth," "safety," and "critical," versus society's definitions of the same. Social policy, the roles of public institutions and the private sector, and the structure of information systems together create a macro system that can introduce change onto the small entrepreneurial firm in a short period of time, and then require certain ethical expectations be followed based on what has been deemed acceptable by the whole of society.[8]

Change can also be introduced by government actions based on shifts in public policy, foreign trade arrangements, taxation laws, new administrations, and diplomatic forces. The political climate can bring about rapid changes in both social and economic areas of concern, and the entrepreneurial firm must recognize that these wider perspectives can have both negative and positive effects on the present direction of product and service markets, and consumer demand.[9] Inherent within the previously described five ethical domains that face entrepreneurs in new ventures, is the important need to recognize and respond to the various forms of change that will accompany the normal cycles of business in these areas. Change will, to some degree, impact the ability of the enterprise to abide by ethical standards in almost every aspect of representation, forecasted market expectations, financing requirements, partnership arrangements, and internal culture. The entrepreneur's ethics and consistent firm behavior will be tested by change from both internal and external forces. The owner will have to respond in a manner that is clear and stable, and yet allows for some forms of flexibility to changes that will modify generally accepted policies and procedures in each of the five primary ethical domains. The interesting reactions between change and ethical behavior will be played out in matters of how rigid or flexible are core, medial, and fringe values, and to what degree does change have an impact on the moral basis for ethical standards.

Change is very difficult to predict, in terms of when it will arrive, to what degree will it impact the firm, and in what manner (positive or negative) will the change affect the functional capabilities of the venture and its strategic positioning in the competitive market. But the entrepreneur can develop general contingency plans that can be accessed in the event of certain types of change. For instance, change can come specifically to the marketing and promotional functions of the firm, and have a negative impact on both firm representation and market forecasts, but have little or no effect on financing requirements or the firm culture, and actually create a positive opportunity for the enterprise in terms of newly emerging partnership arrangements due solely to the introduction of this new event or issue. The decision to maintain core values for the company and adhere to clear guidelines for ethical behavior can also be examined for contingencies in light of possible changes that could occur for the firm. The following discussions deal with the ways in which change can cause entrepreneurs to rethink firm culture, ethics policies, and core values. The decision making process that must remain flexible and highly adaptive to change might also be tempted to make adjustments in the firm's perspectives and interpretations for ethics and moral judgments that affect the long-term viability of the enterprise. And the entrepreneur naturally becomes the center of attention when subjective assumptions about transactions, positions, decisions, communications and such are at stake.

## The Troubling Effects of Change

When changes begin to unfold in the external environment, the entrepreneurial new venture is especially susceptible to alterations in product specifications, pricing policies, distribution arrangements, market shares, production processes, service offerings, and technology innovations for two very important reasons. First, smaller businesses are generally not very diversified in terms of their product and service portfolios. The company has often entered the market with one primary product or service that is not simply a lead item for the firm, but may be their *only* item in the market. There may be one or two versions, or models, of the original concept, but for the most part, the new venture has staked a claim to a market niche with a single product and a fixed set of support options in the established marketing channels. Second, the smaller enterprise is generally capitalized in a manner that is dependent on the single product or service offering. The firm has a fixed asset base that essentially supports the product and distribution of this single product concept group. The newly-launched company did not initially arrange a financial structure to provide support for branching into other areas of manufacturing, nor was it established in a manner that would allow the company to maintain operations through any significant economic downturn in demand, or shifts in consumer buying patterns. These two factors are referred to as *diversifinancial* troubles, where the new venture is often managing a non diversified product/service portfolio, (it is technically not a true "portfolio" because it is singularly structured), and this is backed up by a one dimensional financial plan. The asset investment schedule was planned and designed to produce the one product or service, achieve a point of break even and positive monthly cash flow, and this was all based on certain assumptions that did not include the newly emerging change in the environment. The new venture is essentially living "paycheck-to-paycheck" without a savings account or disability insurance during the formative years. The diversifinancial troubles create a negative compounding effect on the prospects for success in new ventures when significant changes are introduced into the company's marketing mix.

The new venture lacks the product and service diversification to allow shifts in demand in one sector to be covered by increases in other product or service areas, and an adequate financial foundation to provide internal cash flow support for operations during periods of weak sales. Larger companies can many times carry a loss in a product or service group for quite some time due to the positive profit performance in other product/service areas, and a broad financial base of resources, short-term lines of credit, long-term financing, and cash reserves. When the new venture is threatened with diversifinancial troubles, the entrepreneur can become overly focused with trying to remedy the situation as quickly as possible. The weight of the situation can open wide the door to ethical compromise certain positions about what constitutes an acceptable partnership deal, or whether the company should maintain the same climate of internal firm culture. It can force the entrepreneur into a desperate search for financing arrangements that were previously considered unacceptable. Change can also pressure the entrepreneur to make significant alterations in the company's market expectations in order to justify certain financial or partnership proposals. And it can negatively influence the owner's ability to remain objective and entirely forthright in matters of representation in dealing with desperately needed capital providers, market channels, or end-users.

The exposure to diversifinancial concerns brought about by change also opens the possibility that the entrepreneur will experience increased pressure to "fix" things in a quick manner that will sustain repeated impacts from the volatility in the market. This opens up numerous ethical problems for the entrepreneur in two primary areas. Each of these are timing issues linked directly to the entrepreneur's interpretation of the impending change. First, the owner can respond too quickly to the wrong perception of the impending changes. There is a pressure for business owners to be able to immediately recognize change and its accompanying issues, and how and when they will impact the firm. So it follows that many entrepreneurs get caught in a tendency to "jump the gun" and make a quick response to the first glimpse of change. A knee-jerk reaction can be devastating to the non diversified new venture. The owner may seek out an immediate quick fix that in the short run might ease some cash flow worries or inventory backlogs, but the long-term position of the firm could remain in jeopardy due to the lasting impact of the changes in market. The focus is on near-term survival rather than on the longer-term position of the firm in the market. This first timing concern involves "moving too fast and too short-sighted." The urgency factor can affect the entrepreneur's ability to hold on to clearly ethical decision criteria. Second, the entrepreneur can postpone and delay responding to the change, choosing to "play it safe" or "wait and see," but then finds out later on, that the time necessary to make financial investments and marketing adjustments to the company's strategy is longer than the time remaining until the emerging change makes its complete effects felt in all aspects of the market. This is also aimed at short-term survival, because the owner is so concerned about holding on to and protecting what the firm has, that no plans were considered for anything outside the immediate time frame. This is overly cautious position can also open the door to ethical problems in decision making because the individual interpretation can be overly optimistic and simply assume that this present change will "blow over." So this second timing concern involves "moving too slow and too short-sighted." In both cases, responses became short-term oriented, and this can challenge the entrepreneur's ability to think clearly, and remain committed to core values and ethical behavior.

A look back at some of the previously discussed topics from Chapter Two and Chapter Seven will provide some insights into the troubling effects that change can have on the entrepreneur's ethical perspectives. Refer back to Figure 2.2 and a new venture's commitment of resources to a supposed emerging opportunity. In the same way that the individual assesses a new market, so too the owner makes a judgment about the emerging changes in the external environment. The knee-jerk response to change is very similar to assuming a huge market opportunity and making an immediate, full scale commitment of resources to that target (location $A^*$). The entrepreneur runs the risk of missing the true long-term status of the change and being in a poor position once the complete effects of the change arrive. Or, the entrepreneur could wait too long and make no commitment (location $B^*$), only to find out later on that the change requires a significant adjustment in the firm's strategy, but now there is not enough time to do this effectively.

Figure 7.1 showed how the entrepreneur gains greater knowledge of the market based on the interpretation of different types of signals that are received from the external environment. Strong signals are very similar to gradual, methodical changes that occur in the market. They allow quite a bit of time for the firm to respond once the knowledge of the change reaches a relatively high level of understanding about the change. But the biggest concern for ethical behavior is tied to rapid change, or weak signals, where the entrepreneur makes a miscalculated and short-sighted spontaneous reaction that is off the mark, or falls back to a "wait and see" approach. By the time knowledge of the change reaches a critical level, there is not enough opportunity to put together a substantial response, due to the nature of the diversifinancial compounding effect. When the entrepreneur perceives that impending change is like a fuse on a stick of dynamite that is burning down quickly, or a timer ticking down the final seconds prior to an explosion, the temptation to sound ethical behavior is either to make a fast reaction that may not be well thought out for the long term, or offer no response and ignore the change, hoping it will soon go away. In either case, the owner's ability to make clear decisions based on core values and sound ethical choices will be challenged and tested, and the view of the situation could become clouded in light of a perceived urgency in the life of the enterprise. In a similar manner, Figure 7.2 and Figure 7.3 showed how the entrepreneur could misinterpret an emerging opportunity and set in motion a response to a given signal that incorrectly positions the firm for the long term. So too, depending on the level of the change signals, the entrepreneur could do "too much too soon" or "too little too late" by using either a "quick-fix" or "wait and see" strategy. These each create the potential for questionable moral judgments as the entrepreneur may abandon core values and ethical behavior in order to quickly move the venture away from apparent danger, or preserve the firm in the short-term at the expense of sacrificing viability.

## Searching for New Venture Momentum

The entrepreneur would like nothing better than to see the firm make a successful launch followed by a rapid increase in sales growth and profits. But the main issues about new venture development are not so much tied to the feasibility of the launch and the excitement and novelty of a new market introduction, but to the firm's ability to maintain strong performance over the long term. This sustained growth within a large and expanding market is called venture viability and was dealt with in detail in Chapter Five. Momentum is defined as strength or force that keeps growing. Within the context of this discussion of entrepreneurial new ventures, momentum describes the firm's ability to not only maintain a particular pace of business operations, but to include a regular incremental increase in that pace over a relatively long period of time. The momentum process can look something like this. The new venture introduces its product or service, the market begins to adopt the concept, sales begin to grow, some favorable publicity and timely promotions continue to build the trend of widespread market penetration, profitability is attained, and the firm expands its sales efforts from a regional to a national level. But the press toward a certain goal can bring about numerous ethical concerns involving levels of commitment, lack of diversification, and market expectations that are all subject to negative ramifications for the firm's position due to significant change.

Figure 11.1 demonstrates a major concern about the negative effect of momentum and its potential to adversely impact the ethical behavior of the entrepreneur. The horizontal line represents time—the company's life cycle (starting with the launch and moving into periods of various levels of growth). If the business is moving at "full speed ahead" toward significant market penetration, weak or strong signals about potential changes may be detected as the entrepreneur assesses the competitive landscape (see Figure 7.1). At some point in the life of the firm there exists an optimum point of change ($C_o$) at which it is best to make adjustments in the firm's plans relative to the changes that are unfolding. This begins at time period $t_o$ and continues for $n$ number of time periods to $t_{+n}$. This interval R, is the range of time within which the firm will be required to make a shift in its direction due to the critical nature of the change (the window of opportunity for the firm to remain competitive in the market). If the entrepreneur is affected by diversifinancial troubles and is over committed in a singular market, the positive momentum prior to $C_o$ could suddenly become negative momentum that does not allow the company to make the changes in direction until farther down the line at point $C_m$ (change made). The period of time between $t_o$ and $C_m$ shows the skidding effect of negative momentum. The firm has, in essence, applied the brakes to its present course, but cannot safely turn until the residual speed of the prior strategy slows down. Once the turn in direction is made at $C_m$, the firm will have to deal with the gap (the lost time) between when it *should have* made its new strategy move and when it actually did make its move. If the firm is the market leader, the followers might also trail in the leader's path and experience a comparable skidding effect. But if the new venture is a follower, the skid area of negative momentum could be longer than the leader's due to a time lapse between recognizing the change in the leader's course and the entrepreneur being able to execute a similar maneuver.

■ ■ ■ ■

**Figure 11.1
Negative Firm Momentum**

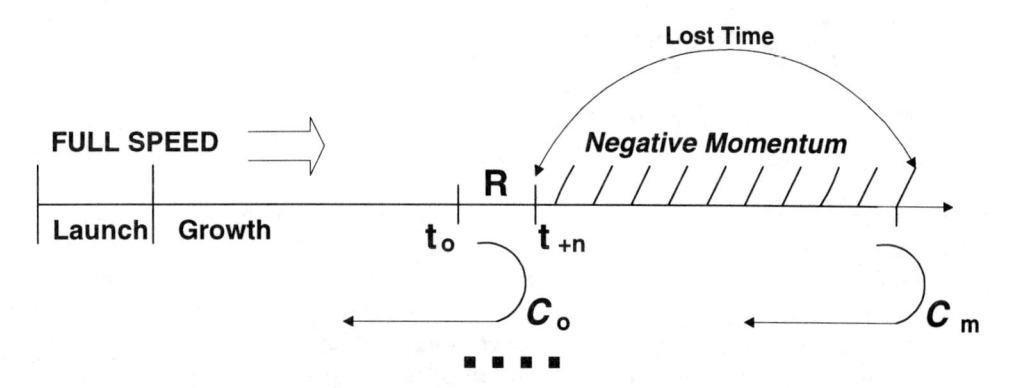

```
                                          Lost Time
                                         ⌒⌒⌒⌒⌒⌒
        FULL SPEED   ⟹              Negative Momentum
                                 R  ////////////
    |     |                      |  |
    Launch  Growth         t₀      t₊ₙ
                           ⌒            ⌒
                           ⌓C₀          ⌓Cₘ
```

■ ■ ■ ■

The new venture could also proceed with their market strategy at a much slower and more conservative pace. This type of controlled momentum is certainly a more risk averse position. Figure 11.2 shows the entrepreneurial new venture following the market leader at a more steady and controlled pace. The rationale behind this approach is that when change occurs, the market leaders will make the first moves and the followers will somehow be able to benefit from the foresight about the impending change that is communicated by the leader through various perceived signals in marketing, production, and financial operations. The entrepreneur could believe that when the leader makes the first move at the optimum point of change $C_o$, the new venture will simply be able to follow in the leader's wake with a change made at point $C_m$ to replicates the other company's strategy. However, this is also very dangerous because the new venture's lack of product diversification and financial strength could make it virtually impossible to closely shadow the leader. It is not so much that the smaller firm has a slower speed (and less momentum), but that it probably lacks the necessary internal capabilities to execute the turn effectively. It takes an oil super tanker, traveling at thirty knots, almost three miles to make a complete ninety degree turn to the left or the right. So too, a fast-growth new venture may not be able to "turn on a dime" in the face of change. Even a slower paced "follower" new venture (Figure 11.2) will lose some competitive positioning ground while making a sharp turn in response to the market leader.

The entrepreneur will generally have to guard against the temptation to misrepresent the firm's true position to the outside stake holders during time of significant change. There will be a two-fold effect of momentum on ethical behavior. First, as the new venture speeds along at a fast-growth pace in the lead position (Figure 11.1), the entrepreneur could be tempted to disregard the attention to every little detail about the company's transactions in the func-

**Figure 11.1
Negative Firm Momentum**

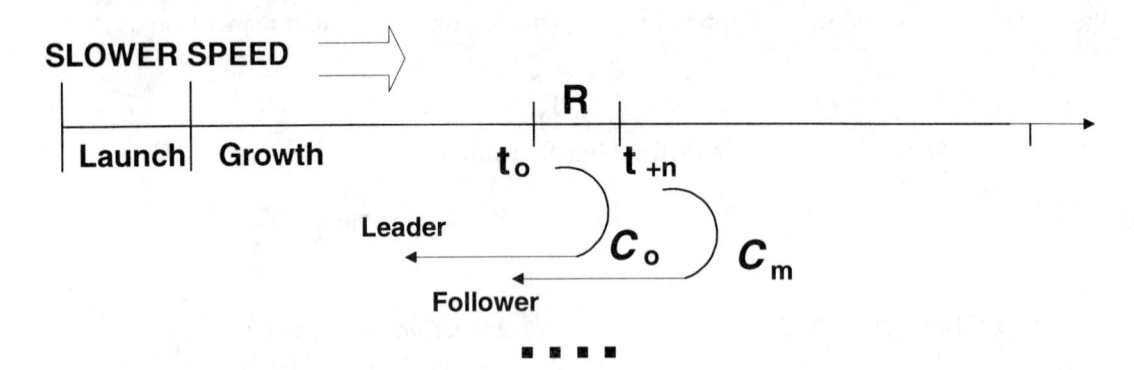

SLOWER SPEED ⇒

| Launch | Growth |  $t_o$  R  $t_{+n}$  
Leader  
$C_o$  $C_m$  
Follower

tional areas because the enterprise is growing so quickly and the main focus is on new sales and expanding the market share. Devoting time and resources to ethics and values could very likely take a back seat to marketing, promotions, and advertising during periods of successful sales and increased profitability. The entrepreneur could also face challenges in accurately representing the company, its market expectations, and its financial requirements when everything about the company is so positive and upbeat. But this type of significant momentum can hurt the company further down the road when immediate and considerable change surfaces in the external environment. Many entrepreneurs are lulled into a temporary false sense of security when sales are growing and forward momentum is building continuously during, and soon after, the launch. When the entrepreneur's attention is singularly focused on the positive aspects of sales growth, additional market share, and increased profitability, concerns about core values and ethical behavior could be easily pushed to the back burner. In fact, there can be a tendency for firm owners to believe that a need for extra attention to ethics and values is more closely related to difficult economic times for the company's sales and profits. Running headlong into rapid market growth soon after the launch can create huge ethical problems later on when significant change is introduced into the market and the firm experiences some degree of negative momentum as it tries to quickly adjust its strategy and positioning (Figure 11.1). Also, partnership arrangements could be placed in jeopardy due to change, but the entrepreneur may not be willing to share information or tell the entire story to outside business partners about the negative effects that change will have on the firm's functional capabilities. And, market expectations and financial requirements could be altered significantly due to change, but the entrepreneur may deny or alter the facts, and abandon core values in order to maintain an external image that the firm is still well positioned and able to meet all its obligations. The entrepreneur will be very vulnerable when change creates negative pressure to adjust and redirect the new venture's original business strategy that has been rendered obsolete by the new trends in the market. It is a difficult task to successfully shift the company's momentum and direction due to the introduction of change and its effects on market positioning and firm viability. It is during periods of initial positive momentum, and difficult times of negative reactionary momentum, that the entrepreneur is most likely to experience challenges to core values and ethical behavior, because the very life of the new venture might be at stake. The normal flow of daily business operations will have to make the necessary adjustments to accommodate change, which will likely affect the entrepreneur's perception about maintaining moral absolutes given the unique circumstances facing the firm.

## Sources of Change and Momentum

There are several places from which change can originate. The internal operations of the new venture can introduce change. This can come from a managerial decision to change a certain policy or procedural parameter. It can come from a new production process or technological development that is ready to be implemented. It can come about from a reorganization of the company's personnel qualifications and functional locations. It can also be the result of a new product or service innovation introduced into the market. In these situations the new venture is imposing its change onto other firms in the external environment. Change can also be thrust upon the new venture from outside forces. These could include a competitor's product or service innovation, a new information systems requirement from different marketing channels, a new form of government regulation, a domestic or international political event, or a shift in certain macro economic trends. The source of change often has a direct impact on the extent of the firm's ability to maintain favorable momentum in the market. For example, change that comes from within the firm's internal environment is generally well-planned with respect to the company's overall marketing, financial, and operations strategies. The venture will guard the critical information about the change from its competition and establish a clear sense of direction and funding support prior to unveiling the change to the public. This is an ideal situation because it allows the entrepreneur to formulate a comprehensive plan to deal with the effects that the change will bring about in the market, the hope being that this will clearly distinguish the new venture as a leader in this particular area of technology, production, or product and service offerings.

Many times, however, the change that impacts the new venture comes from outside the firm. The external environment thrusts change onto the entrepreneur's doorstep and the owner must be both prepared with an accurate assessment of the impact the change will have on the enterprise, and prepared with an appropriate response that will allow the company to avoid negative effects to performance. The uncertainty surrounding potential changes from the external environment, and the risks involved in putting into place the correct response, together create in the entrepreneur either a frustrating sense of apprehension about what to do next, or an emboldened sense of empowerment to quickly respond with a daring and gutsy strategy. In these two cases, the entrepreneur is either placed in a position of having nearly full knowledge of the pertinent information (internal change), or limited knowledge of the relevant information (external change). There are ethical considerations that must be explored regarding how the entrepreneur communicates, negotiates, and positions the firm, for decisions, negotiations, market expectations, and representation to outside stake holders.

## Ethical Exposure, Change, and Momentum

There are distinct ethical concerns for the entrepreneur based on the effects of change and the desire to maintain venture momentum. Table 11.1 lists the basic challenges and obstacles to entrepreneurial ethical behavior that come from changes that impact the new venture. Owners of small firms can easily experience a sense that everything outlined in the original business plan is no longer valid, and the entire scope of the new venture's operations and market strategy must be brought into question. The change can be perceived as both undermining the entrepreneur's confidence in knowing what is best for the firm, and brining into question whether the owner does in fact have the necessary technical and managerial expertise to handle the newly emerging changes in the business. Information becomes a prime resource for assessing the status of the venture, and the entrepreneur's ability to maintain control of operations and future direction. It also can erode the explicit and implicit commitments to various business partners, and may reduce the overall credibility of the venture's expectations for sales and profits now that the market has been affected. The original business plan outlined the feasibility and long term viability of the venture based on assumptions that did not include the effects of the present changes in the environment. All forecasted information and the entrepreneur's representation of that data were tied to a specific point in time, and generally three or four years of projections assumed under somewhat constant conditions. If the entire foundation for the new venture's existence is challenged by the changes in the environment, the business plan is no longer a reliable picture of the venture's prospects and must be disregarded in light of the current information. With the enterprise under intense scrutiny and the entrepreneur's position of control and responsibility disputed by insiders and outsiders alike, there will be pressure to make favorable assessments about the firm's direction and the entrepreneur will be tempted to alter some ethical behaviors in order to conserve the company's resources and support any prior momentum. The five ethical domains will each present different forms of potential compromise as the entrepreneur is burdened with the need to keep the venture in a positive light as capital providers, market channels, and end-users begin to question the overall strength of the company in the face of significant change. To meet and maintain company goals and objectives during tough economic times, many entrepreneurs will face various temptations to cut ethical corners in the various domains of representation, expectations and forecasts, financial matters, partnership arrangements, and even within the internal structure and policies and procedures of the new venture firm culture.[10]

■ ■ ■ ■

### Table 11.1
### The Effects of Change on Ethics

1. *Diminished Entrepreneurial Confidence*
2. *Questioning of Entrepreneurial Expertise*
3. *Increased Propensity to Withhold Information*
4. *Threat to Entrepreneurial Control*
5. *Lack of Commitment to Business Partners*
6. *Reduced Credibility of Market Expectations*

■ ■ ■ ■

## The Ethics Model and Change

Change can be thought of as a comprehensive force that sweeps across the *EVI* matrix for any of the five ethical domains. As such, it disturbs the way the entrepreneur thinks and acts with respect to the seven general business functions. Adjustments will have to be made regarding how the firm is positioned, how situations are assessed, how transactions are executed, how negotiations are handled, how communication is engaged, how decisions are made, and how relationships are maintain. Think of change as a secondary challenge to ethical behavior. Given the original ethical problem areas identified in the *EVI* matrix, the entrepreneur may become sensitive to the potential for compromise during the "normal" course of functional operations. But the secondary difficulty comes when the "normal" course of daily business is significantly altered due to some level of change from the external environment. The established policies and procedures are subject to reevaluation and could be assigned higher or lower priorities with respect to how certain changes affect the viability of the new venture. The effects of change will be felt throughout the new venture, so arguably, it is not possible to use the *EVI* matrix to locate potential problem areas for ethics based on the impact of change and any resultant negative momentum. However, change will exhibit numerous forms of influence on the five ethical domains identified throughout the previous chapters. In the survey, the entrepreneurs were asked about how they perceived change within the recent past, since they first appeared on the *INC. 500*. Two-thirds of the owners (65%) stated that their particular market had generally experienced dramatic changes. This does not try to quantify change or define the type or magnitude of change experienced, but it does provide a basic overview of the subjective interpretations of the entrepreneurs regarding whether they perceived change affecting their companies. The remaining owners (35%) said that their market had generally little or no significant change since their inclusion on the *INC. 500*. And remember, about seven out of ten owners (69%) stated that the combined risks for their new ventures were quite formidable and difficult to manage.

### *Representation Exposure*

As was previously outlined in Chapter Six, the entrepreneur makes various forms of new venture representation to three primary outside constituencies, namely capital providers, marketing channels, and wholesale and retail end-users. The *EVI* matrix outlined in Figure 6.3 highlighted the proposed "problem areas" for entrepreneurial ethics for matters of firm representation. When change is introduced into this mix, the prospects for compromising personal values and ethics are increased. The personal reputation of the entrepreneur is always at stake any time the enterprise makes information available to the outside stake holders. Change usually introduces increased levels of risk and uncertainty which could cause the entrepreneur to withhold pertinent information about the firm's future viability. The entire scope of the company's market opportunity could be substantially reduced or, in some extreme cases, completely eliminated due to a radical change in the external environment. The role of innovator could be severely discounted due to large scale redefinitions of product and service technologies and processes. The business reputation is also at stake as the entrepreneur could seek to preserve a favorable perspective and ward off any adverse opinions about firm performance.

Change might also call into question the degree of control that the entrepreneur maintains in decision making and company strategy. If a major shift in policy direction is necessary, an informal corporate culture and narrow organizational structure could create major problems for both the timely flow and content integrity of information conveyed in firm representation. There might be no greater pressure on the entrepreneur to compromise ethics than when the venture is having to make crucial adjustments in its strategy and position due to change in the market. The key issue is that the matrix may no longer be the best indicator of the potential strengths and weaknesses in entrepreneurial core values, because the level of change could alter the owner's priorities and perspective about what is considered acceptable in "normal" times versus what is deemed acceptable during times of significant change. And it does not always have to be viewed in the context of the negative effects of change. Entrepreneurs could easily cross many ethical boundaries within the context of firm representation when change brings about huge benefits to the company's position in the market.

## *Market Expectations Exposure*

The effects of change will have a very similar impact on the ethical stability of the entrepreneur's moral basis and the firm's core values in dealing with market expectations as it had on firm representation. There is a direct link between the venture's future prospects in the market, how the firm is represented to outsiders, and the level of change that takes place in the external environment. So much of the entrepreneur's representation is based on the individual view toward market opportunity and expectations for sales and profit viability. The owner's market expectations are the direct results of the personal interpretation of several key characteristics that the entrepreneur displays, namely being innovative and being able to spot an opportunity. The ethics of realistic market expectations will likely encounter difficulties and challenges in areas such as *touting* and the entrepreneur-dependent assessments formulated about the scope of the innovation introduced and the impact it is expected to have on the existing market. Figure 7.6 focused in on the proposed problem issues involved in assessing, deciding, and communicating the new venture's prospects for sales growth and degree of profitability. Perhaps the most awkward outcome of change on the entrepreneur's ability to construct market expectations is the way that sweeping changes can be used to provide a subjective cover for the inaccuracy of expectations in the original model. It is quite convenient to suddenly have a new round of change come and alter the existing market, which at one time had been a future *expected* market. The new changes bring about shifts in the entire range of assumptions developed previously, and the entrepreneur's level of accuracy can be shrouded in the volatility of the current changes. This allows for an entirely new set of assumptions to be put forth based on new assessments, when it would have been difficult to introduce new assumptions had their not been volatile activity in the external environment. The entrepreneur can use change as a rationale to bail out prior expectations that were far off the recent actual results. Questions of accuracy, disclosure, and the underlying basis for overly optimistic forecasts can often be conveniently circumvented when the market is experiencing significant change. Personal values associated with forecast accuracy and the ability to justify optimism will be greatly affected by the influx of change, as different situations emerge and render previous expectations and assumptions irrelevant. The entrepreneur's personal interpretation of these events serves as the focal point for how the outside stake holders receive adjustments to expectations based on change. The entrepreneur is obviously in a place that can direct and influence opinion about the venture during times of change and uncertainty.

## *Financial Requirements Exposure*

The entrepreneur normally provides a detailed investment schedule for asset acquisitions and working capital provisions for the launch of the new venture. The perceived requirements are dollar figures that must be qualitatively and quantitatively justified to capital providers in keeping with the overall market expectations of the enterprise and the levels of anticipated feasibility and viability exhibited by the product or service innovation. Change is interesting in this context, because it is often factored into the assumptions that determine the required financing for the launch and the transition to profitability. But what really makes for ethical compromise are both the extent of future *expected* volatility, and the ways that changes are linked to how much financing is needed in certain aspects of the enterprise asset mix. The entrepreneur will be greatly challenged to hold on to the same consistent assumptions that helped to persuade the original capital providers to join the enterprise now that a particular type of change has been introduced into the present scenario. For example, Figure 8.3 proposed the key areas that could affect ethical compromise related to the financial requirements of the new venture. These could be incorporated to some degree in the assumptions that built the original range of potential outcomes that could occur due to various changes in the market. The entrepreneur must now make the subjective assessment as to whether these previously outlined *expected* changes are valid in the present state of flux, and if they are not, can the company's financial picture be modified to fit the real change that is happening, or could the entrepreneur be tempted to represent the current change as that which was built into the original financial plan. The owner might compromise the core values related to disclosure and rapport with outsiders in order to salvage the best possible picture about the firm's financial situation during periods of change that were altogether unanticipated and never planned for.

## *Partnering Exposure*

It should be easily understood that change will have huge impact on the entrepreneur's ability to maintain existing business partnerships. But beyond basic maintenance, the new venture must decide how the changes that are upon the market affect the functional capabilities of the partner firm in light of the goals and objectives that were originally established. The core values that supported the initial rationale for the joint venture must be reexamined in light of the changes taking place in the environment. Perhaps the most formidable test of entrepreneurial ethics involves the determination by only one of the parties that the partnership is no longer valid due to the shift in the market. This can happen two ways. The entrepreneur could feel that now, more than ever, the new venture needs to stay involved with the other company as a hedge against certain risks that are perceived due to the change. But the other firm interprets the change in a different light and believes it is best to terminate the agreement. The new venture sees the on-going partnership as a positive response to the change while the other party views the partnership as an impediment to continued success. One firm wants to draw closer to insure some perceived aspect of stability and the other wants to make a clean break to increase some perceived sense of flexibility. In the first situation, the entrepreneur may want to hold the deal together and is challenged with the ethics of persuading the other firm to remain in the partnership. In the second situation, the owner of the new venture could encounter challenges to personal morals and core values in needing to devise a means of exiting the partnership, when the other firm wants to remain allied. In either case, the problem areas highlighted in Figure 9.3 will be significantly tested when change introduces questions about the necessity of various entrepreneurial partnering arrangements.

### *Firm Culture Exposure*

Finally, change can have a dramatic impact on the inner workings and dynamics of the entrepreneurial new venture. The once informal and casual internal environment could instantly be required to become formalized and highly structured due to the new trends in the market. Figure 10.3 outlined the potential for ethical compromise in the entrepreneur's establishing and managing a distinctive firm culture tied to the owner's personal morals and core values. This book has proposed that the entrepreneurial firm culture can be examined based on the degree of owner value reflectivity. And many prior research studies have found strong evidence that, for most small businesses, ethics generally begin with the entrepreneur's commitment to inculcate clearly defined foundational principles among all levels of the employees.[11] The primary ethical challenges come in how the entrepreneur maintains the balance between mandating a form of corporate morality and simply allowing the enterprise to exist in a "values vacuum," where each employee acts according to their own sense of what is appropriate business procedure relative to each situation. When change arrives, the firm could be forced to adopt policies and procedures that are different from the normal means of daily operations in order to respond to the changes. The entrepreneur will have to weigh the ethical issues of how to manage the flow of internal communications and decision making authority when the existing culture requires significant adjustments to the logistics of operations.

## Conclusions

The entrepreneur is in a unique position relative to change. The firm's five ethical domains will initially take on some form of identity based on the individual biases and moral judgments of the owner's personal values system. Nearly every aspect of how the firm is represented, how market expectations are determined, how financial requirements are established, how partnership deals are structured, and how firm culture is managed is a product of the entrepreneur's subjective choice or position on the matter. The firm owner is comfortable with uncertainty and managing risk, is seeking innovative and significant opportunity, and wants to keep a close watch over business operations and responsibility. The entrepreneur has quite a bit of influence in determining the firm's strategy and direction. Change can provide the owner an opportunity to exercise even greater control and leverage as the firm's original position and growth expectations in the market are brought into question.[12] The entrepreneur can actually use change as an unfair advantage or catalyst for seizing control back from prior areas of delegation. Employees might be less likely to challenge lay-offs, budget cut-backs, and suspended capital improvements during times of change, and the entrepreneur could easily exploit the situation for personal gain at the expense of the greater good of the enterprise. The degree of programmatic checks and balances could also increase the entrepreneur's temptation to use change as a convenient rationale for questionable ethical behavior and adjusting the moral basis and core values of the firm.

# CHAPTER TWELVE

# *Evidences and Interaction of Ethics*

## Introduction

The final pieces of this study that must be examined involve how entrepreneurs perceive their positions on personal values, moral judgments, and ethical behavior versus how they act in certain scenarios derived from the five ethical domains. This final chapter will first provide the remaining summary statistics about personal values and ethical perceptions from the survey data. Then the evidence for whether owners practice ethics will be examined across several interactions using a series of multiple regression functions. The insights about the various effects of the entrepreneur's perceptions and beliefs about morals and ethics when compared with how behaviors and attitudes happen in these various domains is very intriguing. Although there is no way to completely explain how the entrepreneur acts in a given situation, the results do provide an excellent basis for discussion and inferences into the processes of entrepreneurial ethics in successful new ventures. During the course of the research, over sixty separate regressions were performed. Fifteen of these functions were selected because they were both highly significant and offered the greatest insights into entrepreneurial ethical behavior within the new venture environment.

Demographic data about the owner's age, sex, and education level, and the company's number of years in business and relative size based on employment, were tested for each of the functions that were chosen as a secondary examination of whether there were also any differences in the ethical behavior and attitudes between younger and older entrepreneurs, men versus women, education levels, larger firms versus smaller firms (based on employment), or older firms versus younger firms. Where any of this demographic data was found to make significant contributions to the explanation of a given hypothesis, they are noted in the equation summaries. However, in many of the proposed equations, there were no differences between older and younger entrepreneurs, men and women, education levels, larger and smaller companies, or younger and older ventures. These secondary effects are often very provocative, when ethical behavior can be differentiated between how men and women act in a given situation, or how older and younger entrepreneurs behave in certain scenarios.

It can also be very intriguing to see how entrepreneur's in relatively larger new ventures act differently than those in somewhat smaller firms. And in some instances, the longer the new venture has been in existence, the more or less likely the entrepreneur is to act a certain way in a given ethical situation.

So as not to turn this final summary of evidences and interaction effects into a comprehensive quantitative review of advanced econometrics, all of the regression statistics for the equations have been organized in the *Appendix* that immediately follows this chapter. The statistical results for each equation's parameters and significance are summarized in a generally accepted format that corresponds to the narrative of this chapter, where each equation is interpreted in an easy to read manner to draw attention to the qualitative issues and association between the different combinations of variables being analyzed. The following proposed relationships are all based on the primary qualitative data from the previously mentioned *INC. 500* survey. It must be clearly stated that there could literally be dozens of variables that together explain any of the proposed ethical issues from this book. The goal of this chapter is not to provide comprehensive explanations for each of the entrepreneurial ethics issues. That is essentially impossible. But in the following situations, the proposed combinations of variables do explain a relatively significant portion of the variations in the ethics topics, and as such they provide considerable support for insights and inference into the ethical behavior of entrepreneurs.

## The Big Picture for Small Firms

It has been proposed that the process by which entrepreneurial ethics take hold in the new venture is most likely a direct function of the individual owner's commitment to personal moral bases and core values. This is a unique managerial endeavor for the entrepreneur. Competitive management generally defines the transaction-based activity displayed by entrepreneurs in pursuit of present and future profits, and is differentiated from the risky activity of strategic management and vision which incorporate seeing new technologies, product developments, and innovation in future markets, with an eye toward profit potential.[1] But entrepreneurial vision and effective leadership communication are necessary characteristics for owners of new ventures who wish to transfer a strategic view to others in the organization.[2] The decision to make ethics an integral component of the new venture development process requires the entrepreneur to examine the moral basis and fundamental tenets of a personal values system, and then recognize the applications of these as either guidelines or policies for all levels of business activities,[3] including positions, transactions, relationships, communication, negotiations, assessments, and decision making. The premise of this book is then that ethical behaviors, whether merely general guidelines or specific company policies, will be repeatedly challenged across five distinct ethical domains in the entrepreneurial new venture. Company representation, market expectations, financial requirements, business partnering, and firm culture have numerous potential "problem areas" that will test the moral and ethical resolve of the entrepreneur. For example, prior work has shown that entrepreneurs generally *want* to operate their ventures with consideration for external social responsibility, but they often have difficulty putting that concern into practice due to economic and competitive pressures.[4]

## Empirical Evidence of Personal Values and Ethics

When asked about the reasons behind the ultimate success of their new ventures, almost every entrepreneur in the *INC. 500* survey (99%) stated that firm success was closely attributed to their personal value system. This is very significant because it shows clearly that owners of successful new ventures perceive that firm performance is tied to the subjective aspects of *who* they are and *how* they do business. In a separate situation, an almost identical proportion (98%) said that their individual ethical beliefs have a direct impact on the success of the business. This notion of personal impact on the firm appears to be confirmed in that almost nine out of ten entrepreneurs (88%) said that the goals and objectives of the enterprise, its activities in the market, and its company-wide policies and procedures were also closely associated with their own personal values system. The entrepreneurs were also asked about whether the success of the new venture is due to a complementary management team that has a common set of values and ethical beliefs. More than four out of five (83%) agreed with this position and only a few (6%) disagreed. The remaining owners (11%) were not sure and said that it is not always the case in their firm. This evidence about their perceptions mounts a strong initial case for the argument that entrepreneurs believe that their personal moral identity has a strong influence in the performance of the new venture. This builds support for the presence of perceived ethical reflectivity in new ventures, but does not provide an endorsement of whether the firm really acts in a manner consistent with the entrepreneur's values.

These issues must now be addressed, concerning how the entrepreneur's perceptions play out in actual methods used in the business. For example, it was previously shown that about two out of every five entrepreneurs (39%) could not state definitively that they devote regular company time and resources to the development of a common managerial philosophy and distinctive ethical guidelines within the firm. And although seventy percent said there is no difference between their public and private managerial style, thirty percent agreed that they do have a dual personality when dealing with insiders versus outsiders. Another major concern about their "working" ethics, as opposed to their perceived behaviors, is that more than one quarter of those surveyed (27%) said that they do not utilize a firm position or even general guidelines when they are personally confronted with a difficult ethical decision, but that they choose their course of action based solely on the circumstances of the case. For many of those surveyed, this appears to conflict with how they thought of themselves.

Just over three quarters (76%) of the entrepreneurs believed that the intensity of the competitive market environment for new ventures definitely puts pressure on them to "do whatever it takes" to be successful. Now this does not say that they *would* "do whatever it takes," but they certainly appear to recognize that the challenge to ethical behavior is present in the new venture process. In a similar context, only about one in twelve entrepreneurs (8%) agreed that, because new ventures are comprised of so many unknown factors, it is nearly impossible to hold to absolute ethical standards given the wide range of decision situations. Another one in seven (18%) said they were not sure about this, but almost three out of every four owners (74%) disagreed, stating that they believed it was possible to hold to an absolute ethics standard. A similar situation regarding absolute ethical standards had nearly identical responses. Three quarters (75%) of the entrepreneurs said that they would choose to hold to an absolute ethical standard in decision making, rather than compromise their personal values, even if it meant that the venture would experience negative economics consequences. This is a very significant perception, because it can be inferred that the owners are claiming ethical integrity is more important than negative firm performance.

## Venture Success and Personal Values

The market has often informally surmised that the entrepreneurial new venture and the entrepreneur are essentially one and the same.[5] Equation 1.0 shows the first proposed hypothesis, that the entrepreneur's perception of new venture success can be explained by the impact of the owner's personal values on the goals and objectives of the firm, and by whether the entrepreneur utilizes both a public and private personal management style in the firm. More than ninety-nine percent of the entrepreneurs believe that venture success is closely attributed to their own personal values system. The proposed relationship was highly significant.

(1.0)    Success = $\beta_0 + \beta_1$ Goals - $\beta_2$ Style

The two variables together explained about ten percent of the variations in new venture success. The formation of venture goals and objectives was positively associated with the success of the firm being linked to the entrepreneur's personal values. But entrepreneurs who utilized a dual public and private management style were inversely related to the success of the new venture, such that owners who utilized this dual managerial style were less inclined to attribute their firm's success to their own personal values, while those who were consistent in their managerial approach tended to attribute success to their own values system. This is very intriguing, because it lends credibility to the premise that ethical goals for the firm and a straightforward managerial style contribute greatly to the firm's ultimate success in the market.

## Company Goals Defined

Next, it was surmised that the ethical formation and definition of the new venture's goals and objectives might be explained by the entrepreneur's overall impact on the company. Equation 2.0 proposed that the firm's goals are a function of an internal firm culture that is personally representative of the owner's business style, that the firm displays a deliberate company-wide manner of conducting business that directly reflects the entrepreneur's personal values, that the management team fully shares in common the entrepreneur's ethical and moral values, and that owners believed all of their business partners (like their management team) should also share the in their personal manner of business ethics.

(2.0)    Goals = $\beta_0 + \beta_1$ Culture + $\beta_2$ Firm + $\beta_3$ Team + $\beta_4$ Shared

The four variables together explained about fifteen percent of the variations in how the firm's goals were established. The entrepreneur's interest in working with other firms that shared the same morals and ethical beliefs was the most important relative contribution to the firm's moral, and ethical, goals and objectives. The firm's specific manner in doing business was the next most important issue, followed by a unified management team and finally a distinctive firm culture. All four parameters were positively related to the firm's goals and objectives, such that a personally reflective internal corporate culture, a firm manner of doing business that reflected the owner's personal values, a management team with unified morals and ethical beliefs, and the need for outside business partners to share in the entrepreneur's personal sense of business ethics all contribute directly to strong moral and ethical goals and objectives in entrepreneurial new ventures. This is consistent with previous works that advocate an anthropological approach to the nature of people and values as the basis for entrepreneurial success.[6]

## Ethics and Representation

The entrepreneur's decision to represent the firm in a particular manner is a vital component of company operations in the external market environment. Outsiders will construct impressions about the firm based largely on the perceived credibility of the owner's representation of insider information. The first hypothesis in this section addressed the entrepreneur's ability to hold to an *absolute* business ethic even if it would mean negative economic consequences for the firm. Three parameters were proposed to explain the entrepreneur's propensity to hold to an *absolute* position. These included the owner's: a) management style, b) use of conservative or liberal expectations in forecasting, and c) perception of whether to include negative information when speaking with outsiders about firm performance. Equation 3.0 outlines this proposed relationship.

(3.0)   Absolute Values = $\beta_0 - \beta_1$ Style + $\beta_2$ Forecast - $\beta_3$ Performance

The three variables together explained almost eight percent of the variation in the owners' use of an absolute ethic. The owner's use of a dual insider/outsider management style was inversely related (it has a negative sign), and contributed the greatest relative explanation, to the ability to hold to an absolute ethical standard. The means of forecasting firm performance was the next most important issue and was also inversely related (negative sign), such that the choice to withhold negative information was associated with entrepreneurs who would *not* hold to an absolute ethic. The owner's use of conservative or liberal expectations in forecasts was the third most important issue and was directly related (positive sign), such that the use of the "most realistic" expectations was closely associated with holding to an absolute ethical standard. None of the demographic data, such as age, education or employment, was significant.

A second hypothesis was tested regarding firm representation, based on the owners tending to use an *absolute* or *relative* position in making difficult ethical decisions. Four parameters were proposed to explain their ethical leaning. These included: a) the firm's goals, b) the owner's prior experience, c) the owner's managerial style, and d) whether they stated they would hold to an *absolute* ethic (as covered in the previous equation). Equation 4.0 summarizes the proposed relationship of these variables.

(4.0)   Ethic = $\beta_0 + \beta_1$ Goals - $\beta_2$ Experience - $\beta_3$ Style + $\beta_4$ Absolute

The variables together explain almost thirteen percent of the variations in what type of business ethic is used. The owner's use of a dual management style was inversely related, and was the most important contributor, to the use of an *absolute* business ethic. Those who had a dual style tended to use a *relative* ethic, while those who had no distinction in their public or private style tend to use an *absolute* ethic. The firm's goals and objectives being value-driven was the next most important issue and was positively related to the use of an *absolute* ethic. It was very interesting to find that when owners had prior experience in a similar field, they were more likely to use a *relative* ethic. And owners who previously said they would hold to an absolute ethic were consistent in their use of ethics in difficult situations.

The age of the entrepreneur was also found to be a very significant issue and positively related to the use of an absolute ethic, such that older owners are more likely to use an *absolute* ethic, while younger entrepreneurs use a more *relative* ethic. There were no distinctions between the size or age of the firm, or the entrepreneur's education, or men versus women.

## Ethics and Market Expectations

The entrepreneur's ability to accurately assess the new venture's market expectations presents a formidable challenge to personal business ethics. There will always exist the temptation to overestimate the opportunity in the emerging market, and this impacts the owner's ability to be entirely objective in drawing conclusions about the firm's prospects for future sales growth and profitability. Four parameters were proposed regarding the company's future expectations relative to the entrepreneur's previous business experience. These included: a) the idea for the venture, b) the focus of the entrepreneur, c) the difficulty of making initial financial expectations, and d) the use of liberal or conservative assumptions when making forecasts. More than two-thirds of the owners (69%) had experience in a similar or complementary field. Equation 5.0 outlines the proposed interaction of these variables.

**(5.0)**  $\text{Experience} = \beta_0 - \beta_1 \text{ Idea} - \beta_2 \text{ Focus} - \beta_3 \text{ Financial} + \beta_4 \text{ Forecast}$

It was very interesting to find that from the demographic data, the sex of the entrepreneur was also significantly associated with experience, and turned out to make the largest relative contribution as well. Together, the five variables explained about eleven percent of the variations in prior work experience, such that female entrepreneurs were much more likely to have similar or complementary experience prior to the launch of the new venture. The owner's use of more realistic expectations was the next most important issue related to experience. The use of a brand new idea or innovation in the existing market was inversely related to the entrepreneur's experience. The sense that financial expectations were not that difficult to assess was also inversely related to experience. And, the entrepreneur's focus for the firm was also inversely related to experience, such that those with similar prior experience were more near-term oriented in their managerial focus. This opens up numerous issues regarding the propensity for the entrepreneur to be more liberal in assumptions and more likely to mark figures upward when formulating firm expectations. Male entrepreneurs with unrelated prior experience were most likely to inflate expectations, being perhaps overly focused on the long-term issues of the firm, while female entrepreneurs with similar prior experience were most likely to use very conservative expectations and be focused more on the near-term issues of the enterprise.

A second hypothesis dealing with firm expectations proposed that the attitude toward risks would have a telling impact on the owner's expectations for the firm. More than two-thirds of the entrepreneurs (69%) stated that the risk for their venture were quite formidable, while the rest believed the risks to be minimal and somewhat easy to manage. The entrepreneur's perception of the difficulty to make financial projections, and the likelihood to use conservative versus liberal expectations in forecasts were used to explain the owner's risk position. Equation 6.0 summarizes this hypothesis.

**(6.0)** Risks = $\beta_0 + \beta_1$ Financial + $\beta_2$ Forecasts

The entrepreneur's age had a significant and positive impact in explaining the risk position. These three variables together explain over eleven percent of the variance in the entrepreneur's risk position. The number of years in business was extremely close to being significant as well with an inverse relationship (the longer the venture has been operating, the more likely the entrepreneur is to view the risks as formidable and difficult to manage), but it was just outside the cut-off point for inclusion in the equation. It appears that relatively younger entrepreneurs view risk as more substantial, and are likely to say that financial projections are more difficult to make, and they use more liberal estimates in their forecasts, while older entrepreneurs see risks as somewhat minimal, and believe that financial projections are easy to make and are likely to use more conservative estimates in their forecasts. This is quite revealing, as the older entrepreneurs seem more confident that they know what is going on and can handle the risks, whereas younger owners seem to have more concern for the risks of new venture development.

## Ethics and Financing Requirements

The owners of entrepreneurial new ventures are faced with numerous ethical challenges related to the raising of adequate financial resources for operations, and the interaction with outside capital providers. The ability to establish a forecast of the firm's future prospects in the market for sales and profitability is built on numerous assumptions that the owner makes about the market environment, and conveys a personal bias about the firm's likelihood for success in the future. This can have a tremendous impact on the perceptions of outside investors. About two-thirds of the owners surveyed (65%) said they only use the most realistic expectations in their forecasts, but many entrepreneurs will either mark-up their numbers (liberal expectations) or discount their numbers (conservative expectations), and investors must try and determine which position the owner takes in securing financing for the new venture. The propensity for the entrepreneur to either mark-up or discount financial forecasts is presumed to be a function of how the owner views the risks to new venture success, and the management of pertinent information about the financial performance of the enterprise. Equation 7.0 outlines this initial financing hypothesis.

**(7.0)** Forecast = $\beta_0 + \beta_1$ Risks - $\beta_2$ Performance

The entrepreneur's sex was also a significant issue in determining the way financial forecasts are made. The three variables together explain about twelve percent of the variations in entrepreneurial forecasting types. The most important item was whether the owner was male or female, followed by the owner's perspective about risk, and then the way information about financial performance is managed. Female entrepreneurs have a greater propensity to be more optimistic and mark-up expectations when forecasting compared to their male counterparts, as were owners who view the risks of the venture to be formidable and difficult to manage. It was also interesting to see that the entrepreneurs who tend to withhold negative information about the firm's financial performance also tend to be liberal in their forecasts of the firm's financial expectations.

A second hypothesis was proposed concerning entrepreneurial financial requirements in the new venture. The level of funding requested from capital providers requires the entrepreneur to make choices about how much money is really necessary to meet projected cash and investment needs. Almost four out of five surveyed (79%) said that when raising financial support, it is best to secure funding in excess of the amount required in the business plan. This infers that the majority of entrepreneur's are either relatively unsure about how much they really need to make the venture work, or wanting to provide a financial cushion against unforeseen expenses that can surface after the launch. The following four variables were proposed to explain the entrepreneur's likelihood to overfund the new venture: a) the owner's view of changes impacting the enterprise, b) how close were the original financial expectations to the actual results, c) the owner's opinion on whether the capital providers in the market should receive only unbiased information, and d) the owner's opinion about staying focused only on positive aspects of the firm when speaking with potential investors. Equation 8.0 summarizes the parameters in this proposed relationship.

**(8.0)** Funding = $\beta_0 - \beta_1$ Changes + $\beta_2$ Close + $\beta_3$ Unbiased + $\beta_4$ Investor

The sex of the entrepreneur was once again the most significant factor in explaining the entrepreneur's position, such that female entrepreneurs were more likely to request funding in excess of the planned requirements. The five variables together explained about thirteen percent of the variations in the funding perspectives of owners. The next most important factor was the entrepreneur's opinion on whether to provide negative information to investors, followed by how close financial forecasts were to actual results. These first two variables were both directly related to funding, such that those who felt their forecasts were very close to the actual results, and those who stayed focused only on the positive aspects of the firm were most likely to secure only the exact amount of funding necessary. The owner's opinion about providing unbiased information to investors was slightly positive, such that most were "not sure" or believed they should interpret the information for investors. It was very interesting to see an inverse relationship between changes and funding, although the association was only marginal. Entrepreneurs who tended to perceive that their firm experienced dramatic changes were more likely to secure funding in excess of the planned amount, while those owners who said there was little or no change affecting the venture were apt to secure the exact amount of funding.

## Ethics and Partnering Arrangements

The entrepreneur is also subject to numerous ethical issues associated with the new venture partnering process. About three out of five owners (59%) said that they make extensive use of partnerships, joint ventures, and alliances in their business operations. It was proposed that the owner's focus was the main issue that explains the use of partnerships, and that the longer a company has been in business, the *less* likely it is to use business partnering arrangements (due to establishing greater autonomy over the years), whereas the newest firms are expected to make extensive use of partnership deals. Equation 9.0 outlines this relationship.

(9.0)  Partnering = $\beta_0 + \beta_1$ Focus $- \beta_2$ Years

No other demographic data such as the entrepreneur's age or sex, or the size of the firm, had any significant impact on the propensity to utilize partnership deals. These two variables explained only about three percent of the variations in why new ventures use partnerships, but the function was significant. Although marginally close to being material, the entrepreneur's focus was just outside the cut-off point for significance. Entrepreneurs who were primarily focused on the long-term issues of the firm, and whose companies were the relatively youngest, appear to be somewhat more likely to seek out partnership deals, while companies that had been in business for a longer time and had a more near-term focus tended to make little or no use of partnership arrangements. This function was much less definitive than all the others, but was included because it provided some marginal insights into the negotiation process. It was interesting to note that the entrepreneur's desire to structure the partnership deal so that it heavily favored the new venture was *not* associated with the excess negotiation tactic.

Small firm partnership arrangements present ethical challenges to the entrepreneur concerning the negotiation process of securing a deal. As was previously discussed in chapter nine, this also involves some overlap with ethical issues of firm representation, market expectations, and financing requirements. It was reported that almost one third of the owners surveyed (31%) agreed that it was a perfectly acceptable business practice to start partnership negotiations far in excess of expectations and goals in order to ultimately arrive at an acceptable settlement position. An almost equal proportion (29%) disagreed with this, but forty percent were not sure, saying it depended on the circumstances of the situation. The next hypothesis proposed that the entrepreneur's approach to negotiating a partnership deal could be explained by how the owner views both the risks associated with the venture, and whether the intensity of the competitive environment for new venture development puts pressure on individuals to "do whatever it takes" to be successful. Equation 10.0 outlines this scenario.

(10.0)  Negotiate = $\beta_0 + \beta_1$ Risks $+ \beta_2$ Intensity

There was once again a significant difference between male and female entrepreneurs, such that men were less likely to start negotiations far in excess of the targeted agreement. These three variables together explained about seven percent of the variations in how entrepreneurs negotiate a partnership deal. The intensity of the new venture was the most important issue, followed by the perception of the risks involved in the enterprise. Female owners who felt the environment *does* put pressure on the entrepreneur to "do whatever it takes" to be successful, and who perceived the risks to be formidable and difficult to manage, were most likely to employ the excess strategy in negotiating an outside business alliance.

A third area of ethical concern was proposed within the context of entrepreneurial partnering. The question of the owner holding to an absolute ethical standard, even if it meant negative economic consequences for the new venture, seemed intuitively suited for this ethical domain. The prospects of the entrepreneur being caught in a business alliance on the decline would test the moral resolve of the individual's ability to follow through on a contractual agreement. Remember three quarters (75%) of the owners said that they would stand firm on an absolute ethic. It was proposed that the entrepreneur's interpretation about who a partnership deal should benefit most, and whether the business partners share the owner's personal values and business ethics, together would be associated with the entrepreneur's resolve to hold to an *absolute* ethic. Equation 11.0 summarizes this idea.

**(11.0)** Absolute = $\beta_0 - \beta_1$ Benefit + $\beta_2$ Shared

The number of years that the firm has been in business was also found to be a very significant and direct relationship within this function, such that the longer a company had been in operation, the more likely it was that the owner would hold to an absolute ethical standard. It was interesting to see that having a management team with unified morals and ethical beliefs was in no way related to any of the partnership issues. The entrepreneurs who disagreed with the idea that a partnership should be structured to favor their new venture, and those who believed partners should share the same morals and business ethics were most likely to hold to an absolute ethic, while those who felt that partnerships should be arranged in favor of the new venture, and felt it was *not* important for a business partner to share their values were generally those who would not hold to an absolute ethical standard. The ability to structure a successful partnership arrangement appears to be a direct function of the entrepreneur's personal values system, which seems to have a direct association with the relative longevity of the new company.

The last interaction regarding the ethics of small firm partnering deals with the entrepreneur's commitment to recognize and honor an oral agreement versus the opportunity to unilaterally rescind such an agreement in order to pursue a secondary deal that appears more beneficial. Almost one third of the entrepreneurs surveyed (32%) stated that they would try get the other company to back out of the first deal in order to pursue an agreement with the second firm. And another two percent stated it would depend on the circumstances. It was proposed that the entrepreneur's position on whether to maintain a strong stand on difficult ethical issues would provide the first insights into this tendency to want to escape an oral deal. It was also assumed that the degree to which the management team shares unified morals and ethical beliefs, and the entrepreneur's position on absolute versus relative values would also help to explain the owner's position on oral partnership deals. Equation 12.0 shows this functional form.

**(12.0)** Oral = $\beta_0 + \beta_1$ Ethical + $\beta_2$ Team + $\beta_3$ Absolute

Evidences and Interaction of Ethics ■ 201

The demographic data was also tested and it showed that the size of the firm was also related to the entrepreneur's position on oral agreements. This parameter made only a relatively small contribution to the function, but it was very significant. Together, these four variables explained twelve percent of the variations in how entrepreneurs handle oral partnership arrangements. The most important contributor to the issue was the venture's management team. When the team shared unified morals and ethical beliefs, it was very probable that the entrepreneur would honor the original oral agreement. The next most important factor was whether or not the owner maintains a firm position when faced with difficult ethical decisions. Those who maintain a firm position are most likely to honor the agreement. Also, those individuals who hold to an *absolute* ethic are likely to abide by an oral agreement. And finally, it appears that the smaller the firm (in terms of employment) the more likely it is that the entrepreneur will honor an oral contract. Perhaps the smallest new ventures believe they must honor oral contracts because they lack the necessary size and clout to open up a confrontation with another firm. Taken together, it is quite interesting to see that the most likely profile to honor an oral partnership arrangement is the relatively smallest new venture that has a unified management team, with an owner who maintains a firm position in difficult ethical decisions, and who holds to an *absolute* standard even if it means negative economic consequences for the firm. And conversely, the most likely entrepreneur to try and rescind an oral deal is one who does not hold to *absolute* ethical positions, and owns a relatively larger new venture that lacks the unified management team.

## Ethics and Small Firm Culture

The last of the five ethical domains presents many interesting issues for how the firm deals with people, and to what degree the new venture reflects the entrepreneur's personal values system. The primary focus of this study examined whether the owner committed the necessary time and resources to establish, nurture, and maintain a cohesive culture built on clear and unified business ethics. Sixty percent of the entrepreneurs said that they did devote special planning time to the development of a company-wide, and systematic, common managerial philosophy that includes distinctive ethical guidelines for personal and group decision making. Four variables were proposed to explain whether the entrepreneur devoted time to an ethical firm culture. These included: a) the type of firm culture the firm had, b) whether the management team did have unified morals and ethical beliefs, c) the firm's manner of doing business in the market, and d) the entrepreneur's position on *absolute* versus *relative* ethics. Equation 13.0 summarizes this relationship.

**(13.0)**   Devote = $\beta_0 + \beta_1$ Culture + $\beta_2$ Team + $\beta_3$ Firm + $\beta_4$ Absolute

None of the demographic information proved to be significant, such that there were no distinctions between men and women, their age or education, or company profiles. Together, these four variables explained about eight percent of the variations in whether or not the owners devote time to developing a unified and ethical firm culture. The most important factor was the state of the existing culture. Those owners who devoted the time, did have a unified culture, and those who did not devote time had a more fragmented and diverse firm culture. The unity of the management team, the firm's distinctive manner of conducting business, and the entrepreneur's holding to an *absolute* ethic were all positively related, and nearly equal contributors to explaining whether owners devoted time to firm culture or not. The evidence seems very clear. When the entrepreneurs pledged to nurture a unified and ethically sound internal culture, their firms tended to exhibit strong and unified values and ethical behavior.

## Maintain a Strong Ethical Position

As continuous change and momentum impact the new venture, the entrepreneur will likely be confronted with numerous situations where decisions must be made that carry the weight of difficult ethical choices for the firm's internal operations and its prospects in the external environment. Four variables were selected to explain the owner's position on maintaining a strong ethical position in the face of very tough ethical decisions. These were: a) the entrepreneur's defining vision for the venture, b) the type of prior business experience the entrepreneur possesses, c) the perception of whether the external market puts pressure on entrepreneurs to "do whatever it takes" to be successful, and d) the ability to hold to an *absolute* moral standard even if it meant experiencing negative economic effects for the firm. Equation 14.0 summarizes this relationship.

$$(14.0) \quad \text{Ethical} = \beta_0 + \beta_1 \text{ Vision} - \beta_2 \text{ Experience} - \beta_3 \text{ Intensity} + \beta_4 \text{ Absolute}$$

The most important contributor to a strong ethical position was the owner's holding to an *absolute* moral standard. The second most important issue was the entrepreneur's previous business experience, such that those who had similar or complementary backgrounds were less likely to hold to a strong ethic, while those who had experience in another field were more likely to do so. And, owner's whose vision was synonymous with the company's defining vision were most likely to maintain a strong ethical stance as well. It was very intriguing to find that there was no relationship at all between the pressure to "do whatever it takes" and the owner's opinion about holding to a strong business ethic. This infers that the resolve to hold on to moral bases and ethical values is not done in response to outside influences or temptations, but is more closely related to the entrepreneur's inherent decision to act in an ethical manner, irrespective of outside issues.

The demographic data showed no differences between men and women, or firm profiles, but it did reveal that the age of the entrepreneur was positively related and very significant, such that older entrepreneurs were more likely to maintain this strong ethical position during difficult decisions. This is extremely provocative because it infers that the youngest entrepreneurs are most open to compromising their ethical positions when faced with difficult moral decisions. This could be due to several factors. It could be a tendency that younger owners are more cynical in their perception of how hard it is to conduct business in an ethical manner when the rest of the market appears not to operate in the same manner. It could also be that a gradual resolve to hold to strong ethical positions builds within individuals as they grow older. Perhaps decisions and scenarios that younger entrepreneurs consider difficult and compromising of ethics are not viewed in the same manner by owners who are older. Whatever the reasons, there does appear to be a clear and persistent pressure on the entrepreneur to lay aside moral bases and ethical absolutes in order to keep pace with the competition. This idea is captured in Equation 15.0, where the perception of whether it is impossible to hold onto *absolute* ethical standards in the face of so many unknown factors in the new venture process is proposed to be explained by the core strength of the firm, the owner's opinion if it is easy (or not) to neglect ethics when times get tough, and the entrepreneur's age.

**(15.0)** Hard = $\beta_0 + \beta_1$ Strength + $\beta_2$ Neglect - $\beta_3$ Age

The owners who did *not* feel that there was a pressure to neglect ethics were associated with the owners who also felt it was *not* impossible to hold to an *absolute* business ethic. And these were both closely linked with those entrepreneurs who believed that the success of the new venture is based primarily on adhering to a moral code of business conduct. And once again, older entrepreneurs disagreed that it was very hard to hold to an *absolute* ethic. This infers that the youngest owners see the primary strength of the company centered in the products and services, and that the pressures of the external market can cause an entrepreneur to neglect business ethics, and they perceive that the risks and uncertainty make it impossible to hold to an *absolute* ethical standard in new venture development.

## A Final Summary of Insights

It would be virtually impossible to establish hard and fast rules about the "science of ethics in new ventures." There are perhaps countless variables and factors, both recurring and nonrecurring, that affect the entrepreneur's moral bases and world view, formation of personal values, and interpretation of ethical behaviors. This book does not try to explain every nuance and dynamic for each ethical situation that could confront the entrepreneur. And, it does not assert that there are ways to clearly define what constitutes "ethical behavior" in all circumstances. There is no way to establish a universal code of conduct by which all individual small firm owners should manage their ventures. But the core question underlying this topic remains: *"Regarding qualitative characteristics and ethical behaviors, to what degree are the entrepreneur and the new venture one and the same"?* This would be very helpful to understanding morals bases, core values, and the practical applications of business ethics in the new venture development process. The unique profiles and positions of the owner and the new venture, when matched with the relatively volatile external environment for rapid sales growth, form a wide range of potential compromises based upon personal perspectives, moral choice, and interpretations about ethical ideas.

Taken in their entirety, the fifteen functions examined in this chapter paint a very intriguing picture about how ethical choices are determined, who is more apt to act in a certain manner, and what factors appear to be typically associated with various perceptions and actions in the market. The analysis suggests that entrepreneurs believe the success of their venture is closely attributed to their own personal values system, which also explains the firm's goals and objectives, where success is formulated through a unified corporate culture that deliberately reflects the entrepreneur's personality, expectations, and values. Even though holding to an *absolute* ethical does not always produce positive firm results, the entrepreneur generally receives a non pecuniary *residual ethical value* for maintaining moral standards.

## Conclusions

There have been countless attempts to specify empirically those characteristics that define risky, entrepreneurial new ventures as inherently successful. Similar studies have tried to define the entrepreneur (the driver of the risky new venture) with specific personal attributes that are generally conducive to risky endeavors. The premise of the model presented here is that the risk tolerant entrepreneur brings to the enterprise a distinct set of personal values, beliefs, and ethical positions that will ultimately manifest themselves, to some degree, as venture characteristics. These decision making value parameters are intricately associated with the entrepreneur's business idea, namely, the product or service concept to which the opportunity is inherently linked. But an idea alone is not sufficient to mold and shape the entrepreneur's values. It was proposed that the real bonding of the entrepreneur, the idea, values, and opportunity for success is uniquely expressed in the owner's goals and objectives, management style, previous experiences, risk assessments, and general regard for *absolute* ethical standards versus *relative* ethical circumstances. The core inquiry is focused on whether the personal values of the risk tolerant entrepreneur are indistinguishable from the venture's risky activities to bring together an idea and an opportunity. This perceived melding of the individual entrepreneur with the newly launched enterprise may present the notion that the personal values and ethical considerations of the individual might, in fact, become one and the same with the firm's corporate perspective. This phenomenon may then contribute to how the entrepreneur and the venture deal with decision making, core values, moral beliefs, and ethics across the five domains examined throughout the prior chapters. The entrepreneur's value system appears to permeate the corporate culture, the management team, the firm's business conduct, and even stands as a prerequisite to other firms planning to partner with the entrepreneurial venture. But it also appears that values and ethics feel pressures for compromise from inside and outside the firm.

The *values reflection factor*—the melding of the entrepreneur's values and the firm's perspective—might have a direct impact on all aspects of how the content and process of the new business is represented externally in the competitive market, and it may have a direct influence on the degree of future expectations for firm performance. It might direct the relative utilization of various methods for financing the new venture, and it could establish the structure and frequency of a wide range of external business partnerships. It may even determine the nature and effectiveness of the firm's internal corporate culture. The relative extent of impact to these five domains will play a significant role in how the venture is strategically positioned, and ready to deal with, external change in the market. Ultimately, the extent of the company's ethical competence in accommodating change will impact the long-term viability of the venture, as it tries to build and maintain momentum in a competitive environment. And eventually, entrepreneurial ethics and the five domains will be brought together in the context of perpetual change and the impact that the resultant decision making processes can have on the firm's competitive momentum.

The various configurations of ideas, values, opportunity, and risk exhibited in entrepreneurial decision making present a formidable obstacle to developing a universal and objective set of guidelines for ethical entrepreneurial decision policies. The key to entrepreneurial ethics rests squarely with the entrepreneur's perceptions and beliefs about morals standards, values, and ethical behavior. Yet so often there exists a *new venture parallax*, where the venture appears to be in trouble when viewed from the outside looking in, yet from the entrepreneur's viewpoint, everything is fantastic. And maybe there really is some unknown *X-factor* that is needed to convince the entrepreneur that ethical behavior will be rewarded in the market, rather than have a negative impact on the firm's potential for success. It is hoped this model of entrepreneurial ethics, values formation, and decision contexts will establish a basis for discussions about ethics among entrepreneurs, managers and employees of fast-growth entrepreneurial new ventures, as well as teachers and students of entrepreneurship and the new venture development process. The issues of ethics in the small firm are fascinating. The pressures on the entrepreneur to be successful are substantial. As the firm speeds ahead toward the market opportunity, moral appraisals and ethical behaviors will be subject to the unique dynamics of market success, and the underlying systems and processes that make success an attainable goal for the entrepreneur. Hopefully, the individual will not have to utilize compromise and deception to realize the personal dreams and vision that are embodied in the enterprise.

# Appendix

The following regression equations are excerpts from Chapter Twelve and deal with the evidences and interactions of entrepreneurial ethics in the successful new venture. Each equation is numbered to correspond to the proposed equation from the previous chapter. The regression functions are each presented in the following format. First, the function is presented with the quantitative parameters for the independent variables on the right side of the equation (the constant and the beta coefficients), including the respective signs based on whether they contribute to (positive) or detract from (negative) the dependent variable on the left side of the equation. Next, each parameter's *Student's t* statistic is footnoted with its respective *p* value (the probability of being wrong in assuming that the parameter is significant). Then the coefficient of determination ($R^2$) is presented. This states what percentage of the variance in the dependent variable can be explained by the variance in the independent variables together. Finally, the F statistic shows the significance of the regression's overall explanatory power, and includes the probability (*p*) of being wrong in assuming the regression is significant.

## Venture Success and Personal Values

(1.0)   Success = .9285 + .080468[1] Goals - .02992[2] Style

        1. t = 4.0043 (p < .000062)
        2. t = -2.131 (p < .033063)

$R^2$ = 9.27 percent.

F = 10.5768 @ 2,207 df (*p* < .000042)

## Company Goals Defined

(2.0)   Goals = .423 + .0874[1] Culture + .1497[3] Firm + .1012[2] Team + .2363[4] Shared

        1. t = 1.8554 (p < .06505)
        2. t = 3.1819 (p < .00170)
        3. t = 2.2863 (p < .02331)
        4. t = 2.9518 (p < .00354)

$R^2$ = 15.2 percent.

F = 8.7134 @ 4,194 df (*p* < .000002)

## Ethics and Representation

**(3.0)** Absolute = .7098 - .1904[1] Style + .1253[2] Forecast - .1849[3] Perform

        1. $t = -2.226$ ($p < .02712$)
        2. $t = 1.8122$ ($p < .07149$)
        3. $t = -3.048$ ($p < .00262$)

    $R^2 = 7.65$ percent.

    $F = 5.3859$ @ 3,195 df ($p < .001394$)

---

**(4.0)** Ethic = .4238 + .3165[1] Goals - .2336[2] Experience - .318[3] Style + .173[4] Absolute

    1. $t = 1.9778$ ($p < .04936$)
    2. $t = -2.131$ ($p < .03242$)
    3. $t = -2.848$ ($p < .00486$)
    4. $t = 1.8738$ ($p < .06245$)

The entrepreneur's age was also a significant parameter ($t = 1.8738$; $p < .0482$) and had a positive impact ($ß = + .0114$) on ethical behavior.

    $R^2 = 12.67$ percent.

    $F = 5.6566$ @ 5,195 df ($p < .000068$)

## Ethics and Market Expectations

**(5.0)** Experience = .616 - .175[1] Idea - .122[2] Focus - .144[3] Financial + .105[4] Forecast

    1. $t = -2.440$ ($p < .0156$)
    2. $t = -1.692$ ($p < .09221$)
    3. $t = -2.103$ ($p < .03675$)
    4. $t = 1.9054$ ($p < .05823$)

The entrepreneur's sex was also a significant parameter ($t = 2.6451$; $p < .0088$) where females were more closely associated with having related experience in the field ($ß = + .3402$).

    $R^2 = 10.82$ percent.

    $F = 4.6129$ @ 5,190 df ($p < .000538$)

---

**(6.0)** Risks = -.026 + .168[1] Financial + .1419[2] Forecast

    1. $t = 2.4786$ ($p < .01405$)
    2. $t = 2.5880$ ($p < .01039$)

The entrepreneur's age was also a significant parameter (t = 3.6305; p < .00036) where older owners viewed the risks of the new venture as much more formidable and difficult to manage (ß = + .0133), while younger entrepreneurs viewed risks as somewhat minimal and easy to manage.

$R^2$ = 11.39 percent.

$F$ = 8.1845 @ 3,191 df ($p$ < .000037)

## Ethics and Financing Requirements

**(7.0)** Forecast = -.5694 + .2669[1] Risks + .241[2] Performance

1. t = 3.0745 (p < .00241)
2. t = 3.9478 (p < .00011)

The entrepreneur's sex was also a significant parameter (t = 2.2997; p < .02255) where female owners are more likely to use optimistic, or liberal, expectations when making financial forecasts (ß = + .3644), while male entrepreneurs tended to be more pessimistic, or conservative, in their forecasts.

$R^2$ = 11.67 percent.

$F$ = 8.3693 @ 3,190 df ($p$ < .000030)

---

**(8.0)** Funds = .427 - .0954[1] Change + .1439[2] Close + .0635[3] Unbias + .188[4] Invest

1. t = -1.564 (p < .11956) *Falls just outside the realm of being significant.*
2. t = 2.4557 (p < .01500)
3. t = 1.7672 (p < .0788)
4. t = 2.5317 (p < .01219)

The entrepreneur's sex once again a significant parameter (t = -2.2641 p < .02474) where female owners are more likely to seek funding in excess of the targeted amount required in the business plan (ß = - .2617), while male entrepreneurs were more likely to secure the exact amount of funding required.

$R^2$ = 12.79 percent.

$F$ = 5.3409 @ 5, 182 df ($p$ < .000132)

## Ethics and Partnering Arrangements

**(9.0)** Partnering = .6683 + .1218[1] Focus + .00105[2] Years

> 1. t = 1.5815 (p < .11376) *Falls just outside the realm of being significant.*
> 2. t = 1.7734 (p < .07615)

$R^2$ = 2.71 percent.

F = 2.8202 @ 2,202 df (p < .061943)

---

**(10.0)** Negotiate = .0285 + .2442[1] Risks + .2972[2] Intensity

> 1. t = 2.0731 (p < .03948)
> 2. t = 2.3333 (p < .02066)

The entrepreneur's sex once again a significant parameter (t = -1.9718 p < .05006) where female owners are more likely to begin negotiations far in excess of the goals and expectations in order to arrive at an acceptable settlement (b =- .4333), while male entrepreneurs were more likely to begin negotiations near or at the target level for the settlement.

$R^2$ = 6.69 percent.

F = 4.6143 @ 3,193 df (p < .003841)

---

**(11.0)** Absolute = .2064 - .1080[1] Benefit + .2595[2] Shared

> 1. t = -1.943 (p < .05343)
> 2. t = 1.8205 (p < .07018)

The number of years that the new venture has been in business was also found to be a significant direct parameter in explaining the entrepreneur's adherence to an absolute ethical standard in the company (t = 1.7652; p < .0790), such that owners who have relatively older companies are more likely to utilize absolute business

$R^2$ = 2.71 percent.

F = 2.8202 @ 2,202 df (p < .061943)

---

**(12.0)** Oral = .50 + .129[1] Ethical + .16[2] Team + .104[3] Absolute

> 1. t = 2.9187 (p < .00395)
> 2. t = 2.6106 (p < .00979)
> 3. t = 1.8356 (p < .06802)

The firm's employment level proved to be significant (t = -1.7965 p < .07404) where the smallest new ventures tended to honor an oral agreement, while the largest firms were most likely to try and rescind an oral deal (ß = - .000159).

$R^2$ = 11.9 percent.

$F$ = 6.3013 @ 4,185 df ($p$ < .000089)

## Ethics and Small Firm Culture

**(13.0)**  Devote = - .057 + .218[1] Culture + .151[2] Team + .188[3] Firm + .1602[4] Absolute

  1. t = 1.9256 (p < .05560)
  2. t = 1.4770 (p < .14120) *Falls close to the realm of being significant.*
  3. t = 1.6804 (p < .09445)
  4. t = 1.6293 (p < .10485) *Falls right at the edge of being significant.*

The variable "Team" was not even closely associated with any other of the 60+ regressions performed in this study. But it was in this function that it made its best showing. Although there is only an 86% chance that it does contribute to explaining time devoted to firm culture, its marginal status was worth including in this review.

$R^2$ = 7.76 percent.

$F$ = 4.1420 @ 4,197 df ($p$ < .003035)

## Maintain a Strong Ethical Position

**(14.0)**  Ethical = - .645 + .188[1] Vision - .247[2] Exper - .087[3] Intensity + .276[4] Absolute

  1. t = 1.7031 (p < .0902)
  2. t = -2.175 (p < .03082)
  3. t = -.0725 (p < .46895)
  4. t = 3.0138 (p < .00293)

$R^2$ = 10.5 percent.

$F$ = 4.4237 @ 5,187 df ($p$ < .000785)

The entrepreneur's age was also positively related and significant in explaining the ability to maintain strong ethical positions (t = 2.216; $p$ < .0278) such that older owners were more likely to maintain a strong moral position when faced with difficult ethical decisions (ß = .01327).

**(15.0)** =+ .2250 + .1009[1] Strength + .2057[2] Neglect - 1.5746[3] Age

        1. $t = 2.0206$ ($p < .04467$)
        2. $t = 2.9692$ ($p < .00335$)
        3. $t = -3.344$ ($p < .00098$)

$R^2 = 12.1$ percent.

$F = 9.0682$ @ 3, 197 df ($p < .000012$)

# Notes

## Introduction

1. *Economist*, 1991. "The Many Faces of BCCI," July 13, 81-82.
2. Dwyer, P.; Dawley, H. and G. Burns, 1996. "Decent Into the Abyss," *Business Week*, July 1, 28-29.
3. Lee, Peter, 1995. "Lesson One: The Safety Harness," *Euromoney*, August, 34-38.
4. Lesley, Elizabeth, 1995. "Fall From Grace," *Business Week*, (May 29), 60-70.
5. Holland, K.; Himelstein, L. and Z. Schiller, 1995. "The Banker's Trust Tapes," *Business Week*, October 16, 106-111.
6. Maremont, Mark, 1995. "Blind Ambition," *Business Week*, October 23, 78-92.
7. Murphy, Kim, 1987. "How the Big Bubble Burst," *Los Angeles Times*, March 30, Section One, 1, 3-4.
8. Hoaas, David J. and D. C. Wilcox, 1995. "The Academic Coverage of Business Ethics," *American Journal of Economics and Sociology*, July, 289-303.
9. Stark, Andrew, 1993. "What's the Matter With Business Ethics?," *Harvard Business Review*, May, 38-48.
10. Boroughs, D., 1995. "The Bottom Line on Ethics," *U.S. News & World Report*, March 20, 61.
11. Labich, K., 1992. "The New Crisis in Business Ethics," *Fortune*, April 20, 167-176.
12. Dunckel, J., 1989. *Good Ethics, Good Business: Your Plan for Success*, Bellingham: International Self-Counsel Press.
13. Aguilar, Francis J., 1994. *Managing Corporate Ethics: Learning From America's Ethical Companies How to Supercharge Business Performance*, NY: Oxford Press.
14. Hass. R. D., 1994. "Ethics: A Global Business Challenge," *Vital Speeches of the Day*, June 1, 506.
15. Husted, B.; Dozier, J.; McMahon, T. and M. Kattan, 1996. "The Impact of Cross-National Carriers of Business Ethics on Attitudes About Questionable Practices Form of Moral Reasoning," *Journal of International Business Studies*, IIQ, 391.
16. *U.S. News & World Report*, 1995. "Shredding a Myth," March 20, 61.
17. Noe, T.; and M. Rebello, 1994. "The Dynamics of Business Ethics and Economic Activity," *American Economic Review*, June, 531-547.
18. Stark, A., 1993. *ibid*.
19. *Economist*, 1992. "Who Cares Who Wins," May 16, 19.
20. Benjamin, M., 1990. *Splitting the Difference: Compromise and Integrity in Ethics and Politics*, Lawrence, KS: University Press.

21. Choudhury, Masudul Alam, 1995. "Ethics and Economics: A View from Ecological Economics," *International Journal of Social Economics*, Vol. 22, 61-80.

22. Hoffman, M. W.; Frederick, R. and E. Petry, 1989. *The Ethics of Organizational Transformation: Mergers, Takeovers, and Corporate Restructuring*, New York: Quorum Books.

23. Shirref, D., 1995. "Danger: Kids at Play," *Euromoney*, March, 43-46.

24. Cooper, A. and A. Kendall, 1995. "Determinants of Satisfaction for Entrepreneurs," *Journal of Business Venturing*, November, 439-455.

## *Chapter One*

1. Avishai, Bernard, 1994. "What is Business' Social Compact?," *Harvard Business Review*, January, 38-47.

2. Barlow, S. and E. Kotite, 1991. "Entrepreneurs Across America," *Entrepreneur*, June, 60-84.

3. Reynolds, P., 1991. "Sociology and Entrepreneurship: Concepts and Contributions," *Entrepreneurship Theory & Practice*, Winter, 47-70.

4. McGarvey, Robert, 1995. "Natural Wonder," *Entrepreneur*, September, 160-164.

5. McGarvey, Robert, 1995. "Shoe In," *Entrepreneur*, February, 115-119.

6. Beresford, Lynn, 1995. "The Right Stuff," *Entrepreneur*, August, 158-164.

7. Schumpeter, J., 1934. *The Theory of Economic Development*, Cambridge, MA: Harvard University Press.

8. Logue, D., 1973. "Premia on Unseasoned Equity Issues," *Journal of Economics and Business*, Spring-Summer, 133-141.

9. Sharpe, William F., 1963. "A Simplified Model for Portfolio Management," *Management Science*, January, 277-293.

10. Modigliani, F. and G. Progue, 1974. "An Introduction to Risk and Return: Concepts and Evidences, Part I," *Financial Analysts Journal*, March-April, 68-80.

11. Modigliani, F. and G. Progue, 1974. "An Introduction to Risk and Return: Concepts and Evidences, Part II," *Financial Analysts Journal*, May-June, 69-86.

12. Stoll, Hans, 1976. "The Pricing of Underwritten Offerings of Common Stocks and the Compensation of Underwriters," *Journal of Economics and Business*, Winter, 96-103.

13. Mintzberg, Henry, 1989. *Mintzberg on Management*, New York: Free Press.

14. Amit, R. and B. Wernerfelt, 1990. "Why Do Firms Reduce Business Risk?," *Academy of Management Journal*, September, 520-533.

15. Ahmihud, Y. and B. Lev, 1981. "Risk reduction as a Managerial Motive for Conglomerate Mergers," *Bell Journal of Economics*, Number 12, 605-616.

16. Knight, Francis H., 1921. *Risk, Uncertainty, and Profit*, Boston: Houghton Mifflin.

17. Cantillon, R., 1755. "The Circulation and Exchange of Goods and Merchandise," in Higgs, H. 1931, *Essai sur la Nature du Commerce en General*, London: Macmillan.

18. Kihlstrom, R. and J. J. Laffont, 1979. "A General Equilibrium Entrepreneurial Theory of Firm Foundation Based on Risk Aversion," *Journal of Political Economy*, Vol. 87, 719-748.

19. Leibenstein, H., 1968. "Entrepreneurship and Development," *American Economic Review*, No. 58, 72-74.

20. Kirzner, Israel M., 1982. "Uncertainty, Discovery, and Human Action," in *Method, Process, and Austrian Economics: Essays in Honor of Ludwig von Mises*, Lexington, MA: D. C. Heath Publishers.

21. Ahmihud, Y.; Dodd, P. and M. Weinstein, 1986. "Conglomerate Mergers, Managerial Motives, and Stockholder Wealth," *Journal of Banking and Finance*, No. 10, 401-410.

22. Jensen, M. and W. Meckling, 1976. "Theory of the Firm: Managerial Behavior, Agency Costs, and Ownership Structure," *Journal of Financial Economics*, October, 305-359.

23. Anderson, R.; Condon, C. and J. Dunkelberg, 1992. "Are Franchisees "Real" Entrepreneurs?," *Journal of Business and Entrepreneurship*, March, 97-105.

24. Holmstrom, B., 1979. "Moral Hazard and Observability," *Bell Journal of Economics*, No. 10, 74-90.

25. Newton, D., 1991. "The Case of A.V.I. Developers, Inc." in Maroun, J. (editor), *Decision Making in Business*, Los Angeles: Roxbury Publishing.

26. Abrahamson, E., 1991. "Managerial Fads and fashion: The Diffusion and Rejection of Innovations," *Academy of Management Review*, July, 586-612.

27. Newton, D. B., "Concentric Managerial Placement: A Strategic Approach to Problem Intervention in Organizational Structures," in Hamel, Willem A. (editor), 1985, *Association of Human Resource Management and Organization*, Washington, DC: Maximilian Press, 659-663.

## Chapter Two

1. Evans, D. S. and L. Leighton, 1989. "Some Empirical Aspects of Entrepreneurship," *American Economic Review*, Vol. 79, No. 3, 519-535.

2. McCelland, D., 1961. *The Achieving Society*. Princeton, NJ: Van Nostrand Publishing.

3. Mintzberg, H., 1989. *Mintzberg on Management*. New York: Free Press.

4. Mitton, D. G., 1989. "The Compleat Entrepreneur," *Entrepreneurship Theory and Practice*, Spring, 9-19.

5. Ansoff, H. I., 1988. *General Management in Turbulent Environments*, Unpublished manuscript, San Diego, CA: U.S. International University, used by permission.

6. Leff, N., 1978. "Industrial Organization and Entrepreneurship in the Developing Countries: The Economic Groups," *Economic Development and Cultural Change*, No. 26, 537-544.

7. Ansoff, H. Igor., 1987. "The Emerging Paradigm of Strategic Behavior," *Strategic Management Journal*, No. 8, 501-515.

8. Leibenstein, H., 1968. *ibid*.

9. Anderson, R.; Dunkelberg, J. and C. Conden, 1990. "A Comparison of Entrepreneurs, Small Business Owners, Corporate Executives, and Public Sector Managers," *Journal of Business and Entrepreneurship*, October, 41-50.

10. Gartner, William B., 1989. " 'Who is an Entrepreneur?' is the Wrong Question," *Entrepreneurship Theory and Practice*, Summer, 47-68.

11. Stewart, A.; Learned, K. and F. F. Martinello, 1991. "Entrepreneurial Organizing and the Accumulation of Asset Stocks," *Unpublished Manuscript*, used by permission.

12. Rothwell, R. and W. Zegveld, 1982. *Innovation and the Small and Medium Size Firm: Their Role in Employment and in Economic Change*, London: F. Pinter Publishing Company.

13. McNeil, R. D. and P. S. Burgar, 1991. "Entrepreneurship Success or Failure: Can We Identify the Causes?," *Journal of Business and Entrepreneurship*, March, 35-46.

14. Cook, D. L., in N. MacRae, 1982. "Intrapreneurial Now," *Economist*, April 17, 67-72.

15. Schednel, D. E. and C. Hofer, 1979. *Strategic Management and Organization Types: A New View of Business Policy and Planning*, Boston, MA: Little, Brown and Company.

16. Pinchot, G., in N. MacRae, 1982, *ibid*.

17. Pinchot, G., 1985. *Intrapreneuring: Why You Don't Have to Leave the Corporation to Become an Entrepreneur*, New York: Harper and Row.

18. Schwartz, R., 1985. "Secrets of Intrapreneurship," *INC*, January, 69.

19. Dunphy, S. M., 1990. "Entrepreneur and Intrapreneur: Why One is Not the Other and the Other Does Not Exist," *Journal of Business and Entrepreneurship*, March, 81-90.

20. MacRae, N., 1982, *ibid*.

21. Lowe, E., "Transferring the Edward Lowe 'Cell System' to Entrepreneurial Activities in Latin America," in Reed, D. (editor), 1990, *Spirit of Enterprise: The 1990 Rolex Awards*, Bern, Switzerland: Buri International.

## Chapter Three

1. Schwab, B., 1996. "A Note on Ethics and Strategy: Do Good Ethics Always Make for Good Business?," *Strategic Management Journal*, Vol. 17, No. 6, 499-512.

2. Toffler, B. L., 1986. *Tough Choices: Managers Talk Ethics*. New York: John Wiley & Sons.

3. Aplander, G.; Carter, K. and R. Forsgren, 1990. "Managerial Issues and Problem-Solving in the Formative Years," *Journal of Small Business Management*, April, 9-19.

4. Gartner, William B., 1989. *ibid*.

5. Lussier, Robert N., 1995. "A Nonfinancial Business Success versus Failure Prediction Model for Young Firms," *Journal of Small Business Management*, January, 8-20.

6. Gartner, William B., 1991. "Acting As If: Differentiating Entrepreneurial from Organizational Behavior," *Entrepreneurship Theory and Practice*, Winter, 13-27.

7. Gatewood, E.; Shaver, K. and W. Gartner, 1995. "A Longitudinal Study of Cognitive Factors Influencing Start-Up Behaviors and Success at Venture Creation," *Journal of Business Venturing*, September, 371-387.

8. Humphreys, N.; Robin, D.; Reidenbach, E. and D. Moak, 1993. "The Ethical Decision Making Process of Small Business Owner/Managers and Their Customers," *Journal of Small Business Management*, July, 9-22.

9. Fagenson, Ellen, 1993. "Personal Value Systems of Men and Women Entrepreneurs Versus Managers," *Journal of Business Venturing*, September, 409-422.

10. Posner, B., 1992. "Values and the American Manager," *California Management Review*, Spring, 80-94.

11. Kinnear, James W., 1995. "The Ethics of International Business: Foreign Policy and Economic Sanctions," *Vital Speeches of the Day*, September 15, 561-565.

12. Johnson, P. and D. Cathcart, 1979. "The Founders of New Manufacturing Firms: A Note on the Size of Their Incubator Plants," *Journal of Industrial Economics*, December, 219-224.

13. Curtis, D., 1983. *Strategic Planning for Smaller Businesses*. Lexington, MA: D. C. Heath.

14. Hall, William K., 1980. "Survival Strategies in a Hostile Environment," *Harvard Business Review*, September-October, 75-85.

15. Bailey, J., "Intrapreneurship: Sources of High Growth Start-Ups or Passing Fad?," in Hornaday, J. (editor), 1984. *Frontiers of Entrepreneurship Research*. Wellesley: Babson Press.

16. Blake, R. and J. Mouton, 1962. "The Managerial Grid," *Advanced Management Office Executive*, Vol. 1, No. 9, 62.

17. Newton, D., 1992. "Schumpeterian Entrepreneurship Versus Intracorporate Entrepreneurship: A Differentiation Based on Risk Transfer and Assignment Vesting," in Kao, Raymond (ed.), *Enterprising in Partnership with the Environment*. Toronto: Federal Business Development Bank.

18. Blake, R.; Mouton, J.; Barnes, L. and L. Griener, 1964. "Breakthrough in Organizational Development," *Harvard Business Review*, No. 42, 135-155.

19. Dugan, K. W., 1989. "Ability and Effort Attributions: Do They Affect How Mangers Communicate Performance Feedback in Organization," *Academy of Management Journal*, March, 87-114.

20. Sonfield, M. and R. Moore, 1990. "Innovative Turning Points in the Path to Entrepreneurial Success," *Journal of Small Business Strategy*, February, 60-64.

21. Locke, E.; Shaw, K.; Saari, L. and G. Latham, 1981. "Goal Setting and Task Performance: 1969-1980," *Psychological Bulletin*, No. 70, 474-484.

22. Keys, B. and T. Case, 1990. "How to Become an Influential Manager," *Academy of Management Executive*, November, 38-51.

23. Tubbs, M. and S. Ekeberg, 1991. The Role of Intentions in Work Motivation: Implications for Goal-Setting Theory and Research," *Academy of Management Review*, January, 180-199.

24. Miller, D. and P. H. Friesen, 1982. "Innovation in Conservative and Entrepreneurial Firms: Two Models of Strategic Momentum," *Strategic Management Journal*, No. 3, 1-25.

25. Miller, D. and P. H. Friesen, 1984. "A Longitudinal Study of the Corporate Life Cycle," *Management Science*, October, 1161-1183.

## Chapter Four

1. Lin, Bin-Shan and J. Vasser, 1990. "Issues in Managing Small Business Information Systems," *Journal of Small Business Strategy*, February, 27-42.

2. Rabin, Afzalur, 1996. "Stress, Strain, and Their Moderators," *Journal of Small Business Management*, January, 46-56.

3. Longenecker, J.; McKinney, J. and C. Moore, 1989. "Ethics in Small Business," *Journal of Small Business Management*, January, 27-31.

4. Cunningham, Barton, 1991. "Defining Entrepreneurship," *Journal of Small Business Management*, January, 45-61.

5. Hyatt, J., 1991. "Mapping the Entrepreneurial Mind," *INC.*, August, 26-31.

6. Koppensteiner, R. and T. McAdams, 1992. "The Manager Seeking Virtue: Lessons from Literature," *Journal of Business Ethics*, July, 627-634.

7. Whipple, T. and D. Swords, 1992. "Business Ethics Judgment: A Cross-Cultural Comparison," *Journal of Business Ethics*, September, 671-678.

8. Sims, R., 1992. "The Challenge of Ethical Behavior in Organizations," *Journal of Business Ethics*, July, 505-513.

9. Evans, R., 1991. "Business Ethics and Changes in Society," *Journal of Business Ethics*, November, 871-879.

10. Paine, L. S., 1991. "Corporate Policy and the Ethics of Competitor Intelligence Gathering," *Journal of Business Ethics*, June, 423-436.

11. Van Wensveen Siker, L., 1991. "Does Your Religion Make a Difference in Your Business Ethics?," *Journal of Business Ethics*, November, 819-832.

12. Magill, G., 1992. "Theology in Business Ethics: Appealing to the Religious Imagination," *Journal of Business Ethics*, February, 129-135.

13. Nesteruk, J., 1991. "The Ethical Significance of Corporate Law," *Journal of Business Ethics*, September, 723-727.

14. Noe, T. and M. Rebello, 1994. *ibid*.

15. Avishai, B., 1994. "What is Business' Social Compact?," *Harvard Business Review*, January, 38-47.

16. Reynolds, P., 1991. "Sociology and Entrepreneurship: Concepts and Contributions," *Entrepreneurship Theory and Practice*, Winter, 47-70.

17. File, K.; Moriya, F. and B. Judd, 1991. "Social Responsibility in the Smaller Enterprise," *Journal of Business and Entrepreneurship*, October, 23-32.

18. Hoffman, M.; Frederick, R. and E. Petry, 1989. *The Ethics of Organizational Transformation*, New York: Quorum Books.

19. Gartner, William, 1991. "Acting As If: Differentiating Entrepreneurial from Organizational Behavior," *Entrepreneurship Theory and Practice*, Winter, 13-27.

20. Donham, W., 1992. "Business Ethics: A General Survey," *Harvard Business Review*, September/October, 160-173.

21. Schell, J., 1991. "In Defense of the Entrepreneur," *INC.*, May, 28-30.

22. Brown, G., 1992. "Are Profits Deserved?," *Journal of Business Ethics*, Fall, 105-114.

23. *Economist*, 1992. "Who Cares, Wins," May 16, 19.

24. Hoaas, D. and D. Wilcox, 1995. "The Academic Coverage of Business Ethics," *American Journal of Economics and Sociology*, July, 289-303.

25. Aguilar, Francis, 1994. *Managing Corporate Ethics*, New York: Oxford Press.
26. Boroughs, Donald., 1995. "The Bottom Line on Ethics," *U.S. News & World Report*, March 20, 61.
27. Thorbeck, John, 1991. "The Turnaround Value of Values," *Harvard Business Review*, January, 52-64.
28. Powell, Michael, 1996. "Betrayal," *INC.*, April, 23-24.
29. Longenecker, J. et al., 1989. *ibid*.
30. Pideril, J., 1993, *The Ethical Foundations of Economics*. Washington, DC: Georgetown University Press.
31. Dunckel, J., 1989. *ibid*.
32. Hornsby, J.; Kuratko, D.; Naffziger, D.; Lafollette, W. and R. Hodgetts, 1994. "The Ethical Perceptions of Small Business Owners: A Factor Analytic Study," *Journal of Small Business Management*, October, 9-16.
33. Smith, P. and E. Oakwood, 1994. "A Study of the Ethical Values of Metropolitan and Non metropolitan Small Business Owners," *Journal of Small Business Management*, October, 17-27.
34. Stark, Andrew, 1993. *ibid*.
35. Labich, Kenneth, 1992. "The New Crisis in Business Ethics," *Fortune*, April 20, 167-176.
36. Haas, Robert, 1994. "Ethics: A Global Business Challenge," *Vital Speeches*, June 1, 506.
37. Whipple, T. and D. Swords, 1992. *ibid*
38. Husted, B.; Dozier, J.; McMahon, T. and M. Kattan, 1996. "The Impact of Cross-National Carriers of Business Ethics...," *Journal of International Business Studies*, QII, 391.
39. Choudhury, M. Alam, 1995. "Ethics and Economics: A View from Ecological Economics," *International Journal of Social Economics*, Vol. 22, 61-80.
40. Case, John, 1996. "Corporate Culture," *INC.*, (November), 42-53.
41. Noe, T. and M. Rebello, 1994. *ibid*.

## *Chapter Five*

1. Hoffman, R., 1988. *Biblical vs. Secular Ethics: The Conflict*. Buffalo, NY: Prometheus Books.
2. Jonsen, A. R., 1988. *The Abuse of Casuistry: A History of Moral Reasoning*. Berkeley, CA: University of California Press.
3. Caplan, A., 1984. *Darwin, Marx, and Freud: Their Influence on Moral Theory*. NY: Plenum.
4. Edwards, J., 1982. *Ethics Without Philosophy*. Tampa, FL: University Presses of Florida.
5. Little, David, 1978. *Comparative Religious Ethics*. New York: Harper and Row.
6. Hauerwas, Stanley, 1977. *Truthfulness and Tragedy: Further Investigations in Christian Ethics*. Notre Dame, IN: University of Notre Dame Press.
7. Ryn, Claes, G., 1990. *Democracy and Ethical Life*. Washington, DC: Catholic University Press.
8. Gert, Bernard, 1988. *Morality: A Justification of the Moral Rules*. New York: Oxford Press.

9. Hetzer, B., 1996. "The Heavy Burden of Light Fingers," *Business Week Enterprise*, November, 28-35.

10. Mount, Jeffrey, 1996. "The Blood Knot," *INC.*, February, 19-20.

11. Chuang, J., 1995. "On Balance," *INC.*, (July), 33-34.

12. Phillips, M. and Salli Rasberry, 1981. *Honest Business*. New York: Random House.

13. Mayo, Michael, 1991. "Ethical Problems Encountered by U.S. Small Business in International Marketing," *Journal of Small Business Management*, April, 51-59.

14. Peterson, Robin, 1991. "Attitudes of Small Business Managers Regarding the Importance of Various Social Responsibility Themes," *Journal of Business and Entrepreneurship*, October, 1-8.

## *Chapter Six*

1. Pratt, C., 1991. "Public Relations: The Empirical Research on Practitioner Ethics," *Journal of Business Ethics*, March, 229-236.

2. Vitell, S. J. and J. Muncy, 1992. "Consumer Ethics: An Empirical Investigation of Factors Influencing Ethical Judgments on the Final Consumer," *Journal of Business Ethics*, August, 585-597.

3. Danley, J. R., 1991. "Polestar Refined: Business Ethics and Political Economy," *Journal of Business Ethics*, December, 915-933.

4. Labich, Kenneth, 1995. "SEC to Investors: Watch Out, Speak Up," *Fortune*, May 15, 133-138.

5. Phillips, M. and Salli Rasberry, 1981. *ibid*.

6. Jones, D. G., 1982. *Doing Ethics in Business*. Cambridge: Oelgeschlager, Gunn, and Hain.

7. Toffler, Barbara L., 1986. *ibid*.

8. Liebig, J. E., 1990. *Business Ethics: Profiles in Civic Virtue*. Golden, CO: Fulcrum Publishers.

## *Chapter Seven*

1. Anderson, Elizabeth, 1993. *Value in Ethics and Economics*. Cambridge, MA: Harvard University Press.

2. Thorbeck, J., 1991. "Turnaround Value of Values," *Harvard Business Review*, January, 52-64.

3. Stodder, Gayle S., 1995. "Entrepreneurial Fables," *Entrepreneur*, August, 120.

4. Braendel, Gregory G., 1994. "How I Lost It," *INC.*, July, 21-22.

5. *Economist*, 1995. "Management Focus: Business Ethics," April 8, 57.

6. Smeltzer, L. R., 1991. "Analysis of the Use of Advisors as Information Sources in Venture Start-Ups," *Journal of Small Business Management*, July, 10-20.

7. Bride, Amar, 1994. "How Entrepreneurs Craft Strategies That Work," *Harvard Business Review*, March, 150-163.

8. File, K.; Moriya, F. and B. Judd, 1991. "Social Responsibility in the Smaller Enterprise," *Journal of Business and Entrepreneurship*, October, 23-32.

9. Ansoff, H. Igor., 1988. *ibid*.

10. Hall, William, 1980. *ibid*.

## Chapter Eight

1. Brokaw, Leslie, 1993. "The Truth About Start-Ups," *INC.*, March, 56-64.
2. Hood, J., and J. E. Young, 1993. Entrepreneurship's Requisite Areas of Development: A Survey of Top Ten Executives in Successful Entrepreneurial Firms," *Journal of Business Venturing*, March, 115-135.
3. Hornsby, J; Kuratko, D.; Naffziger, D.; Lafollette, W. R., and R. Hodgetts, 1994. "The Ethical Perceptions of Small Business Owners," *Journal of Small Business Management*, October, 9-16.
4. Susbaver, J. and R. Baker, 1989. "Strategies for Successful Entrepreneurial Values," *Journal of Business and Entrepreneurship*, October, 56-66.
5. Coady, Roxanne, 1996. "The Cobbler's Shoes," *INC.*, January, 21-22.
6. Baechler, Mary, 1994. "The Cash-Flow Quagmire," *INC.*, October, 25-26.
7. Murphy, Anne, 1995. "True Value," *INC.*, January, 66-72.
8. McMahon, Christopher, 1995. "The Political Theory of Organizations and Business Ethics," *Philosophy and Public Affairs*, Vol. 24, No. 4, 292.
9. Williams, O.; Reilly, F. and J. W. Houck, 1989. *Ethics and Investment Industry*. Savage, MD: Rowan and Littlefield Publishers.
10. Simon, R. 1996. "NASD's Top Cop Vows to Crack Down...," *Money*, May, 24-31.
11. Templeton, John M. and J. Ellison, 1987. *The Templeton Plan: 21 Steps to Success and Happiness*. San Francisco: Harper and Row.
12. Copeland, T. and J. F. Weston, 1983. *Financial Theory and Corporate Policy*. Menlo Park, CA: Addison-Wesley Publishing Company.
13. *Economist*, "Pulp Research," February 3, 65.
14. Sen, Amarlya, 1993. "Money and Value: On the Ethics and Economics Finance," *Economics and Philosophy*, October, 203-227.
15. McDougall, Patricia, 1996. "New Venture Internationalization, Strategic Change, and Performance: A Follow Up Study," *Journal of Business Venturing*, January, 23-36.
16. Modigliani, F., and M. Miller, 1958. "The Cost of Capital, Corporation Finance, and the Theory of Investment," *American Economic Review*, June, 261-297.

## Chapter Nine

1. Porter, M. E. , 1991. *Michael E. Porter on Competition and Strategy*. Boston: Harvard Business School Press.
2. Minus, P., 1993. *The Ethics of Business in a Global Economy*. Dordrecht: Kluwer Academic.
3. Koslowski, P., 1992. *Ethics in Economics: Business and Economics Policy*. NY: Springer.
4. Burton, Lloyd, 1990. "Ethical Discontinuities in Public-Private Sector Negotiation," *Review of Social Economy*, Winter, 23-40.
5. Stack, Jack, 1996. "Mad About Lay-Offs," *INC.*, May, 21-22.

6. Chandler, S. & W. Sellner, 1996. "Prime Time for Sweatshops," *Business Week*, June 17, 44.
7. Hoffman, M. W.; Frederick, R. and E. Petry, 1989. *The Ethics of Organizational Transformation: Mergers, Takeovers, and Corporate Restructuring*, New York: Quorum Books.
8. Collins, Jim, 1996. "Looking Out For Number One," *INC.*, June, 29-30.
9. Hyatt, Joshua, 1995. "Guaranteed Growth," *INC.*, September, 68-78.
10. Welles, Wedward, 1994. "Blood Fued," *INC.*, November, 60-69.
11. Gilbert, Nick, 1994. "Just Business," *Financial World*, (August 18), 86-87.
12. Olson, Philip D. and Donald Bokor, 1995. "Strategy Process-Content Interaction: Effects on Small, Start-Up Firms," *Journal of Small Business Management*, January, 34-44.

## Chapter Ten

1. Shusall, Sumantra, 1995. "Changing the Role of Top Management: Beyond Structure to Processes," *Harvard Business Review*, January-February, 86-96.
2. Darling, J., 1990. "Team in the Small Business Firm," *Journal of Small Business Management*, July, 86-91.
3. Enderle, G., 1991. "Business Ethics and Market Failure," *Journal of Business Ethics*, Volume 2, 67-85.
4. Noe, T.; and M. Rebello, 1994. "The Dynamics of Business Ethics and Economic Activity," *American Economic Review*, June, 531-547.
5. Dunckel, J., 1989. *ibid*.
6. Frederick, W., 1995. *Values, Nature, and Culture in the American Corporation*, New York: Oxford Press.
7. Hamlin, Alan P., 1996. *Ethics and Economics*. Brookfield: Elyar Publishers.
8. Sauer, James B., 1995. "Economics and Ethics: Foundations for a Transdisciplinary Dialogue," *Humanomics*, Volume 11, 5-91.
9. Miller, Gary, 1992. "Ethics and New Game Theory," *Ruffin Series in Business Ethics*, 117-126.
10. Eriksson, R. and M. Janlli, 1995. *Economic Value and Ways of Life*. Brookfield: Ashgate.
11. Lewis, A. and K. Warneryd, 1994. *Ethics and Economic Affairs*. London: Roulledge.
12. Murphy, A., 1994. "The Seven (Almost) Deadly Sins of High-Minded Entrepreneurs," *INC.*, July, 47-49.
13. Case, John, 1990. "Honest Business," *INC.*, January, 65-69.
14. Canarroe, R. R., 1972. *Bravely, Bravely in Business*. New York: American Management Association.
15. Andrews, K. (editor), 1989. *Ethics in Practice*. Boston, MA: Harvard Business School Press.
16. Jones, D. G., 1982. *Doing Ethics in Business*. Cambridge: Oelgeschlager, Gunn, and Hain.
17. Longo, T., 1996. "The Cost of Rebuilding a Career," *Kiplinger's Personal Finance*, February, 140.
18. Aguilar, Francis J., 1994. *Managing Corporate Ethics: Learning From America's Ethical Companies How to Supercharge Business Performance*, New York: Oxford Press.

19. *Corporate Ethics: A Prime Business Asset*, 1988. New York: The Business Roundtable.
20. Pastin, M., 1986. *The Hard Problems of Management*. San Francisco, CA: Jossey-Bass.
21. *Economist*, 1995. "Whistle Blowers and Business Ethics," August, p. 5.
22. Powell, Michael, 1996. "Betrayal," *INC.*, April, 23-24.
23. Ballenger, J.; Franklin, G. M., and R. K. Robertson, 1992. "Accommodating the Disabled Customer: Perceptions of Small Business Owners and Managers Toward the Law," *Journal of Business and Entrepreneurship*, March, 43-51.
24. Carney, Daren and Stephanie Gruner, 1993. "The INC Network," *INC.*, December, 184-185.
25. Stark, Andrew, 1993. "What's the Matter With Business Ethics?," *Harvard Business Review*, May, 38-48.
26. Burgleman, R., 1984. "Managing the Internal Corporate Venturing Process," *Sloan Management Review*, Winter, 33-48.
27. Burgleman, R., 1986. *Inside Corporate Innovation*. New York: The Free Press.

## *Chapter Eleven*

1. Millins, John W., 1996. "The Influence of Competency and Prior Performance Under Changing Market Conditions," *Journal of Business Venturing*, March, 89-104.
2. Pearlstein, S., 1987. "The Corpracy's Last Gasp," *INC.*, October, 31-33.
3. Young, T. A., 1992. "Ethics in Business," *Vital Speeches of the Day*, September 15, 725.
4. Bauman, Andrea, 1992. "Strictly Confidential," *Entrepreneur*, October, 126-131.
5. Baumol, William J., 1996. "Entrepreneurship: Productive, Unproductive, and Destructive," *Journal of Business Venturing*, January, 3-22.
6. Evans, W., 1981. *Management and Ethics: An Intercultural Perspective*. Boston, MA: Martimus Nijhoff.
7. Peters, Tom, 1989. "The Trouble With Business Ethics," in Richardson, J. E. (editor), 1995. *Annual Editions: Business Ethics*. Guilford, CT: Dushkin Publishing Group.
8. Novak, Michael, 1980. *Democracy and Mediating Structures*. Washington, DC: American Enterprise Institute for Public Policy Research.
9. Kugel, Y., 1977. *Ethical Perspectives on Business and Society*. Lexington: Lexington Books.
10. Labich, Kenneth, 1992. "The New Crisis in Business Ethics," *Fortune*, April 20, 167-176.
11. Serwinek, P., 1992. "Demographic and Related Differences in Ethical Views Among Small Businesses," *Journal of Business Ethics*, (July), 555-566.
12. Jackall, Robert, 1988. *Moral Mazes: The World of Corporate Managers*. NY: Oxford Press.

## *Chapter Twelve*

1. Conger, J. A., 1991. "Inspiring Others: The Language of Leadership," *Academy of Management Executive*, February, 31-45.

2. Smith, R. and B. Miner, 1983. "Type of Entrepreneur, Type of Firm, and Managerial Motivation," *Strategic Management Journal*, No. 4, 325-340.

3. Langan, John, 1990. "The Ethics of Business," *Theological Studies*, March, Vol. 51, No. 1, 81.

4. Blake, D. and D. Newton, 1994, "Do Entrepreneurs Believe They Can Impact Society Through Socially Responsible Behavior?," Proceedings, 7th Annual *International Academy of Business Disciplines*, April 6-9, Los Angeles, CA.

5. Williams, O.; Reilly, F., and J. Houck, 1989. *Ethics and the Investment Industry*. Savage: Rowan and Littlefield Publishers)

6. Stewart, Alex, 1991. "A Prospectus on the Anthropology of Entrepreneurship," *Entrepreneurship Theory and Practice*, Winter, 71-83.

# Glossary

*The following terminology is based entirely within the context of entrepreneurial ethics and the tenets of this book in particular. The author readily acknowledges that some of these concepts may have different meanings in other settings.*

*Absolutism* - An *a priori* decision making principle based upon a predetermined set of guidelines that establishes what is good and right and acceptable behavior.

*Active Risk Management* - The belief that certain levels of business and financial risk exposure can be navigated successfully, and even avoided altogether, through the use of various strategies of diversification and contingency plans. It recognizes that extraneous risk variables may exist outside the new venture, but it focuses entirely on specific, identifiable risks that are controlled or impacted by the entrepreneur's decisions. It assumes that success in the new venture development process is dependent on accurately assessing negative prospects and implementing appropriate strategies to reduce their impact on the firm.

*Assignment Vesting* - The process that describes how the risk management oriented entrepreneur secures the rights to all open-ended potential outcomes (both profit and loss) generated through the operations of the new venture, and serves as a primary motivating factor for pursuing entrepreneurial new venture development. This vesting is the result of a transfer to the entrepreneur from risk averse stake holders who wish to minimize their economic exposure in exchange for guaranteed income paid to them by the entrepreneur.

*Assumption-based Model Building* - The construction of a simulated representation of reality incorporating one or more inferences about the relationship(s) between certain variables involved in the proposed decision. The main issue is the sensitivity of the decision outcome to slight changes in the assumptions that are incorporated.

*Asymmetric Information* - This describes the situation where the stake holders in the new venture do not possess the same information that is known by the entrepreneur as it relates to product or service technology, financial performance, or the status of pending contracts. The entrepreneur is placed in the position of information originator and the investors, marketing channels, and end-users are placed in the position of information receptors. The firm owner may recognize that there are benefits to sending partial, or even entirely false, signals pertaining to the firm's performance and plans. The receptors must decide on the perceived veracity of the entrepreneur's representation and then respond according to their interpretation of the information received. (See *Insider Information*.)

*Bootstrapping* - The process by which an entrepreneur supports business operations without the influence or resources of any outside assistance, even though it may appear that the internal capabilities of the enterprise cannot provide an adequate foundation. Derived from 19th century western American literature that described how an individual could rescue himself from rising waters if he picked himself up by his own bootstraps.

*Bridge Loan* - Short term working capital financing that works like a "bridge" to transport the new venture across a relatively short time period (normally between ninety days and one year) during which a timing gap exists between paying for current labor, materials, and company overhead necessary for manufacturing and delivering a product or service, and the actual future date when payment is received from customers.

*Business Plan* - A 30-to-50 page document that describes all aspects of launching and managing a business venture. It includes separate sections with forecasts of the product or service innovation concepts, market development, promotion and advertising, accounting and financial statements, human resource requirements, the executive managerial team, logistics and operations, the company vision and mission, and an offer of ownership shares to potential investors.

*Business Risk* - Also referred to as nonsystematic risk, it describes the new venture's inherent obstacles that, to various degrees, adversely impede the relative success of an entrepreneurial enterprise effort. It encompasses aspects that are unique to the firm's internal structure and capabilities including the relative strength of the products or services, the management team and other functional personnel, the capital structure, and various marketing and production capabilities.

*Coinvestment Mutualism* - This represents both the financial and vested interest link between the entrepreneur and the new venture, and describes one of the fundamental bases for certain ethical behavior on the part of entrepreneurs. The asset vesting supports the development of a fiduciary capacity that supposedly causes the owners of small firms to act in a manner that preserves all interested stake holder positions. However, it is also argued that this can actually sanction more risky behavior because the entrepreneur has spread personal risk exposure to others through diversification.

*Competitive Equilibrium* - The fourth phase in the life of an entrepreneurial new venture, it occurs when the business experiences a leveling off in both sales and market share growth, accompanied by good profitability and an established presence in the competitive market. During this phase, the firm must establish reliable procedures, consistent managerial policies, and highly efficient functional capabilities. Many firms will require a new round of innovation in order to once again initiate growth in sales and market share (see also *Seed*, *Launch*, and *Fast-Growth*).

*Concentric Managerial Placement* - A management model that places the entrepreneur at the center of a series of sequentially overlaid concentric circles and employees placed at each successive concentric level of decision responsibility. Managerial directives originate with the entrepreneur at the core level and proceed outward across the subsequent employee levels aimed at a specific decision area. This format allows entrepreneurs to maintain a "hands-on" approach to decision implementation and monitoring by limiting the span of responsibility along the directive at each concentric level.

*Conceptual Ethical Advocacy* - This describes the necessary awareness, vested interest, and realistic expectations that must be nurtured in the firm's employees in order for a formal ethics plan to improve its chances of successful implementation in the entrepreneurial new venture. Without this, a newly initiated ethics plan would collapse due to a lack of formality with respect to the design and implementation.

*Continuous Innovation* - A newly introduced non substantive improvement in features, performance, and utility of a product or service that incorporates only minor changes in design that do not radically alter the function and use of the related predecessor products or services already in the market.

*Corporate Venturing* - The formal process of initiating new corporate-level activity to generate new businesses through the use of internal resources employed by individuals working under the authority of the large corporation, but specifically equipped and funded to generate new venture opportunities. It is promoted as a systematic process that allows big business to recapture the original determination, creativity, innovation, and imagination of the entrepreneurial spirit. (See also *Intracorporate Entrepreneurship*.)

*Discontinuous Innovation* - A newly introduced substantive improvement in features, performance, and utility of a product or service that is based upon entirely new technology or structure that has no prior representation in any existing related predecessor products or services already in the market.

*Disinterested Innovation* - One of four degrees in the *Market Innovation Matrix* that evaluates the scope of users as well as the degree of penetration within the market channels to determine how a market accepts new products, services, or process technologies. This describes a type of innovation with applications to only a very small segment of the market, and then within that niche, there is little use throughout the marketing channels. (See also *Market Innovation Matrix*.)

*Diversifinancial Troubles* - This describes how the new venture often manages a non diversified product or service portfolio, and their operations are backed up by a one dimensional financial plan. The asset investment schedule was based on certain assumptions that did not include any newly emerging change in the environment. Diversifinancial troubles create a negative compounding effect on the prospects for success when significant changes are introduced into the company's marketing mix because the firm lacks the product and service diversification to allows shifts in demand in one sector to be covered by increases in other product or service areas, and an adequate financial foundation to provide internal cash flow support for operations during periods of weak sales.

*Due Diligence* - The process of objective investigation and verification of claims, statements, and forecasts associated with an entrepreneurial new venture. This responsibility falls to each individual capital provider to complete prior to investing funds in the business.

*Econometrics* - The use of quantitative models that incorporate numerous variables within a hypothesis that is believed to accurately describe the relative variations of success and failure for a business. The most popular model utilizes multiple regression for descriptive and predictive results.

228 ■ Glossary

*Entrepreneur* - The individual who recognizes an opportunity in a either a new, emerging, or established market, and then conceives of an idea and vision for a new business venture, and ultimately undertakes to manage the various relative risks of organizing the entire range of resources necessary to launch a new enterprise that can successfully deliver specific products or services to the market in a timely manner and at a profit.

*Entrepreneur-Dependent Assessment (EDA)* - The method by which the individual entrepreneur assesses the magnitude of potential impacts regarding business uncertainty in entrepreneurial new ventures. It reflects the personal opinion of the entrepreneur who assigns a weight to a matter of uncertainty so as to determine its impact on the firm. A perception bias will tend to affect whether issues are taken seriously in business decisions and can cause issues of uncertainty in new ventures to be highly suspect.

*Entrepreneurial Fraternizing* - The process whereby an entrepreneur actively seeks involvement in external organizations, societies, or clubs in order to secure business-related contacts that may serve the new venture in the future. There is no interest in developing true personal friendships, only in promoting the nature of the venture among individuals and groups that may have resources necessary to the success of the firm.

*Entrepreneurial Pioneering* - This describes the activities of the new venture in a market landscape that is wide open, with few (if any) predecessor firms having gone on ahead into the new competitive region. Uncertainty abounds due to extremely limited information about the environment, and any information that is available is generally not current or reliable with regard to its source. Pioneers are either extremely visionary and incredibly opportunistic because they believed in the possibilities that eventually came to fruition before anyone else was willing to make a move, or they are ill-prepared and foolish, lacking in common sense. The final verdict will be based completely on hindsight gained some time after the uncertainty has passed away and the new market comes into clear focus.

*Erosion Factor* - A subjective planning tool measured across the two separate dimensions of speed and magnitude, it attempts to forecast the rate of decrease in the initial entrant's beginning market share as newly emerging competitors stake claims to various pockets of distinction around the position of the new venture innovator. It provides a basis for the entrepreneur to predict several future market scenarios, although it cannot guarantee to determine the actual results. (See *Ultimate Market Composition*.)

*Ethics* - A system of moral principles or standards for personal conduct relative to interaction with other individuals or organizations. This system is the outward manifestation of managerial business decision making that is related to, and based upon, the particular ethos within which the individual entrepreneur functions (See *Values*).

*Ethical Patronage* - Describes the three levels of commitment or involvement by which the entrepreneur may choose to promote awareness and adherence to moral standards and ethical behavior for the new venture as it engages in normal business operations.

*Ethics Decision Realm* - Because of the routine nature of the many decision scenarios and options presented in the new venture, entrepreneurs may create a separate area that tends to discriminate between decisions that exhibit obvious ethical implications, and alternatives that are perceived as not implying any outright moral judgments or values-oriented choices. This is a poorly constructed paradigm for entrepreneurial decision making, because it denies the position that *all* decisions draw upon some aspect of the individual's personal perspectives and biases, so they always contain an ethical component. The reason that entrepreneurs think in this bifurcated mode is that they have either intentionally or unknowingly placed a subjective level of importance to groups of decisions based upon their own value judgments of what is deemed a pertinent ethical matter and what is not.

*Exit Strategy* - The plan by original investors in a new venture to liquidate their equity ownership for cash through a purchase by other owners or an outside capital provider. This proposed process is often chronicled in the financial section of the business plan in order to communicate the intentions of the entrepreneur with respect to funding from outside investors.

*Explicit Forfeiture* - This describes how, during partnership negotiations, the entrepreneur unequivocally states that a certain condition has been conceded by the other party. Although this is clearly agreed upon, it does leave open the possibility that certain conditions might be implied as going along with this issue, and this could resurface at a later date and create a disagreement based not on the explicit condition, but on the presumed accompanying conditions. (See *Implicit Forfeiture*.)

*Factoring* - The process by which entrepreneurial new ventures sell their accounts receivable to a financial intermediary at a steep discount from the face value in order to secure immediate cash flow toward current expenses. The intermediary can either accept responsibility to ultimately collect the receivables, or merely accept receivables on a consignment basis.

*Fast-Growth Market* - The third phase in the entrepreneurial new venture development process characterized by a rapidly expanding customer base and sales growth in excess of five percent (5%) per month. After the firm is successfully launched and the approachment process between buyers and the business gains momentum, many new ventures experience a near-term (12-18 months) or intermediate term (2 to 3 years) where a large and accepting market is readily adopting the new product or service at several levels. Most firms begin to show a profit within, or near the end of, this phase. (See *Seed, Launch, Hyper-Growth,* and *Competitive Equilibrium*.)

*Fatalism* - The attitude that many entrepreneurs can experience when it appears that the many assumptions necessary to the success of the new venture may not transpire as expected causing the future feasibility and viability of the entire enterprise to be placed in jeopardy.

*Feasibility* - The initial hurdle that all entrepreneurial new ventures must clear, it describes the relative degree with which the business idea can actually be translated into a real, marketable product or service. It deals only with the ability for venture operations to get started and does not address the issue of whether the firm will experience success in the market. Many new ideas lack feasibility due to technological and logistical impracticalities. (See also *Viability*.)

*Figurative Delegation* - This describes how the entrepreneur presents the outward appearance of passing along certain aspects of decision making authority to others, but the process is only procedural and lacks any form of true content responsibility. In one situation, the delegated issue is actually a *non*issue, but it outwardly resembles a critical matter in order to foster a sense of decision involvement on the part of support personnel. In the other situation, a truly critical issue is supposedly delegated to the staff, but the entrepreneur never relinquishes control of implementing and monitoring the directive. Although it was seemingly delegated, the entrepreneur maintains a continuous review and close eye on every aspect of the decision.

*Financial Risk* - The probability that adverse circumstances related to the capital structure and cash flow of the new venture will severely decrease the firm's ability to function successfully as a going concern. This is also stated as the likelihood that the new venture will fail as bankrupt due to the lack of long-term financial viability.

*Firm Culture* - The atmosphere developed within an organization that establishes the manner with which employees interact, make decisions, and work together. It is the defining environment of how the venture operates and functions and includes channels of communication, policies and procedures, and lines of authority and internal controls.

*Guaranteeism* - A problem exhibited by many entrepreneurs, it describes an attitude and overall business mentality that knowingly assures and convinces related stake holders that the new venture will not experience anything short of its intended target goals for sales, profitability, and market share. It is the product of overly optimistic business expectations on the part of the entrepreneur that willingly disregards any negative effects and essentially recognizes only positive benefits from firm operations.

*Hyper-Growth* - This near-term (12-18 months) period after the launch of the new venture can decimate the firm as it experiences a distorted amplification of immediate demand for that newly introduced product or service that completely outpaces the company's ability to keep up with production supply. It is characterized by exponentially expanding sales and market share penetration, but generally does not include increasing profitability. Rates of monthly increases in sales are double-digit and supply cannot keep pace with market demand. The firm experiences rising negative cash flow because production costs are payable now, but receipts from growing sales are due in future periods. Production facilities approach capacity while marginal costs can increase dramatically due to asset diseconomies of scale (see also *Seed*, *Launch*, *Fast-Growth*, and *Competitive Equilibrium*).

*Implicit Forfeiture* - This describes how, during partnership negotiations, the entrepreneur might assume that a certain condition has been conceded by the other party due to its being subjectively linked to another issue that is currently under discussion. Although never specifically stated, the owner proceeds, believing that a condition does exist with respect to the condition, when in fact nothing has been explicitly decided. (See *Explicit Forfeiture*.)

*Initial Public Offer (IPO)* - Also referred to as "going public," it is the first sale of a significant proportion of a corporate firm's common stock to investors in the formal equity capital market, and is exclusively represented to the market in a formal written prospectus that must be filed with the *Securities and Exchange Commission*. The sale is generally underwritten by an investment bank that accepts the risk of disseminating the shares to a relatively wide cross-section of investors, thus creating a ready liquid market for buying and selling the stock on either a regional or national market basis.

*Initiator Proxy* - This is established by the new venture entrepreneur, it provides a detailed description of the forecasted ultimate market composition, but is essentially a personal commentary on the relative strength of the original market penetration, the potential for holding onto market share, and the anticipated final resting spot for the venture in terms of product leadership and regulatory impacts. It defines the prospects for achieving significant gains in an emerging market opportunity.

*Innovation* - A newly introduced product or service that substantially improves the features, performance, and utility of an existing product or service in the established market. It can be either continuous or discontinuous in features content, depending on the level of performance improvement attained relative to prior entrants in the market. It can also represent either objective and substantive performance improvements, or subjective and intangible perceptions subject to personal preferences. (See also *Continuous Innovation, Discontinuous Innovation, Level I Innovation,* and *Level II Innovation*).

*Innovator Trap* - This exists as a potential detriment for entrepreneurial behavior, and is characterized by the belief that *all* innovations will be readily recognized and accepted in the market. Innovation does not necessarily translate into immediate market acceptance, rapid growth in sales, and venture success. The trap describes the pull on the individual entrepreneur to overemphasize a positive evaluation of an innovation, and the pressure to convince everyone that the innovation will radically reshape the market. (See *Star Quality*.)

*Insider Information* - This describes the information that the entrepreneur possesses about firm operations, financial performance, the status of a proposed contract, or capital requirements that is not known by the stake holders outside the company. Because the owner knows the true nature of this information, it normally has significant value relative to the expectations (or partial information) that non-insiders possess.

*Internal Security* - This describes the new venture's ability to support continued expansion, asset investments, and growth in sales through internally generated cash flow from existing operations. If sales are strong and marginal costs are under control, the firm may have the financial strength to support new product development and market expansion plans. If the existing levels of working capital are already stretched to the limit, the firm lacks internal security and becomes dependent upon outside sources of capital to support continued growth.

*Interpretive Perspective* - A form of new venture representation where the entrepreneur either responds to a request for information or voluntarily offers information about the enterprise to an outside stake holder in a manner whereby what is considered negative and positive news is based purely on the subjective viewpoint of the entrepreneur and the personal discretion to frame the representation in a specific light. In certain cases it can be considered a form of misrepresentation.

*Intracorporate Entrepreneurship (Intrapreneurship)* - A concept introduced in the early 1980's that seeks to create new ventures entirely from within the large, established corporation. Funds and support resources are specifically designated by the firm for a relatively small and quasi- autonomous new venture division that is supposed to foster creative thinking, risk taking, and innovation targeted at creating new products and services for newly emerging markets. This system is often referred to as "intrapreneurship" and the individuals charged with these tasks are nicknamed "intrapreneurs."

*Joint Venture* - When two firms enter into an agreement to pursue a specific business project together, and this deal is tied solely to this one project, and describes how each company will have jurisdiction to handle certain aspects based on the agreed upon functional capabilities that each organization recognizes in the other. The structure is based on a formal demarcation of decision making authority and responsibility for specifically designated components of the functional operations necessary to accomplish a certain project within a required time period to meet a target completion date.

*Keepers* - Business ideas for new ventures that exhibit both exceptional feasibility for formation and launch, as well as long-term viability for sustained growth in a large, expanding competitive market. Investors in entrepreneurial new ventures actively search out these types of business opportunities.

*Kirk Syndrome* - Named for the fictional intergalactic starship captain, symptoms include a thrill and excitement experienced in taking a product or service innovation into a newly emerging market, and an overly emboldened sense of confidence to achieve success due to a willingness to pursue uncertainty while others are content to merely operate in well-defined markets, with known products, and clear channels of distribution. The entrepreneur is credited as one who "boldly goes where no one else has gone before," but this invitation to uncertainty can be incorrectly viewed as a positive attribute of entrepreneurs, when in fact it may be the one factor that is most likely to destabilize the new venture. An entrepreneur displaying symptoms of Kirk Syndrome may be more likely to disregard objective, outside advice about the firm's potential problems, and be more apt to head straight into a new market even if certain research indicators are present that define the market as highly volatile and nearly impossible to define.

*Laissez-Faire* - A French term that literally means "let persons do as they please," it commonly describes a managerial economic behavior and attitude present in most entrepreneurs that desires freedom to pursue new product or service market innovations without any interference from overly stringent government regulations, competitors, and organizational bureaucracy.

*Latent Risk Management* - The belief that certain levels of business and financial risks will increase and decrease due to the interaction of numerous extraneous variables outside the new venture that cannot be controlled or impacted by the entrepreneur's decisions or strategies. It can also describe the ill-advised entrepreneurial notion that "things tend to work themselves out" over time and that exposures to certain risks are unavoidable and change on their own during the course of new venture development.

*Launch* - The second phase of establishing a viable entrepreneurial new venture, it is often characterized by slow sales growth, high expenses for initial production, promotion, and distribution, and negative cash flow. During this period, the venture requires a reliable source of working capital to support daily operations until adequate sales are generated (See also *Seed*, *Hyper-Growth*, and *Competitive Equilibrium*).

*Level I Innovation* - The tangible, physical properties of a newly introduced product, service, or manufacturing process that produce objective, measurable performance improvements relative to the similar products, services, or technologies in the existing market. Examples include superior speed, greater fuel efficiency, quieter operations, real time savings, improved communication quality, maintenance cost reductions, and longer useful life.

*Level II Innovation* - The intangible, non-material properties of a newly introduced product, service or manufacturing process that produce highly subjective improvements to existing similar products, services, or processes that are difficult, or even impossible, to measure because they are based solely on individual personal interpretation and perspective. Examples include improved care in handling, greater prestige, less confusion, enhanced appearance, and easier operation.

*Limited Innovation* - One of four degrees in the *Market Innovation Matrix*, this describes a type of innovation with applications to only a very small segment of the market, but within that niche, there is widespread use throughout all the marketing channels. (See also *Market Innovation Matrix*.)

*Limited Liability Myth* - The belief that the corporate form of business organization will sufficiently limit the new venture's exposure to all forms of business and financial risks because it restricts the reach of creditors and other lien holders to business assets alone, protecting the entrepreneur's personal assets from having to be liquidated to satisfy outside claims. Entrepreneurs often assume this provides a sufficient risk management shield to support the successful operation of the firm.

*Managerial Hedge* - This describes how the entrepreneur shows outward signs of being receptive to input and feedback from staff personnel, but a structural buffer of committees, meetings, and administrative assistants has been crafted within the organization to insulate the entrepreneur from comments and concerns. The other form is where the entrepreneur attributes the lack of staff input and feedback into decisions to the urgency with which certain decisions have to be made and implemented, so that there is not enough time to consult everyone about the matter and therefore the decision had to be made quickly, and singularly.

*Market Efficiency* - The manner by which many buyers and sellers engage in the rational pricing of goods and services based on common and equal access to all pertinent information related to the goods and services, the producers, the suppliers, and the end users. A market is *inefficient* when the information is not equally accessible to all interested buyers and sellers.

*Market Forecast* - The sub component of the market potential it is the reasonable aggregate expectation for *all* sellers in a market. It is the anticipated combined annual purchases made by end-users. Market potential yields the market forecast, which yields the firm's sales potential, which yields the firm's annual sales forecast.

*Market Innovation Matrix* - Comprised of four degrees of innovation adoption, it evaluates the scope of users as well as the degree of penetration within the various levels of the marketing channels to determine how a market accepts and adopts new products, services, or process technologies.

*Market Potential* - The most liberal aggregate expectation for combined annual sales in a market if every possible end-user that meets the buyer profile were to purchase their respective allocation of the product or service. It represents the highest prospective saturation of the market. (A sub component of market potential yields the market forecast, which yields the firm's sales potential, which yields the firm's annual sales forecast.)

*Misrepresentation* - The deliberate deception of an individual or venture's true position relative to their dealing with a related or interested business contact. This includes both the omission of pertinent factual details related to the business deal, as well as the inclusion of erroneous information that misleads the interest contact.

*Mission Statement* - A concise commentary that summarizes the underlying principles and expectations upon which a venture is founded. It captures the nature and essence of the fundamental goals, values, and environment that have application in all aspects of how the enterprise functions.

*Modified Rationality* - The negative impact to decisions among stake holders of entrepreneurial new ventures caused by the abstract concept of anticipated future prospects. It alters individual ethical alternatives, moral choices, and value judgments in tangible business decisions based on the potential for future gain for those who can persevere through uncertainty.

*Monotony Fallacy* - A common problem encountered by entrepreneurs once the new venture has seemingly stabilized and attained a plateau of reliable sales revenues, profitability, and cash flow. The tendency can be to slip into a false sense of security and contentment believing that the venture can easily maintain this seemingly invariable performance trend, when in fact the apparently steady monotony of daily operations is really a signal that the firm has lost its innovative vitality and ability to stay sharp and well-focused.

*Negotiable Standards* - The apparent oxymoron that describes how certain individuals function with seemingly objective moral guidelines, but these "principles" are subject to changes and adjustments due to the nature and complexity of extenuating circumstances that impact the decision process.

*New Venture Parallax* - The phenomenon where, from the perspective of most interested stake holders, the entrepreneurial business appears to be poorly positioned and in need of significant strategic and managerial restructuring, but when viewed through the eyes of the founding entrepreneur the ventures appears to be well positioned, well managed, and successful.

*Operational Ethical Failure* - This describes the disintegration of a recently initiated ethics plan at the fourth stage in the ethics implementation sequence. Even though awareness, vested interest, and realistic expectations were achieved, the firm was unable to effectively implement ethical behavior into the functional areas of the enterprise because it lacked sufficient operational support systems. Although the idea gained conceptual momentum, there was no way to operationalize ethics into readily applicable functional policies and procedures.

*Operational Management* - The process of making business decisions that impact the near-term operating concerns of the entrepreneurial venture. This addresses functional capabilities such as accounting and information systems, production, customer service, and internal day-to-day activities.

*Opportunism* - A problem exhibited by many entrepreneurs, it describes an attitude and overall business mentality that knowingly seeks to exploit other individuals and organizations in order to secure a personally advantageous position with respect to both pecuniary and non pecuniary benefits that result from obtaining a primary position relative to competing individuals and firms.

*Opportunity Overreaction* - This happens when the entrepreneur is too optimistic about the prospects for moving successfully into a new market and commits too many resources to the effort. The biggest problem is that the entrepreneur will not become aware of this miscalculation until personnel, funds, and time have already been allocated toward a losing proposition. Many times, it is difficult to determine when to pull the plug on an overreaction or when to allow more time for new developments to transpire.

*Opportunity Under Reaction* - This happens when the entrepreneur becomes overly pessimistic about what appears to be a very limited market potential. The decision is then made to restrict personnel, funding, and time allocations toward this effort because the initial sales response is not adequate to support a fully funded strategy. Problems occur if the market improves and requires large scale allocation of resources, but the time to respond is less than the time required to implement the strategy, or there is enough time to respond, but the required resources are no longer available.

*Optional Commitments* - An apparent oxymoron that describes how certain individuals function on two levels in matters of business negotiations. The first level seemingly secures an agreeable position relative to the other party; yet, the second level intentionally reserves the right to rescind the first level agreement if a superior opportunity or position is made available elsewhere.

*Over-Dependency Risk Factor* - This describes the situation where the start-up company has just one or two supply and distribution connections due primarily to its limited production capacity, lack of significant capitalization, or minor market penetration. The enterprise depends almost exclusively on this small number of outside firms for component parts, raw materials, or other supplies and the timely distribution of its product or service.

*Perception Connections* - The four possible responses that the market can have in response to the introduction of an innovation by an entrepreneurial new venture. The market will either agree or disagree with the message being sent by the innovator, and as such will either have a similar interpretation to the offering firm's view and adopt the product or service, or arrive at a contrary perception and choose not to adopt the innovation.

*Post-modern* - The world view regarding the nature of man, societal interactions, personal relationships, and subjective values developed during the period after the 20th century philosophical movement to the new "modern" era of art, literature, philosophy, theology, commerce, and organizations. Its tenets include a systematic reevaluation and methodical skepticism about any values or morals that are founded in religious or theological bases, and an onus to challenge such prior theories of man.

*Prospective Paradox* - Inherent in new ventures, it defines both the anticipation of future prospects that fuels various degrees of optimism and perseverance among stake holders, while at the same time this optimism for future potential distorts and modifies rational decision making among stake holders due to the subjective perception of whether these unrealized future prospects can actually be obtained due to perseverance and effort.

*Quantum Effect* - The phenomenon whereby an entrepreneurial new venture will supposedly accomplish a significant increase in sales, managerial performance, profitability, and operating efficiency due to a proposed infusion of capital provided by an outside investor. This is often a false hope, based on the belief that most (if not all) of the firm's problems can be instantly corrected given adequate financial resources; however, the firm really requires adjustments to many subjective and qualitative factors.

*Reciprocity Illusion* - The tactic by which an entrepreneur enjoys substantive measurable benefits derived from a business partnership, but is only able to deliver an apparently comparable outcome in principle alone. A non substantive response lacks tangible results to the other party and is merely a procedural appearance of compliance with the negotiated deal.

*Relativism* - A decision making process that is not based upon a predetermined set of guidelines that establishes what is good and right and acceptable behavior, but instead assesses each situation relative to the immediate benefits and costs, and chooses an appropriate path that maximizes the benefits irrespective of any established principles of conduct.

*Representation Disclosure Content* - This describes the type or level of plain and truthful information that is included in the entrepreneur's representation of information to capital providers, market channels, and end-users. It is measured as either a *full* disclosure (a completely open representation), a *partial* disclosure (truthful components mingled with embellishments or outright false information), or *non*disclosure (an outward image of representation that contains no element of truth).

*Residual Ethical Value* - Within the context of entrepreneurial ethics, it describes the remaining moral benefit that accrues to an individual decision maker after having implemented a specific course of action that did not generate the greatest pecuniary benefits, but did adhere to a foundational principle of conduct that provides personal gratification, a sense of doing the right things, and other non pecuniary benefits.

*Risk* - The chance of experiencing economic damage or loss due to adverse circumstances that impact the entrepreneurial new venture. This is weighed with respect to all significant managerial decisions as a function of the degree of adverse effects versus any potential accrued benefits or gain.

*Risk Premium* - The payment made from the party accepting a specified risk and its entire range of potential outcomes, to the party discharging the risk and its various prospects. The risk averse party would generally rather receive some form of guaranteed income (rent, salary, royalty) instead of holding onto both the possibility of loss and gain.

*Risk Transfer* - The process whereby various interested stake holders in a new venture shift the entire range of potential outcomes (both positive and negative) related to the decision making responsibility for the firm, from themselves to the individual entrepreneur who accepts the assignment of the actual results as an incentive for rational action (See *Risk Premium*).

*Sales Forecast* - The sub component of the firm's sales potential that represents the most realistic expectation for annual purchases of a product or service among buyers in the competitive market. (A sub component of market potential yields the market forecast, which yields the firm's sales potential, which yields the firm's annual sales forecast.)

*Sales Potential* - The sub component of the aggregate market forecast that represents the highest possible expected sales for the firm, based on the maximum saturation level of one firm's product or service in the competitive market. (A sub component of market potential yields market forecast, which yields the firm's sales potential, which yields the firm's annual sales forecast.)

*Saturated Innovation* - One of four degrees in the *Market Innovation Matrix*, this describes a type of innovation with applications across a wide range of market sectors, and there is widespread use throughout all the marketing channels. (See also *Market Innovation Matrix*.)

*Seed* - The initial phase (of four) in establishing a viable entrepreneurial new venture, it includes the primary process of examining the fundamental feasibility of a prototype for the proposed business organization. It does not involve any systematic manufacturing or sales and is focused on determining what components must be in place prior to the initiating of regular business operations (see also *Launch*, *Hyper-Growth*, and *Competitive Equilibrium*).

*Situation Ethics* - An apparent oxymoron that describes how an individual makes decisions based on assessing the immediate circumstances of each separate predicament, deciding not what is the most appropriate course of action, but rather what is the most expedient given the decision context.

*Star Quality* - It describes the pressure placed on innovation by entrepreneurs to demonstrate immediate recognition and acceptance as a clear leader by the market. The entrepreneur tries to convince everyone that the innovation will have the same degree of impact that the internal combustion engine had on the transportation markets, or that Microsoft Corporation had on the market for personal computers.

*Strategic Issue Management* - The formal process whereby the firm listens to, and watches, the external competitive environment for various signals that are indicators of the company's expected future market. These signals can be either weak or strong in both structure and content, based on the time it takes to attain full knowledge of the actual market situation. The duration of the timing component dictates the window of opportunity for the enterprise as it considers its response relative to certain perceived market expectations.

*Strategic Management* - The process of making business decisions that impact the competitive positioning of the entrepreneurial venture relative to other firms in various expected external market environments. This addresses how well internal capabilities are postured with respect to what is required for success in the forecasted business conditions still to come.

*Strategic Plan* - It assesses the internal capabilities of an entrepreneurial new venture and the expected volatility of the future competitive market in which it operates. The plan determines what actions have to be taken, a time frame for implementations, and the costs associated with obtaining the necessary skills and competencies that are required by firms wishing to be well-positioned in the newly emerging competitive market environment.

*Strategy* - The specific actions to be implemented for a business to achieve predetermined levels of internal functional capabilities deemed necessary to be well-positioned and successful in a newly emerging, anticipated external competitive environment. This represents the formal plans for closing the gaps between existing capabilities and targeted capabilities for a future time period that requires systematic resource allocations and periodic monitoring.

*Suggestive Interpretation* - A managerial negotiation ploy whereby an entrepreneur feigns uncertainty about performance in a proposed business deal to gain concessions from the counter party. These are knowingly presented in a manner that enhances the supposed lack of structure and resources in the entrepreneurial venture to invoke more lenient expectations from the partner. Issues include: an expected growth rate for sales, project completion times, payment dates and amounts for financial obligations, the ability to deliver product modifications, and attracting capital to a project.

*Sunk Costs* - Those expenditures that are invested during the *Seed* phase of the entrepreneurial new venture development process. The costs deal with research, permits, and market testing aimed at establishing the feasibility of the enterprise. They do not generate sales and are not recoverable, especially if the venture is not ever able to begin operations due to lack of feasibility, lack of long-term viability, or lack of capital.

*Surface Innovation* - One of four degrees in the *Market Innovation Matrix*, this describes innovation with applications to many segments of the market, and within these various segments, there is only sporadic use throughout all levels of the marketing channels. (See also *Market Innovation Matrix*.)

*Systematic Optimism* - A prevailing positive attitude throughout all levels of the stake holders associated with new ventures due to future, anticipated positive gains for those who persevere and stay focused in the early stages of venture uncertainty. It generally finds its source in the entrepreneur's assessment of expectations for company growth in sales and profitability.

*Tactical Positioning* - Describes the most favored stance the entrepreneur desires within a partnership agreement, and targets one or two alternative positions that are acceptable by using the partnership focus and influence parameters. The entrepreneur states what issues are open to discussion and what issues are not. The tactic is based on the subjective value assessments made about the costs and benefits for each issue during the negotiation process. The entrepreneur wants to manipulate a final consent that gives up less than what is gained to create a net gain position.

*Target Pricing* - The practice whereby the new venture deliberately experiments with economic price discrimination in order to determine the highest possible price that users will pay for a newly introduced product or service. It creates a pricing schedule based solely on the demographic profiles of various target groups in the prospective market. This method can be highly suspect in the early phases of market development, especially if different users learn of the price discrepancies offered by the new venture.

*Touting* - The practice whereby an entrepreneur knowingly deviates from, and embellishes, formal written information contained in a business prospectus pertaining to the future potential of the new venture, through seemingly informal oral discussions that are represented as privileged knowledge for only a select constituency. The is designed to create in the minds of potential investors the appearance that they have received insider information that can provide an advantage relative to other interested parties.

*Ultimate Market Composition* - This describes the eventual configuration of the relative placement of the entrepreneurial new venture, the competitive positioning of other firms (both existing companies and subsequent new entrants), the structure of the marketing distribution channels, and the scope of any government regulations dealing with the product or service, its manufacture, and its dissemination. Perceptions about this can greatly vary the opportunity expectations of the interested stake holders.

*Underfunded Adjustments* - Substantive changes made in the assumptions of the asset investment schedule used in the successful launch of a new venture. When the entire funding for the initial operations of the enterprise cannot be secured, the entrepreneur adjusts the investment downward to accommodate the lower capital raised from investors. This happens in two ways and places in jeopardy the potential success of the business.

- *Type I Underfunded Adjustment* - The entrepreneur removes assets from the investment schedule in order to have the funds raised match the funds needed for launch of the venture. The underlying rationale is that after being reviewed, certain items were deemed unnecessary and the entrepreneur decided that the venture can manage without such capabilities.

- *Type II Underfunded Adjustment* - The entrepreneur discounts the original acquisition costs of several or all of the assets listed on the investment schedule in order to have the funds raised match the funds needed for launch of the venture. The underlying rationale is that after being reviewed, certain costs were determined to be overestimated and could be secured at lower costs than originally expected.

*Values* - The collection of specific moral judgments and perspectives of what is right and good and desirable, they constitute the basis for how the entrepreneur views the relationship of the new venture to the market, society in general, and personal goals and objectives. Personal actions, or ethical behaviors, are the resultant outcomes of values (see also *Ethics*).

*Values Reflection Factor* - Describes the degree to which the ethical actions and attitudes of the new venture are a direct function of the moral basis and ethical behavior of the founder-entrepreneur. It can be either completely unrelated, a vague likeness, or a direct image of the individual.

*Values Vacuum* - Without a strong commitment from the owner to formulate and maintain a systematic approach to business ethics within the firm culture, the new venture is susceptible to developing a *values vacuum*, where employee ethical relativity and ambiguity reign supreme due to the lack of no clear moral basis or focus initiated by the entrepreneur. The owner shies away from trying to mandate a corporate morality, and yet ends up doing nothing, which allows the firm to be devoid of any form of absolute ethics or values identity.

*Venture Capital* - Equity funds invested in an entrepreneurial new venture from an outside source other than the founders of the enterprise. It generally refers to money obtained from a venture capital firm which actively pursues investments in fast-growth emerging companies.

*Venture Paroxysm* - The first form of entrepreneurial market expectations attitude that describes a sudden but sustained sense of euphoria that the company is literally going to explode on the scene of the competitive landscape and completely revolutionize an industry. This attitude believes that the company will experience a Type A innovation-target scenario where radical discontinuous innovation creates an entirely new fast-growth market.

*Viability* - Another initial hurdle that all entrepreneurial new ventures must clear, it describes the ability of the product or service innovation and the new venture to maintain a strong competitive position in the market over the long term. It addresses the issues related to the size of the market, whether the market is growing sufficiently, and the staying power of the firm relative to competitors and market demand for the product or service.

*Vision* - The ability of the entrepreneur to see and recognize the far reaching opportunity available in a product or service market at a time when the market either does not yet exist, or is in its infancy. It describes the view of the new venture as a mature leader, operating successfully in the market even at a time when the firm remains an unrealized entity in the planning stages prior to launch.

*Voluntary Omission* - A form of new venture representation where the entrepreneur knowingly excludes the release of certain information that is deemed negative in order to maintain a more favorable rendering of the firm to the outside stake holders. Depending on the type of information omitted, this can constitute a form of misrepresentation.

*Weathering Capability* - A calculated non response to certain types of financial and operating problems that confront the entrepreneurial new venture. This common practice involves utilizing a "wait and see" approach regarding how to address various types of risk, such that the enterprise does not engage in planned responses to a potentially negative issue, but instead keeps focused on the existing operating plan that is in place and, to some degree, disregards any form of directly addressing the risk in question because it is deemed as exogenous to the management function, residing outside of the realm of the firm's control.

*X-Factor* - The one missing element necessary for the entrepreneur to implement a company-wide ethics program in the new venture. It represents the necessary assurance that values-based decision making and ethical behavior will be rewarded and not cause any form of economic downturn in the financial performance of the firm.

# Index

## A
absolute   201
absolute business ethic   195, 203
absolute ethic   196
absolute ethical standards   204
absolutism   46
active risk management   22
affirmative action   52
agency   5
alliance   149, 150, 156, 199, 200
American Management Association   160
Andreeson, Marc   87
Ansoff, H. Igor   106
assignment vesting   5, 40
assumption-based model building   111
assumptions   74
asymmetric information   72, 88
autonomy   19, 199

## B
bankruptcy   3, 6
bargaining power of new customers   143
bargaining power of suppliers   143
benefit-to-cost (BC) ratio   147
Boesky, Ivan   xi
bootstrapping   129
Borrowed Culture, the   170
bridge financing   76
bridge loan   131
Buddhism   68
bureaucratization of ethics   161
Burgleman, Robert   22
business ethics   163
business plan   vii, 11, 26, 41, 42, 43, 186, 198
business risk   5, 6
business uncertainty   69
*Business Week*   57

## C
Cantillon, R.   5
capitalization   75
captured market expectations   109

catch-22   131
cause-related marketing   106
champion   162
character   xi, 46, 47, 49, 66, 103, 168, 169
charisma   11, 86
co-investment mutualism   19
compatibility   113
competitive equilibrium   95, 96
competitive settling   10
concentric managerial placement   15
concentric positioning   16
conceptual ethical advocacy   63
conservative   118
consortium   147, 149
continuous change   75
continuous innovation   38
contractual arrangements   145
CORE values   51, 162
corporate culture   50, 78, 79, 174, 175, 188, 195, 203, 204
corporate venturing   22
corporate white lie   88
"covering all the bases"   154

## D
degree of optionality   53
demanded   96
dilemma of capitalization   127, 128
disclosure   188
discontinuous change   75
disinterested innovation   25
distributor accord   147, 151
diversifinancial   180
"don't ask, don't tell"   141
due diligence   11

## E
Eagle Computer   178
early departure   42
econometrics   192
entrepreneur-influencer   164
entrepreneurial bias   112

entrepreneurial confidence  186
entrepreneurial control  186
entrepreneurial ethics wedge  59
entrepreneurial expertise  186
entrepreneurial fraternizing  158
entrepreneurial idea generation  34
entrepreneurial pioneering  24, 119
entrepreneurship  3
erosion factor  11
ethical behavior  v, vi, xi, xii, xiii, xiv, 26, 33, 34, 39, 40, 41, 46, 47, 48, 49, 50, 51, 54, 63, 65, 66, 68, 69, 72, 78, 81, 83, 87, 88, 93, 119, 122, 126, 130, 138, 140, 159, 160, 161, 162, 163, 165, 166, 167, 168, 169, 170, 171, 172, 174, 177, 179, 181, 182, 183, 184, 185, 186, 187, 190, 191, 192, 193, 202, 203, 204, 205
ethical detractors  61
ethical domain(s)  71, 72, 156
ethical facilitators  61
ethical "fuzziness"  165
ethical hurdle  11
ethical limitations  105
ethical mandates  171
ethical patronage  162
ethics  61, 191
Ethics and Values Interaction (EVI)  86
ethics decision realm  55
ethics wedge  58, 61
evangelical  68
excessive market expectations  108
exit strategy  128
Expectations  3, 117, 118, 121
expectations  1, 3, 6, 8, 12, 25, 27, 39, 40, 56, 61, 63, 71, 72, 73, 74, 88, 89, 91, 101, 105, 106, 107, 108, 110, 111, 112, 113, 114, 116, 117, 118, 119, 121, 122, 123, 126, 127, 128, 130, 132, 134, 137, 141, 144, 145, 147, 153, 154, 156, 158, 160, 163, 166, 168, 169, 170, 174, 175, 178, 179, 180, 184, 186, 188, 189, 190, 192, 195, 196, 197, 198, 199, 203
expected return  2, 3, 4, 5, 16, 67, 136, 137
explicit forfeiture  158
external environment  7, 24, 49, 52, 56, 68, 85, 106, 109, 115, 132, 177, 179, 181, 184, 185, 187, 188, 202, 203
extraneous risk variables  23

## F

factoring  89
false negative representation  73, 88
false positive representation  73, 88
false sense of security  184
false weak signal  108
fast-growth  95
fatalism  102
feasibility  37, 74, 113
feasible  37
figurative delegation  29
financial risk  19
financing  vi, xiii, 39, 47, 56, 75, 76, 89, 91, 102, 125, 126, 127, 128, 129, 132, 133, 137, 140, 158, 179, 180, 189, 197, 199, 204
firm culture  xiii, xv, 39, 65, 69, 71, 78, 79, 87, 126, 159, 160, 161, 162, 163, 164, 165, 166, 167, 168, 169, 170, 171, 172, 173, 174, 175, 176, 179, 180, 186, 190, 192, 194, 195, 201, 202
forecasting  vi, 81, 120, 195, 198
formal compromise  77
*Fortune*  57
franchisees  6
free-agency seed money  130
Freud  68
FRINGE values  51, 162
full disclosure  72, 93
funds allocation  146

## G

Gates, Bill  87
"go(ing) through the motions"  66, 172
going public  76
guaranteeism  103
guarded optimism  112
gut feeling  57, 116

## H

Hall, William  75, 109
Hinduism  68
"hit-or-miss" tactic  167
Hybrid Culture, the  171
hyper-growth  76, 96, 134

## I

IBM  178
implicit forfeiture  158
"in the works"  43
*INC.*  57
incremental discovery basis  57
incremental seed money  129
influencer  162
informal compromise  77

information   146
infrastructure   146
initial public offer (IPO)   133
initiator proxy   10
innovation   v, vi, xii, 2, 7, 8, 9, 10, 16, 22, 23, 24, 25, 35, 37, 38, 39, 40, 41, 67, 68, 73, 75, 92, 96, 98, 102, 105, 109, 110, 111, 112, 113, 114, 115, 122, 123, 125, 127, 130, 150, 177, 178, 185, 188, 189, 192, 196
innovator trap   24
insider information   72, 88
internal environment   vi, 2, 12, 16, 67, 68, 185, 190
internal security   132, 133
interpretive perspective(s)   73, 95
intracapital   22
intracorporate   21
intracorporate entrepreneurship   22, 41, 168
intrapreneur   22
intrapreneurship   168
intrusive erosion   11
IPO mirage   134

## J

Jesuits   68
Jobs, Steven   87
jockeying principle   151, 154
joint venture   147, 148
Judeo-Christian   68

## K

Keating, Charles   xi
keepers   27
"Kirk Syndrome"   23
knee-jerk reaction   180
knee-jerk response   181
Knight, Frank   5

## L

laissez-faire   54
latent risk management   22
launch   76, 95
less than expected   43
Lesson, Nick   xi
Level I Innovation   7
Level II Innovation   7
Levi Strauss and Company   49
limited innovation   25
limited liability   64
limited liability myth   64

Longenecker, Justin   45, 49
"loose cannon"   168
Lopker, Pam   87

## M

managed morality   172
management   vi, vii, xiii, 2, 3, 5, 7, 12, 13, 15, 21, 23, 30, 33, 38, 41, 42, 45, 46, 48, 55, 57, 65, 66, 70, 72, 89, 90, 93, 98, 101, 107, 126, 128, 137, 144, 149, 159, 166, 168, 175, 176, 192, 193, 194, 195, 196, 197, 200, 201, 204
managerial communication   12
managerial fads   7
managerial hedge   29
managerial support   146
manipulation enigma   151, 154
market breadth   25
market depth   25
market efficiency   123
market forecast   112
market opportunity   69
market potential   112
marketing chain   77
marketing life cycle   92
Marxism   68
massive erosion   11
maverick   168
MEDIAL values   51, 59, 162
Microsoft   25
Milken, Michael   xi
Miller, Merton   127
Minkow, Barry   xi, 87
minority   153
minority position   147
misrepresentation   xi, 47, 72, 73, 87, 88, 93, 154, 155
missed market expectations   109
"missing a piece"   42
mission   78
mission statement   78
modified rationality   2
Modigliani, Franco   127
momentum   184, 185, 186
monotony fallacy   122
*Moody's Industrial Manual*   57
moral choice   2, 203
morality   xiii, 55, 160, 161, 172, 175, 176, 190
morals   191
mutual coinvestment   5

## N

National Conference on Business Ethics   68
natural selection   68
naturalists   68
negative momentum   183
negotiable standards   175
neutral observer   162, 163, 164, 169
new venture development process   34
new venture parallax   204
niche   34
nondisclosure   72, 93

## O

"open-door" policy   13
operational ethical inability   63
operational management   98
opportunism   158
opportunity overreaction   27
opportunity underreaction   27
optional commitments   176
organizational structure   1, 12, 29, 63, 67, 167, 172, 175, 188
"outsider" perception   135
over-dependency risk factor   91

## P

partial disclosure   72, 93
partner   30, 39, 55, 77, 89, 91, 145, 154, 189, 200, 204
partnership   xiii, 39, 76, 77, 134, 143, 144, 145, 146, 147, 148, 149, 150, 151, 152, 153, 154, 155, 156, 157, 158, 179, 180, 184, 186, 189, 190, 199, 200, 201
perception connections   9, 110
perceptions   193
personal interpretation   133
pessimism   162
Peters, Tom   178
Porter, Michael   143
post-modern   68
preemptive release   96
price sensitivity   113
"private" style   101
prospective paradox   1
Protestantism   19
prudent market expectations   108
"public" manner   101

## Q

qualitative quandary   116
quantitative legend   116
quantum effect   141

## R

random "noise"   107
realistic   118
realistic expectations   117
reciprocity illusion   158
reflectivity   165, 174
relational transactions   2
relative   201
relative ethic   196
relative ethical circumstances   204
relativism   46
Replicate Culture, the   170
representation   xiii, xv, 8, 29, 39, 71, 72, 73, 74, 75, 77, 80, 85, 86, 87, 88, 89, 90, 91, 92, 93, 94, 95, 96, 97, 98, 100, 101, 102, 103, 104, 111, 112, 113, 114, 118, 123, 126, 127, 129, 132, 134, 139, 141, 144, 153, 154, 155, 156, 159, 160, 161, 178, 179, 180, 185, 186, 187, 188, 192, 195, 199
representation disclosure content   72, 93
requested   96
residual ethical value   203
resources   7, 11, 15, 22, 27, 29, 30, 33, 37, 38, 39, 40, 41, 46, 52, 53, 57, 69, 72, 73, 74, 75, 76, 79, 89, 106, 108, 109, 114, 119, 129, 130, 135, 144, 146, 147, 148, 149, 151, 158, 160, 161, 165, 166, 167, 170, 178, 180, 181, 184, 186, 193, 197, 201
ripple effect   98
risk   3
Risk assumption   5
risk management   3, 7
risk premia   4
risk premium   5
risk transfer   4, 40

## S

sales forecast   112
sales potential   112
saturated innovation   25
Schumpeterian   3
Schumpeterian entrepreneur(ship)   5, 6, 21, 40
Securities and Exchange Commission   85, 86, 133
Seed phase   75

Seed stage  95
self-employment  20
seniority  153
seniority position  147
shirking  161
signal  107
situation ethics  169
skidding effect  183
social responsibility  2, 178
socialism  68
solicited transfer  96
"specific-relative" influencer  164
sponsor  162
stabilization  96
stake holders  5
*Standard and Poor's*  57
star quality  24, 72
start-up company  115
steady erosion  11
strategic alliance  147, 149
strategic behavior  20
strategic issue management  106
strategic management  192
strategic plan  89
strategy  xiii, 3, 23, 27, 38, 40, 47, 52, 55, 57, 74, 86, 89, 90, 97, 101, 102, 105, 106, 108, 110, 112, 113, 121, 126, 128, 135, 143, 144, 145, 146, 153, 156, 165, 166, 168, 181, 182, 183, 184, 185, 186, 187, 188, 190, 200
structural heuristic  166
suggestive interpretation  158
Summists  68
sunk costs  129
supplier accord  147, 150
surface innovation  25
systematic optimism  1, 102

## T

tactical positioning  147, 148, 151, 158
target niche  73
Templeton Plan  126
10-K  86
10-Q  86
Thomas, Dave  87
tolerance  69
"too little too late"  182
tout  153
touting  88, 92, 103, 130, 158
trampled seed money  129
true weak signal  108

## U

ultimate market composition  10
uncertainty  vi, xi, xii, xiv, 2, 5, 6, 7, 10, 16, 20, 22, 23, 24, 26, 28, 45, 49, 67, 68, 69, 89, 90, 97, 98, 101, 118, 119, 121, 122, 123, 125, 126, 127, 129, 139, 168, 175, 177, 185, 187, 188, 190, 203
underfunded adjustments  76
underreaction  27

## V

valuation  87
value judgments  xiv, 1, 2, 3, 8, 17, 35, 39, 46, 48, 51, 55, 57, 68, 71, 75, 79, 86, 96, 105, 117, 118, 132, 144, 145, 155, 167, 170
*Value Line*  57
value of information  126
value transfers  78
values  45, 78
values and ethics interaction matrix  70, 81
values reflection factor  65, 204
values vacuum  175, 190
venture enthusiasm  112
venture origination  34
venture paroxysm  1, 112
vertical marketing chain  90
viability  37, 74, 113, 186
viable  37
vision  20, 37, 38, 130
volatility  10, 22, 27, 115, 117, 180, 188, 189
voluntary omission(s)  73, 95, 158

## W

weathering capability  23, 140
whistle blowers  161
"win-win" situation  150

## X

X-factor  205

## Z

ZZZZ Best  87